Lecture Notes in Computer Science 1649

Edited by G. Goos, J. Hartmanis and J. van Leeuwen

T0223315

Springer

Berlin
Heidelberg
New York
Barcelona
Hong Kong
London
Milan
Paris
Singapore
Tokyo

Ron Y. Pinter   Shalom Tsur (Eds.)

Next Generation Information Technologies and Systems

4th International Workshop, NGITS'99
Zikhron-Yaakov, Israel, July 5-7, 1999
Proceedings

 Springer

Series Editors

Gerhard Goos, Karlsruhe University, Germany
Juris Hartmanis, Cornell University, NY, USA
Jan van Leeuwen, Utrecht University, The Netherlands

Volume Editors

Ron Y. Pinter
IBM Research Laboratory in Haifa
Matam – Advanced Technology Center
Haifa 31905, Israel
E-mail: pinter@il.ibm.com

Shalom Tsur
SurroMed, Inc.
1060 East Meadow Circle
Palo Alto, CA 94303, USA
E-mail: tsur@surromed.com

Cataloging-in-Publication data applied for

Die Deutsche Bibliothek - CIP-Einheitsaufnahme

Next generation information technology and systems : 4th
international workshop ; proceedings / NGITS '99, Zikhron-Yaakov,
Israel, July 5 - 7, 1999. Ron Pinter ; Shalom Tsur (ed.). - Berlin ;
Heidelberg ; New York ; Barcelona ; Hong Kong ; London ; Milan ;
Paris ; Singapore ; Tokyo : Springer, 1999
    (Lecture notes in computer science ; Vol. 1649)
    ISBN 3-540-66225-1

CR Subject Classification (1998): H.2, H.3, H.4, H.5, C.2

ISSN 0302-9743
ISBN 3-540-66225-1 Springer-Verlag Berlin Heidelberg New York

Typesetting: Camera-ready by author
SPIN: 10703935   06/3142 – 5 4 3 2 1 0   Printed on acid-free paper

Foreword

The Next Generation Information Technologies and Systems (NGITS) workshop series is a biannual event held in Israel since 1993. Like its predecessors, NGITS'99 brings together active members of the international research community interested in information technology and knowledge based systems. Many of the base technologies in the traditional areas of database management systems, information retrieval, and resource optimization, are being deployed nowadays in novel systems and applications that flourish with the astonishing increase in computational power, storage capacity, communication, and – of course – the advent of the world-wide web. These new fronts, in turn, present an ever growing set of challenges to the technologies, such as data availability, information integrity, and knowledge extraction, fuelling an exciting set of activities.

Our workshop clearly reflects this trend, offering a rich sample of the state of the art at the close of the millennium and a glimpse of what is to come in the next one. In response to the call for papers, we received 34 high quality submissions, 22 of which were carefully selected by the Program Committee for presentation at the workshop and inclusion in these proceedings. These include 17 full length papers as well as 5 short papers (that will be accompanied by demonstrations during the workshop). In addition, it is our pleasure to feature two invited talks, given by Professor J. Ullman of Stanford University and IBM Fellow C. Mohan.

We classified the selected papers into a number of broad topics, which were also used to organize the workshop sessions:

- Exploring the World Wide Web
- Database Technology
- Storage, Meta Information, Ontologies, and Software Engineering
- Agent and Workflow Management Technology
- Data Warehousing and Mining

We would like to extend our thanks to the many individuals who spared no time or effort to contribute to the success of this event:

The authors, the Program Committee members, and the technical reviewers,
Tova Berger, Antje Endemann, Dagan Gilat, Danna Pascal,
and Nilly Schnapp for their support in organization and logistics.

Finally, we would like to recognize the NGITS'99 institutional sponsors (listed in alphabetic order) and would like to thank them for their generous support:

The IBM Research Lab in Haifa,
The Tandem Labs Israel, a Compaq Company,
The Technion, Israel Institute of Technology, Haifa, Israel.

Haifa, Israel　　　　　　　　　　　　　　　　Ron Pinter, Shalom Tsur
May 1999　　　　　　　　　　　　　　　　　　Program Co-chairs

　　　　　　　　　　　　　　　　　　　　　　　　Opher Etzion
　　　　　　　　　　　　　　　　　　　　　　　General Chair

Steering Committee

Ami Motro   Arie Segev
Avi Silbershatz   Peretz Shoval

General Chairs

Opher Etzion   Moshe Tennenholtz

Program Committee

Israel Ben-Shaul	[Israel]	Francois Bry	[Germany]
Asuman Dogac	[Turkey]	Ronald Fagin	[USA]
Ronen Feldman	[Israel]	Avigdor Gal	[USA]
Ehud Gudes	[Israel]	Pierre Huyn	[USA]
Sushil Jajodia	[USA]	Frank Leymann	[Germany]
Rajeev Motwani	[USA]	Frank Olken	[USA]
Dino Pedreschi	[Italy]	Ron Pinter	[Israel]
Allen Reiter	[Israel]	Mori Rimon	[Israel]
Doron Rotem	[USA]	Eyal Shimoni	[Israel]
Oded Shmueli	[Israel]	Shalom Tsur	[USA]
Ouri Wolfson	[USA]	Beat Wuthrich	[Hong-Kong]
Carlo Zaniolo	[USA]		

Additional Reviewrs

Sena Arpinar	Patrizia Asirelli
Francesco Bonchi	Fazli Can
Nihan Cicekli	V. Cho
Martin Ester	K. Jim
Junyi Jin	Eliezer Kantorowitz
David Konopnicki	Jianzhong Li
Gianni Mainetto	Giuseppe Manco
Mirco Nanni	J. Pun
Salvatore Ruggieri	Nesime Tatbul
Jamel Tayeb	Hakki Toroslu
Ozgur Ulusoy	Bo Xu

Local Arrangements Chair

Nilly Schnapp

Table of Contents

Storage, Meta Information, Ontologies, and Software Engineering

Invited Talk II

Agent and Workflow Management Technology

Data Warehousing and Mining

Some Advances in Data-Mining Techniques

Jeffrey D. Ullman

Department of Computer Science,
Stanford University
Stanford, CA 94305, USA
ullman@cs.stanford.edu

Research in the MIDAS project at Stanford explores new ideas in data-mining. One early result was a new algorithm for Web search, that resulted in a recently turned commercial search engine, called Google.

A second area of interest is in generalizing the techniques such as "a-priori," which were developed by Rakesh Agrawal and his associates at IBM Research in Almaden to allow "market-basket analysis," or "association-rule mining." The latter problem deals with finding items that customers frequently buy together. We have developed a framework called "query flocks." In this system, we can phrase highly complex data-mining queries, including many that are not handled well by commercial SQL systems. We then compile the "query flock" into a sequence of SQL queries that are simple enough to be optimized by commercial systems.

A third interesting challenge is summarizing the knowledge of the Web in a form that resembles conventional relational data. We describe some experiments that have been carried out to exploit the redundancy of the Web and discover the patterns in which facts of a certain kind tend to exist.

Finally, we shall talk about extending the techniques for association-rule mining to extract relationships that are not based on "high support," i.e., sets of items that appear very frequently in market baskets. Important example include intelligence-gathering, where we want to find terms that are highly correlated in documents, but that do not appear in very many documents. The MIDAS group has recently developed some techniques to process very large amounts of data and detect efficiently items that are highly correlated but not very frequent. We can even find implications, similar to causal relationships, without requiring high support for the associated items.

Querying Semantically Tagged Documents on the World-Wide Web*

Ziv Bar-Yossef[1], Yaron Kanza[2], Yakov Kogan[2], Werner Nutt[3], and
Yehoshua Sagiv[2]

[1] Department of Electrical Engineering and Computer Science,
U.C. Berkeley, Berkeley CA 94720
zivi@cs.berkeley.edu
[2] Dept. of Computer Science
Hebrew University, Jerusalem, Israel
{yarok, yakov, sagiv}@cs.huji.ac.il
[3] German Research Center for Artificial Intelligence
(DFKI GmbH), 66123 Saarbrücken, Germany
nutt@dfki.de

Abstract. QUEST is a system for Querying Semantically Tagged documents on the World-Wide Web. The advent of new markup languages, such as XML, facilitates authoring of Web documents that contain not just HTML tags for instructing a browser how to view a document, but also contain objects that represent the semantic structure of the document. When such documents become widely available, more powerful methods to access and query information on the Web will be possible. The QUEST system was designed and implemented for querying and manipulating documents written in the markup language OHTML. OHTML combines HTML and objects of the OEM data model. QUEST has several new features. First, QUEST can be used to query a combination of hypertext and object structures. Second, The results of queries are OHTML pages and thus of the same type as the data being queried. Third, QUEST implements a new approach for querying semistructured data that produces meaningful answers even when the input data is incomplete, i.e., when some variables of the query cannot be bound to database values. Finally, the experience of developing and using QUEST for querying semantic documents on the Web can be useful for the design and implementation of query languages for XML. This paper provides an overview of the QUEST system and its components.

1 Introduction

The enormous growth in the usage of the World-Wide Web as an information source suggests that the Web will evolve into a platform with more database tools. One major obstacle in the evolution of the Web into one giant database

---

* This research was supported by Grants 8528-1-95 and 9481-1-98 of the Israeli Ministry of Science.

is the lack of semantics in HTML pages, which makes it difficult to distinguish between different pieces of information in Web pages. To overcome this problem, we have used OHTML [KMSS98], which enriches HTML with semantic tags that define an object structure. In OHTML, the semantic tags are hidden as HTML comments and, hence, their existence is transparent to HTML browsers. The object structure imposed by OHTML on the data of the Web is in the style of the *object exchange model* (OEM) that was proposed for *semistructured data* (see [Abi97,Bun97,PGMW95]). The development of OHTML started before the advent of XML. However, we believe that the techniques developed in QUEST for OHTML are also applicable to documents formulated in XML.

This paper describes QUEST, a system for QUErying Semantically Tagged documents on the Web. The QUEST system was developed and implemented at the Hebrew University of Jerusalem. QUEST treats a set of OHTML pages as a semistructured database. The usage of semantic tags allows one to pose more precise queries than is possible over untagged HTML pages. We consider tagged pieces of information in Web pages as atomic values. QUEST queries refer both to the structure of objects and to their atomic values.

The novel aspects of QUEST include: (1) a graphical query language; (2) the possibility to specify queries that retrieve incomplete information, thus taking into account the incompleteness of semistructured sources; and (3) answers of queries may become extensions of the initial database.

Motivated by the growing use of the World-Wide Web as a heterogeneous information source, many systems for querying the Web were developed. Among them W3QL [KS97,KS95], WebLog [LSS96], WebSQL [MM97,MMM97], and WebOQL [AM98]. As a further development, systems were designed for Web site management, e.g., Strudel [FFK+98] and Araneus [AMM97,MAM+98]. In comparison to these systems, QUEST has the advantages of (1) using semantic tags for more accurate querying, and (2) dealing robustly with incomplete information. The second novelty is also an advantage when comparing QUEST to query languages, such as Lorel [AQM+97,MAG+97,QWG+96] and UnQL [BDHS96], that were developed for querying semistructured data in general, and not just in the context of the Web.

Today, as XML [Con98] is becoming a standard, querying semantically tagged documents is an important research issue. Languages such as XML-QL [DFF+98] and XQL of Microsoft have been proposed recently. These languages are at an early stage of implementation, and we believe that our experience can be useful for the design and implementation of query languages for XML.

2   Data Model

QUEST is a system for querying hypertext documents that also embed some object structures. Due to the diversity of the Web, we cannot expect that documents with object structures will conform to a fixed schema, as in a classical database. Object structures that show some regularity, but do not follow a strict explicit schema, are captured by semistructured data models [Abi97].

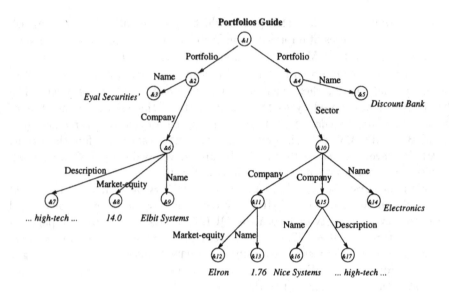

Fig. 1. A Portfolios Guide as an OEM database

We chose the *Object Exchange Model* (OEM) of [PGMW95] as the data model for the semantic layer in our system. OEM is a semistructured data model that represents databases as labeled directed graphs. Each node of a graph is an *object* with a unique *object identifier* (oid). Some objects have *names* and are called *named objects*. The named objects are the entry points to the database, and the names serve as aliases to those objects. Each object in the database must be reachable from some named object through a path in the database graph. An object that is not reachable cannot be accessed and is therefore ignored. An *atomic object* is an object that has no outgoing edges. It contains a value of an atomic type, such as *integer, real, string, gif, html, audio, java*, etc. Objects that have outgoing edges are *complex objects*. Figure 1 shows, as an example, a database graph of a portfolio guide.

Since databases and queries are graphs of a similar structure, we introduce a common abstraction, called skeletons. A *skeleton* is a directed graph with a partial function ν that assigns names to some of the nodes in the graph, such that distinct nodes have distinct names and each node is reachable from a named node. A *database* is a skeleton with two functions, one that maps edges to labels, and one that maps atomic nodes to values.

Using skeletons as a common abstraction of the basic components provides a high degree of uniformity, at both the conceptual level and the implementation level. In the implementation of QUEST, this is reflected in the class hierarchy, where databases, query graphs and result graphs are all extensions of the "skeleton" class.

One purpose of the recently proposed markup language XML is to express the semantics of certain parts of a document by means of markup tags. We

```
<HTML>
    <TITLE> Index of Portfolios Guide </TITLE>
    <BODY>
    <!-- (LABEL)Portfolios Guide(/LABEL) -->
    <!-- (OBJ id=&1 type=set name="Portfolios Guide") -->
        <H3>Portfolios Guide:</H3>
        <UL>
          <LI><A HREF="eyal.html">
            <!-- (LABEL) -->portfolio<!-- (/LABEL) --></A>
            <!-- (OBJREF)eyal.html#&0(/OBJREF) -->
          <LI><A HREF="discount.html">
            <!-- (LABEL) -->portfolio<!-- (/LABEL) --></A>
            <!-- (OBJREF)discount.html#&0(/OBJREF) -->
        </UL>
    <!-- (/OBJ) -->
    <HR>
    <CENTER> This page is a simplified version of the
            OHTML page with portfolio suggestions.   </CENTER>
    </BODY>
</HTML>
```

Fig. 2. An OHTML page with tags

started our project before the advent of XML and created the tagging language OHTML [KMSS98]. OHTML is an extension of HTML that superimposes an OEM object structure on top of an HTML page, by adding semantic tags that are hidden inside HTML comments. Thus, one can tag an HTML document without affecting the display of the document by a browser. The tags are used to define objects and references among those objects. Thus, a set of OHTML document contains a textual representation of an OEM database.

Figure 2 shows OHTML code that defines a Portfolios Guide object with two portfolio subobjects, similarly to the Portfolios Guide database of Figure 1. Note that the tags of a subobject are nested inside the tags of the parent object.

In order to interpret OHTML documents as OEM graphs, we add object identifiers (oid's) to the objects defined by OHTML tags. Thus, objects can be referenced, and each object has a unique oid. The oid of an object is a combination of a uniform resource locator (URL) and the offset of the object from the beginning of the page. URLs also provide entry points to the database, since browsers are capable of reaching a Web page through its URL.

In OHTML one can also use references to object id's. In Figure 2, for example, there are references to two subobjects having the oid's eyal.html#&0 and discount.html#&0. These two subobjects are children of the object having the oid &1 and are connected to their parent via edges labeled with portfolio. Since the two subobjects are not located physically immediately after the labeled edges leading into them, oid references are used. Finally, OHTML also allows one to declare the type of each atomic node, e.g., *integer*, *gif*, *java*, etc.

3   QUEST and How It Is Used

In this section we give an overview of QUEST from the user's perspective. We show how a user can formulate queries and view their results. In later sections, we will describe QUEST's query language and its components in more detail.

To illustrate the usage of our system, we rely on a running example based on the Web site of the Israeli economic magazine GLOBES [GLO], which holds information about the Israeli economy. We concentrate on the part of the site that deals with stock portfolios recommended by financial analysts. A portfolio consists of a group of companies recommended for investment. There is a general style in the design of the HTML documents that describe portfolios. However, each one of the portfolios has its own particular schema. The schemas differ in the attribute names and in the hierarchies of the objects they contain. For example, some portfolios are flat lists of companies preceded by a short introduction while other portfolios group companies by sectors, e.g., "Electronics," "Chemical," etc. The portfolio pages are a good practical example for semistructured data. They contain incomplete data without a strict schema, and they contain concrete information, such as prices, dates, etc., along with descriptions, images, links, etc. It seems natural that one would like to ask queries against these pages. For our experiments, we copied pages of the GLOBES site to our computer, tagged these pages with OHTML tags, and queried them in QUEST.

3.1   Overview of the Querying Process

We consider a set of OHTML documents as a *database.* A database has two aspects. The *visual view* is the visualization of the HTML part of the documents as shown by a browser. The *semantic view* is the second aspect, and it is the graph structure of the set of objects contained in the database. Figure 3 shows how QUEST provides simultaneously the two views of the GLOBES database. The existence of two parallel views for each OHTML document is due to the combination of HTML tags and OEM structures in the documents.

The display of the database graph in the visual view familiarize the user with the structure of the database and thus, gives her the ability to design meaningful queries. A QUEST query essentially consists of two graphs, the *query graph* and the *result graph*. The query graph determines how the object graph of a database is explored and how data are retrieved. The result graph describes the object structure produced by the query. Both, the query and the result graph are drawn using a graphical user interface. In Section 4 we discuss query graphs and their evaluation over a database. In Section 5 we cover the usage of a result graph for the creation of result pages when submitting a query.

QUEST is a client-server system. The query is created in the client part, and when submitted, it is transferred to the server for evaluation over the database. After evaluating a query, the server creates the query result, which is an extension of the given database. That implies that the result is a set of OHTML documents. The location of the result in the database is then sent to the client as a URL and that part of the extended database is displayed. The display of the result

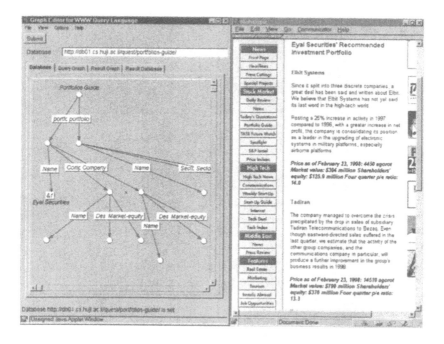

Fig. 3. The two aspects of a database—semantic (left) and visual (right)

contains both the semantic view and the visual view. As a query system that facilitates the querying process we just described, QUEST is a combination of tools that allow a user to browse a database, to construct a new or edit an existing query, to evaluate a query over a given database, and to construct the result.

A query in QUEST is evaluated in three phases. The first phase is the *search phase* in which information is extracted from the database. In this phase the query graph is matched to the database graph in search for similarity of patterns. We thus call *matchings* to the result of the search phase. The second phase is the *filtering phase* in which the extracted information is subjected to additional constraints. We call *solutions* to the matchings that remain after the filtering phase. The third phase is the *construction phase* in which an extension of the existing database is constructed from the extracted information. The result of the construction phase is called the *query answer*.

QUEST allows incomplete answers when querying incomplete information. Yet, we require an answer to have a maximal information content. The distinction between searching and filtering is necessary in order to apply some constraints only to matchings that contain maximal information (see Section 4).

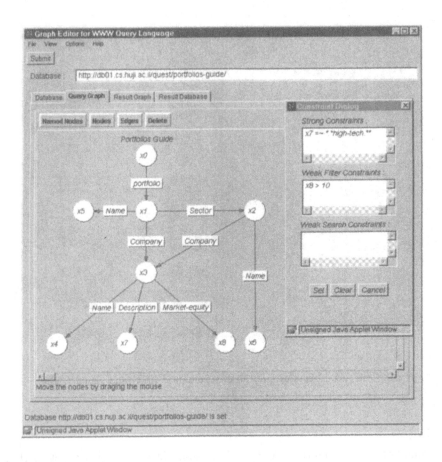

Fig. 4. The query graph

3.2 The Components of a Query

A query consists of two main parts. The first part defines the information to be
extracted from the database and the constraints for filtering that information.
This part plays similar roles as the FROM and the WHERE clauses in an SQL
query. The evaluation of this part is the search phase and the filtering phase.
The second part defines how to create the result from the information that was
found in the first phase. That role is similar to the SELECT clause in SQL and is
used for the construction phase.

The main parts are further divided into the following components:

The Query Graph is a graph that is matched against the database graph
during the search phase. Figure 4 shows the graph of a query that searches
the Portfolios Guide database for high-tech companies whose market per equity
value is greater than 10.

The Search Constraints are a set of constraints that further specify how to
match the query against a database.

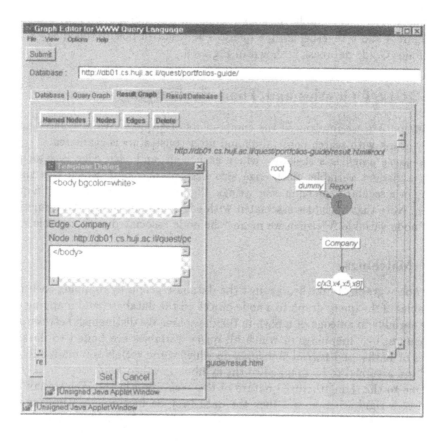

Fig. 5. The result graph and a node template

The Filter Constraints are applied during the filtering phase and filter the information that was found in the search phase.

The Result Graph is a graph that defines the graph structure of the result database. It defines which new database objects are to be created as the result of a query, and how to connect these objects to each other and to existing database objects. The result graph defines the semantic view of the result database. An example of a result graph is given in Figure 5.

The Templates are textual entities that specify how to construct the HTML part of the result database and how to combine the OEM structure of the result with HTML segments to create OHTML pages. The templates define the visual view of the result database. In the graphical user interface, one can decorate every node in the result graph with a *node template,* as shown in Figure 5. Alternatively, one can create template files (see e.g. Figure 7) that also contain a description of the result graph.

The result database, similarly to the original database, is a set of OHTML documents. The system displays the graph of the result database as an answer to the query. The query graph, the constraints, the result graph, and the templates in Figure 4 and 5 together form a query. The result of posing this query to the Portfolios Guide database is shown in Figure 6.

4 QUEST Queries and Their Evaluation

In Section 3.2, we introduced the components of a query. We now show how a query graph with search constraints and filter constraints is evaluated.

A *query graph* is a skeleton, where each node and each edge is associated with a distinct variable. Each edge also has an *edge label,* which is a simple string or a regular expression over strings. Figure 4 shows an example of a query graph. Note that variables associated with edges are not shown. We sometimes say "node variable X" when we mean "the node associated with variable x."

4.1 Matchings

The query graph is matched against the database graph by mapping each node variables of the query graph to a node object on the database, and mapping each edge variable to an edge or a path in the database. We distinguish between *total matchings,* i.e., mappings in which all query variables are bound to database nodes or paths, and *partial matchings* in which some variables remain unbound (and are assumed to be mapped to the symbol $\perp$, called *null*).

Due to the semistructured nature of the Web, data in the Web do not conform to a rigid schema, and thus the data may be incomplete. Allowing only total matchings for a query is too restrictive, since this would assume that information appears in certain concrete patterns and is complete. For this reason, QUEST has been designed so that it can handle incomplete information and return incomplete answers.

The definition of matchings is based on viewing edge labels in a query as constraints. The label of an edge in a query graph is a constraint, since only certain edges or, more generally, paths of the database match that label; furthermore, the topology of the matching portion of the database must be the same as the topology of the query graph. More precisely, suppose that e is an edge variable in the query graph, such that l is the label of e (l is a string or, in general, a regular expression) and e links the node variable x to the node variable y. Let μ be an *assignment* to the variables of the query, i.e., μ maps node variables to database objects and edge variables to paths in the database graph. We say that μ *satisfies* the edge constraint of e if the path $\pi = \mu(e)$ that is assigned to e satisfies the following.

1. π is a path in the database from $\mu(x)$ to $\mu(y)$, i.e., the source of e is mapped to the source of π, and the target of e is mapped to the target of π;
2. the sequence of edge labels on the path π satisfies the regular expression l.

If the label l of the edge e is just a string, the last condition means that $\mu(e)$ consists of a single database edge that is labeled with the same string l.

We also view the names of the named nodes in the query graph as constraints. We say that the *name constraint n* is satisfied if the query node with the name n is mapped to a database object with the same name.

Usually, query languages consider only total matchings, i.e., partial information is ignored when answering a query. Total matchings are defined as follows.

Definition 1 (Total Matchings). *A total matching is an assignment of objects and edges of the database to the variables of the query, such that each name constraint is satisfied and each edge constraint is satisfied.*

That is, a total matching requires all variables in a query to be bound and all constraints to be satisfied.

In *partial assignments,* node and edge variables may remain unbound, i.e., variables are mapped either to database entities or to $\perp$. Thus, the requirement that all edge constraints and name constraints be satisfied has to be relaxed. Essentially, we require that name and edge constraints be satisfied only when the corresponding variables are assigned non-null values; moreover, we also require that the portion of the query graph that is assigned non-nulls will be a skeleton.

Formally, we say that a partial assignment is *defined* for a node (edge) variable if it maps the node (edge) to a non-null object (database edge). Partial matchings are defined as follows.

Definition 2 (Partial Matchings). *A partial assignment μ is a partial matching if it has the following properties.*

1. *if μ is defined for a named node of the query, then the name constraint is satisfied;*
2. *if μ is defined for an edge of the query, then the edge constraint is satisfied;*
3. *the edges and nodes for which μ is defined form a skeleton.*

Condition 3 means that if x is either a node or an edge that is assigned a non-null value, then there is a path from a named node to x, such that μ assigns non-null values to all nodes and edges on that path.

4.2 Constraints

In addition to the constraints implicit in the query graph, explicit constraints can be specified. Explicit constraints are either *search constraints* or *filtering constraints*. Furthermore, in the presence of nulls, constraints can be satisfied either *weakly* or *strongly*. We first define weak and strong constraints.

Constraints are expressions combined of Boolean operators and *atomic expressions*. Atomic expressions are either constants or variables that occur in the query graph. A variable in a constraint can be bound either to a value of an atomic database node or to an object identifier of a node. Thus, we have two sets of comparison operator: $C_v = \{<, \leq, >, \geq, ==, ! =, = \}$ for comparing values and $C_i = \{=o=, !o=\}$ for comparing the identities of database objects. A *simple constraint* is a constraint of the form $a_1 \theta a_2$, where a_1 and a_2 are atomic expressions and θ is a comparison operator from C_v or C_i.

To take into account partial matchings, we define two ways to evaluate constraints with respect to an assignment: *strong evaluation* and *weak evaluation*. The point is that we still want to evaluate constraints if the assignment is undefined for some query variables.

Consider a simple constraint $a_1\theta a_2$ and a partial assignment μ for the variables in the query. For the sake of simplicity, we adopt the convention that μ is defined for all constants and maps a constant to itself. The comparison operators in C_v expect atomic values as arguments. If the variable in the argument position is bound to a complex database object, the constraint is not satisfied. In the other cases, the constraint can be evaluated in the following two ways:

1. *Strong Evaluation*: the constraint $a_1\theta a_2$ is satisfied if μ is defined for both a_1 and a_2 and the values to which a_1 and a_2 are bound by μ satisfy θ;
2. *Weak Evaluation*: the constraint $a_1\theta a_2$ is satisfied if one of the following is true: (1) the assignment μ is not defined for a_1 or μ is not defined for a_2; (2) the assignment μ satisfies $a_1\theta a_2$ under strong evaluation.

If $\perp$ is assigned to some variable of a simple constraint, then the constraint is never satisfied under strong evaluation and is always satisfied under weak evaluation. If a constraint is satisfied under strong (weak) evaluation, we say that it is *strongly satisfied* (*weakly satisfied*). Satisfaction of Boolean combinations of simple constraints can be defined in the obvious way. Each constraint in a query is entered either as a weak or as a strong constraint.

4.3 Search Constraints and Maximal Matchings

For each explicit constraint, the user specifies whether it is weak or strong and, furthermore, whether it is to be used in the search phase or in the filtering phase.

During the search phase of the query evaluation, QUEST constructs matchings for the variables of the query graph. These matchings must satisfy Definition 2 and, furthermore, each explicit search constraint must be satisfied either weakly or strongly, as specified by the user.

The partial matchings constructed during the search phase may exhibit some redundancies, since a partial matching μ may yield another partial matching μ' by making μ defined for fewer variables. Formally, we say that μ *subsumes* μ' if for every variable x for which μ' is defined, $\mu(x) = \mu'(x)$. In other words, μ is the same as μ', except that μ may be defined for some entities in the query-graph for which μ' is not defined. We say that a matching is *maximal* if it is not subsumed by any other matching. To avoid redundancies as well as unnecessary computations, the search phase should only construct maximal matchings. Note that maximal matchings cannot be extended over the given database without violating some constraint. Intuitively, maximal matchings contain maximal information, which is the best we can expect when information in the database may be incomplete. Maximal matchings can be viewed as a generalization of the notion of full disjunction [RU96,GL94].

Consider the query graph in Figure 4. Table 1 shows the maximal partial matchings produced by the query, when evaluated over the database depicted in

Figure 1. For easier comprehension, we have replaced the oid's of atomic objects by their values. We only show the assignments to the node variables, since (in this example) these assignments uniquely determine the assignments to the edges.

No.	x0	x1	x2	x3	x4	x5	x6	x7	x8
1	&1	&2	⊥	&6	Elbit Systems	Eyal Security	⊥	"..high-tech.."	14.0
2	&1	&4	&10	&11	Elron	Discount Bank	Electronics	"..high-tech.."	1.76
3	&1	&4	&10	&15	Nice Systems	Discount Bank	Electronics	⊥	⊥

Table 1. Maximal matchings of the query in Figure 4

The partial matchings in Table 1 are maximal, since none of the null values in each matching can be replaced by a database object in a way that will satisfy the edge constraint in the query graph.

4.4 Filter Constraints

During the second phase of the query evaluation, the maximal matchings from the search phase are filtered. Filter constraints are either strong constraints or weak constraints, as specified by the user. The maximal matchings that satisfy all the filter constraints are called *solutions*.

There is a need for both strong constraints and weak constraints due to the presence of partial information. The basic difference between the two is that strong constraints are only satisfied if variables are bound, and thus certain information is required to be present in order to satisfy strong constraints. Weak constraints do not require information to be present. If information is available in a given matching and that information violates the constraint, then the matching is dismissed; however, if the information is not available, then the matching gets the benefit of the doubt and is retained. For example, if a query asks for companies that have a market value of at least 500 million dollar, then we will not receive in the result companies for which it is known that their market value is below that figure, but we may receive companies for which the market value is unknown.

For strong constraints, it does not matter whether they are applied during the search phase or during the filtering phase. The reason for that is that a strong constraint is satisfied only if all the variables in the constraint are assigned non-null values. Consequently, it is advisable to apply strong constraints as early as possible during the search phase in order to prune the search space.

For weak constraints the situation is different, since a weak constraint may be satisfied by changing the assignments of some variables to nulls. Therefore, it makes a difference whether a weak constraint is applied during the search phase or during the filtering phase. Note that if a new weak constraint is added to a query as a search constraint, then it may change the result by forcing some null assignments to variables that previously were assigned non-nulls. However,

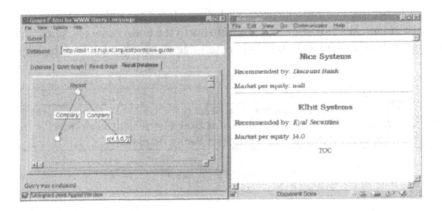

Fig. 6. The result database produced when evaluating our example query (the query graph of Figure 4 and the result graph of Figure 5) over the database of Figure 3

the new weak search constraint will not decrease the number of solutions to the query. If the same weak constraint is used in the filtering phase, then it may decrease the number of solutions to the query. Intuitively, weak search constraints have the effect of luring maximal matchings to be as large as possible. Once the maximal matchings are produced, the filter constraints are used to eliminate some of those matchings. In fact, one reason for having maximal matchings as the result of the search phase is in order to give as much elimination power as possible to the weak filter constraints.

Note that the edge constraint and the name constraint (Definition 2) are a form of weak search constraint.

The set of solutions, which is obtained as the outcome of the filtering phase, is used for the creation of the result. We discuss this topic in the next section.

5 Constructing Results

The result of a query in QUEST is a set of OHTML pages that extend the database over which the query is posed. Since the search and filtering phases produce sets of partial matchings, we need a mechanism to convert those partial matchings into OHTML pages. When creating OHTML pages, we must take into account the two aspects of OHTML, namely, the semantic view and the visual view. Thus, the answer returned by a query must include an OEM graph, and that graph must be embedded in HTML pages by means of OHTML tags.

In principle, there are two ways to combine the two aspects, depending on which aspect is given priority. The first approach is to produce an OEM graph and decorate its nodes and edges with HTML. The second is to create HTML pages, and embed in those pages objects and edges of the OEM structure. Both approaches lead to OHTML pages. In QUEST, there are mechanisms realizing each of the two approaches. We will discuss only the first one, which gives priority to the semantic structure when constructing the answer.

We use two formalisms in the creation of the result. The first is a *result graph* that determines the OEM structure of the answer. The second is a set of OHTML templates that are used to decorate the OEM structure with HTML tags.

5.1 Result Graph

When creating an OEM structure out of the solutions to the query, two main tasks have to be fulfilled. The first is to create new objects, and the second is to create edges among these new objects and edges from the new objects to other database objects.

These two functions are accomplished by means of a result graph. A *result graph* is essentially a skeleton with edges that are labeled with *edge labels* and nodes that are labeled with flat terms. A *flat term* is either a variable or a term of the form $f[x_1, \ldots, x_n]$, where f is a Skolem function and $x_1, \ldots, x_n$ are node variables occurring in the query graph. The idea is that new objects are generated by applying Skolem functions to existing objects.

The solutions of a query are (partial) assignments of database objects to node variables of the query. Suppose that $f[x_1, \ldots, x_n]$ is a flat term in the result graph. If μ is a solution, then $[\mu(x_1), \ldots, \mu(x_n)]$ is a tuple of database objects with oid's, say, $o_1, \ldots, o_n$. For each solution μ, we create a new object with the oid $f[o_1, \ldots, o_n]$. Note that if two solutions μ_1 and and μ_2 are equal on all the x_i, then only one object is created for them.

There are different ways to handle tuples with nulls. One approach is to create new objects only when all the variables of a term are bound to non-null values. However, this approach is too restrictive. Instead, we treat each null value as a unique database object. In this way, we take into account partial solutions that may not bind all variables, and we utilize this partial information in order to create new objects.

Summarizing, new objects are generated as follows. First, in each solution μ, replace every null with a new unique non-null value. Secondly, for each solution μ and each flat term $f[x_1, \ldots, x_n]$, create a new object having the oid $f[\mu(x_1), \ldots, \mu(x_n)]$ (duplicates are removed).

Once the result objects are generated, edges are introduced between them according to the edges in the result graph. Suppose that there is an edge, labeled with l, from node n_1 of the result graph to node n_2. If there is a solution μ, such that μ generates objects o_1 and o_2 from the flat terms of n_1 and n_2, respectively, then we create an edge, labeled with l, from o_1 to o_2.

Suppose that n is a leaf node (i.e., a node without any outgoing edges) of the result graph, and let t be the flat term of n. If o is an object created from a solution μ and the flat term t, then o is an atomic object. Since atomic objects have values, each leaf node of the result graph has an associated string s. The string can include variables of atomic nodes of the query graph. Such variables should be enclosed by the $ sign, i.e., x. Note that the string may be just a variable. The variables in the string are instantiated according to the solution

μ, and the instantiated string becomes the value of the atomic object generated from μ and the leaf node. Since an atomic object can have just a single value, each variable appearing in the string of a leaf node of the result graph must also appear in the flat term of that leaf node. This requirement guarantees that an atomic object is created for each distinct value that is produced by applying solutions to the string of the leaf node.

A special case of a flat term is a variable, e.g., x. In this case, no new objects are created, since no Skolem function is applied to existing oid's. Therefore, when a variable is used as a term, it actually defines connections between result objects and objects of the database over which the query is evaluated. Since we want to avoid situations in which the result graph implies that a new outgoing edge has to be added to an existing object, we allow a variable as a term only in leaf nodes of the result graph. This requirement guarantees that new edges are added only between two new objects, or between a new object and an object that already exists in the database.

QUEST requires result graphs to be acyclic. In addition, the list of variables in the term of each node must include all the variables of its parent. This requirement is due to the following reason. Assume, for example, that $f[x]$ is a parent term and $g[y]$ is a child term. Let $\mu_1 = \{x/o_1, y/o_e\}$ and $\mu_2 = \{x/o_2, y/o_e\}$ be two solutions. Then $f[o_1]$, $f[o_2]$ and $g[o_e]$ are the newly generated objects. When OHTML pages are created they contain these objects, and each one of the objects $f[o_1]$ and $f[o_2]$ must encapsulate in its OHTML representation the representation of the object $g[o_e]$. Thus, we need to have the ability to break an HTML page into pieces stored in more than one physical location. This resemble the usage of parameter entities in XML, but is not an HTML feature.

QUEST automatically adds missing variables to flat terms, when those variables are needed according to the requirements specified in this section.

Since only one object can exist in the uppermost level of each OHTML page, a dummy root object is created for each OHTML page produced in the result. Such a root object encapsulates the objects in the uppermost level of the page and the HTML text that appears before and after those objects. In order to create root objects, the root of the result graph is required to have a flat term that has the Skolem function symbol *root* and some variables. Each instantiation of this flat term by some solution μ will create a new root object that will reside in a new OHTML page. Thus, the *root* term defines the partition of the result database into pages.

5.2 OHTML Templates

QUEST uses OHTML templates to create the HTML that embeds the OEM structure of the result. In the query interface, one can add to a given node a preceding and a succeeding HTML text. Actually, the text is HTML with references to variables of atomic nodes of the query. The variables in the text segments are instantiated to the atomic values to which they have been bound, and the instantiated text segments surround the result objects that are created from the given node.

```
<HTML>
<!-- (LABEL)Report(/LABEL) -->
<!-- (OBJ id=report[] type=set name="Report") -->
    <BODY bgcolor=white>
    <!-- (LABEL)Company(/LABEL) -->
    <!-- (OBJ id=company[x3] type=set) -->
        <HR>
        <P>
        <H3><CENTER>$x4$</CENTER></H3>
        <P>
        Recommended by: <I>$x5$</I>
        <P>
        Market per equity: $x8$
    <!-- (/OBJ) -->
    </BODY>
<!-- (/OBJ) -->
</HTML>
```

Fig. 7. A textual representation of a template

In the actual implementation, the system produces, for each node in the result graph, a *node template* that consists of the term of the given node and the surrounding HTML text. The node template defines the visual display of the objects that are created from that node. Each node template consists of parameterized HTML text and OHTML tags that define the objects to be created from the template, as well as the edges leading to immediate subobjects and to other objects that are referenced by the given object. Hence, each node template is essentially an OHTML document with variables from the query. The node templates are combined into a *query template*, which may consist of one ore more OHTML pages (with variables).

New OHTML pages are generated from a query template by evaluating the template over the solutions to the query. For each solution, each variable of the template is bound either to a complex database object (more precisely to an oid reference), to the value of an atomic object, or to a null.

Figure 7 shows a query template, where **report** and **company** are two Skolem functions, and **x4**, **x5** and **x8** are variables embedded in the text.

6   Conclusions

We have designed and implemented QUEST—a graphical query language for semantically tagged pages on the Web. QUEST was implemented in Java and thus has the benefits of Java applications, such as system independence, object oriented design, etc. QUEST has a client-server architecture, where the client is a Java applet. It uses a main memory approach when querying the Web.

The most novel feature of QUEST is its ability to query incomplete information and return incomplete maximal answers as a result. We believe that the ability of QUEST to query incomplete information is of great importance, due to the semistructured nature of the Web. We also believe that the mechanism of finding maximal matchings is natural for querying partial information in general, and not just in QUEST. For more details on the foundation of query processing in QUEST see [KNS99].

QUEST provides a graphical query language. We believe that the graphical interface facilitates easy and succinct formulation of complex queries that may involve a number of path expressions and constraints. Similar queries are not expressed as easily in textual query languages, such as Lorel [AQM+97]. Moreover, the graphical interface also facilitates construction of new Web pages that have both HTML tags and object structures. Hence, the principles of this graphical interface may also apply to querying XML documents and generating new pages for the result by means of style sheets.

Currently, our main effort is to alter the system to support XML. We believe that the principles used in QUEST are sufficiently general and important to be carried over to query languages for XML documents.

References

[Abi97]   S. Abiteboul. Querying semi-structured data. In *International Conference on Database Theory*, volume 1186 of *Lecture Notes in Computer Science*, pages 1–18, Delphi (Greece), January 1997. Springer-Verlag.

[AM98]   G.O. Arocena and A.O. Mendelzon. WebOQL: Restructuring documents, databases, and webs. In *Proc. 14th International Conference on Data Engineering*, pages 24–33, Orlando (Florida, USA), February 1998. IEEE Computer Society.

[AMM97]   P. Atzeni, G. Mecca, and P. Merialdo. To weave the web. In *Proc. 23nd International Conference on Very Large Data Bases*, pages 206–215, Athens (Greece), August 1997. Morgan Kaufmann Publishers.

[AQM+97]   S. Abiteboul, D. Quass, J. McHugh, J. Widom, and J.L. Wiener. The Lorel query language for semistructured data. *International Journal on Digital Libraries*, 1(1):68–88, 1997.

[BDHS96]   P. Buneman, S.B. Davidson, G.G. Hillebrand, and D. Suciu. A query language and optimization techniques for unstructured data. In *Proc. 1996 ACM SIGMOD International Conference on Management of Data*, pages 505–516, Montreal (Canada), June 1996.

[Bun97]   P. Buneman. Semistructured data. In *Proc. 16th Symposium on Principles of Database Systems*, pages 117–121, Tucson (Arizona, USA), May 1997. ACM Press.

[Con98]   World Wide Web Consortium. Extensible markup language (XML) 1.0. http://www.w3.org/TR/REC-xml, 1998.

[DFF+98]   A. Deutsch, M. Fernandez, D. Florescu, A. Levy, and D. Suciu. Applications of XML-QL, a query language for XML. http://www.w3.org/TR/NOTE-xml-ql, 1998.

[FFK+98]   M.F. Fernandez, D. Florescu, J. Kang, A.Y. Levy, and D. Suciu. Catching the boat with Strudel: Experiences with a web-site management system. In *Proc. 1998 ACM SIGMOD International Conference on Management of Data*, pages 414–425, Seattle (Washington, USA), June 1998. ACM Press.

[GL94] C.A. Galindo-Legaria. Outerjoins as disjunctions. In *Proc. 1994 ACM SIGMOD International Conference on Management of Data*, pages 348–358, Minneapolis (Minnesota, USA), May 1994. ACM Press.

[GLO] GLOBES. http://www.globes.co.il.

[KMSS98] Y. Kogan, D. Michaeli, Y. Sagiv, and O. Shmueli. Utilizing the multiple facets of WWW contents. *Data and Knowledge Engineering*, 28(3):255–275, 1998.

[KNS99] Y. Kanza, W. Nutt, and Y. Sagiv. Queries with incomplete answers over semistructured data. In *"Proc. 18th Symposium on Principles of Database Systems"*, *"Philadelphia (Pennsylvania, USA)"*, may 1999. ACM Press.

[KS95] D. Konopnicki and O. Shmueli. W3QS: A query system for the world-wide web. In *Proc. 21st International Conference on Very Large Data Bases*, pages 54–65. Morgan Kaufmann Publishers, August 1995.

[KS97] D. Konopnicki and O. Shmueli. W3QS—A system for WWW querying. In *Proc. 13th International Conference on Data Engineering*, page 586, Binghamton (United Kingdom), April 1997. IEEE Computer Society.

[LSS96] L.V.S. Lakshmanan, F. Sadri, and I.N. Subramanian. A declarative language for querying and restructuring the web. In *Proc. 6th International Workshop on Research Issues on Data Engineering - Interoperability of Nontraditional Database Systems*, pages 12–21, New Orleans (Louisiana, USA), February 1996. IEEE Computer Society.

[MAG+97] J. McHugh, S. Abiteboul, R. Goldman, D. Quass, and J. Widom. Lore: A database management system for semistructured data. *SIGMOD Record*, 3(26):54–66, 1997.

[MAM+98] G. Mecca, P. Atzeni, A. Masci, P. Merialdo, and G. Sindoni. The Araneus web-base management system. In *Proc. 1998 ACM SIGMOD International Conference on Management of Data*, pages 544–546, Seattle (Washington, USA), June 1998. ACM Press.

[MM97] A.O. Mendelzon and T. Milo. Formal models of web queries. In *Proc. 16th Symposium on Principles of Database Systems*, pages 134–143, Tucson (Arizona, USA), May 1997. ACM Press.

[MMM97] A.O. Mendelzon, G.A. Mihaila, and T. Milo. Querying the world wide web. *International Journal on Digital Libraries*, 1(1):54–67, 1997.

[PGMW95] Y. Papakonstantinou, H. Garcia-Molina, and J. Widom. Object exchange across heterogeneous information sources. In P.S.Yu and A.L.P. Chen, editors, *Proc. 11th International Conference on Data Engineering*, pages 251–260, Taipei, March 1995. IEEE Computer Society.

[QRS+95] D. Quass, A. Rajaraman, Y. Sagiv, J. Ullman, and J. Widom. Querying semistructured heterogeneous information. In *Proc. 4th International Conference on Deductive and Object-Oriented Databases*, volume 1013 of *Lecture Notes in Computer Science*, pages 319–344, Singapore, December 1995. Springer-Verlag.

[QWG+96] D. Quass, J. Widom, R. Goldman, K. Haas, Q. Luo, J. McHugh, S. Nestorov, A. Rajaraman, H. Rivero, S. Abiteboul, J.D. Ullman, and J.L. Wiener. Lore: A lightweight object repository for semistructured data. In *Proc. 1996 ACM SIGMOD International Conference on Management of Data*, page 549, Montreal (Canada), June 1996.

[RU96] A. Rajaraman and J.D. Ullman. Integrating information by outerjoins and full disjunctions. In *Proc. 15th Symposium on Principles of Database Systems*, pages 238–248, Montreal (Canada), June 1996. ACM Press.

WWW Exploration Queries

David Konopnicki and Oded Shmueli*

Computer Science Department
Technion, Haifa, 32000, Israel
(konop, oshmu)@cs.Technion.AC.IL

Abstract. The World-Wide Web presents new challenges to database researchers, especially in the area of query processing. Currently, querying the World-Wide Web is done by using *online indices*. These sites employ search engines, known as "robots", that scan the network periodically and form text based indices. A severe limitation of these search services is that the structural information, namely the organization of documents into parts pointing to each other, is lost. Several tasks, ranging from data mining to Intranet management, require the analysis of the hypertext structural organization.

In this paper, we propose a simple graph based query language. In this language, both the query and its target are graphs. We present and evaluate the efficiency of a general class of algorithms for answering graph queries. The algorithms' definitions take into account two important facts of the WWW: (1) efficient algorithms must minimize the communication needed to answer a query and (2) query evaluation involves a process of data graph *exploration*.

1 Introduction

The World-Wide Web presents new challenges to database researchers, especially in the area of query processing. Currently, querying the World-Wide Web is done by using *online indices* such as Lycos, Infoseek, AltaVista[1] and others. These sites employ search engines, known as "robots", that scan the network periodically and form text based indices. A severe limitation of these search services is that the structural information, namely the organization of documents into parts pointing to each other, is lost. Several tasks, ranging from data mining to Intranet management, require the analysis of the hypertext structural organization.

Many data organizations resemble directed graphs, especially hypertext. This has resulted in the design of query languages that view their target data as graphs [6, 11]. In the context of object oriented databases, path expressions can

---

* Work supported by grant 8528-95-1 of the Israeli Ministry of Science and the Arts and by the Fund for the Promotion of Research at the Technion.

[1] www.lycos.com, www.infoseek.com and www.altavista.digital.com

also be viewed as traversing graphs [9]. Such languages are also closely related to the semi-structured databases of [1].

In this paper, we propose a simple graph based query language. In this language, both the query and its target are graphs. We present and evaluate the efficiency of a general class of algorithms for answering graph queries. The algorithms' definitions take into account two important facts of the WWW: (1) the dominating cost is that of communication, (2) the structure of the data graph is usually unknown prior to query evaluation. The consequences of these facts are that: (1) efficient algorithms must minimize the communication needed to answer a query and (2) query evaluation involves a process of data graph *exploration*.

Consider the following example. In a CS Dept., the faculty WWW pages are organized as follows. There is an index page containing a hypertext link for each faculty member. These links lead to pages that contain general information about the faculty members. These pages point, in turn, to the faculty members' home pages. Home pages point to pages of the courses taught by the faculty members. An example of a graph query is: find pairs of faculty members' home pages that point to the same course page. Given the WWW data graph, the query graph is shown in Figure 1. The solution of the query is a set of mappings from the query graph to the data graph such that: node I is mapped to the site's index page, nodes a and b are mapped to the information pages of the two faculty members, nodes a' and b' are mapped to their home pages and C is their common course page.

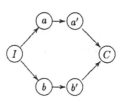

Fig. 1. An Example of a Query Graph

Related Work There exist several query languages for hypertext systems that address the problem of analyzing hypertext structural information. *Graphlog* [5] can be used for the graphical specification of search patterns. In [3], Beeri and Kornatzky define a logic-based language to state queries on hypertext structures. A query language on a dynamically changing hypertext is proposed in [15]. W3QL [11] and WebSQL [14] are two languages defined especially for the WWW. Weblog is a language, based on Datalog, to query and restructure WWW information [12]. However, to date, little has been done in defining what are the requirements from a general hypertext query language, what are the basic problems involved in answering such queries and what optimization techniques should be used.

We have built *W3QS* [11], a query system for the World-Wide Web which uses W3QL, a graph based language. W3QS is limited to simple queries and uses naive algorithms for query processing. Extending W3QL's query processing capabilities was the primary motivation for this paper. It is also conceivable that the techniques developed here will be useful for handling queries on semi-structured data [1, 10] and queries on XML [4] data.

In [13], the authors propose an algorithm to answer a particular class of graph queries: the *regular simple path* queries. Their algorithm does not take into account the cost of building the data graph and considers it as free. Data graph creation is certainly *not* free in the context of the WWW.

Paper Organization Section 2 presents the main definitions and the class of algorithms being studied. Sections 3 describes several techniques for optimizing graph queries. Section 4 presents results of experimenting with optimization techniques. Section 5 introduces extensions such as content conditions and embedded XML objects. Finally, section 6 presents future work and conclusions.

2 Graph Queries

In this section we introduce graph queries with no *content conditions*, i.e., graph queries that focus on the hypertext structure. In section 5, we show how the algorithms presented here can be adapted to handle conditions on the content of the hypertext nodes and links.

2.1 Basic Definitions

A graph query instance is defined by two graphs[2]: the *query graph* and the *data graph*. The answer to a graph query instance is a set of subgraphs of the data graph onto which the query graph is *mapped*. These notions are formalized in the following definitions.

Since the World-Wide Web may be viewed as a directed graph (as in [11]), it can serve as the data graph of a graph query instance where the query graph corresponds to the searched hypertext structure.

In [2], the authors consider the WWW as infinite. Without making this assumption, our model takes into account the size of the WWW by defining *practically computable graph query instances*. In these queries, the query graph search is restricted to a subset of the WWW by the *Starting Point Function (SPF)* which maps nodes in the query graph to sets of nodes in the data graph. The SPF models information on hypertext nodes whose possible addresses (URLs) in the WWW are known. Therefore, the definition of practically computable query instances using the SPF avoids the problem of an infinite search space.

Definition 1. *A* Starting Point Function *(SPF), say f, from graph $G = (V, E)$ to graph $G' = (V', E')$ is a finite partial function from V to sets of nodes of V', i.e. $f : V \mapsto 2^{V'}$.*

We denote the starting point function
$f(a_1) = \{b_1, \ldots, b_n\}, \ldots, f(a_m) = \{c_1, \ldots, c_l\}$ by
$f = \{a_1 \mapsto \{b_1, \ldots, b_n\}, \ldots, a_m \mapsto \{c_1, \ldots, c_l\}\}$

A *mapping function* defines how the query graph is to be mapped on the data graph. There are two different semantics for the mapping function: *Distinct* and *Non-Distinct*.

---

[2] By *graph*, we mean finite directed graph with no self edges.

Definition 2. *A* Mapping Function *(MP) in the Non-Distinct semantics, say m, from graph $G = (V, E)$ to graph $G' = (V', E')$ is a total function from $V \cup E$ to $V' \cup E'$ that maps nodes in G to nodes in G' and edges in G to edges in G' such that $\forall e \in E$, $e = (v_i, v_j) \Rightarrow m(e) = (m(v_i), m(v_j)) \in E'$.*

For the Distinct semantics, the definition is identical to definition 2, except that m also satisfies $\forall v_i, v_j \in V, v_i \neq v_j \Rightarrow m(v_i) \neq m(v_j)$.

Definition 3. *A* Graph Query Instance *is a triple (G, G', f) where $G = (V, E)$ and $G' = (V', E')$ are graphs and f is a SPF from G to G'. G is called the* query graph *and G' is called the* data graph.

Definition 4. *The* restriction *of the graph $G = (V, E)$ to the set of node V' where $V' \subseteq V$, denoted $G[V']$, is a graph $G_r = (V_r, E_r)$ such that $V_r = V'$ and $\forall v, v' \in V', (v, v') \in E \Leftrightarrow (v, v') \in E_r$. We say that $G[V']$ is the subgraph of G that is induced by V'.*

With some abuse of notation, we will write $G[t]$, where t is a tuple containing nodes, instead of $G[T]$, where T is the set of nodes contained in t.

A *Graph Query Solution* is defined as a table in the relational model[3].

Definition 5. *The* solution *of the graph query (G, G', f), where $G = (V, E)$ and $G' = (V', E')$, denoted $S_{(G, G', f)}$, is a relation $r(V)$ such that the tuple $t \in r$ if:*

- $\forall v \in V, t[v] \in V'$ *(i.e for each node in V, there is an associated node in V').*
- *There exists a mapping function, say m, from G to the restriction of G' to the nodes in t, $G'[t]$, such that $\forall v \in V$:*
  - $t[v] = m[v]$ *(i.e, the association is determined by m).*
  - *if f is defined on v, $t[v] \in f(v)$ (i.e, the association respects the SPF constraints).*

If the mapping function respects the Distinct (resp., Non-Distinct) semantics, we say that the solution is in the Distinct (resp., Non-Distinct) semantics.

For example, if the query graph is $G = (\{1, 2, 3\}, \{(1, 2), (1, 3)\})$, the data graph is $G' = (\{a, b, c\}, \{(a, b), (a, c)\})$ and the SPF is $f = \{1 \mapsto \{a\}\}$ then $S_{(G, G', f)}$ in the Distinct semantics is $R(1, 2, 3) = \{(a, b, c,), (a, c, b), (a, b, b), (a, c, c)\}$

For any node $v \in V$, $\Pi_v(S_{(G, G', f)})$ is called the *solution for v*. For example, the solution for 2, in the previous example, is $\{b, c\}$.

Definition 6. *The* partial graph query solution *of the graph query instance (G, G', f) where $G = (V, E)$, for the set of nodes $V_r \subseteq V$, is the solution of the graph query instance $(G[V_r], G', f_r)$ where f_r is the restriction of f to the nodes of V_r.*

In this paper, we consider algorithms that build the query solution progressively, by joining partial query solutions.

---

[3] We denote by $r(R)$ that the schema for relation r is R.

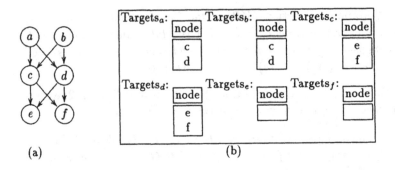

Fig. 2. A Data Graph and the Data Graph Tables

2.2 Finding the Graph Query Solution

We now describe how the graph query solution (in the Non-Distinct semantics) can be found[4]. We define a general class of algorithms, called *progressive algorithms*. These algorithms model an important feature of *WWW query processing*, i.e., the discovery of the topology of the data graph during query execution.

We use relational algebra to describe the algorithms, and therefore, we need first to describe the graph query instance as a relational database.

Definition 7. *Let $G = (V, E)$ be a graph and let V_1 be a subset of V, $V_1 \subseteq V$. The target (resp., source) set of V_1, denoted $T(V_1)$ (resp., $S(V_1)$), is the set $\{ v_2 \mid \exists v_1 \in V_1, (v_1, v_2) \in E \}$ (resp., $\{ v_2 \mid \exists v_1 \in V_1, (v_2, v_1) \in E \}$).*

Definition 8. *The graph query schema for the graph query instance (G, G', f), where $G = (V, E)$ and $G' = (V', E')$, denoted $D_{(G,G',f)}$, is composed of:*

- *The Data Graph tables: for all $v' \in V'$, $D_{(G,G',f)}$ contains a table $Targets_{v'}(node)$, i.e a single column table whose column name is node.*
- *The Query Graph tables: for all $v \in V$ such that v has outgoing edges, let $T(\{v\}) = \{v_1, \ldots, v_k\}$, $D_{(G,G',f)}$ contains a table, $Solutions_v(v, v_1, \ldots, v_k)$.*

In the following sections, we describe how the graph query schema is used to build the graph query solution. In the algorithms described below, for a given data graph $G' = (V', E')$, the content of the data graph tables is fixed and defined in the following way: $Targets_{v'} = \{ (v'_t) \mid v'_t \in V' \land (v', v'_t) \in E' \}$. For example, the data graph tables for the data graph in Figure 2(a) are presented in Figure 2(b). The schema of the query graph tables for the query graph in Figure 1 is $Solutions_I(I, a, b)$, $Solutions_a(a, a')$, $Solutions_b(b, b')$, $Solutions_{a'}(a', C)$ and $Solutions_{b'}(b', C)$. The data graph tables, and the tuples contained in them, model the WWW pages and the embedded hypertext links. The query graph tables are used in the algorithms for holding temporary results.

---

[4] Transforming the algorithms to handle the Distinct semantics is straightforward and it is briefly described in a subsequent section.

Capturing Query Graph Nodes The central concept of progressive algorithms is the *capture* of query graph nodes[5]. Let v be a node of the query graph in the query instance $I = (G, G', f)$. There are edges from v to the nodes in $T(\{v\})$. If we know that the solution for v, $\Pi_v(S_{(G,G',f)})$, is contained in a given set, say Sol, we can use the tables $Targets_{v'}$, where $v' \in Sol$, to find a superset of the solution set for each node in $T(\{v\})$. This superset, say S, is the same for all such nodes in $T(\{v\})$: $S = \bigcup_{v' \in Sol} Targets_{v'}$. Therefore, it is possible to use Sol to build a superset of the query solution for the restriction of instance I to the nodes $\{v\} \cup T(\{v\})$. This operation is called *capturing v*.

For example, let Q be a query instance whose query graph is presented in Figure 3 and whose data graph is presented in Figure 2(a). The SPF is $\{1 \mapsto \{a, b\}\}$. We know that $\Pi_1(S_Q) \subseteq f(1) = \{a, b\}$. Therefore, by capturing node 1, we learn that $\Pi_2(S_Q) \subseteq Targets_a \cup Targets_b = \{c, d\}$. Similarly, $\Pi_3(S_Q) \subseteq \{c, d\}$.

The capture of a node is described in Function 2.1, *capture_node*[6]. For example, let Q be a graph query instance whose query graph is presented in Figure 3 and whose data graph is presented in Figure 2(a). The SPF is $f = \{1 \mapsto \{a, b\}\}$. The function call *capture_node(1,f(1))* returns the table $Solutions_1(1, 2, 3) = \{(a, c, c), (a, d, c), (b, c, c), (b, d, c), (a, c, d), (a, d, d), (b, c, d), (b, d, d)\}$. Observe the (potentially) large size of the table generated by the Cartesian product in line 4 of the *capture_node* function. The function execution can be optimized and we have presented here a simplified version for the sake of clarity.

Fig. 3.

The progressive algorithms cannot be applied to arbitrary graph query instances. Therefore, before continuing the description of the progressive algorithms, we define the class of graph query instances that can be solved (using progressive algorithms).

Practically Computable Graph Query Instances An exhaustive search for graph patterns in the WWW is infeasible. Therefore, for a query to be practically computable, every query graph node must be reachable from some node on which the SPF is defined.

Definition 9. *Let (G, G', f) be a graph query instance, $G = (V, E)$. (G, G', f) is a practically computable graph query instance if there exists a set of nodes $\{v_1, \ldots, v_n\} \subseteq V$, denoted $St_{(G,G',f)}$, such that $\forall i \in [1, n]$, $f(v_i)$ is defined, and $\forall v \in V$, there is a directed path in G from some node in $\{v_1, \ldots, v_n\}$ to v. $v_1, \ldots, v_n$ are the Starting Points of (G, G', f).*

---

[5] This is conceptually similar to the capture of nodes in [17] in the context of rule/goal graphs.

[6] In the description of the algorithms, the statement <u>for</u>$(a \in A)$ is a loop that iterates over the elements of set A, assigning the value of the current element to the variable a.

\ is the set difference operator.

Function 2.1 *capture_node*

Input:

- A query graph node, v.
- A set of potential solutions for v, *Sol*.

Output: The query graph table, $Solutions_v$.
Method:

```
1  begin
2      Solutions_v = ∅
3      for (v' ∈ Sol) do                          d is the arity of Solutions_v
4          Solutions_v = Solutions_v ∪ ({(v')} × (Targets_{v'})^{d-1})
5      od
6      return(Solutions_v)
7  end
```

This definition captures the following fundamental fact. The only source of WWW addresses (URLs) in WWW query processing is the user. All other addresses encountered during query execution are found in pages reachable from the pages whose addresses are explicitly defined in the query by the user (using the SPF). We concentrate now on how to find solutions for practically computable graph query instances.

The Progressive Algorithms The core of all the progressive algorithms is a loop in which each node of the query graph is captured in turn. At each iteration of the loop, the partial query solution is updated using the query graph tables. Before we explain the algorithms in detail, the following facts are noteworthy.

1. As we show in the query optimization section, the cost of query execution depends on the data graph tables accessed in building the query solution. During query execution, *capture_node(v,Sol)* is called for each node of the query graph. *Sol* is a *superset* of the solution for v computed using the SPF and the query graph tables of the nodes captured thus far. Let v' be a node in *Sol*. *Capture_node* uses $Targets_{v'}$ to compute the query graph table. If v' is not in the solutions for v, this step is superfluous and inserts, in the query graph tables, tuples that do not contribute to the query solution; v' is a *dangling* data graph node (for v). Dangling data graph nodes are analogous to *dangling tuples* when optimizing transmission cost by semijoins in distributed RDBMS [17]. To optimize the execution of the query, we try to reduce the number of dangling data graph nodes.

2. If a query graph node v has no outgoing edges (it is a *sink* of the query graph), then it is not necessary to capture it. The solution for v may be computed using the data graph tables of the nodes pointing to v. We do not care where nodes that correspond to v point to.

When a progressive algorithm begins, the nodes that are candidates for capture are the starting points of the graph query instance, i.e. the nodes in $St_{(G,G',f)}$. If *captured* is the set of the captured nodes at some iteration of a progressive algorithm loop, the node that is captured next is either a starting point or a node in $T(captured)$ that is not already captured, i.e a node in the set $((St_{(G,G',f)} \cup T(captured)) \setminus captured)$. Since there is no need to capture nodes whose out-degree is zero, we denote by V_c the set of nodes of the query graph whose out-degree is not zero, and at an iteration of a progressive algorithms the candidates for capture are given by $((St_{(G,G',f)} \cup T(captured)) \setminus captured) \cap V_c$

Definition 10. *Let (G, G', f) be a graph query instance. $(v_1, \ldots, v_n)$ is a capture ordering if:*

- *$v_1, \ldots, v_n$ are the vertices of the query graph G that have outgoing edges.*
- *$(\forall i \in [1, n])(v_i \in St_{(G,G',f)} \vee v_i \in T(\{v_1, \ldots, v_{i-1}\}))$.*

A progressive algorithms must choose a capture ordering. In the worst case, if the query graph is a clique and the SPF is defined on all the query graph nodes, then there are $n!$ possible capture orderings.

The core of the progressive algorithms is presented in Function 2.2. The important variables of the main function are *captured*, the set of captured nodes, and S, the partial query solution for the captured nodes. At line 5, a node $v \in V$ is chosen among the current candidates for capture[7]. Lines 7-10 compute the set of candidate solutions for v. If v is a starting point and *captured* does not contain nodes pointing to v (Line 7), the candidate solutions for v are given by $f(v)$ (Line 8). Otherwise, some node pointing to v has already been captured. Therefore, column v of S contains the candidate solutions for v (Line 9) (We will see below why, if v is a starting point, $\Pi_v(S) \subseteq f(v)$). Next, v is captured (Line 11). Lines 13-15, select from $Solutions_v$ the tuples that comply with f[8], and, in line 16, $Solutions_v$ is joined to S. Therefore, $\forall u \in St_{(G,G',f)} \cap captured, \Pi_u(S) \subseteq f(u)$. Finally, v is added to *captured*. When all the nodes in V_c have been captured, S is the query solution[9].

We have not described the *Choose* function. This will be the subject of the next section on graph query optimization.

The solution in the Distinct semantics is obtained by slightly modifying the main function of the algorithm. Recall that in the Distinct semantics, different query graph nodes must map to different data graph nodes. This is achieved by selecting tuples in S that have different values in all their columns. That is, if τ is the relational algebra select expression: *Every two different columns have different values in t*, the statement $S = \sigma_\tau(S)$ must be added after line 16 in Function 2.2.

3 Optimizing Graph Queries

The various progressive algorithms are differentiated by the way they choose nodes to capture. At each iteration of the while-loop, a node is chosen and, as

---

[7] We do not explain here how this choice is made. In fact, the various instantiations of progressive algorithms are differentiated in the way they choose the node to capture.

[8] The condition $vs \in f(vs)$ stands for $\vee_{st \in f(vs)}(vs = st)$.

[9] Due to space limitation, the proof of correctness of the progressive algorithms is not included.

Function 2.2 *Main* (The general form of progressive algorithms)

Input:

- A Graph Query Instance: (G, G', f). Let $G = (V, E)$ and let let $V_c \subseteq V$ be the nodes in V whose out-degree is not zero (i.e. these are the nodes to capture).
- The Graph Query Schema: $D_{(G,G',f)}$.

Output: The Query Solution: $S_{(G,G',f)}$.

Method:

```
1   begin
2       captured = ∅
3       S = {()}
4       while (captured ≠ Vc) do
5           v = Choose(((St(G,G',f) ∪ T(captured)) \ captured) ∩ Vc)
6                                                   S({v}) is the source set
7           if (v ∈ St(G,G',f) ∧ (S({v}) ∩ captured = ∅))
8               then Sol = f(v)
9               else Sol = Πv(S)
10          fi
11          Solutionsv = capture_node(v, Sol)
12                                                  T({v}) is the target set
13          for (vs ∈ St(G,G',f) ∩ T({v})) do
14              Solutionsv = σvs∈f(vs)(Solutionsv)
15          od
16          S = S ⋈ Solutionsv
17          captured = captured ∪ {v}
18      od
19      return(S)
20  end
```

---

will be shown, the choice policy may have a crucial effect on the algorithm's performance.

3.1 Cost Model

In the WWW, the dominating cost is that of communication. We are mainly interested in measuring only the influence of choice policies on the amount of communication. Therefore, our cost model considers only the communication costs and not the cost of performing the local table joins required by the algorithm[10]. Furthermore, the local table joins may be optimized independently.

In the algorithms as presented thus far, it is unclear where exactly communication over the network is performed. In a network context (over the WWW), the graph query schema and the progressive algorithms are interpreted in the following way; a data graph table corresponds to a HTML page and the content of the data graph table is the set of hypertext links in the page which point to other pages; the query graph tables are used only for local query processing. Therefore, the communication part of the algorithms is "hidden" in the use of

---

[10] Query optimization in relational databases is an extensively studied problem [8, 16].

the data graph tables. In fact, line 3 of the *capture_node* function can be re-written as:

$Request(Targets_{v'})$
$Solutions_v = Solutions_v \cup ((v') \times (Targets_{v'})^{d-1})$

$Request(Targets_{v'})$ may be interpreted as *get the HTML page v' and collect the outgoing hypertext links*. Therefore, we assume the existence of a function $Cost : V' \rightarrow N$, that models the cost of requesting a data graph table (N denotes the integers).

Another factor affecting performance is the *caching policy*. If a data graph node appears in the solutions of several query graph nodes, it is useful to put the corresponding data graph table (i.e., the HTML page) in a cache in order not to access it over the network more than once. Studying complex caching policies is beyond the scope of this work. We only examine two extreme cases: *no cache* and *infinite cache*. If there is no cache, the cost of execution is calculated by transforming line 3 of the *capture_node* function to:

$Request(Targets_{v'})$
$Cost = Cost + Cost(v')$
$Solutions_v = Solutions_v \cup ((v') \times (Targets_{v'})^{d-1})$

If there is an infinite cache, the cost of execution is calculated by transforming line 3 of the *capture_node* function to:

---

if $(v' \notin cached)$ **then**
$\qquad\qquad Request(Targets_{v'})$
$\qquad\qquad cached = cached \cup \{v'\}$
$\qquad\qquad Cost = Cost + Cost(v')$
fi
$Solutions_v = Solutions_v \cup ((v') \times (Targets_{v'})^{d-1})$

In both cases, the cost of execution is the value of the *Cost* variable when the algorithm terminates. The fundamental problem of graph query optimization is to find a capture ordering that leads to the minimum cost. We assume a serial execution; parallel execution is beyond the scope of our study.

In the WWW context, the value of $Cost(v')$, where v' is a query graph node, may be interpreted in different ways. We may take $Cost(v')$ to be the time it takes to bring v' from the network. In this case, $Cost(v')$ is unknown to the optimization algorithms before the completion of the request operation. We may also consider that $Cost(v')$ is the size of the WWW page corresponding to v'[11]. In the latter case, an optimization algorithm can compute the cost before the actual request by using the HTTP *HEAD* network request [7]. Our optimization algorithms model the two possibilities.

---

[11] Practically, the *relative* size of a WWW page may be used to approximate the *relative* request time.

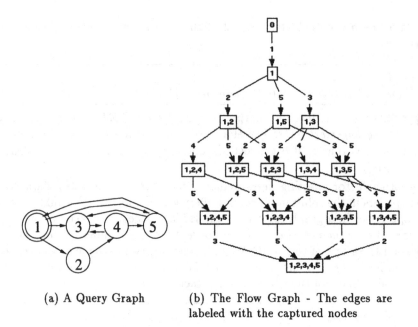

(a) A Query Graph

(b) The Flow Graph - The edges are labeled with the captured nodes

Fig. 4. A Query Graph and the Corresponding Flow Graph

3.2 The Flow Graph

Our main tool for studying graph queries optimization, called the *flow graph*, models the different possible states of query execution by considering the possible contents of the *captured* set. Consider the query graph presented in Figure 4(a)[12]. The corresponding flow graph is presented in Figure 4(b) and is interpreted as follows. The upper node (labeled with 0) corresponds to the empty *captured* set. Since the SPF is defined only on the query graph node 1, node 1 must be captured and the next state into which every progressive algorithm will enter (*captured* = {1}) corresponds to the flow graph node labeled 1. It is then possible to capture the query graph nodes 2, 3 or 5, leading, respectively, to the states *captured* = {1, 2}, *captured* = {1, 3} or *captured* = {1, 5}. Each path in the flow graph, from node 0 to node 1,2,3,4,5, corresponds to a possible capture ordering.

If the query graph contains n nodes, there are $n!$ possible capture orderings. The use of the *flow graph* reduces the number of tested orderings. The flow graph considers only the possible contents of the *captured* set instead of the possible orderings leading to them. The number of possibilities is reduced to 2^n. This technique was used to optimize joins in System-R [16]. Formally:

Definition 11. *The* flow graph *of the graph query instance* (G, G', f), *where* $G = (V, E)$, *is the graph* $G_f = (V_f, E_f)$ *defined in the following way:*

---

[12] The SPF is defined on the double-circled nodes

- *The nodes of V_f are the possible contents of the captured set. This is defined inductively as:*
  - $\emptyset \in V_f$
  - $\forall v \in V_f, \forall v_{new} \in (St \cap T(v)) \setminus v$, *such that* $T(\{v_{new}\}) \neq \emptyset$, *the flow graph contains the node* $v \cup \{v_{new}\}$.
- *There is an edge from u to v if the captured set v is obtained by capturing a node when captured $= u$, that is $\|v \setminus u\| = 1$.*

3.3 Optimized Progressive Algorithms

We can build a taxonomy of the optimization algorithms along several dimensions.

- Local vs. Global Algorithms. Local optimization algorithms do not build the entire flow graph. Instead, a local optimization algorithm considers a node in the flow graph, calculates the cost for each out-edge (i.e., each possible capture) and moves along an edge with the minimal cost to a new flow graph node. A global optimization algorithm builds the whole flow graph, associates a cost with each flow graph edge and searches for the least cost path from its current node to the node with *captured $= V$*.
- Offline vs. Online Algorithms. An offline algorithm does the optimization prior to query execution while an online algorithm may change the capture ordering during query execution. Also, an online algorithm can gather statistical information, on the part of the network being explored, in order to improve its initial estimates.
- Rule-Based vs. Cost-Based Algorithms. Rule-based optimization algorithms use heuristic rules for choosing the capture ordering, whereas Cost-based optimization techniques use (estimated) costs.

We now present in detail four typical optimization algorithms.

The Greedy Algorithm The Greedy algorithm chooses the cheapest node to capture at each iteration. Greedy is a local, online, cost-based algorithm. Greedy can be defined in two different "flavors". In the first case, it is assumed that the cost of a data graph node cannot be computed prior to accessing it. Therefore, Greedy chooses the query graph node whose *Sol* set is the smallest. The *Choose* function is presented in Function 3.1. If the cost of a data graph node can be computed prior to its capture, line 5 of the Greedy algorithm is replaced by:

$cost = 0$
for $(v' \in Sol \setminus cached)$ **do**
    $cost = cost + Cost(v')$
od

Recall that the cost function is different if the data graph tables are cached. If there is no cache, the cost of each capture is simply the cost of the nodes in the *Sol* set. If there is a cache, the cost of the capture is the cost of the nodes in *Sol* that are *not* in the cache.

Function 3.1 *Choose* - The Greedy Algorithm

Input: $V = ((St \cup T(captured)) \setminus captured) \cap V_c$

Output: The next node to capture.

Method:

```
 1  min = ∞
 2  for (v ∈ V) do
 3      if ((v ∈ St) ∧ (S({v}) ∩ captured = ∅))
 4          then Sol = f(v) else Sol = Πᵥ(S) fi
 5      cost = ‖Sol \ cached‖                          If there is no cache, cached = ∅
 6      if (cost < min) then
 7                          min = cost; current = v
 8      fi
 9  od
10  return(current)
```

The Best-Source Algorithm Greedy does not use the topology of the query graph in order to reduce the number of accessed data graph tables. The potential solutions for a node are in the intersection of the columns found in the *Solutions* table of the captured nodes that point to it. Therefore, it is better to choose in the set of candidates for capture, a node that maximizes $\|S(\{v\}) \cap captured\|$ since the intersection is more likely to be small and there will be less dangling data graph nodes in the potential solutions for v. This optimization idea is independent of the cost of the capture and is therefore considered to be rule-based. The rule of thumb can be stated as: *Capture the node with the largest fraction of captured source nodes.*

The Global Best-Source Algorithm (GBS) GBS uses the same heuristics as BS. But, instead of minimizing the fraction of non-captured source nodes at each stage, GBS minimizes the sum of the fractions of non-captured source nodes for *all* the nodes in an ordering. This is done in the following way. The flow graph corresponding to the query graph of the query is constructed. Each flow graph node corresponds to a possible content of the *captured* set. Each edge (u, v) is labeled with the fraction of the non captured source nodes when the captured node is in $(v \setminus u)$. Global Best-Source finds the cheapest path from node $captured = \emptyset$ to node $captured = V$.

The Approx Algorithm As in GBS, Approx labels the edges of the flow graph and finds the least cost path from node $captured = \emptyset$ to node $captured = V$. The difference is that each edge (u, v) is labeled with the *approximated cost* of capturing the node in $(v \setminus u)$.

To compute the approximate cost, Approx operates under the following assumptions:

- Every starting point is mapped to a data graph nodes.
- The out-degree of every data graph node (i.e. the size of every data graph table) is m.

- The data graph contains p data graph nodes (p is, for example, the (approximated) size of the "site" against which the query is evaluated).
- Let v be a data graph node. The m edges that emanate from v are constructed by choosing randomly m different target nodes, out of the $p - 1$ possible nodes, with an equal probability.
- All the pages of the site have the same size (namely 1).

In order to describe how Approx computes the approximative cost, we first establish the following lemma.

Lemma 1. *Let A be a set containing p elements. Let $A_1, \ldots, A_n$ be n sets such that A_i, $i \in [1, n]$, is constructed by choosing at random and uniformly m_i different elements out of A, then:*

1. *The expected number of elements in $\cap_{i=1}^n A_i$ is $p\Pi_{i=1}^n (m_i/p)$.*
2. *The expected number of elements in $\cup_{i=1}^n A_i$ is $p(1 - \Pi_{i=1}^n (1 - m_i/p))$.*

Therefore, given a node v, the cost of capturing v, say *cost*, is evaluated (inductively) in the following way:

- If v is a starting point then *cost* is a.
- if v is not a starting point, let $v_1, \ldots, v_n$ be the captured nodes that point to v, i.e. $\{v_1, \ldots, v_n\} = S(\{v\}) \cap captured$. Consider a node v_i, $i \in [1, n]$, and assume that we know that v_i is mapped to s_i data graph nodes. Each one of these data graph nodes points to m data graph nodes that are potential solutions for v. That is, the potential solutions for v are in the union of the s_i sets of m data graph nodes each. Denote this set of potential solutions for v induced by v_i as S_i. From the preceding lemma (part 2), we know that the expected number of potential solutions for v found in the s_i sets, each with m data graph nodes, is $p(1 - \Pi_{i=1}^{s_i}(1 - m/p)) = p(1 - (1 - m/p)^{s_i})$. Define $d = (1 - m/p)$. So, $E(\|S_i\|) = p(1 - d^{s_i})$, where s_i is the number of potential solutions for v_i.
For a data graph node v' to be a potential solution for v, it must belong to $\cap_{i=1}^n S_i$ where $E(\|S_i\|) = p(1 - d^{s_i})$. It can be easily shown that, from the preceding lemma (part 1), the expected number of data graph nodes that are solutions for v is $p(\Pi_{i=1}^n \frac{p(1-d^{s_i})}{p}) = p(\Pi_{i=1}^n 1 - d^{s_i})$. Therefore, *cost* is $p(\Pi_{i=1}^n 1 - d^{s_i})$.

For example, consider the data graph in Figure 5 and let each starting point be mapped to 10 data graph nodes ($a = 10$), let the out-degree of each data graph node be 10 ($m = 10$) and let the size of the site on which the query is evaluated be 100 ($p = 100$). The number of potential solutions for each starting point is 10. The sets S_1, S_2 and S_3, i.e. the potential solutions for 4 induced by 1, 2, and 3, respectively, contain each $100(1 - 0.9^{10}) \approx 65$ potential solutions for 4. The potential solutions for 4 are in the intersection of S_1, S_2 and S_3. Therefore, the expected number of potential solutions for 4 (and the approximated cost of capturing 4) is $100((1 - (0.9)^{10})^3) \approx 27$.

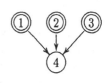

Fig. 5. A Query Graph

4 Experiments

We built a query execution simulator to evaluate the performance of the different optimization algorithms. The simulator enables the setting of the different parameters and calculates the cost of executing synthetic or user-defined query graphs on random, or abstractions of real WWW sites, data graphs.

We present the results of several optimization experiments. We simulated the execution of 30 query graphs. The query graphs are constructed thus. The basic query graph is $G = (\{1, 2, 3, 4, 5\}, \{(1, 2), (1, 3), (2, 4), (3, 5)\})$. We formed three sets, of 10 graphs each, by adding to G n randomly chosen edges in each set ($n = 3, 6, 9$, resp.). We have tested these query graphs on three types of data graphs.

- **Tree Data Graphs.** The data graph is a tree of depth d in which the out degree of each node was chosen at random between min and max. Furthermore, r random edges are added to the tree.
- **Levels Data Graphs.** The data graph consists of d sets of nodes (the *levels*). The first level contains one node and all the other levels contains *width* nodes. The maximum in-degree (id) and out-degree (od) of a node are defined and the nodes of two consecutive levels are linked, accordingly, at random.
- **Actual sites.**

Before executing a query, 10 query solutions are planted in the data graph. The cost of each (non cached) data table access is 1. We present the results of simulations for three data graphs[13]: G_1 is a tree data graph with $d = 3, min = 2, max = 15, r = 200$, G_2 is a levels data graph with $d = 3, width = 50$ and G_3 is the graph of an actual site. We used the set of all the pages accessible from the URL http://www.cs.technion.ac.il/p-f-off.html. The organization of this site is similar to the site described in the first example (Fig 1). The simulations were done (1) with an infinite cache and (2) with no cache. The results of the simulations are shown in Figure 6. Pairwise comparisons of the algorithms (without cache) are presented in Table 1.

Analysis From these results we can make the following observations:

- Caching is obviously very important.
- The differences in performance between the algorithms are significant and "wrong" capture orderings can result in very expensive query plans.
- GBS has only a slight advantage over BS. Since GBS tends to capture query graph nodes that are "far" from starting points, it sometimes creates very expensive orderings.
- Approx and GBS are usually better than Greedy.

---

[13] We present the results for three data graphs, however similar results have been obtained when experimenting with other data graphs (created in the same way).

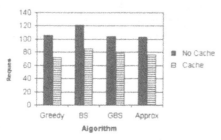

(a) Average number of requests per algorithm over all data sets for G_1

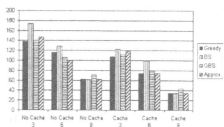

(b) Average number of requests per algorithm and per data set for G_1

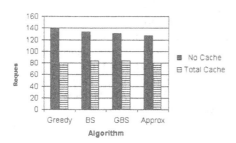

(c) Average number of requests per algorithm over all data sets for G_2

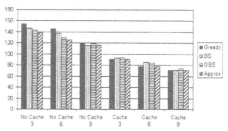

(d) Average number of requests per algorithm and per data set for G_2

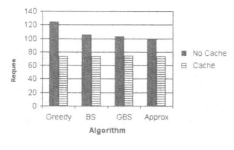

(e) Average number of requests per algorithm over all data sets for G_3

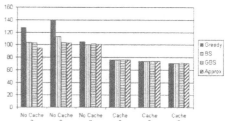

(f) Average number of requests per algorithm and per data set for G_3

Fig. 6. Results of simulations.

	G_1			G_2			G_3		
	N	%	Diff %	N	%	Diff %	N	%	Diff %
BS vs. GBS									
BS better	2	6.6	143	7	23.3	12	4	13.3	28
Equal	14	46.6	-	16	53.3	-	20	66.6	-
GBS better	14	46.6	-28	7	23.3	-16.2	6	20	-22
Greedy vs. Approx									
Greedy better	2	6.6	54	0	0	-	0	0	-
Equal	19	63.3	-	15	50	-	16	53.3	-
Approx better	9	30	-14	15	50	-16	14	46.6	-34.7
Greedy vs. GBS									
Greedy better	3	10	123	6	20	14	2	6.6	17
Equal	14	46.6	-	9	30	-	15	50	-
GBS better	13	43.3	-15	15	50	-17	13	43.3	-21

Table 1. Some Pairwise Comparisons of the Algorithms. The table is read as follows. For each data graph, pairs of algorithms are compared (A vs. B). The line "A better" analyzes the cases in which algorithm A costs less than algorithm B. Columns "N" and "%" contain the number, and the percentage, of query graphs on which A is better. Column "Diff (%)" contains the difference of costs between the two algorithms. For example, in the comparison between BS and GBS on the data graph G_1, BS is better than GBS on 2 query graphs (6.6%) and GBS is better than BS on 14 query graphs (46.6%). When BS is better than GBS, GBS costs, on average, 143% more than BS. When GBS is better than BS, GBS costs, on average, 28% less than BS.

- The differences between the offline algorithms and Greedy when there is an infinite cache is very small. The reason for this may be that the offline algorithms do not take into account the content of the cache.
- When the query graph is highly constrained ($n = 9$), very few data graph nodes are "dangling" and, therefore, the differences between the algorithms is small.

The experimentation suggests the development of online algorithms that use the topology of the query graph (as do BS and GBS) and use the flow graph to "look ahead" using approximated costs (like Approx). Adaptive algorithms, i.e. algorithms that improve their initial assumptions as they navigate the WWW, refine their knowledge, and dynamically redefine the execution plan, are worth checking.

5 More Expressive Languages

5.1 Content Conditions

Users do not usually search for just hypertext structures. Rather, they impose content conditions on the WWW pages they access. In order to model such queries, we consider edge and node labeled data graphs. The query graph is augmented with a set of *content conditions*. For example, a content condition may state that some query graph node must be mapped to data graph nodes that contain a specified string. The progressive algorithms can be adapted to handle queries with content conditions.

The optimization algorithms presented above have natural extensions to queries with content conditions. For example, BS may be modified as follows. Given a candidate node for capture, say v, let a be the number of captured nodes pointing to v. Let c be the content condition defined on v and s be the selectivity of c^{14}. The *constraining factor* of v is defined as $\alpha a + \beta s$ where α and β are weighting factors. BS captures the node with the largest constraining factor.

Note that (1) conditions on edges can be treated in a similar way, and (2) the algorithms can be refined further to handle "join" conditions between query graph nodes, e.g. "query graph nodes 1 and 2 must be mapped to HTML pages that have the same title".

5.2 XML Objects and Semi-Structured Data

It is possible to consider the case in which the query graph nodes correspond to (semi-structured) objects embedded in pages (encoded, for example, using XML [4]). In this case, a WWW page may contain several query graph nodes, and edges between query graph nodes may be local (i.e., link data graph nodes that appear in the same page) or external (i.e., link data graph nodes that appear in different pages).

To understand how the progressive algorithms can be used in this framework, consider the following example. An index page points to publication pages in which publication objects are organized on a per author basis (i.e., all the publications of one author are contained in the same page). The publication objects point to journal issue objects that are found in other pages which are organized per year. We search for authors that have at least two publications in two different journal issues in the same year. This query is shown in Figure 7 (and must be evaluated under the Distinct semantics). The dotted boxes contain objects that must appear in the same page. The dotted arrows represent links between pages that are induced by the links between the embedded objects. The dotted boxes and the dotted arrows form a *superstructure graph* that may be used to obtain pages from the network by using a progressive algorithm.

Obviously, the progressive algorithms must be adapted to handle queries involving objects embedded in pages. In particular, the cost model and the optimization algorithms must take into account the possibility of requesting several objects in one page request. However, the global approach of the progressive algorithms is still a promising approach for these cases.

---

[14] For example, if c is "v must be mapped to nodes that contain the string t", s can be approximated by checking the number of HTML documents containing t in the corpus of pages under consideration.

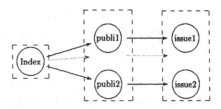

Fig. 7. Example of a graph query involving embedded objects

6 Conclusions

We have defined the class of *graph queries* and a class of algorithms for solving them. We showed how these algorithms can be optimized. Further work on this subject includes:

- **Defining New Optimization algorithms**. The algorithms presented here use only one optimization technique at a time. We intend to develop algorithms that use several techniques, i.e., algorithms that use simultaneously the information gathered from the actual data graph (as Greedy), the topology of the query graph (as BS and GBS) and the flow graph labeled with approximated costs (as Approx).
- **Testing other query graph and data graph topologies**. We plan to examine if some optimization algorithms are more suited for particular query graph or data graph topologies.
- **Analyzing caching policies**. We began to analyze caching policies using standard caching algorithms (FIFO and LRU) and specialized algorithms for graph queries.
- **Simulating Query graph with content conditions**. We plan to examine how to modify the optimization algorithms in the presence of content conditions on the query graph nodes and links.
- **Defining and testing parallel query processing algorithms**. World-Wide Web browsers usually open several network connections in order to load concurrently several World-Wide Web objects. The same technique may be used to speed up query processing.
- **Analyzing the effect of projections**. Graph queries with *projections* are graph queries in which the user is interested only in the solutions for a proper subset of the query graph nodes.
- **Finding appropriate query algorithms when the query graphs are extended with regular expressions**. Query languages for semi-structured data [1] use regular expressions to specify queries on data graphs whose organization is not completely known. We plan to extend the progressive algorithms to handle regular expression constructs.
- **Taking into account the local processing cost**.
- **Defining standard server services**. Optimization algorithms benefit from the availability of statistics on the data being queried. The progressive algorithms will help in defining what is the information that servers should provide in order to make a site "query friendly".

References

1. S. Abiteboul, D. Quass, J. McHugh, J. Widom, and J. Wiener. The lorel query language for semistructured data. *Journal on Digital Libraries*, 1(1):68–88, 1996.
2. S. Abiteboul and V. Vianu. Queries and computation on the web. In *ICDT*, 1997.
3. C. Beeri and Y. Kornatzky. A logical query language for hypertext systems. In *Proceeding of the European Conference on Hypertext*, pages 67–80, 1990.
4. T. Bray, J. Paoli, and C. M. Sperberg-McQueen. Extensible markup language (xml). W3C Recommendation, http://www.w3.org/TR/WD-xml.
5. M. P. Consens and A. O. Mendelzon. Expressing structural hypertext queries in graphlog. In *Proc. Hypertext'89*, 1989.
6. M. P. Consens and A. O. Mendelzon. Graphlog: a visual formalism for real life recursion. In *Proc. PODS*, pages 404–416, 1990.
7. R. Fielding, J. Gettys, J. Mogul, H. Frystyk, and T. Berners-Lee. Rfc 2068: Hypertext transfer protocol http/1.1, January 1997.
8. M. Jarke and J. Koch. Query optimization in database systems. *Computing Surveys*, 16(2), June 1994.
9. M. Kifer, W. Kim, and Y. Sagiv. Querying object-oriented databases. In *Proc. SIGMOD*, pages 393–402, 1992.
10. Y. Kogan, D. Michaeli, Y. Sagiv, and O. Shmueli. Utilizing the multiple facets of www content. In *Proc. NGITS*, 1997.
11. D. Konopnicki and O. Shmueli. Information gathering in the world-wide web: The w3ql query language and the w3qs system. TODS, to appear.
12. Laks V. S. Lakshmanan, Fereidoon Sadri, and Iyer N. Subramania. A declarative language for querying and restructuring the web. In *Sixth International Workshop on Research Issues in Data Engineering - Interoperability of Nontraditional Database Systems*, 1996.
13. A. O. Mendelzon and P. T. Wood. Finding regular simple paths in graph databases. *SIAM J. Comp.*, 24(6), 1995.
14. G. A. Mihaila, A. O. Mendelzon, and T. Milo. Querying the world-wide web. In *Proc. PDIS96*, pages 80–91, 1996.
15. T. Minohara and R. Wanatabe. Queries on structure in hypertext. In *Proc. FODO*, pages 394–411, 1993.
16. P. G. Selinger, M. M. Astrahan, D. D. Chamberlin, R. A. Lorie, and T. G. Price. Access path selection in a relational database management system. In *Proc. SIGMOD*, pages 23–34, 1979.
17. J. D. Ullman. *Data and Knowledge-Base Systems - Volume II*. Computer Science Press, 1989.

Strategies for Filtering E-mail Messages Combining Content-Based and Sociological Filtering with User-Sterotypes

Peretz Shoval, Bracha Shapira and Uri Hanani,

Information Systems Engineering Program
Department of Industrial Engineering & Management
Ben-Gurion University of the Negev, Beer-Sheva 84105, Israel

Abstract. A prototype system was developed to test the applicability of a dual-method information-filtering model for filtering e-mail messages: content-based filtering and sociological filtering implemented with user stereotypes. This paper reports the main results of experiments that were run to determine the effects of combining the two methods in various ways. A major outcome of the experiments is that the combination of both methods yields better results than using each method individually. The optimal combination of the two filtering methods is stereotype dependent.

1 Introduction

Information filtering systems differs from traditional information retrieval systems, in that their users have long-term information needs that are described by means of user profiles, rather than ad-hoc needs that are expressed as queries. There exist two main filtering approaches [3], [5]: *content-based* filtering and *sociological filtering*. The two approaches differ in the methods used for constructing user profiles and the techniques used to calculate relevance of data items (documents). In content-based filtering, the user profile and the filtering technique are based solely on the content of information. The user's profile consists of a list of keywords that represent his areas of interest, and the filtering process is aimed at finding out to what extent the content of a candidate document is close to that profile. Most commercial filtering systems employ content-based filtering, since the method is relatively easy to implement, and produces reasonable results [4].

Sociological filtering is usually (e.g. [1] and [8]) interpreted as a collaborative process that bases the filtering on "similar" users. For a given user, a group of users is found whose feedback, recommendations, or content-based profile is most similar to his. The filtering consists of calculation of a document's rank, as based on comparison of the user profile or the evaluated document to corresponding parameters of "similar users". However, similarity of users in most systems is content-based since it is calculated on the basis of similarity of their content-based profiles or on feedback.

We adopt a different interpretation of sociological filtering: we claim that demographic parameters of the user, such as education, occupation and work experience, influence his preferences and habits in consuming or filtering information. For example, a researcher and a programmer may have the same area of interest (i.e. same content-based profile), but owing to their affiliation, education and occupation, different documents may be relevant to them. To cope with such differences, the user profile must include demographic information in addition to a content-based profile.

We assume that users who share demographic parameters also have common preferences and habits with respect to their information needs. This idea is expressed by means of "user-stereotypes". A user-stereotype is a "centroid" for users who have similar demographic background and similar information filtering behavior. This behavior is represented by a set of filtering rules that are common to those users. A user is assigned to a stereotype on the basis of commonality (closeness) of demographic parameters, and the filtering rules of "his" stereotype are applied to determine the relevance rank of documents. This forms the sociological filtering method, which is applied in addition to content-based filtering.

Our filtering model combines content-based and sociological filtering in various ways. A prototype system that implements the model was developed, to examine its applicability and effectiveness. The model and the system that implements it are overviewed in section 2. Section 3 describes how we implement sociological filtering. Section 4 describes experiments conducted to test the model with various filtering strategies in the domain of e-mail messages. Section 5 analyses the results of the experiments, and Section 6 provides conclusions and discusses further research.

2 The Model and the Prototype System

The filtering model is described in greater detail in [6]; here we provide a brief overview only. The model contains four databases:

D1: Raw Database - contains incoming documents (e-mail messages) to be filtered.

D2: Represented Documents – a document is represented as a weighted-vector of keywords.

D3: User Profiles - contains two types of profiles for each user: a) a content-based profile - presented as a weighted-vector of keyword, and b) a sociological profile - includes demographic parameters of the user, e.g., education, occupation and age.

D4: Stereotype Data & Rules: contains descriptions of known user stereotypes. Each stereotype is represented by a set of demographic parameters that are common to users who "belong" to the stereotype, and by a set of filtering rules that are typical to those users. Each rule refers to a parameter in documents. For example, for an e-mail message, the parameters may include its goal (purpose), source and length. A rule specifies the relevancy of a document to a user who belongs to the stereotype, with respect to a certain parameter. For example, the rule
If (goal = 'conference') then rank ← 5.9 determines that, for a certain stereotype, messages announcing conferences are of high relevance (on a 0-7 scale).

The model contains three main processes:

F1: Representation Process - converts raw documents to a vector of weighted-terms.

F2: Filtering Process – this main process of the model calculates the relevance rank of each document. As said, it incorporates two main methods: 1) Content-based filtering, where a document is examined for relevancy to the user on the basis of his areas of interest. This is accomplished by calculating the statistical correlation between the vector of keywords representing the user interests and the vector of keywords representing the document. 2) Sociological filtering, where relevance of a document is calculated by applying relevant filtering-rules of the user's stereotype. Each filtering method produces a relevance rank for the examined document. The overall rank is some combination of the two ranks. One of our goals is to find combinations of both filtering methods that yield best relevance ranks.

F3: Learning Process - Based on feedback from the user and filtering process, this process may update the user's profile, his stereotype's rules, and even re-assign the user to a different stereotype. (We do not elaborate on this process.)

We examine two combinations of the filtering methods: *consecutive* and *parallel:*

- In the *consecutive* combination, one of the filtering methods is considered "primary", i.e. more important. Thus, a document is first filtered by the primary method, and only if its resulting rank is above a certain relevance threshold, the second filtering method is applied, providing a second relevance rank. The overall relevance rank of the document is a weighted-average of the two ranks, with more weight given to the primary method. If the relevance rank of the primary method is below a relevance threshold, this rank is considered as the overall rank of that document.

- In the *parallel* combination, each of the filtering methods is applied on every document, providing its relevance rank. The overall rank of a document is the average of the two ranks.

As already stated, one of our objectives is to examine the different filtering approaches and find out optimal strategies for different user stereotypes. We have implemented the filtering model in a prototype system, designed to enable experimentation, i.e., evaluation and ranking of documents using different filtering strategies. For the purpose of this research the system was implemented to evaluate e-mail messages. The messages are initially evaluated by their users (recipients) who use special software that serves as a front-end interface to various e-mail systems: users who receive e-mail messages from various list servers utilize that software to evaluate and rank the relevancy of their incoming messages on a 1-7 scale. The user-evaluated messages are saved. At the experimentation stage, the system computes the relevancy of each of these messages several times, according to the different filtering strategies that are examined. The objective of the filtering system is to evaluate the relevance of documents (messages) as close as possible to the users evaluations.

The main component of the prototype system is a filtering module that implements the two filtering methods in various ways. The filtering module utilizes two main engines: the *content-based engine*, and the *sociological engine*. The prototype system enables the experimenter to evaluate each e-mail message according to the following filtering strategies: 1) Content-based filtering alone; 2) Sociological filtering alone; 3) Two-phase parallel combination (both content-based and sociological filtering); 4) Two-phase consecutive combinations, with either filtering method as the "primary" (i.e. content-based followed by sociological, or sociological followed by content-based), with different weights to each method.

3 Implementation of Sociological Filtering

In order to implement the model and perform experiments, we have to create user profiles (both content-based and sociological), form user stereotypes, and for each stereotype define filtering rules and sociological parameters to represent it.

This process is based on user interviews. We need to interview users (i.e., recipients of e-mail messages) in a certain domain, in order to identify their sociological parameters and information filtering rules. The environment domains for the implementation and the following experiments are information technology departments at universities. The information users are academic researchers, information specialists, graduate students, and computer technicians. We have interviewed forty e-mail users from that domain who subscribe to several list-servers each. The interviews were based on a questionnaire consisting of two main parts:

The first part includes questions on sociological parameters that might affect users in their information seeking and filtering behavior. These parameters will found a basis for defining stereotypes' sociological parameters, and for assigning new users to existing stereotypes. For each question/parameter we provided a set of possible answers (values). Table 1 presents the sociological parameters, their possible values and their numerical decoding. The result of this part of the interview is sociological profiles of the forty users. As an outcome of this part of the interviews, a set of eight rules with identical parameters, but with different value, was defined. Table 2 presents the parameters of the eight rules and their meaning.

Table 1. Sociological Parameters of Users

Parameter	Possible Values (and their numerical decoding)
Education	Ph.D. (1), M.Sc. (2), Engineer (3), B.Sc.(4), Technician (5)
Occupation	researcher (1), information specialist (2), computer professional (3), student (4)
Level	junior (1), intermediate (2), senior (3)
Computer knowledge	novice user(1), experienced user (2), professional (3), computer scientist (4)
Age	up to 25 (1), between 25-40 (2), above 40 (3)
No. of lists subscribed	up to 2 (1), between 2-7 (2), above 7 (3)
Use of e-mail	once in a couple of days (1), once a day (2), several times a day (3)
Weekly use of Internet	up to 5 hours (1), between 5-10 hours (2), above 10 hours (3)
% of e-mail filtering	no filtering (1), up to 20% (2), between 20%-50% (3), above 50% (4)

Table 2. Filtering Rules

Parameter	Meaning of the rule
conference	Announcement of a conference
paper	Call for papers
internet	Reference to sites on the Internet
technical	Technical message
job	Job offer
fund	Announcement on funds (research grants, etc.)
length > 2 screens	Message whose length is above two screens
history > 2	Message topic already discussed (replied) more than twice

We used a clustering technique [2] for the partition of the users to stereotypes. Clustering is a suitable data-analysis technique for stereotype formation [7] since clusters and stereotypes share the basic idea of setting groups whose members are similar in various parameters. The similarities among users who form a stereotype are based on commonalties in patterns of information usage, as deduced from the values of filtering rules assigned by the users. Each rule provides one parameter in the similarity calculation, and its value is the numeric value for the calculation.

The next step was to determine the rules that are applicable to each of the stereotypes and their values, where value of a rule actually means the relevance-rank that will be given to an evaluated message by this rule. To determine the rules that are applicable to a certain stereotype, the statistical average of each rule's values for all users that belong to that stereotype was calculated. Only rules whose standard deviation is **below** a certain threshold are selected to represent the stereotype. The justification for this is that a low standard deviation implies unity of the rule value among members of the stereotype. The value of each rule for a certain stereotype is the average of the values of its rules. Table 3 displays the rules that represent each stereotype and their average values. As can be seen, the stereotypes differ in the set of the rules that represent them, and in the average values of their rules.

Each rule is implemented by special procedures, which determine how to evaluate and rank messages. Ranking is based on multiplication of two factors: the average value of that rule for the stereotype (as shown in Table 3) and a certainty factor which indicates to what degree is the rule relevant to the evaluated message. Hence, if a rule is not relevant at all, its rank is 0; if it is 100% relevant, its rank is equal to the average value for that stereotype (as in Table 3); otherwise, its rank equals to the multiplication of the two factors.

Table 3. Rules of Stereotypes and their Average Values

Rule	Average values of rules per stereotypes			
	Stereotype 1	Stereotype 2	Stereotype 3	Stereotype 4
conference	5.83	2.45	4.78	4.38
paper	5.92	1.36	2.00	1.38
Internet	4.25	-	4.89	-
technical	-	-	1.89	6.63
job	2.08	-	2.22	1.5
fund	6.5	1.82	-	1.88
length	-	-	-	1.5
history	1.92	1.73	1.44	-

To compute the certainty factor of a rule, the system looks for specific indicators in the message that enables it to determine the pertinence of the message to the rule. The indications are based on the occurrences of appropriate terms in e-mail messages. For example, to determine with 100% certainty that a message announces a conference, at least one of the following must hold: 1) The body of the message includes more than one occurrence of terms from a pre-defined list of "conference terms", and at least one occurrence of a date. 2) The subject header of the message includes at least one occurrence of a "conference term". Partial fulfillment of conditions will result with lower certainty.

We need to define the sociological parameters and values that represent each stereotype, so as to enable the assignment of new users to the right stereotypes. To accomplish this, the frequency of values of each of the sociological parameters is calculated for users who belong to a given stereotype. Only parameters whose frequency is **above** a certain threshold are considered as representative of a stereotype. The most common value of the parameter is selected to represent that parameter in that stereotype. For example, if the most common value of education of stereotype 1 is "technician", then "technician" represents this stereotype on that parameter. Table 4 presents the sociological parameters and their values for each stereotype.

Table 4. Representing Sociological Values for the Stereotypes

Parameter	Stereotype 1	Stereotype 2	Stereotype 3	Stereotype 4
Education	1 (Ph.D.)	2 (M.Sc.)	-	-
Occupation	1 (researcher)	2 (information specialist)	4 (student)	3 (technical staff)
Level	-	1 (junior)	1 (junior)	3 (senior)
Computer knowledge	-	2 (experienced user)	-	3 (professional)
Age	3 (above 40)	-	-	-
No. of lists	2 (2-7 lists)	-	1 (up to 2 lists)	2 (2-7 lists)
Use of e-mail	2 (once a day)	2 (once a day)	3 (more than once a day)	-
Weekly use of Internet	-	-	1 (up to 5 hours)	-
% of e-mail filtering	3 (20%-50%)	-	1 (no filtering)	3 (20%-50%)

4 Experimentation

We conducted a series of experiments with the prototype system, aimed at examining the applicability of the model, especially the applicability of sociological filtering integrated with stereotypes, the impact of using dual-method filtering (i.e., various combinations of sociological and content-based filtering), and the optimal filtering strategy for different user stereotypes. The experiments involved ten users from the same domain that was used to define the stereotypes and filtering rules.

To enable content-based filtering, we had to prepare a content-based profile of each of the ten participants, describing his areas of interest. Each participant received a proposed list of terms generated from several dozen of his incoming e-mail messages. The list included the most frequently occurring terms in those messages. (It was prepared with the aid of special software that extracts terms from messages, employing look-up tables and a stop-list, and counts the frequency of meaningful terms). Each participant was asked to review the proposed list of terms, add or drop terms, and weigh each term for its degree of interest to him, using a 0-100 scale.

To enable sociological filtering, we had to prepare a sociological profile of each of the ten participant users, and then assign each of them to an appropriate stereotype. The sociological profile of each participant was created with a questionnaire; similar to the way it was created for the forty original users. The assignment procedure that relates a user to a stereotype calculates the Euclidean distance between the user's sociological profile and the vectors of sociological parameters that represent each of the existing stereotypes (see Table 4). The stereotype whose vector of sociological parameters is closest to the user's profile is chosen to be "his" stereotype.

For the actual experiments with the various filtering strategies, each of the ten participants evaluated the relevancy of about 200 e-mail messages that came in from list-servers dealing with professional matters. This was done with the aid of front-end software that was developed for this purpose. The users used a 1-7 scale to rank the relevancy of each message. Once a user evaluated a message, its rank, along with the message and the user identification, were saved to a special file. The same messages were evaluated later by the filtering system; each message was evaluated several times - each time using a different filtering strategy. The output of these runs were a file for each participant user, containing for each message, the user's evaluation (rank) and the ranks produced by each of the filtering strategies.

The following is an example for the evaluation of a certain e-mail message obtained by a certain user. The message announced an opening for a post-doctoral fellowship. That user (who was assigned to stereotype 1 – researchers - as based on his sociological profile) ranked the relevancy of this message as 3, possibly because he was not looking for a job. His partial interest in the message may be a result of the information it provides on job openings in his working area.

In **content-based filtering**, the system evaluates this message by computing the correlation between the weighted-terms in the user's content-based profile and the frequency of those terms in the message, relatively to the message length. (The system identifies and counts the frequency of meaningful terms, as described earlier for the construction of content-based profiles.) For this message the relevance rank is **4.27**. (The correlation is actually 0.61 in a -1 to 1 scale; 4.27 is its transformation onto a 1-7 scale.) This rank is high compared to the user's rank, because the message contains terms that appear in the user's profile, but – as indicated by the user - the message is not so relevant to him (rank 3). This example shows that content-based filtering alone may not be sufficient, and may even be misleading.

In **sociological filtering**, the system evaluates this message by applying the six filtering rules of stereotype 1 (that user's stereotype). Each of these rules may provide one rank/value, and the overall sociological rank for the message is the average of the applicable rules' ranks. The rules of stereotype 1 yielded the following ranks:
• Conference = 0: system found no evidence that the message is about a conference.

- Paper = 0: system found no evidence that the message is about a call for papers.
- Internet = 0: the message does not include an Internet address.
- Job = 2.08: system found that the message is definitely about a job opening, and therefore rated the message according to the value of this rule for stereotype 1.
- Fund = 4.5: system found that the message is about funding with 70% certainty, which is multiplied by the value of the rule - 6.5. (70% certainty is because the stem "fund" appears in the message body, but not in the subject header).
- History = 0: the message does not refer to earlier messages having the same subject obtained by the user (i.e. no "reply" with same subject in the message header).

Thus, the overall rank of this message, according to the sociological filtering method, is the average of the applicable rules' ranks, i.e., $(2.08 + 4.5)/2 = 3.29$. In this example, the sociological filtering rank is closer to the user's evaluation, because this message is more related with the user's sociological profile (and hence with the filtering rules that apply to his stereotype) than with his content-based profile.

The rank of this message according to the **parallel filtering** strategy is calculated as the average of content-based and sociological ranks: $(4.27 + 3.29)/2 = 3.78$, which is better (i.e. closer to the user's evaluation) than content-based filtering, but worse than sociological filtering. The result for **consecutive filtering** strategy where content-based filtering is the primary method, with weight 70%, followed by sociological filtering is: $.7*(4.27) + .3*(3.29) = 3.976$. For consecutive filtering strategy where sociological filtering is the primary method the rank is **3.29**, equal to sociological filtering alone. This is because the relevance threshold for sociological filtering is 3.5; since the rank obtained by sociological filtering is lower than the threshold, it becomes the overall rank of the message.

In conclusion, for this particular example, the best strategy is sociological filtering, then comes a consecutive strategy where sociological filtering is the primary method, and followed by the parallel filtering strategy. Content-based filtering is worst strategy for this case. Of course, for different users (in the same or different stereotypes) and different messages, different results may be obtained, meaning that different filtering strategies may be more appropriate.

The overall goal was to find out which filtering strategy generates evaluations that are mostly correlated with the user evaluations, and if any filtering strategy is consistently more effective than other for different user stereotypes. The comparison of filtering strategies was done within stereotypes because the experiments are meant to examine the effect of sociological filtering as integrated with stereotypes. To do so, for every filtering strategy, a vector that includes the ranks of messages given by users that belong to a certain stereotype was correlated with the system-produced ranks for the same messages.

5 Analysis of Results

The main results of the experiments are summarized in Table 5. It is divided into 4 main sections, each referring to one stereotype. Rows shows the correlation between the system's rankings of the messages (Y) and the users' rankings (X). Each row refers to a different filtering strategy. In the two-phase consecutive strategies the weights of the methods are 70% for the primary and 30% for the secondary. $r(X,Y)$ is the correlation coefficient; r^2 - the coefficient of determination; t – the statistic of significance test; and p – the level of significance of the correlation ($p < .05$ is considered significant). N is the number of messages. The results are interpreted as follows: the higher the correlation between rankings of a filtering strategy and of the users belonging to a given stereotype – the better it is, because the system's evaluation of messages is similar to the user's evaluation of the same messages.

Table 5. Correlation Results for the Four Stereotypes

Filtering Strategy	r(X,Y)	r²	t	p
Correlation Results for Stereotype 1 - Researchers; N=429				
Content-based	.5753*	.3309*	14.533*	.0000*
Sociological	.4767*	.2273*	11.207*	.0000*
Parallel	.5875*	.3451*	15.002*	.0000*
Content-based + Sociological	.6066*	.3680*	15.766*	.0000*
Sociological + Content-based	.5160*	.2262*	12.447*	.0000*
Correlation Results for Stereotype 2 - Information Specialists; N=469				
Content-based	.5048*	.2548*	12.636*	.0000*
Sociological	.4828*	.2331*	11.914*	.0000*
Parallel	.6387*	.4079*	17.938*	.0000*
Content-based + Sociological	.4420*	.1953*	10.647*	.0000*
Sociological + Content-based	.0646	.0042	1.399	.1624
Correlation Results for Stereotype 3 - Students; N=179				
Content-based	.4686*	.2194*	7.053*	.0000*
Sociological	.4342*	.1885*	6.412*	.0000*
Parallel	.5884*	.3462*	9.682*	.0000*
Content-based + Sociological	.6153*	.3786*	10.385*	.0000*
Sociological + Content-based	.5056*	.2556*	7.797*	.0000*
Correlation Results for Stereotype 4 - Technical Staff; N=350				
Content-based	.4062*	.1650*	8.292*	.0000*
Sociological	.6521*	.4252*	16.045*	.0000*
Parallel	.7051*	.4971*	18.548*	.0000*
Content-based + Sociological	.5301*	.2810*	11.663*	.0000*
Sociological + Content-based	.6598*	.4353*	16.378*	.0000*

Based on those tables, here are our main observations on the results per stereotype:

- **Stereotype 1**: Content-based filtering alone is better than sociological filtering alone, but parallel filtering is better than either method alone. The best strategy is consecutive filtering with content-based as primary method. The worst strategy is sociological filtering alone, while second to worst would be consecutive filtering with sociological as primary. At any rate, sociological filtering improves performance when applied in parallel with or following content-based filtering.
- **Stereotype 2**: Parallel filtering yield the best results, followed by content-based filtering alone and then sociological filtering alone. Surprisingly, the results for the two consecutive methods are lower than for each method alone. (Particularly low are the results when sociological filtering is the primary method.)
- **Stereotype 3**: Here again, the consecutive strategy with content-based filtering as primary method yields the best results, followed by parallel filtering. Then comes consecutive with sociological filtering as primary method. Last again is sociological filtering alone, and second to last be content-based filtering alone.
- **Stereotype 4**: Again, parallel filtering is best, but second best is consecutive with sociological as primary method. Following that is sociological filtering alone. The worst strategy for this stereotype is content-based filtering alone and second to worst is consecutive with content-based filtering as primary method.

There results are summarized in Table 6 which shows the strategies within each stereotype by descending order of correlation with the users' evaluations. The following interesting observations on the results concern all stereotypes:

Table 6. Order of filtering strategies within stereotypes

Order	Stereotype 1	Stereotype 2	Stereotype 3	Stereotype 4
1	Content-based + Sociological	Parallel	Content-based + Sociological	Parallel
2	Parallel	Content-based	Parallel	Sociological + Content-based
3	Content-based	Sociological	Sociological + Content-based	Sociological
4	Sociological + Content-based	Content-based + Sociological	Content-based	Content-based + Sociological
5	Sociological	Sociological + Content-based	Sociological	Content-based

1. For all stereotypes, all system's evaluations (except one) correlate significantly with the users' evaluations. This suggests that all filtering methods yield effective results, that match with the users needs to a certain extent. (The correlation coefficients range between 0.406 to 0.705.)
2. For most stereotypes (1, 2 and 3), content-based filtering alone provides higher correlation than sociological filtering alone. Hence, sociological filtering cannot substitute content-based filtering, which is based on the contents of documents.
3. For most stereotypes (1, 2 and 3), the consecutive strategy where content-based is primary filtering method provides higher correlation coefficients than the consecutive strategy where sociological is primary method.
4. In **no** case are content-based or sociological filtering alone better than some combination of content-based and sociological (either consecutive or parallel).
5. For two stereotypes (2 and 3), parallel filtering turned out to be best, and for the other two (1 and 4) - second best. Consequently, in all cases parallel filtering is better than content-based alone or sociological alone.
6. Most of the two-phase filtering results have higher correlation coefficients than the corresponding one-phase filtering method. I.e., parallel filtering is compared to either of the filtering methods, while consecutive combination is compared in each run to the filtering method that was considered as "primary" method on that run.

In conclusion, for every stereotype there is at least one significantly better result when the strategy is to combine the two filtering methods in some way. So, dual-method filtering is definitely vital. However, there is no single strategy that is "best" in all cases; the best strategy is stereotype-dependent. In other words, for every stereotype the best strategy needs to be discovered. This can be done by means of experimentation or after gaining experience with the system.

6 Conclusions

We implemented sociological filtering by means of rules attached to user stereotypes. We showed that sociological filtering, even as a single filtering method is significantly correlated with user evaluations, implying that it can be used to predict the relevance of documents. However, we found that in most cases content-based filtering alone is more correlated with user evaluations than sociological filtering alone. This should not be taken as a surprise; after all, content-based filtering is about the content of documents, which is obviously a major criterion for relevance.

We found it clearly that for every stereotype, there exists at least one combination of the two filtering methods (consecutive or parallel) that is better than either filtering method alone. The conclusion from that is that dual-method filtering is better than any single-method filtering.

The experiments show that there is no single "best" strategy for combining content-based and sociological filtering. For different stereotypes there may be different "best" combinations: parallel, content-based followed by sociological, or sociological followed by content-based. Hence, the optimal filtering strategy may be considered as a stereotype characteristic, which can be inferred by experimentation and experience.

Our experiments did show the applicability of dual-method filtering model, including the integration of sociological filtering with stereotypes. Furthermore, the consistent results, which are based on about 200 messages per participant, certainly show the correctness of the approach. However, because of the small number of participants, we can not claim for external validity of the results. For that, more experiments, encompassing more users and involving a variety of application domains, are needed. We plan to implement the model in other domains, such as digital libraries, and test the various filtering strategies with more users. Other domains may enable us to identify different user stereotypes and more filtering rules.

The filtering model includes a learning process, but we have addressed it only partially. In the future, we plan to extend the learning process, so that it will become possible to detect new rules or change existing rules as based on user feedback, as well as due to changes in the user population and their information needs.

In the current model, a user is assigned to one stereotype only. In further research we plan to extend this to enable assignment of a user to multiple stereotypes. This may be problematic, because there may be conflicting rules or rule values in each of those stereotypes; appropriate methods to resolve such conflicts must be investigated.

Another issue for further research is the effectiveness of stereotype-based sociological filtering. In the current model sociological filtering is determined according filtering rules attached to user stereotype. An alternative approach could be to have personal filtering rules attached to each user. Such rules may be defined similar to the way the user's content-based profile is defined. The research issue is to compare the two alternative approaches. It may be found out that a combination of the two approaches is desired, so that at the beginning (i.e. for a new user) sociological filtering will be based on a stereotype and it's filtering rules. Later on, as the user gains experience, the system may assist him to define his personal filtering rules, which will be used instead of the stereotype's rules.

References

[1] Balabanovic M. and Shoham Y. (1997), 'Fab: Content-Based Collaborative Recommendation System'. *Comm. of the ACM*, Vol. 40(3), pp. 66-72.
[2] Jain A.K., Dubes R.C. (1988), *Algorithms for Clustering Data*. Prentice Hall Advanced Reference Series.
[3] Malone T., Grant K., Turbak F., Brobst S. and Cohen M.: 1987, 'Intelligent Information Sharing Systems'. *Comm. of the ACM*, Vol. 30(5), pp. 390-402.
[4] McLeary H. (1994), 'Filtered Information Services - A Revolutionary New Product or a New Marketing Strategy?' *Online*, Vol. 4(18), pp. 33-42.
[5] Morita M. and Shinoda Y. (1994), 'Information Filtering Based on User Behavior Analysis and Best Match Retrieval'. In: *Proceedings of the 17th Annual Intl. ACM SIGIR Conference for Research and Development*, pp. 272-281.
[6] Shapira B., Hanani U., Raveh A. and Shoval P. (1997), 'Information Filtering: A New Two-Phase Model Using Stereotypic Profiling'. *Journal of Intelligent Information Systems*, Vol.8, pp. 155-165.
[7] Shapira B., Shoval P.and Hanani U. (1997). 'Stereotypes in Information Filtering Systems'. *Information Processing & Management*, Vol. 33(3), pp. 273-287.
[8] Shardanand U. and Maes P. (1995), 'Social Information Filtering Algorithm for Automating "Word of Mouth"'. *Proceedings of the 1995 ACM Conference on Human Factors in Computing Systems*, pp. 210-217.

Interactive Query Expansion in a Meta-search Engine

Claudia Oliveira, Luis Gustavo Varges Resende and Roberto Lehmann

Instituto Militar de Engenharia - Departamento de Engenharia de Sistemas
Praça General Tibúrcio, 80, 4o andar Rio de Janeiro, R.J., CEP 22290, Brazil
{cmaria,varges,lehmann}@de9.ime.eb.br

Abstract. In this article we describe a method for refining an initial set of search results, obtained through a meta-search engine, based on *relevance feedback*. The idea is to interactively obtain from the user a subset of relevant documents in an ongoing query, thereby providing a sample of the related vocabulary. Terms acquired in this way are combined with the terms initially in the query, in order to improve retrieval precision. In our method the user is also asked to select a subset of irrelevant documents, so that terms may be combined negatively in the query. A model of compatible architectures, in which the method can be implemented, is presented. An instance of such model, the system Web Query Reformulator (WQR), is described, with some of its performance results.

1. Introduction

The World Wide Web has become a global source of information in all areas of human interest, ranging from commerce to science. Nevertheless, the potential for exchange and sharing is not yet matched by the ability to actually access and retrieve specific information of interest to the user. Keyword searching is a particularly challenging task, due to the enormous volume of information that can be returned. In general, the bulk of matching results is completely irrelevant. This situation gets worse by the week and consequently, improving the ratio of the number of hits to number of retrievals is at the top of the agenda for any search tool.

Keyword searching has been implemented in library information systems for decades and as a result there is a fair amount of ground covered by the information retrieval community on the subject. Although the conventional library techniques are ready to use in the context of Web searching, there are two major factors that distinguish the usual centralised library information system. First, the scale of magnitude of the Web is unique. Because of this size discrepancy, the application of such early techniques can be profitable but only if coupled with additional mechanisms for filtering and ranking the search results. Secondly, the Web is a totally distributed collection of multimedia documents, which is not completely indexed by any one of the available spiders' databases. The fact that these indexing systems cover overlapping portions of the Web motivates the concept of meta-search engine, which queries a number of underlying search engines in parallel.

In this article we describe a method for refining an initial set of search results, obtained through a meta-search engine, based on *relevance feedback* [1]. The principle of this approach to the refinement of search results is asking the user to select a subset of documents, which are relevant to an ongoing query, thereby providing a sample of the related vocabulary. Terms are acquired and ordered with the use of standard methods of information retrieval, such as stemming, term co-occurrence, term length and document frequency. The resulting terms are combined with the terms initially in the query, in order to improve retrieval precision. In our method the user is also asked to select a subset of irrelevant documents, so that terms may be combined negatively in the query.

Although our method is completely general, for a number of reasons related to the dynamics of the interactive querying process and to performance issues, a suitable underlying search system must have a few desirable properties. In particular, the systems we have in mind comply with a client-server architecture that includes features such as storage structures to support learning and history log and availability of computing power on the client side to cope with expensive string processing tasks.

The paper is organised as follows. In section 2, the application of information retrieval techniques to Web searching is discussed and the main features of publicly available search engines are presented. In section 4 we present our method for refining search results inside a "query session" and the general architecture of the meta-search engine in which our query expansion technique can be incorporated. In section 5 we present preliminary test results. Finally, in section 6 we discuss the most closely related works and in section 7 we draw our conclusions.

2. Web Searching

Most of the techniques used for indexing and searching in the Web derive directly from the legacy of traditional Information Retrieval. Although much research has been focusing on knowledge-intensive approaches to Information Retrieval, indexing and searching in the Web still relies heavily on very basic techniques, going back over 20 years, such as document frequency/inverse document frequency, stop words and stemming. But the Web poses new and tough challenges to these techniques, due to its sheer volume, great diversity and accelerated volatility.

One novel aspect of indexing in the Web is spamming, and all the heuristics that have to be built in to try to neutralise it. The specifics of the Web also have effects over stop word lists, which have to be dynamic in order to adjust to the changing nature of the collection. Despite increasing efforts to define structural standards, such as the use of metadata, retrieval on the Web relies heavily on the traditional vector and probabilistic representation models. Term weighting is widely used, which takes into account the location of the term inside the document (title, use of keywords like "summary", "conclusion", etc) or ad-hoc heuristics like capitalisation, bold faces, etc.

In such a massive volume of documents, it is especially important to contextualise the user's information need. One of the strategies that are being very successfully used for that purpose is query expansion, particularly when it has the benefit of the user's relevance feedback. Query expansion is thus a form of adding terms to the original query presented by the user, which is typically very short, so that the augmented query can be better compared to documents in the proper context. The selection of additional terms may be based on a few documents that the user assessed as adequate or employing other techniques such as thesaurus, domain databases, etc. When using relevance feedback the user may or may not be directly involved in the term selection process. Some systems will automatically select the "best" terms out of the "relevant" documents.

Attempts have been made to use query expansion techniques in Web search engines, but the results are less than impressive. In particular, relevance feedback implementations, like "more like this" are very ineffective.

2.1. Search Engines

Ordinarily, the Web user employs one or more search tools as a starting point to access Web pages of interest. These tools, AltaVista, Yahoo, etc, have different degrees of user-friendliness, effectiveness and range. They offer a variety of search facilities, in the user interface, in the actual query language, and sometimes in the structural organisation exhibited in directories.

Pro-active search engines have their own or robots, which periodically traverse the Web's hypertext structure, to build and maintain their own massive database of indexes. These databases turn out to be quite different from one another because the robots use different strategies: what documents to consider, what links to follow, what words to index, what weights to use for each word, etc.

Subject trees offer a browsing service, where the user can follow subject trees or ontological directories to find information. Typically these catalogues are built with human selection of documents and judgement of which subject the document belongs to, as well as links to pages that offer wide coverage of that subject and contain a useful number of further links. An example of a subject tree is Yahoo. Because subject trees rely on humans for their overall design and maintenance, they typically provide links to a smaller number of documents than a keyword query made against a spider-automated index.

Meta-search engines, instead of keeping their own indexes, route the query in parallel to various other search engines. The answer pages of each of those different search engines are collected and subsequently the result is consolidated into a list with new rankings and a uniform presentation.

In MetaCrawler [2] and Fusion [3] the user chooses from a list of search engines with the option *all*, the aggregation by normalising the score provided by each search engine. Pro-fusion [4] and SavvySearch [5], on the other hand, select the engines that they will use based on the query and some other heuristics.

Relevancy Rankings - Most of the search engines return results with confidence or relevancy rankings. The majority uses mainly term frequency to whether a document is relevant, with possibly the position of keywords in the document being taken into account. Another common criterion is whether the document is frequently linked to other documents on the Web.

3. Refining Search Results

In order to describe our approach to refining search results, first we describe a typical query session, the processes involved and the assumptions we make. Secondly we present the architecture of a system capable of hosting such a query session.

3.1 The Query Expansion Method

A typical query made by the user of a retrieval system is made up of very few terms. From these terms, an initial set of documents is fetched from various index systems, each contributing with a specific number of documents. Typically, there is a reasonable amount of duplicates. Some are easily recognisable as such (same URL, for instance) but most have deceptively distinct descriptions. The more these duplicates are eliminated the wider the range of search results. Also, as it will become clear, fewer duplicates make our method more sound.

From the entries list of retrieved documents – titles, abstracts and other bits of information – the user may select a subset of relevant ones and another subset of irrelevant ones. From this assessment, the full versions of those selected documents are fetched. Each document selected is individually analysed. The terms are clustered by stem and their frequency of occurrence is computed. After going through all the documents two global data structures are created, one related to the documents assessed as relevant and the other to the documents assessed as irrelevant. The structures contain, for each stem, its document frequency (number of documents containing the stem) and total frequency (total number of occurrences of the stem in the retrieved collection).

The terms to be positively added to the query are amongst those extracted from the relevant documents, and are ranked in order of document frequency, length (number of component stems) and total frequency. This is a variation of the algorithm proposed in [6]. Conversely, the terms to be negatively added are amongst those extracted from the irrelevant documents and are ranked in order of total frequency provided they do not occur in any of the relevant documents.

At this point we have two possible routes to follow: 1. the automatic construction of the new query with the highest scoring terms; 2. involving the user's judgement with respect to which terms to add, positively or negatively, to the query. There are arguments for both approaches and we leave the choice open.

The expanded query is broadcast again to the available indexing systems and another cycle of interaction takes place.

3.2 Compatible Architectures

The basic architecture of meta-search engines is shown in fig. 1. An interface receives the user's input of keywords and possibly some search options. These specifications generate URLs, which are broadcast to a list of search engines. Upon receiving the answer pages, the fusion of the results takes place and an answer page is produced.

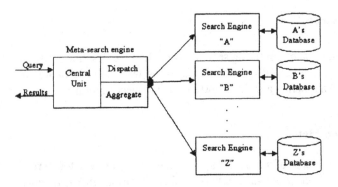

Fig. 1. meta-search engine architecture

This architecture does not support – as our does - the concept of a query session, which is a slice of time and computer resources totally dedicated to one particular user with a specific information need. A more suitable architecture is one that complies with a client-server model as shown in fig. 2.

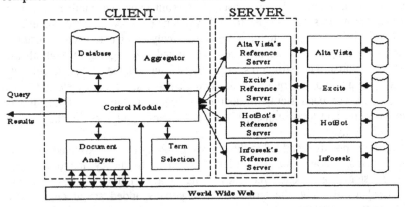

Fig. 2. client-server based architecture

On the client side, the basic functional modules are described as follows.

The **Control** module is responsible for dispatching the query to the reference servers and managing the local database, as well as controlling all the interactions with the user.

The **Aggregator** module performs the consolidation of the results, which basically involves re-ranking and identifying duplicates originated by different reference servers. The output of this module is the list of ranked documents, with normalised scores. In case the same document is returned by more than one reference server, its ranking reflects the addition of individual scores in order to reward the agreement between search tools. The reference server itself filters duplicates from the same search tool

Identifying duplicate results may be crucial in obtaining a sound list of results. There are a number of methods for performing such a task, of which we found the Dice proximity measurements over terms of the title, abstract and URL, a particularly cost-effective one.

The **Document Analyser** processes the documents that were singled out by the user, extracting the terms of the HTML document, grouping them by stemming and computing their frequency of occurrence. Phrases may be taken into account, regardless of number of terms. The resulting global term vector is kept by the Control Module, which will be processed by the Term Selection Module.

The main attributions of the **Term Selection** module are: 1) to eliminate redundancies, i.e. terms already accounted for within phrases; 2) to rank the remaining terms based on their document frequency, length of phrase and frequency inside each document. Nevertheless, there are a number of highly profitable techniques that can be incorporated here, mainly related with previous interactions, user profile and domain knowledge. The term selection process may also take into account all the documents assessed as relevant within a query session.

Although not essential, we strongly recommend the maintenance of a database containing a broad range of historic information, which can be used as a training set in **machine** learning for filtering responses and other relevancy measures.

On the server side, the **reference servers** are responsible for the exchanges between the meta-search system and the Web search mechanisms with their own databases. Each search mechanism has a corresponding reference server, which have knowledge of the specific details of that particular mechanism. One of the parameters passed to the server is the number of desired hits on results. It is up to the reference server to guarantee that the requested number of distinct results is returned, i.e., if a duplicate is identified another document is solicited. When a query is provided to the system on the client side, that same query is dispatched to all the configured reference servers. The server also receives the time constraint for the retrieval operation.

In summary, the reference servers' role is twofold:
- Processing the query, by the translating and forwarding it to the corresponding Web search mechanism;
- Parsing the results' page(s), extracting structured fields, such as title, abstract and URL.

3.2.1 WQR

Based on the architecture blueprinted above, we implemented WQR - Web Query Reformulator. In particular, some important characteristics of the WQR are:
- it is a Java application with heavy usage of multi-threading;
- there is no limit to the number of words (stems) that can be combined into a phrase. Any sequence of terms can be considered a phrase, provided it occurs more than once and starts and ends with terms that are not stop words. Imposing a limit produces very artificial constructs. For example, limiting phrases to three terms [7] would partition "Fourth Annual International World Wide Web Conference" into "Fourth Annual International", "Annual International World", "International World Wide", "World Wide Web" and "Wide Web Conference".
- duplicate documents are eliminated with the Dice similarity measure.

The concept of using query reformulation with relevance feedback in Web searching was originally proposed by Smeaton [3] in the Fusion system. The basic differences between WQR and Fusion are:

- in Fusion, most of the processing is performed at the server side. In the client side concentrates the heaviest burden, so that a much larger number of users can be accommodated with limited processing power;
- Fusion only takes into account documents assessed as relevant;
- WQR indicates the operators that should be applied to the suggested terms;
- WQR provides suggestions of phrases;
- WQR can be naturally expanded to make use of learning mechanisms based on user relevance assessments.

4. Analysis of Search Results

In order to assess the potential benefits of WQR we adopted the following procedure.
- A specific information need was selected: conferences with call for papers, in the area of textual information retrieval for the Web.
- The following query was formulated: +"call for papers" "information retrieval" web www "world wide web".
- The query was executed in 8 other search mechanisms available as well as in WQR, using all possible result enhancing features available.
- We computed the precision of the first twenty references presented by each system. They were classified as relevant, irrelevant or somewhere in between – documents that were not precisely what we wanted but had links to relevant documents.
- We performed two sets of tests with our system, one with automatic query expansion and the other with user interaction.

Fig. 3 depicts the best results obtained in a single session for each system. For each search mechanism there is a vertical bar divided into 3 sections. The height of the black bottom section indicates the percentage of relevant documents retrieved by the search mechanism; the grey middle section indicates the not quite irrelevant documents; the white top section indicates the percentage of irrelevant documents. From left to right, the vertical bars correspond to MetaCrawler, SavvySearch, ProFusion, Fusion2, Infoseek, Excite, Hotbot, Altavista and WQR.

The results of a single session show that our system had the highest precision, considering relevant and average documents (12 among 20 using interactive query expansion). This result was obtained after two interactions with the system, which resulted in 8/20 and 10/20 ratios, respectively. After the third interaction the precision deteriorated, going back to a 10/20 ratio. In our experiment, interactive query expansion had better performance than automatic query expansion.

Although the experiment had a limited scope we noticed some important points.
- Most of the other search engines returned to the user a significant number of duplicate references to the same conference.
- For this particular query none of the enhancement features offered by the different search engines was effective.

We feel that more experimentation is needed to effectively assess the benefits that our system is capable of providing, but we found these preliminary results very encouraging.

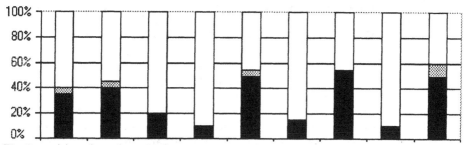

Fig. 3. precision of search mechanism

5. Conclusions

We propose a method of expanding user queries in the Web, using relevance feedback. Based on the assessment made by the user of the relevancy of documents presented to him as a result of his original query, we produce a ranked list of terms that may be added to the query, preceded or not by operators (+, -).

Experiments indicated that the proposed method enhanced the performance of the search session as perceived by the user.

One way to further improve the precision of our method is to apply filtering/categorisation techniques to the intermediate results, in order that documents that are clearly irrelevant can be moved down or excluded from the list. Another promising development is to provide mechanisms for creating profiles based on typical queries and relevance judgements of an individual user and use them to contextualise both the processing of the query and the filtering/categorisation mechanisms.

References

1. Gerard Salton and C. Buckley. Improving Retrieval Performance by Relevance Feedback. Journal of the American Society for Information Science, 41(4):288-297. 1990.
2. Oren Etzioni e Erik Selberg. Multi-Service Search and Comparison using the MetaCrawler. Proceedings of the 1995 WORLD WIDE WEB Conference . 1995.
3. Alan F. Smeaton e Francis Crimmins. Relevance Feedback and Query Expansion for Searching the Web: A Model for Searching a Digital Library. Research and Advanced Technology for Digital Libraries, ECDL'97. 1997.
4. Susan Gauch, Guijun Wang e Mario Gomez. Profusion: Intelligent Fusion from Multiple, Distributed Search Engines. Journal of Universal Computer Science. 1997.
5. Adele E. Howe e Daniel Dreilinger. SavvySearch: A Meta-Search Engine that Learns which Search Engines to Query. AI Magazine, 18(2). 1997.
6. Efthimis N. Efthimiadis. User Choices: A New Yardstick for the Evaluation of Ranking Algorithms for Interactive Query Expansion. Information Processing & Management, 31(4):605-620. 1995.
7. Alan F. Smeaton e Fergus Kelledy. User-Chosen Phrases in Interative Query Formulation for Information Retrieval. Proceedings of the 20th BCS-IRSG Colloquium. 1998

On the Optimization of Queries Containing Regular Path Expressions

Andreas Henrich[1] and Stefan Jamin[2]

[1] Otto-Friedrich-Universität Bamberg, Fakultät Sozial- und
Wirtschaftswissenschaften, Praktische Informatik, D-96045 Bamberg, Germany,
Andreas.Henrich@sowi.uni-bamberg.de
[2] CENIT AG Systemhaus, Schulze-Delitzsch-Str. 50, D-70565 Stuttgart, Germany,
S.Jamin@cenit.de

Abstract. One of the main characteristics of object-oriented database management systems is the explicit representation of relationships between objects. A simple example for a query addressing these relationships arises, if we assume the object types *Company*, and *Division* with the relationship *has_division* from *Company* to *Division*. In this case a query might ask for the companies which have a division called *"strategy"*. The query might start with the companies and navigate to the divisions which can be reached via the *has_division* relationship. Finally the query has to check if the *name* attribute of the *Division* object is *"strategy"*. Since there is no direct condition for the companies in the query, this query execution will be costly. If we assume that there is a reverse relationship *division_of* from *Division* to *Company*, an alternative execution plan might start with the *"strategy"* divisions and follow this reverse relationship. In this case an index structure for the *name* attribute of the *Division* objects can be exploited to speed up query processing.

In the present paper we describe a query optimizer which exploits this potential invertibility of navigational operations in queries. Our approach is based on, but not limited to the context of the ISO and ECMA standard PCTE and P-OQL.

1 Introduction

In contrast to relational database management systems object-oriented database management systems (ooDBMS) allow for the explicit representation of the relationships between the maintained objects. The various ooDBMS differ mostly in the expressive power of their modeling facilities for these relationships. Some systems allow only special attributes which consist of a set of objects. Other systems provide the means of a link to represent a relationship between objects. Furthermore some systems provide different link categories to represent different types of relationships, or they allow for the application of key- and/or non-key-attributes to the relationships.

Such relationships are often addressed in queries to the database. Assume for example an object base with the object types *Student*, *Course* and *Lecturer*

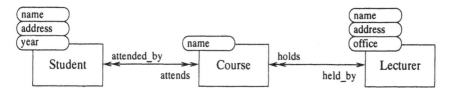

Fig. 1. Simple example schema with relationships

and the relationships *attends* from *Student* to *Course* and *held_by* from *Course* to *Lecturer*. This schema is illustrated in figure 1.

On this object base we could e.g. ask for the names of all students which attend a course held by lecturer *"Smith"* together with the corresponding course names. The straight forward way to evaluate this query would be to address all *Student* objects stored in the database and to check for each student if there is a path consisting of an *attends* and a *held_by* link referencing a lecturer named *"Smith"*. Under the natural assumption that there are far less lectures than courses, and far less courses than students, this is obviously an extremely costly operation. If there are, on the other hand, reverse relationships for the relationships *attends* and *held_by* — as in our example schema — another query processing plan might start with the lecturers. Only for those lecturers with the name *"Smith"* the students attending a course held by the lecturer would have to be addressed in this case. Especially in the case where an index for the *name* attribute of the lecturers exists this query processing plan would be much more efficient than the first one.

To exploit this potential invertibility of navigational operations in queries the query optimizer should consider query execution plans based on such inverted navigational operations in addition to the conventional query optimization techniques. To this end, the query optimizer has to determine invertible path expressions and to select the most beneficial inversion. Thereby the query optimizer should consider the available index structures and select the structure (or structures) which should be applied.

We have developed such a query optimizer for the P-OQL query language. P-OQL [8, 9] is an OQL-oriented query language for the object management system of PCTE [19], which in turn is the ISO and ECMA standard for an open repository [17, 18]. The environment consisting of PCTE and P-OQL is extremely challenging for the sketched optimizer facility, because the data model of PCTE contains extremely powerful facilities for the representation of relationships. The relationships can have key and non-key attributes, and there are different categories of relationships. The query language P-OQL allows to define navigational operations by regular path expressions addressing the attributes and the categories of the relationships and providing various iteration facilities.

In the following we first describe the essential concepts of PCTE and P-OQL (c.f. section 2). Thereafter we give various examples for the inversion of regular path expressions in P-OQL, which might allow for a more efficient query processing. In section 4 we present the architecture of our query optimizer. Section 5 deals with the cost estimation techniques employed to choose from the different possible query formulations and in section 6 we present some experimental results. Finally section 7 gives a short discussion of related approaches and section 8 concludes the paper.

2 Example Environment

2.1 PCTE

As mentioned PCTE (*Portable Common Tool Environment*) is the ISO and ECMA standard for a public tool interface (PTI) for an open repository [17–19]. As one of its major components PCTE contains a structurally object-oriented object management system (OMS) designed to meet the special requirements of software engineering environments.

The data model of PCTE can be seen as an extension of the binary Entity-Relationship Model. The object base contains objects and relationships. Relationships are normally bi-directional. Each relationship is realized by a pair of directed links, which are reverse links of each other. The type of an object is given by its name, a set of applied attribute types, and a set of allowed outgoing link types. New object types are defined by inheritance.

A link type is given by a name, an ordered set of attribute types called key attributes, a set of (non-key) attribute types, a set of allowed destination object types, and a category. PCTE offers five link categories: *composition* (defining the destination object as a component of the origin object), *existence* (keeping the destination object in existence), *reference* (assuring referential integrity and representing a property of the origin object), *implicit* (assuring referential integrity) and *designation* (without referential integrity).

Throughout this paper we will use the schema given in figure 2 as the basis for our examples. It consists of the object types *Student*, *Course*, *Employee*, *Thesis* and *Project*. The attribute types applied to each object type are given in the ovals at the upper left corner of the rectangle representing the object type.

The link types are indicated by arrows. A double arrowhead at the end of a link indicates that the link has cardinality *many*. Links with cardinality many must have a key attribute. In the example the numeric attribute *no* and the string attribute *problem* are used for this purpose. For example the link type *attends* from *Student* to *Course* has such a key attribute and is hence described as *"no.attends"*. Therefore an instance of this link type can be addressed by its *link name* which consists of the concrete value for the key attribute and the type name separated by a dot – e.g. *"3.attends"*. Link types with cardinality *one* do not need a key attribute and are given in the schema by a dot followed by the link type name. An *'E'* or *'R'* in the triangles at the center of the line representing a pair of links, indicates that the link has category *existence* or *reference*.

Finally the schema contains the link type *has_advisor* as an example for a link type with a non-key attribute. In our case this is the attribute *meeting*.

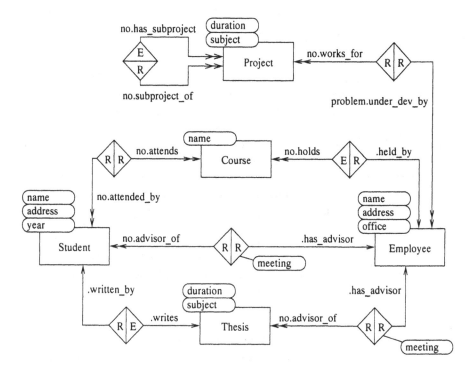

Fig. 2. Example schema

With respect to the query optimizer presented in this paper some further characteristics of the PCTE data model have to be stressed: (1) The reverse link type of a link type is non-ambiguous. I.e. each link type has exactly one reverse link type and a link type can be the reverse link type for only one link type — except for *designation* links. (2) A link type may have multiple destination object types which may or may not be leaves of the inheritance hierarchy. (3) Since links with category *designation* are an exception of the rule that each link has a reverse link a navigation traversing a *designation* link cannot be inverted.

2.2 P-OQL

P-OQL [8] is an OQL-oriented query language for PCTE, and OQL (*Object Query Language*) [2] is the ODMG proposal for a query language for object-oriented database management systems. The main differences between P-OQL and standard OQL are due to the adaptation to the data model of PCTE. Hence, especially the treatment of links is specific to P-OQL.

A query in P-OQL is either a select-statement, or the application of an operator (like *sum*).

Assume that we search for pairs with the name of a student and the name of an employee, where the student attends a course held by the employee and the student is in the fourth year. The following query in P-OQL yields these pairs:

```
select    A:name, B:name
from   A in Student, B in (A:_.attends/.held_by/->.)
where A:year = 4
```

In the **from-clause** of this query two base sets are defined: Base set A addressing all students in the object base and base set B addressing all objects which can be reached from the actual object of base set A via a path matching the regular path expression "A:_.attends/.held_by/->.". In this path expression the prefix "A:" means that the actual element of base set A is used as the starting point of the definition. "_.attends/.held_by" means that exactly one link of type *attends* and one link of type *held_by* must be traversed. The underscore "_" is used as a wildcard for numerical key attributes denoting that arbitrary key values are allowed. In addition intervals can be specified for numerical key attributes and regular expressions can be used for string key attributes. Since there is no key attribute defined for the link type *held_by*, the notation ".held_by" is used to specify that a *held_by* link has to be traversed. The notation "/->" is used in the regular path expression "A:_.attends/.held_by/->." to address the destination object of the path. In addition "->" can be used to address the last link of the path. The dot "." at the end of the regular path expression means that the object under concern is addressed. It is also possible, to address an attribute or a tuple of values (see [8] for more details).

Due to the definition of an *independent* base set (base set A) and a *dependent* base set (base set B), each student is combined with each employee, which can be reached from the object representing the student via a path matching the regular path expression.

Altogether, a base set can be defined in P-OQL in five different ways: (1) giving an object type name or an object type name suffixed by a "^" meaning that objects of all subtypes are addressed as well; (2) using a link type name to address all links of a given type; (3) defining a set of objects or links using a regular path expression, as with base set B in our example; (4) defining a set of objects or links via a sub-select; or (5) passing a set of objects or links via the API (*application programming interface*) when submitting a query.

In the **where-clause** of our example query the considered combinations of students and employees are restricted to those for which the *year* attribute of the student has the value "*4*". Besides such simple conditions P-OQL for example allows the use of quantifiers and subqueries in the where-clause.

The **select-clause** of the example query states that a multiset of pairs is requested. Each pair consists of the name of the student and the name of an employee who holds the course the student attends.

An additional facility of P-OQL — which is relevant to our optimization problem — allows for the iteration over one or more links of the same type. Assume for example that we are interested in the subprojects of a project with subject "*Workflow*". These subprojects can be determined in P-OQL as follows:

```
select    A:subject, A:[_.has_subproject]+/->subject
from   A in Project
where A:subject = "Workflow"
```

Here the regular path expression "A:[_.has_subproject]+/->subject" is used to create a (multi-)set with the subjects of all subprojects of the project addressed in base set A. The meaning of "[_.has_subproject]+" is that one or more links matching the link definition "_.has_subproject" have to be traversed. Alternatively P-OQL knows the iteration facilities "[path_definition]*" to indicate that zero or more paths matching *path_definition* have to be traversed and "[path_definition]" to indicate that a path matching *path_definition* is optional. After traversing an arbitrary number of *has_subproject* links, the *subject* attribute of the destination object is addressed using "/->subject".

In addition to the link definitions used in the above example, which have been based on a given link type name and a definition of the allowed values for the key attributes, P-OQL allows the specification of a set of link categories instead, meaning that all links having one of the given categories fulfill this link definition. E.g. the expression "[{c,e}]+/->." addresses all objects which can be reached via a path consisting only of links with category *composition* or *existence*. Furthermore, not only the category of the link itself, but also the category of its reverse link can be specified using "@" as a prefix for the category.

Finally it has to be mentioned that the ODMG standard OQL also permits the definition of reverse links and the use of path expressions for the definition of base sets. However, since the ODMG data model does not include attributes for links or link categories, the path expressions in OQL can be seen as a special case of the regular path expressions in P-OQL.

3 Inverting Regular Path Expressions

3.1 Simple Cases

First let us consider a slightly extended version of the example query given in section 2.2. In addition we require that the address of the employee is "Cologne":

   select   A:name, B:name
    from A *in* Student, B *in* (A:_.attends/.held_by/->.)
   where A:year = 4 *and* B:address = "Cologne"

In the first base set this query addresses all students and in the second base set the corresponding employees are addressed starting from the student actually under concern via the regular path expression "A:_.attends/.held_by/->.". In this way each student is combined with each employee which can be reached via a path matching the path expression. Furthermore, due to the semantics of P-OQL, this means that when a student attends two courses held by the same employee, this student/employee pair is considered twice. However, the same result can be achieved as well when the query addresses all employees and inverts the regular path expression "A:_.attends/.held_by/->." in order to address the corresponding students in a second base set. In this way we yield the equivalent P-OQL query:

   select   A:name, B:name
    from B *in* Employee, A *in* (B:_.holds/_.attended_by/->.)
   where A:year = 4 *and* B:address = "Cologne"

To see that both queries are equivalent, first we have to note that the data model of PCTE assures that for each path matching the regular path expression "_.attends/.held_by/->." there is a reverse path matching the regular path expression "_.holds/_.attended_by/->.". Hence, if an employee e is reached from a student s via a path matching "_.attends/.held_by/->.", there is always a reverse path from e to s matching "_.holds/_.attended_by/->.". If there are multiple paths from a student s to an employee e, we have exactly the same number of reverse paths. As a consequence, we have the same pairs in the base sets of both queries and each pair has exactly the same number of occurrences.

If there is an index for the attribute *address* of the object type *Employee* which is more selective than the index for the attribute *year* of the object type *Student*, the second query will lead to a more efficient query execution plan.

The above example might suggest that an inversion of a regular path expression used to define a base set can always be performed easily without any effects on the select-clause and the where-clause of the query. Unfortunately this is not true. The situation becomes much more complicated whenever one of the following cases occurs: (1) The values of the key attributes are restricted in the regular path expression. (2) One of the iteration facilities of P-OQL is used. (3) The destination object type of a link is ambiguous. (4) A link definition in the regular path expression is stated by the allowed link categories. In the following sections we describe how these more complicated cases can be handled.

3.2 Conditions for Link Key Attributes

As mentioned in section 2.2 there are different facilities to restrict the allowed key attribute values for traversed links. In the following query we use two of these facilities in order to navigate from the student addressed in base set A to some specific projects. Furthermore we require that the student should be in the fourth year and that the duration of the project should be at least 36 month:

select A:name, B:subject
  from A *in* Student, B *in* (A:[2..4].attends/.held_by/1.works_for/->.)
  where A:year = 4 *and* B:duration >= 36

Due to the conditions for the link key attributes which are integrated in the regular path expression we cannot invert the path expression "A:[2..4].attends/.held_by/1.works_for/->." in one step. Rather we have to split up the expression when inverting it, in order to address the key attributes of the reverse links, for which the conditions have to be enforced. In consequence, this means that the conditions which are integrated in the original regular path expression are moved into the where-clause of the inverted query:

select A:name, B:subject
  from B *in* Project, H1 *in* (B:*.under_dev_by->.),
          H2 *in* (H1:/.holds/_.attended_by->.), A *in* (H2:/.)
  where A:year = 4 *and* B:duration >= 36
          and H1:@no = 1 *and* H2:@no >= 2 *and* H2:@no <= 4

In the inverted query we first navigate from the project under consideration to all outgoing *under_dev_by* links [1]. These links are addressed in the auxiliary base set H1. In the where-clause we have to assure that the key attribute value of the reverse link of the link addressed in base set H1 is *"1"*. In P-OQL the *"@"*-sign can be used to switch from a link to its reverse link. Hence, the condition "H1:@no = 1" assures that the value of the key attribute of the reverse link is *"1"*. Starting with base set H1 we then navigate to the *attended_by* links which are addressed in base set H2. The first "/" in the regular path expression "H1:/.holds/_.attended_by->." used for this purpose specifies that we navigate from the current link in base set H1 to its destination object. Starting at this destination object we then traverse a *holds* links and reach the *attended_by* link. For the reverse links of these *attended_by* links the condition "H2:@no >= 2 *and* H2:@no <= 4" assures that the key attribute value is in the interval [2..4]. Finally the base set definition "A *in* (H2:/.)" addresses the destination objects of these links in base set A.

3.3 Iteration Facilities

For each employee living in Cologne the following example query calculates a set with the subjects of the projects with a duration of at least 36 month he works for. To this end the query iteratively follows the *subproject_of* links:

> *select*   A:name, B:subject
> *from*   A *in* Employee, B *in* (A:_.works_for/[_.subproject_of]*/->.)
> *where* A:address = "Cologne" *and* B:duration >= 36

The inversion of this regular path expression does not cause major problems, since we can use analog iteration facilities in the inverted version:

> *select*   A:subject, B:name
> *from*   B *in* Project, A *in* (B:[_.has_subproject]*/*.under_dev_by/->.)
> *where* A:address = "Cologne" *and* B:duration >= 36

This alternative query formulation exploits that for each path p_1 matching the expression "_.works_for/[_.subproject_of]*/->." there is a reverse path p_2 matching the expression "[_.has_subproject]*/*.under_dev_by/->.". Unfortunately the situation becomes much more complicated as soon as the iteration facilities are combined with conditions for the key attribute values.

3.4 Iterations Facilities and Conditions on Link Keys

The following query directly corresponds to the query considered in section 3.3 except that we traverse only the first link of type *subproject_of* for each project — that means we traverse only links with the key attribute value *"1"*:

---

[1] Recall that the notation "->." at the end of a regular path expression addresses the last link of the path, whereas the notation "/->." addresses the destination object. Further note that the "*" is used in "B:*.under_dev_by->." to allow arbitrary string key attribute values.

select   A:name, B:subject
   from   A *in* Employee, B *in* (A:_.works_for/[1.subproject_of]*/->.)
   where A:address = "Cologne" *and* B:duration >= 36

If we combine the solutions presented in the previous sections for conditions on link keys and for iteration facilities in a straight forward manner to invert the regular path expression "A:_.works_for/[1.subproject_of]*/->.", we yield:

select   A:name, B:subject
   from   B *in* Project, H1 *in* (B:[_.has_subproject]*->.),
          A *in* (H1:/*.under_dev_by/->.)
   where A:address = "Cologne" *and* B:duration >= 36 *and* H1:@no = 1

Unfortunately this query is not equivalent to the original query, because the condition "H1:@no = 1" is checked only for the last link of each path matching the regular path expression "B:[_.has_subproject]*->.".

Therefore, we have to apply a different approach in situations where conditions for the key attribute values occur inside an iteration. To this end, we recall the basic aim of the query inversion. This aim is to apply an index structure for the destination object type of the original path expression. Let us assume for example that there is no index for the *address* attribute of the employees. Then in the above example query the base set definition "A *in* Employee" means that we have to scan all employees. On the other hand, there might be an index structure for the *duration* attribute of the projects. If we assume that the condition "B:duration >= 36" is rather restrictive, there will be only few employees working in such projects. Therefore it might be useful to consider not all employees, but only the employees working in such projects. The objects representing these employees can be determined by the following select statement:

select distinct H2:.
   from   H1 *in* Project, H2 *in* (H1:[_.has_subproject]*/*.under_dev_by/->.)
   where H1:duration >= 36

Two aspects have to mentioned with respect to this query: (1) We use a *select distinct* here to avoid duplicates in the result. (2) The query will in general return more employees than actually needed, because the conditions for the link key attributes given in the original query are not reflected here.

Now we simply use this query instead of the object type *Employee* to define base set A in the original query:

select   A:name, B:subject
   from   A *in* (*select distinct* H2:.
               from   H1 *in* Project,
                     H2 *in* (H1:[_.has_subproject]*/*.under_dev_by/->.)
              where H1:duration >= 36),
        B *in* (A:_.works_for/[1.subproject_of]*/->.)
   where A:address = "Cologne" *and* B:duration >= 36

Using this query an index structure for the *duration* attribute of the projects can be employed to speed up query processing.

3.5 Ambiguous Destination Object Types

Another problem caused by the inversion of regular path expressions, is the existence of ambiguous destination object types for some link types. In the schema given in figure 2 the link type *advisor_of* is such a link type with two destination object types (*Student* and *Thesis*). So by inverting a regular path expression it may be necessary to address objects by using such a link type, but not all destination object types should be considered. The following example uses the link type *has_advisor* to define the dependent base set B:

select A:name, B:name
  from A *in* Student, B *in* (A:.has_advisor/->.)
 where B:address = "Cologne"

If we invert the regular path expression "A:.has_advisor/->.", we have to use the link type *advisor_of*, but only destination objects of type *Student* should be addressed. To this end, we can use a type test predicate of P-OQL:

select A:name, B:name
  from B *in* Employee, A *in* (B:_.advisor_of/->.)
 where B:address = "Cologne" *and* A:. *is of type* Student

Similar situations can arise due to inheritance. To illustrate such a situation, we extend our university schema given in figure 2 by two subtypes for the object type *Employee* as shown in figure 3. As usual, in PCTE a subtype t_1 of an object type t_0 inherits the applied attribute types and the allowed outgoing link types. Furthermore, if t_0 is defined as the destination object type of a link type, links of this type can as well point to objects of type t_1, because an object of type t_1 can be used wherever an object of type t_0 is required.

Fig. 3. Two subtypes of the object type *Employee*

To see the effects of inheritance for the inversion of regular path expressions, we reconsider the example query given in section 3.1 combined with the inheritance situation given in figure 3:

select A:name, B:name
  from A *in* Student, B *in* (A:_.attends/.held_by/->.)
 where A:year = 4 *and* B:address = "Cologne"

Now the inverted query has to address the object type *Employee* and its subtypes in the first base set. To this end, we can use the notation *ObjectType^* which addresses an object type and his descendant object types:

> *select*   A:name, B:name
> *from* B *in* Employee^ , A *in* (B:.holds/_.attended_by/->.)
> *where* A:year = 4 *and* B:address = "Cologne"

3.6   Link Categories Used in Regular Path Expressions

The last feature of P-OQL we want to consider here, is the definition of the allowed link categories in a regular path expression. This feature is extremely useful when combined with the document retrieval facilities included in P-OQL [9]. Unfortunately we cannot present these facilities here due to the space limitations. As a consequence, the following example may seem relatively artificial.

Assume the following query starting with projects and following *reference* links, which in this case lead to employees:

> *select*   A:subject, B:name
> *from* A *in* Project, B *in* (A:{r}/->.)
> *where* B:address != "Cologne"

Since there is only one link type with category *reference* originating from the object type *Project* we can invert this query as follows:

> *select*   A:subject, B:name
> *from* B *in* Employee, A *in* (B:{@r}/->.)
> *where* B:address != "Cologne" *and* A:. is of type Project

Here the regular path expression "B:{@r}/->." enforces, that the reverse link of the traversed link has the category *reference*. Since this condition is true for multiple outgoing link types of the object type *Employee*, we have to add the condition "A:. *is of type* Project" in the where-clause of the query.

In general the situation is a bit more complicated, because there will be multiple destination object types for links with the required category. In this case the query optimizer has to look for a unifying supertype or it can build the union of the objects of the various types which can be accessed via sub-selects.

4   The Optimizer Architecture

In section 3 we have given various examples for situations where a query can be inverted to use another object type as the starting point for query processing. In the present section we will describe the architecture of our query optimizer which tries to exploit such inverted query formulations to speed up query processing.

The query optimizer is implemented as a preprocessor. This preprocessor receives a query in P-OQL syntax and it returns a query in P-OQL syntax with some extensions specifying the index structures to be used. The different steps performed by our optimizer are shown in figure 4. The solid lines with the numbers (1) to (7) represent the main control flow whereas the dashed lines identified by the letters (a) to (e) represent the information transfer between those components of the optimizer which provide additional information for the optimization process. The main components can be described as follows:

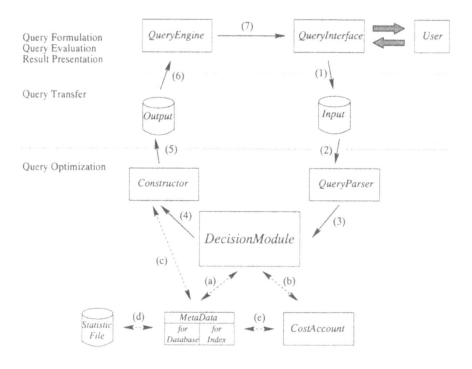

Fig. 4. The optimizer architecture

QueryInterface: The *QueryInterface* stores the P-OQL query in the *Input*-file (1) and expects the result for presentation to the user (7).

QueryParser: This component parses the original query from the *Input* (2) and creates an internal representation which is passed to the *DecisionModule* (3). Thereby the *QueryParser* checks whether there are base set definitions using regular path expressions. In case, the corresponding base sets are marked.

DecisionModule: The *DecisionModule* analyses the base sets of the actual query to detect interdependent base sets. For each group of interdependent base sets the definitions of the dependent base sets are scanned in order to evaluate whether they can be inverted. When the definition of a dependent base set e.g. includes a complex sub-select or a navigation over a *designation* link, an inversion is regarded as impossible. On the other hand in the cases explained in section 3 an inversion is possible. For each invertible base set definition the destination object type is determined. These destination object types and the object type addressed in the independent base set of the original query formulation built a set with object types which can be used as starting points of the query formulation. For these alternatives the query execution costs are estimated based on the information provided by the *CostAccount* module (b). For this cost estimation information about the cardinality of the base sets, information about the available index structures, and information about the conditions in the where-clause of the query is considered. The decision for the alternative with the lowest expected costs is thereafter passed to the *Constructor* module (4).

Constructor: This module actually performs the inversion of the query. To this end, the *Constructor* depends on information from the *MetaData* module (c), e.g. to determine the name of a reverse link type.

MetaData: This module provides an interface to retrieve the relevant meta data for the database and the index structures.

StatisticFile: To assure a minimum of information even if there exists no index structure for an object type, this file contains e.g. an estimation of the number of instances of each object type.

CostAccount: The *CostAccount* module computes the relative costs of the original query plan and the potential alternative query plans by using the available information from the MetaData module (e). The details of this module are discussed in section 5.

QueryEngine: This module evaluates the final query by means of a nested-loop approach. For the base sets for which an index structure has been selected the index structure is employed. The result of the evaluation is sent to the QueryInterface (7), which presents it to the user.

5 Cost Estimation and Index Selection

For the discussion of the applied cost estimation technique it is important to mention that our implementation uses a multi-dimensional index structure. This index structure is presented in detail in [11, 10]. For the present paper it suffices to know that this index structure allows to address multiple attributes in one access structure [2]. A corresponding index definition might e.g. look as follows:

Index for object type Student: *1.* name, *2.* year, *3.* address

Since the index structure is symmetric, the same selectivity is provided for all supported dimensions. Furthermore the index structure is well suited for situations where multiple attributes are addressed in the where-clause of a query, because in these cases the selectivity for all supported attributes is combined.

In this context some administrative information is maintained for each index structure: (1) an *object counter* containing the number of instances of the indexed object type, (2) the *number of dimensions* of the index structure, (3) the indexed attributes, and (4) an *object type hierarchy* specification, defining whether the index is created only for objects of the defined object type itself, or for objects of the defined type and all descendent types.

Based on this information for each object type j which could be used as the starting point of the query formulation the existing index structures are

---

[2] It should be obvious that the use of this multi-dimensional index structure is by no means a prerequisite for the application of our query optimization approach. If the approach is used with one-dimensional index structures — like the B-tree [5] — only the formulas presented in this section have to be slightly adapted.

determined. Now two cases have to be distinguished: (1) For none of the object types an index exists: In this case we use the information from the *StatisticFile* to select the object type with the fewest instances as the starting point of the query formulation. (2) Otherwise we always choose to apply an index structure. To select this index structure we proceed in two steps: In the first step we try to determine the *"best"* index structure for each object type j, for which index structures exist. In the second step we select the object type which should be used as the starting point of the query formulation.

1. **step:** This step is performed for each object type which could be the starting point of the query and for which at least one index structure is defined with an *object type hierarchy* specification corresponding to the query. For the index structures of object type j we proceed as follows:
   1. We collect the conditions from the where-clause which refer to object type j. We denote the number of these conditions by q_j.
   2. For each index i we count those conditions, which can be supported by the index. We denote this number by $h_{j,i}$.
   3. For each index i of object type j we calculate $r_{j,i} = \frac{h_{j,i}}{q_j}$ (the share of the conditions for object type j which are supported by index i).
   4. Now we assume that the index structure with the highest value for $r_{j,i}$ is the *"best"* index structure for object type j. If there are multiple index structures with this highest value, we choose the index which has the fewest dimensions. If this is not unique as well, we choose an arbitrary index out of these index structures. Let i_j^* denote the chosen index structure for object type j.

2. **step:** Now we can choose the object type j which should be used as the starting point of the query formulation: For each object type j we calculate the value $C_j = object\ counter \times \max(0.01, 1 - r_{j,i_j^*})$, where *object counter* is taken from the administrative information of the index structure i_j^*. Since small values for *object counter* and high values for r_{j,i_j^*}, which always is a value out of $[0, 1]$, are desirable, we use $1 - r_{j,i_j^*}$ in the formula. We use $\max(0.01, 1 - r_{j,i_j^*})$ because otherwise this factor would be zero for $r_{j,i_j^*} = 1$, i.e. when all conditions are supported by the index structure. So to assure that the *object counter* can always influence the formula we use $\max(0.01, 1 - r_{j,i_j^*})$. Finally the *DecisionModule* chooses the object type j with the lowest value for C_j as the starting point of the query formulation.

6 Experimental Results

In this section we present some experimental results achieved with our optimizer. The tests were performed on a Sun Sparc20 with two processors and 96 MB of main memory. The database for the tests was filled with synthetic data created for the university schema given in figure 2 and extended in figure 3. Table 1 summarizes the existing index structures for the object types *Student* and *Employee* which occur in our example queries.

First we examined the example query explained in section 3.1:

Table 1. Index structures defined for the tests

object type	object counter	index number	number of dimensions	attributes	object type hierarchy
Student	6040	1	2	name, term	this type only
Student	6040	2	3	name, address, term	this type only
Student	6040	3	2	name, address	this type only
Employee^	1995	1	2	name, address	with subtypes
Employee^	1995	2	3	name, address, office	with subtypes
Employee^	1995	3	1	office	with subtypes

select   A:name, B:name
  from   A *in* Thesis, B *in* (A:_.attends/.held_by/->.)
  where A:year = 4 *and* B:address = "Cologne"

For this query the optimizer returned the following query, where the base set definition "B *in* #1# Employee^ " specifies that index 1 has to be used to speed up the loop over the employees:

select   A:name, B:name
  from   B *in* #1# Employee^ , A *in* (B:.holds/_.attended_by/->.)
  where A:year = 4 *and* B:address = "Cologne"

Table 2. Performance results for the first test query

using the index structures for the object type Student		
index number	number of read index pages	relative execution time
1	225	72 %
2	192	66 %
3	188	66 %
using the index structures for the object type Employee^		
index number	number of read index pages	relative execution time
1	47	23 %
2	51	26 %
3	115	100 %

The performance results presented in table 2 show that the optimizer in fact selected the best possible query plan for our example query. Without the inversion of the query the execution time would have been nearly three times higher. So the optimizer selected the correct object type to start with and it selected the best possible index structure for this object type.

In the second test query we are searching for the subjects of all theses advised by an employee named *"Brubeck"*:

select   A:subject
  from   A *in* Thesis, B *in* (A:.has_advisor/->.)
  where B:name = "Brubeck"

In this case the optimizer returned the following query:

select   A:subject
  from   B *in* #1# Employeeˆ , A *in* (A:_.advisor_of/->.)
  where B:name = "Brubeck" *and* A:. *is of type* Thesis

Here the condition "A:. *is of type* Thesis" is inserted into the where-clause because of the ambiguous destination object types of the link type *advisor_of*.

Table 3. Performance results for the second test query

without using index structures for the object type Thesis		
index number	number of read index pages	relative execution time
—	—	100 %
using the index structures for the object type Employeeˆ		
index number	number of read index pages	relative execution time
1	5	6 %
2	6	8 %
3	115	75 %

Table 3 shows the performance results for the second test query. Since there is no index structure defined for the object type *Thesis* we have included the time for the query execution without an index structure in the table. Again the optimizer chose the best possible query plan for our example query.

It remains to mention that we have performed various other tests as well. The optimizer selected the best possible plan in over 80 % of the cases, and whenever the selected plan was not the best one, it was only slightly worse.

7 Related Work

Although there is a great number of approaches for query optimization problems in the field of ooDBMS, to our best knowledge this is the first approach which tries to invert complex regular path expressions in order to exploit index structures defined for the destination object types of the paths.

For a general overview on query optimization problems in ooDBMS we refer to [13]. In [15] Mitschang presents the basic concepts and implementation aspects of query processing and query optimization. Furthermore multiple interesting articles dealing with various aspects of query optimization can be found in [7]. Finally some rule-based approaches to query optimization are presented in [6], [14] and [1]. However, all these papers do not address topics related to the potential inversion of regular path expressions.

On the other hand some work dealing with path expressions and related aspects has been published, even though it is not directly concerned with the inversion of the path expressions.

In [4] Christophides, Cluet and Moerkotte extend an object algebra with two new operators and present some interesting rewriting techniques for queries featuring generalized path expressions. However, their approach does not address the problem of determining applicable access structures or aspects of the inversion of regular path expressions.

Ozkan, Dogac, and Evrendilek present a heuristic to determine the optimum execution order for the joins needed to process a path expression [16]. In contrast to our approach they assume that the references to objects are maintained as implicit joins which are converted to explicit joins during the optimization phase. Since we assume that the navigation via a link in PCTE is an extremely efficient operation supported by the physical structures of the OMS, these considerations are not applicable in our context.

Other approaches deal with the exploitation of materialized views for query processing [3] or with a general architecture for a query optimizer for OQL [12].

Summarizing, all the aforementioned approaches do not address the aspect that regular path expressions can be inverted in order to exploit index structures defined for the destination object types of the paths.

8 Conclusion and Future Work

In this paper we have presented an approach which exploits the potential invertibility of regular path expressions in order to apply index structures defined for the destination object types of the original path expressions. The approach has been described for the environment of PCTE and P-OQL, but it can be easily adapted for ooDBMS with simpler link concepts than PCTE.

Our future work will be concerned with an extension of the presented approach to other facilities of the query language. One important point in this respect are sub-selects, which can often be eliminated or flattened and processed in the same way as regular path expressions. Another aspect are quantifiers. Especially existence quantifiers seem to be well suited for an integration in our approach. Also improved cost estimation techniques are an interesting research area, and finally a formal framework for our optimization approach is needed.

References

1. L. Becker and R.H. Güting. Rule-based optimization and query processing in an extensible geometric database system. *ACM Transactions on Database Systems*, 17(2):247–303, Juni 1992.

75

2. R. Cattell, editor. *The Object Database Standard: ODMG-93.* Morgan Kaufmann, San Mateo, Cal., USA, 1993.
3. C.M. Chen and N. Roussopoulos. The implementation and performance evaluation of the ADMS query optimizer: Integrating query result caching and matching. In *Advances in Database Technology - EDBT'94. 4th Int. Conf. on Extending Database Technology, Proceedings*, volume 779 of *LNiCS*, pages 323–336, Cambridge, UK, 1994.
4. V. Christophides, S. Cluet, and G. Moerkotte. Evaluating queries with generalized path expressions. In *Proc. ACM SIGMOD Int. Conf. on Management of Data*, pages 413–422, Montreal, Canada, 1996.
5. D. Comer. The ubiquitous B-tree. *ACM Computing Surveys*, 11(2):121–137, June 1979.
6. J.C. Freytag. A rule-based view of query optimization. In *Proceedings of the ACM SIGMOD Int. Conf. on Management of Data*, pages 173–180, San Francisco, Cal., USA, 1987.
7. J.C. Freytag, D. Maier, and G. Vossen, editors. *Query Processing for Advanced Database Systems.* Morgan Kaufmann, San Mateo, Cal., USA, 1994.
8. A. Henrich. P-OQL: an OQL-oriented query language for PCTE. In *Proc. 7th Conf. on Software Engineering Environments*, pages 48–60, Noordwijkerhout, Netherlands, 1995. IEEE Computer Society Press.
9. A. Henrich. Document retrieval facilities for repository-based system development environments. In *Proc. 19th Annual Int. ACM SIGIR Conf. on Research and Development in Information Retrieval*, pages 101–109, Zürich, 1996.
10. A. Henrich. A homogeneous access structure for standard attributes and document representations in vector space. In *Proc. 3rd Int. Workshop on Next Generation Information Technologies and Systems*, pages 154–161, Jerusalem, Israel, 1997.
11. A. Henrich and J. Möller. Extending a spatial access structure to support additional standard attributes. In *Proc. 4th Int. Symp. on Advances in Spatial Databases*, volume 951 of *LNiCS*, pages 132–151, Portland, ME, USA, 1995.
12. A. Heuer and J. Kröger. Query optimization in the CROQUE project. In *Proc. 7th Int. Conf. on Database and Expert Systems Applications*, volume 1134 of *LNiCS*, pages 489–499, Zürich, 1996.
13. Y.E. Ioannidis. Query optimization. *ACM Computing Surveys*, 28(1):121 – 123, März 1996.
14. M.K. Lee, J.Ch. Freytag, and G.M. Lohmann. Implementing an interpreter for functional rules in a query optimizer. In *Proc. 14th Int. Conf. on Very Large Data Bases*, pages 218 – 229, Los Altos, Cal., USA, 1988.
15. B. Mitschang. *Query Processing in Database Systems (Anfrageverarbeitung in Datenbanksystemen).* Vieweg Verlag, Braunschweig, Wiesbaden, 1995. in German.
16. C. Ozkan, A. Dogac, and C. Evrendilek. A heuristic approach for optimization of path expressions. In *Proc. 6th Int. Conf. on Database and Expert Systems Applications*, volume 978 of *LNiCS*, pages 522–534, London, UK, 1995.
17. Portable Common Tool Environment - Abstract Specification / C Bindings / Ada Bindings. Standards ECMA-149/-158/-165, 3rd edition, 1993.
18. Portable Common Tool Environment - Abstract Specification / C Bindings / Ada Bindings. ISO IS 13719-1/-2/-3, 1994.
19. L. Wakeman and J. Jowett. *PCTE - The standard for open repositories.* Prentice Hall, Hemel Hempstead, Hertfordshire, UK, 1993.

A Database Array Algebra
for Spatio-Temporal Data and Beyond

Peter Baumann

FORWISS (Bavarian Research Center for Knowledge-Based Systems)
Orleansstr. 34, D-81667 Munich, Germany
baumann@forwiss.de

Abstract. Recently multidimensional arrays have received considerable attention among the database community, applications ranging from GIS to OLAP. Work on the formalization of arrays frequently focuses on mapping sparse arrays to ROLAP schemata. Database modeling of further array types, such as image data, is done differently and with less rigid methods. A unifying formal framework for general array handling of image, sensor, statistics, and OLAP data is missing.

We present a cross-dimensional and application-independent algebra for the high-level treatment of arbitrary arrays. An array constructor, a generalized aggregate, plus a multidimensional sorter allow to declaratively manipulate arrays. This algebra forms the conceptual basis of a domain-independent array DBMS, RasDaMan, which offers an SQL-based query language with extensive algebraic query and storage optimization. The system is in practical use in neuro science.

We introduce the algebra and show how the operators transform to the array query language. The universality of our approach is demonstrated by a number of examples from imaging, statistics, and OLAP.

1 Introduction

In principle, any natural phenomenon becomes spatio-temporal array data of some specific dimensionality once it is sampled and quantised for storage and manipulation in a computer system; additionally, a variety of artificial sources such as simulators, image renderers, and data warehouse population tools generate array data. The common characteristic they all share is that a large set of large multidimensional arrays has to be maintained. We call such arrays *multidimensional discrete data* (MDD), expressing the variety of dimensions and separating them from the conceptually different multidimensional vectorial data appearing in geo databases.

As arrays obviously form both an important and a very clearly defined information category, it seems natural to describe them in a uniform manner through a homogeneous conceptual model. Preferably this is done in a way that the array model smoothly fits into existing overall models.

From a database perspective (and history), several separate information categories can be distinguished. Sets comprise the first category, well addressed by relational algebra and calculus. Semantic nets form the second one, being fundamentally different in structures and operations, although mappings to the relational model have been studied extensively. The third fundamental category is text, addressed by information retrieval (IR) technology. This distinction is not withstanding the fact that techniques to map object nets to relations with foreign keys are well-known, that IR techniques have found their way into relational products (e.g., Oracle8), and that hypertext combines nets and text into so-called semi-structured data. Arrays represent a separate fourth category, substantially different from the previous three. Again, mappings have been developed to the relational model, however, involving a significant semantic transformation. For sparse business data these are star, galaxy, and snowflake techniques [1], for image data these are blobs [2] (where a particularly high loss of semantics is incurred). A clear indicator for the semantic mismatch of SQL-based multidimensional queries is the resulting lack of functionality and performance, leading to several suggestions for extending the relational model – e.g., [3, 4, 5].

Multidimensional database research has history, as statistical databases have been studied since long [6, 7]; more recently, OLAP continues this tradition with a strong focus on business data [8]. Several proposals exist to formalize array structures and operations for OLAP [4, 3, 9, 10, 11, 5], for scientific computing [12] and for imaging [13]. The Discrete Fourier Transform (DFT) has been studied from a database viewpoint [14]. Often, however, formal concepts have not been implemented in an operational system and they have not been evaluated in real-life applications. Moreover, many of the formal models have been designed specifically with the goal of mapping arrays to relation tuples and in a way that, in practice, makes sense only for sparse arrays.

In this paper, we propose an algebraic framework (see [15] for a first version) which allows to express cross-dimensional queries, i.e., operations on arrays of any number of dimensions, simultaneously in one and the same expression and symmetric in all dimensions. Essentially, this algebra consists of only three operations: an array constructor, a generalized aggregation, and a multidimensional sorter. This core model does not rely on recursion and is safe in evaluation, yet it is sufficient to express a wide range of imaging, statistical, and OLAP operations. Therefore, our algebra can be seen as a "universal" framework, independent from the particular application domain. The concepts are implemented in the domain-independent array DBMS RasDaMan[1] [16, 15, 17], hence the name *RasDaMan Array Algebra*, or short: *Array Algebra*.

The remainder of this paper is organized as follows. In Section 2, Array Algebra is presented, together with practical examples from diverse application fields to illustrate its applicability. The step to an SQL-embedded array query language, RasQL, is shown in Section 3. Section 4 surveys related work, and Section 5 summarizes our findings.

---

[1] <u>Ras</u>ter <u>Da</u>ta <u>Man</u>ager; see *www.forwiss.de/~rasdaman*

2 Array Algebra

We treat arrays as functions mapping n-dimensional points (i.e., vectors) from discrete Euclidean space to values. This is common in imaging for a long time – see, e.g., [18] – and has been transposed to database terminology in [16, 15]. To smoothly embed Array Algebra into existing overall algebrae we use a set-oriented basis. Due to space constraints we have to omit most proofs here.

Operations on such arrays frequently apply a function simultaneously to a set of cells, requiring second-order functionals in the algebra. In practice they are necessary to allow for binding variables to points for iterating coordinate sets and also to aggregate arrays (or part thereof) into scalar values. The latter operation corresponds very much to relational set aggregators; however, instead of providing a limited list of aggregation operations as in the relational algebra, a general constructor is introduced by Array Algebra which is parametrized with the underlying base operation.

2.1 N-Dimensional Interval Arithmetics

We first introduce some notation for n-dimensional integer interval arithmetics. We call the coordinate set of an array its *spatial domain*. Informally, a spatial domain is defined as a set of n-dimensional points (i.e., algebraic vectors) in Euclidean space forming a finite hypercube with boundaries parallel to the coordinate system axes.

We assume common vector notation. For a natural number $d>0$, we write $x=(x_1,..., x_d) \in X \subseteq \mathbf{Z}^d$ for some d-dimensional vector x, x+y for vector addition, etc. The point set forming the geometric extent of an array is called its *spatial domain*. A spatial domain X of dimension d spanned by $\underline{l}$ and $\underline{h}$ is defined as

$$X = [l_1:h_1,...,l_d:h_d] \quad := \quad \overset{d}{\underset{i=1}{\bigtimes}} \{x_i : l_i \le x_i \le h_i\} \text{ if } \forall 1 \le i \le d: l_i \le h_i$$

$$:= \quad \{\} \qquad\qquad\qquad \text{otherwise}.$$

Functions lo, hi: $\mathbf{P}(\mathbf{Z}^d) \rightarrow \mathbf{Z}^d$ (where $\mathbf{P}$ is the Powerset) defined as $lo(X)=\underline{l}$ and $hi(X)=\underline{h}$ for some spatial domain X given as before denote the bounding vectors. We will abbreviate $lo_i(X)=l_i$ and $hi_i(X)=h_i$ for the ith component. Function $dim(X)=d$ denotes the dimension of spatial domain X.

On such hypercubes, point set operations can be defined in a straightforward way. We admit only those operations which respect closure, such as intersect and union*, whereby the asterisk "*" denotes the hull operation applied to the result:

```
intersect*(X,Y) :=
    [ max(low_1(X),low_1(Y)) : min(hi_1(X),hi_1(Y)),...,
        max(low_d(X),low_d(Y)) : min(hi_d(X),hi_d(Y)) ]
```

```
union*( X, Y ) :=
    [ min(low₁(X),low₁(Y)) : max(hi₁(X),hi₁(Y)),...,
      min(low_d(X),low_d(Y)) : max(hi_d(X), hi_d(Y)) ]
```

union*$(X, Y) :=$
$$[\min(low_1(X),low_1(Y)) : \max(hi_1(X),hi_1(Y)),...,$$
$$\min(low_d(X),low_d(Y)) : \max(hi_d(X), hi_d(Y))]$$

Obviously these operations are commutative, associative, and distributive.

The `shift` operator allows to change a spatial domain's position according to a translation vector $\underline{t}$:

$$shift_{\underline{t}}(X) := \{ \underline{x}+\underline{t}: \underline{x}\in X \}$$

Let X be spanned by d-dimensional vectors 1 and h. For some integer i with $1 \leq i \leq d$ and a one-D integer interval $I=[m:n]$ with $1_i \leq m \leq n \leq h_i$, the *trim of* X *to* I *in dimension* d is defined as

$$\tau_{i,I}(X) := \{ \underline{x}\in X: m \leq x_i \leq n \} = [1_1:h_1,...,m:n,...,1_d:h_d]$$

Intuitively speaking, trimming slices off those parts of an array which are lower than m and higher than n in the dimension indicated; the dimension is unchanged. As opposed to this, a section cuts out a hyperplane with dimension reduced by 1. Formally, for some X as above, an integer p with $1 \leq p \leq d$, the *section of* X *at position* p *in dimension* i is given by

$$\sigma_{i,p}(X) := \{ \underline{x}\in Z^{d-1}: \underline{x}=(x_1,..., x_{i-1}, x_{i+1},..., x_d),$$
$$(x_1,..., x_{i-1}, p, x_{i+1},..., x_d)\in X \}$$
$$= [1_1:h_1,..., 1_{i-1}:h_{i-1}, 1_{i+1}:h_{i+1},..., 1_d:h_d]$$

Trimming is commutative and associative, whereas a section changes dimension numbering and, therefore, has neither of these properties.

2.2 The Core Algebra

Let $X \subseteq Z^d$ be a spatial domain and F a homogeneous algebra. Then, an F-*valued d-dimensional array over spatial domain* X − or short: (*multidimensional*) *array* − is defined as

$$a:X \rightarrow F \text{ (i.e., } a\in F^X), \quad a = \{ (\underline{x},a(\underline{x})): \underline{x}\in X, a(\underline{x})\in F \}$$

Array elements $a(\underline{x})$ are referred to as *cells*. For notational convenience, we also allow to enumerate the components of a cell coordinate vector, e.g., $a(x_1,x_2,x_3)$. Auxiliary function sdom(a) denotes the spatial domain of some array a; further, we lift function dim to arrays. For an array $a:X \rightarrow F$, sdom and dim are defined as

```
sdom(a) := X
dim(a)  := dim( sdom(a) )
```

The ith dimension range of an array's spatial domain we will denote by $\mathrm{sdom}_i(a)$.
Example: For a 1024×768 image a with lower left corner in the origin of the coordinate system, $\mathrm{sdom}(a)=[0:1023,0:767]$, $\mathrm{dim}(a)=2$.

The first functional we introduce is the *array constructor* MARRAY. It allows to define arrays by indicating a spatial domain and an expression which is evaluated for each cell position of the spatial domain. An iteration variable bound to a spatial domain is available in the cell expression so that a cell's value can depend on its position. Let X be a spatial domain, F a value set, and v a free identifier. Let further e_v be an expression with result type F containing zero or more free occurrences of v as placeholder(s) for an expression with result type X. Then, an *array over spatial domain* X *with base type F* is constructed through

$$\mathrm{MARRAY}_{X,v}(e_v) \;=\; \{\;(\underline{x},a(\underline{x})):\; a(\underline{x})=e_{\underline{x}},\underline{x}\in X\;\}$$

Example: Consider scaling of a greyscale image a with $\mathrm{sdom}(a) = [1{:}m,1{:}n]$ by a factor $s\in R$. We assume componentwise scalar division and rounding on vectors and write

$$\mathrm{MARRAY}_{[1:m*s,1:n*s],v}(\;a(\;\mathrm{round}(\;v/s\;)\;)\;)$$

For $0<s<1$ the image is sized down; the interpolation method then corresponds to "nearest neighbor", the simplest interpolation technique used in imaging.

The operation which in some sense is the dual to the MARRAY constructor is the *condenser* COND. It takes the values of an array's cells and combines them through the operation provided, thereby obtaining a scalar value. Again, an iterator variable is bound to a spatial domain to address cell values in the condensing expression. Let o be a commutative and associative operation with signature o: F, F $\rightarrow$ F, let further v be a free identifier, $X = \{\;\underline{x}_1,...,\underline{x}_n \mid \underline{x}_i \in Z^d\}$ a spatial domain consisting of n points, and $e_{a,v}$ an expression of result type F containing occurrences of an array a and identifier v. Then, the *condense of a by o* is defined as

$$\mathrm{COND}_{o,X,v}(e_{a,v}) \;:=\; \underset{x\in X}{\mathrm{O}}\, e_{a,\underline{x}} \;=\; e_{a,\,\underline{x1}} \;o\;\cdots\; o\; e_{a,\,\underline{xn}}$$

Examples: Let a be the image as defined in the above example. Average pixel intensity is given by

$$\mathrm{COND}_{+,\mathrm{sdom}(a),v}(a(v)) \;/\; |\mathrm{sdom}(a)| \;=\; \sum_{x\in[1:m,1:n]} a[x]/(m*n)$$

For color table computation needed, e.g., for generation of a GIF image encoding, one has to know the set of all values occurring in array a. The condenser allows to derive this set by performing the union of all cell values:

$\text{COND}_{\cup,\text{sdom}(a),v}(\ \{\ a(v)\ \}\ )$

The third and last operator is an array sorter which proceeds along a selected dimension to reorder the corresponding hyperslices. Function sort_s rearranges a given array along a specified dimension s without changing its value set or spatial domain. To this end, an order-generating function is provided which associates a "sequence position" to each (d-1)-dimensional hyperslice. Let a be a d-dimensional array, $i \in N$ with $1 \le i \le d$ a dimension number, and $f_{s,a}: \text{sdom}_s(a) \to N$ a total function which, for a given array a, inspects a in the sorting dimension s and delivers an ordering measure for each hyperslice. Further, let $\text{perm}(\underline{x},\underline{y})$ be a predicate indicating that vector $\underline{x}$ is a permutation of vector $\underline{y}$ (and vice versa). Then, the two sorters $\text{sort}_{s,f}^{\text{asc}}$ and $\text{sort}_{s,f}^{\text{desc}}$ for ascending and descending order, resp., are given as those arrays which consist of permutations of the hyperslices in the sort dimension and, additionally, fulfil the sorting criterion given by f:

$\text{sort}_{s,f}^{\text{asc}}(\ a\ )\ :=$
$\{\ (\underline{y},b(\underline{y})):\ \underline{y} \in \text{sdom}_s(a),$

$\qquad \forall p,q \in \text{sdom}_s(a):\ p<q\ \Rightarrow\ f_{s,b}(p) \le f_{s,b}(q),$

$\qquad \text{perm}(\ (\ (b(x_1,...,x_{s-1},\text{sdom}_s(a).\text{lo},x_{s+1},...,x_d),\ ...,$

$\qquad\qquad\qquad b(x_1,...,x_{s-1},\text{sdom}_s(a).\text{hi},x_{s+1},...,x_d)\ ),$

$\qquad\qquad\quad (\ (a(x_1,...,x_{s-1},\text{sdom}_s(a).\text{lo},x_{s+1},...,x_d),\ ...,$

$\qquad\qquad\qquad a(x_1,...,x_{s-1},\text{sdom}_s(a).\text{hi},x_{s+1},...,x_d))\ )\ \}$

$\text{sort}_{s,f}^{\text{desc}}(\ a\ )\ :=$
$\{\ (\underline{y},b(\underline{y})):\ \underline{y} \in \text{sdom}_s(a),$

$\qquad \forall p,q \in \text{sdom}_s(a):\ p<q\ \Rightarrow\ f_{s,b}(p) \ge f_{s,b}(q),$

$\qquad \text{perm}(\ (\ (b(x_1,...,x_{s-1},\text{sdom}_s(a).\text{lo},x_{s+1},...,x_d),\ ...,$

$\qquad\qquad\qquad b(x_1,...,x_{s-1},\text{sdom}_s(a).\text{hi},x_{s+1},...,x_d)\ ),$

$\qquad\qquad\quad (\ (a(x_1,...,x_{s-1},\text{sdom}_s(a).\text{lo},x_{s+1},...,x_d),\ ...,$

$\qquad\qquad\qquad a(x_1,...,x_{s-1},\text{sdom}_s(a).\text{hi},x_{s+1},...,x_d))\ )\ \}$

The resulting array has the same number of dimensions, spatial domain, and base type as the input array. Note that function $f_{s,a}$ has all degrees of freedom to assess any of a's cell values for determining the measure value of a hyperslice on hand - it can be a particular cell value in the current hyperslice, the average of all hyperslice values, or even neighbored slices (e.g., for relative increases of sales values).

Example: Let a be a 1-D array with spatial domain $D=[1:d]$ where cell values denote sales figures over time. Let further sorting function $f_{s,a}$ be given as $f_{s,a}(p)$ $= a[p]$. Then, $\text{sort}_{0,f}^{\text{desc}}(a)$ delivers the ranked sales.

As an aside we note that the sort operator includes the relational *group by*. Below we will demonstrate that slice and roll-up operations arising from array access based on dimension hierarchies can be expressed, although - not very comfortably - by indicating the cell coordinates pertaining to a particular member set. Concepts for an intuitive, symbolic treatment of dimension hierarchies are currently under investigation.

2.3 Derived Operators

Several useful operations can be derived from the above ones. We present a selection of those which have turned out particularly important in practical applications.

2.3.1 Trimming and Section

The previously introduced spatial domain operations trimming and section give rise to corresponding array operations. For some array a, an 1-D interval I, and two natural numbers $1 \leq t \leq \dim(a)$ and $p \in \text{sdom}_d(a)$ they are defined as

$$\text{TRIM}_{t,I}(a) := \text{MARRAY}_{X,v}(a(v)) \quad \text{for } X = \tau_{t,I}(\text{sdom}(a)) \text{ and } d < \dim(a)$$
$$\text{SECT}_{t,p}(a) := \text{MARRAY}_{X,v}(a(v)) \quad \text{for } X = \sigma_{t,p}(\text{sdom}(a)) \text{ and } d < \dim(a)$$

Example: Slicing of an OLAP cube c with spatial domain $\text{sdom}(c) = D \times R \times P$ to extract subcube $D' \times R' \times P' \subseteq \text{sdom}(c)$ is denoted as

$$\text{TRIM}_{1,D'}(\text{ TRIM}_{2,R'} (\text{TRIM}_{3,P'}(c)))$$

2.3.2 Induced Operations

A basic set of operations is induced by the algebra of the underlying value sets. If $a, b \in F^X$ are arrays and o is a binary operation on F, then o induces a binary operation on F^X denoted by o_{ind} such that, if $c = a \ o_{\text{ind}} b$, then $c \in F^X$ and, for all $x \in X$, $c(x)$ $= a(x) \ o \ b(x)$. Along this line, we also allow to induce unary operations. Notably, these operations are not axiomatic; for a unary function f and a binary function g,

$$\text{IND}_f(a) \quad = \text{MARRAY}_{X,v}(f(a(v))) \qquad \text{for } X = \text{sdom}(a)$$
$$\text{IND}_g(a,b) \quad = \text{MARRAY}_{X,v}(g(a(v),b(v))) \text{ for } X = \text{sdom}(a) = \text{sdom}(b)$$

Algebraic properties of F transform to corresponding structures on the set F^X of induced functions. If F is a field, then F^X is a vector space; for a ring F, F^X is a module for suitably defined spatial domains.

Examples: Let a be a grayscale image over spatial domain X. Increasing intensity by 5 can be accomplished through induction on unary "+5":

$$\texttt{IND}_{+5}\texttt{(a)} = \{ (\underline{x}, b(\underline{x})) : b(\underline{x}) = a(\underline{x}) + 5, \underline{x} \in X \}$$

Consider now another grayscale image b over the same spatial domain X. Then, pixel addition can be induced to obtain image addition:

$$\texttt{IND}_{+}\texttt{(a,b)} = \{ (\underline{x}, c(\underline{x})) : c(\underline{x}) = a(\underline{x}) + b(\underline{x}), \underline{x} \in X \}$$

When used in a query, binary induction obviously implies a spatial join.

Let now *c* be a color image where the cell type is a three-integer record of red, green, and blue intensity, resp. Such a *pixel-interleaved* image is transformed into a *channel-interleaved* representation, i.e., three separate color planes, through induction on the record access operator ".", obtaining

```
< c.red, c.green, c.blue >
```

The above type of induction is also referred to as pointwise induction, as points pairwise match for each application of the base function.

2.3.3 Aggregation

Obviously, the condenser provides the appropriate basis for aggregation over arrays. Table 1 lists some of the most common aggregations and their definition in Array Algebra.

Table 1: Some possible aggregate operators on arrays. Assumed are array expressions a (without restriction), b of result type Boolean, and c with a numerical result type.

Array aggregate definition	Meaning
Count_cells(a)	The number of cells in a
Some_cells(b)	Is there any cell in b with value true?
All_cells(b)	Do all cells of b have value true?
Sum_cells(c)	The sum of all cells in c
Avg_cells(c)	The average of all cells in c
Max_cells(c)	The maximum of all cells in c

2.4 Further Application Examples

A basic requirement in the development of Array Algebra has been to cover all applications of arrays in databases, the most important ones being statistics, OLAP, and imaging. To illustrate applicability of Array Algebra to these areas, we now present some advanced examples.

2.4.1 Statistics

Example *matrix multiplication*: Let a be an $m{\times}n$ matrix and b an $n{\times}p$ matrix. Then, the $m{\times}p$ matrix product

$$a*b \;=\; \sum_{j=1}^{n} a_{i,j} * b_{j,k}$$

in Array Algebra is expressed as

$$\text{MARRAY}_{[1:m,1:p],(i,k)}(\text{ COND}_{+,[1:n],j}(\text{ } a(i,j)*b(j,k) \text{ }) \text{ })$$

Example *auto correlation*: For two observation vectors x and y of dimension n, empirical covariance $m_{x,y}$ is defined as

$$m_{x,y} \;=\; \frac{1}{n-1}\sum_{i=1}^{n} (x_i - x_{avg})(y_i - y_{avg})$$

In Array Algebra, the mean is given by $x_{avg} = \text{COND}_{+,[1:n],i}(x(i))\,/\,n$ and $y_{avg} = \text{COND}_{+,[1:n],i}(y(i))\,/\,n$. Then, $m_{x,y}$ is described in a straightforward manner:

$$\text{COND}_{+,[1:n],i}(\text{ }(x(i)-x_{avg})*(y(i)-y_{avg})\text{ })\,/\,(n-1)$$

Example *histogram*: A histogram contains, for each possible value, the number of cells conveying this value. For some n-D one-byte integer array with intensity values between 0 and 255, the histogram is computed as

$$\text{MARRAY}_{[0:255],n}(\text{}$$
$$\text{COND}_{+,\text{sdom}(a),v}(\text{ if } a(v){=}n \text{ then } 1 \text{ else } 0 \text{ fi}) \text{ })$$

As we can see, the combination of MARRAY and COND appears in quite different contexts. Indeed, this type of operation forms the basis for an extremely wide range of analysis functions, such as statistical analyses, advanced OLAP consolidation operations like roll-up, slice&dice, as well as scaling, convolutions and filtering in image processing. It is capable of completely changing dimensionality, size, and cell types of arrays.

2.4.2 OLAP

Example *roll-up*: Let c be a sales datacube with $D{\times}R{\times}P{=}[1{:}d,1{:}r,1{:}p]$ as spatial domain where dimension 1 counts days from 1 to today, dimension 2 enumerates sales regions, and dimension 3 contains products sold; cell values shall represent sales figures. The weekly average of sales per product and region, then, is expressed as

$$\text{MARRAY}_{[1:\text{today}/7]\times R\times P,\,(w,r,p)}\big($$

$$\text{COND}_{+,[0:6],d}\big(\ c(7*w+d,r,p)\ /\ 7\ )\ )$$

Aggregating over all products leads only to a slight change in the expression

$$\text{MARRAY}_{[1:d/7]\times R,\,(w,r)}\big($$

$$\text{COND}_{+,[0:6]\times P,(d,p)}\big(\ c(7*w+d,r,p)\ /\ 7\ )\ )$$

Notably, such queries can be of considerable length when formulated relationally, and usually involve several joins.

Example *top performers*: On the same cube, the top performing weeks are determined as follows. We use the notation `<s:sales,w:week>` to describe a two-component record with component names `sales` and week. With function f_c given as $f_c(i)=$ `c[i].sales`, the following expression rolls up this cube from days to weeks and delivers the accumulated sales over all regions and products of the top 3 weeks:

$$\text{sort}_{0,f_c}^{\text{desc}}\big(\ \text{MARRAY}_{[1:d/7],w}\big($$

$$<\text{COND}_{+,[0:6]\times R\times P,(d,r,p)}(c[7*w+d,r,p]):\text{sales},\ \text{w:week}>\ )\ )$$

$$[1:3].\text{week}$$

The last query heavily makes use of the fact that coordinate and cell values (dimension and measure elements in OLAP terminology) can be used interchangeably.

2.4.3 Imaging

Example *skewed section*: A skewed section through a 2-D image where the cutting line is not axis-parallel (Fig. 1) can be described by placing a skew factor $s>1$ on the indexing point $\underline{x}$, resulting in the shifted point position $(s*x_1,x_1)$:

$$\text{MARRAY}_{\text{sdom2(a)},v}\big(\ a(s*v_1,v_1)\ )$$

Using the contents of another (1-D) array for indexing allows to pick arbitrary cells. Let `a` have `sdom(a)=` $[1:m,1:n]$ and `s` be a 1-D array with spatial domain $X=[1:n]$. Cell values of array `s` are used to index `a` (Fig. 1):

$$\text{MARRAY}_{\text{sdom1(a)},x}\big(\ a(s(x),x)\ )$$

Example *filtering*: The following expression, parametrized over array `a` and mask `m` (such as the edge detector illustrated in Fig. 2) can be used as a template for general filtering operations:

$$f(a,m) = \text{MARRAY}_{sdom(a),x}(\text{COND}_{+,sdom(m),y}(a(x+y))*m(y)))$$

1	1	1	1	1	1	1	1	1	1	1	1	1	1
1	1	1	1	1	1	1	1	1	1	1	1	1	1
1	1	1	1	1	1	1	1	1	1	1	1	1	1
1	1	1	1	1	1	1	1	1	1	1	1	1	1
1	1	1	1	1	1	1	1	1	1	1	1	1	1
1	1	1	1	1	1	1	1	1	1	1	1	1	1
1	1	1	1	1	1	1	1	1	1	1	1	1	1

2	1	1	1	s	1	1	1	1	1	1	1	1
3	1	1	1	1	1	1	1	1	1	1	1	1
2	1	1	1	1	1	1	1	1	1	1	1	1
4	1	1	1	1	1	1	1	1	1	1	1	1
7	1	1	1	1	1	1	1	1	1	1	1	1
5	1	1	1	1	1	1	1	1	1	1	1	1
0	1	1	1	1	1	1	1	1	1	1	1	1

a   s   b

Fig. 1: Skewed section (left) $\text{MARRAY}_{[0:6],x}(a(x*2,x))$ of 2-D array a with $sdom(a)=[0:12,0:6]$ and user-defined section (right) $\text{MARRAY}_{[0:6],x}(b(s(x),x))$ of 2-D array b with $sdom(b)=[0:10,0:6]$; selected cells are shaded.

1	3	1
0	0	0
-1	-3	-1

Fig. 2: 2-D Sobel filter mask m = { ((-1,1),1), ((0,1),3), ((1,1),1), ((-1,0),0), ((0,0),0), ((1,0),0), ((-1,-1),-1), ((0,-1),-3), ((1,-1),-1) }.
The spatial domain center (0,0) is marked by a double box.

Through instantiation with mask s_1 as given by Fig. 1 and mask s_2 as the transpose of s_1, we can express the Sobel edge detector (see Fig. 2 for mask definition, Fig. 3 for an application example):

$$(\mid f(a,s_1) \mid + \mid f(a,s_2) \mid) / 9$$

Fig. 3: Sobel filter applied to a 2-D raster image.

We observe that in many cases operations can be formulated without explicitly referring to the array dimension, allowing to develop parametrized cross-dimensional, domain-independent query libraries which go well beyond the capabilities of object-relational ADTs [19].

3 From Array Algebra to RasQL

In this Section, we sketch how Array Algebra translates to the query language RasQL. Array Algebra has been developed in the course of implementing this fully-fledged, domain-independent array DBMS based on an SQL-based query language, obeying strict data independence. Arrays are embedded as a data abstraction allowing, e.g., to define array-valued object or tuple attributes, depending on the hosting data model.

Arrays can be defined either concisely with dimension and extent per dimension fixed, or with a fixed number of dimensions but free lower or upper bounds in some dimension(s), or with dimension and boundaries left completely open. Runtime range checking on instances, then, is performed according to the amount of information provided in the data dictionnary.

RasDaMan commits itself to the ODMG standard [20], hence the RasDaMan query language RasQL also follows the flavour of ODMG's OQL which, in turn, leans itself on standard SQL-92. Queries range over collections which contain the class extents. Array expressions can appear both in the select and in the where clause of a query. The MARRAY equivalent in RasQL has the structure

```
marray <iterator> in <spatial domain>
values <expression>
```

The COND statement is somewhat extended. In the syntactic structure

```
condense <op>
over     <iterator> in <spatial domain>
where    <condition>
using    <expression>
```

The where condition allows to further restrict the cell set inspected. This makes thresholding and similar tasks more elegant to phrase and, in particular, supports optimization.

Optimizing MARRAY and COND expressions is not easy (although not impossible) due to the generality of the operators. We therefore continuously investigate on special cases where particularly efficient solutions exist; a rich set of over 100 rules has been identified and implemented yet [21]. For optimizability reasons and due to their practical importance, trimming, section, and induction are supported by special constructs; likewise, the condenser specializations mentioned in Table 1 are supported directly. Table 2 demonstrates some of these constructs with the help of application examples.

Table 2: Sample RasQL queries. We assume array-valued attributes for 2-D Landsat satellite images, 3-D volumetric images, and 3-D OLAP cubes, to be embedded in object classes (or relations, resp.).

Algebra operator	RasQL example	Explanation
IND_f	`Select img + 5` `from    LandsatImages as img`	The red channel of all Landsat images, intensified by 5

IND_g	`Select oid(br)`
	`from    BrainImages as br,`
	`        BrainAreas as mask`
	`where   br * mask > t`
		OIDs of all brain images where, in the masked area, intensity exceeds threshold value t

TRIM	`Select w[ *:*, y0:y1, z0:z1 ]` `from    Warehouse as w`	OLAP slicing ("*:*" exhausts the dimension)
SECT	`Select v[ x, *:*, *:* ]` `from    VolumetricImages as v`	A vertical cut through all volumetric images

MARRAY	`Select marray n in [0:255]`
	`       values`
	`           condense +`
	`           over    x in sdom(v)`
	`           using   v[x]=n`
	`from    VolumetricImages as v`
		For each 3-D image its histogram [2]

COND	`Select condense +`
	`       over    x in sdom(w)`
	`       using   w[x] > t`
	`from    Warehouse as w`
		For each datacube in the warehouse, count all cells exceeding threshold value t

A trim expression in the left-hand side of an update assignment indicates the array part to be updated:

```
update <collection>
set    <array attribute>[<trim expression>]
assign <array expression>
where  ...
```

Besides updating part of an array, this statement can also be used to extend an array by appending data (e.g., during periodical warehouse population or slicewise insertion

---

[2] RasQL supports the interpretation of Boolean values as numerics as is usual in many programming languages.

into a 3-D image), provided the affected dimension has been defined variable in the attribute definition. Formally the process of extending an array a in direction i with another array b matching a in all dimensions (with a possible exception in dimension i) and base type is governed by the algebra expression as follows.

Let $\underline{t}=(0,...,0,\text{sdom}_i(a),0,...,0)$ be the translation vector consisting of zeros except for component $i \leq d$. Then,

```
extend(a,b,i)  :=
```

$$\text{MARRAY}_{\text{sdom}(a) \cup \text{shift}\underline{t}(\text{sdom}(b)), v}\big($$
$$\text{if } v \in \text{sdom}(a) \text{ then } a(v) \text{ else } b(v-\underline{t}) \text{ fi}$$
$$\big)$$

4 Related Work

In this Section we survey related work in formalization of arrays in databases; in part we rely on the classification published in [22] which gives particular attention to the independence of array formalisms from their implementation.

Let us start, however, with APL [23,24] as a prominent representative from the programming languages area, dedicated to n-dimensional array manipulation. APL basically has to be compared not with the algebra but with the query language RasQL. On this level, both share interesting implementation problems which, however, are out of scope here. Conceptually, Array Algebra functionality has its respective counterparts in APL: the *enclose* operator "⊂" corresponds to the MARRAY constructor; the *reduction* operator "/" corresponds to the condenser, but is applied only to the outermost dimension; the *each* operator "¨" and, to some extent, *scalar functions* correspond to unary and binary induction. As a programming language with procedural constructs and recursion, APL is more powerful than Array Algebra, but not safe.

In the database world, the algebra underlying the EXTRA/EXCESS database system supports 1-D, variable-length arrays [25]. As for the operators, there is a function SUBARR corresponding to the Array Algebra operator SECT, and ARR_APPLY corresponding to our unary induce IND_f. Aggregation is not supported.

Gray et al. [4] propose an SQL cube operator which generalizes *group-by*. It is based on a particular mapping of sparse arrays to relations. There is no clear separation between conceptual (multidimensional) model and the proposed SQL extensions; specifically, no formal algebra is provided.

In [3] a formal model for sparse array maintenance in relational systems (ROLAP) is presented. Array data are organized into one or more hypercubes whereby a cell value can either be an n-tuple (i.e., one nesting level of record elements) or a Boolean value denoting existence of the respective value combination. The algebra consists of a set of basic operations which are parametrized by user-defined functions. For example, operations pull and push increase/decrease, resp., a cube's dimension by changing coordinate values to cell contents and vice versa; in our example *top performers* we demonstrate how this is done in Array Algebra. Further, there is a join operation to combine two arrays sharing k dimensions. The "join partners" are specified through user-defined functions outside the formalism. The same way aggregation is handled through functions outside the formalism as opposed to Array Algebra where the condenser serves to describe aggregation.

Cabibo and Torlone [9] propose a more "cube-oriented" formal multidimensional model and a corresponding query language based on a logical calculus. The data model relies on the notion of n-dimensional *f-tables*, i.e., (mathematical) relations where each cell is represented by a tuple of n coordinates and the cell value itself, which must be atomic. Aside of the usual logical quantifiers and connectors there are scalar and aggregation functions which are user-defined, hence outside the formalism. The equal treatment of coordinates and cells like in Array Algebra is possible.

Li and Wang [10] formalize a multidimensional model for OLAP. Core is an algebraic query language called grouping algebra which treats arrays as sets of relations plus an associated cell value which must be scalar. Operations on arrays are *add dimension, transfer, union, aggregation, rc-join* (relation/cube join), and *construct* (build array from relation). The algebra includes relations so that it can be seen as an extension of relational algebra. The model is very powerful, particularly in grouping, ordering, and aggregation. In [11] an algebra and calculus for multidimensional OLAP is presented. A multidimensional tabular database is defined as a set of tables. The model is close to the way OLAP arrays are mapped to relational star schemata. No direct mechanism is provided for join and aggregation; as by definition all first-order definable classification and aggregation functions are incorporated, these constructs can be expressed, too. Implementation of the model relies on an SQL mapping. Further important recent work in the field is described in [26, 27, 28].

In [12], an array query language, AQL, relying on Lambda calculus is presented which is geared towards scientific computing. AQL offers powerful operations on multidimensional arrays, with only slightly less generality in the aggregation mechanism than Array Algebra. The model has been implemented as a front end for querying arrays maintained in files using a geo scientific data exchange format.

An Array Manipulation Language, AML, is introduced in [13]. Two operators serve to subsample and interleave, resp., arrays based on bit sequences governing cell selection. The third operator, APPLY, corresponds to induce operations modulo the bit pattern for cell selection. Bit patterns are modeled in Array Algebra through 1-D bit arrays executing the same control function. AML is more restricted than Array Algebra in that such control arrays cannot contain arbitrary values (e.g., weights), and moreover are constrained to 1-D. According to the authors, the main application area of AML is seen in imaging.

In summary, most array frameworks nowadays are geared towards OLAP tasks, without regarding, e.g., spatio-temporal array application fields. Conversely, frameworks such as AML aiming at imaging do not consider OLAP. Sometimes array iteration or aggregation retracts to user-defined functions which, in an implementation, makes optimization difficult. All operations such as aggregation and spatial join found in these approaches are expressible in Array Algebra, too, except that dimension hierarchies usually are supported by convenient mechanisms, a feature still to be included in Array Algebra.

5 Conclusion

Let us be philosophic for a moment. Loosely speaking, for every data abstraction a corresponding basic operation exists. For instance, component access by name corresponds with records (in C/C++: "structs"), whereas linear traversal relates to lists and sets. For arrays, usually (nested) loops are seen as the "natural" operation, exploiting the per dimension linear ordering of cell indices. Ordering, however, is not the essence. Instead, the neighborhood defined by the indices is the crucial property: consolidation of a data warehouse cube, say, to derive weekly figures from daily data, involves seven neighbored array cells for every derived cell value. Likewise, edge detection in a 2-D raster image involves an n×n neighborhood of each pixel for computation of the result pixels. Hence, we claim that not iteration is the operation characteristic for arrays, but (conceptually) simultaneous computation of all result array cells, in general based on the evaluation of some neighborhood for each cell.

RasDaMan Array Algebra has been designed as an algebraic framework for multidimensional arrays of arbitrary dimension and base type. Essentially two functionals and a sorter are sufficient for a broad range of statistics, OLAP, and imaging operations. They are declarative by nature and do not prescribe any iteration sequence, thereby opening up a wide field for query optimization and parallelization. Array Algebra is minimal in the sense that no subset of its operations exhibits the same expressive power. It is also closed in application: any expression is either of a scalar or an array type. Finally, Array Algebra does not rely on any external array handling functionality ("user-defined functions") aside of the operations coming with the algebraic structure of the cell type. By making all operations explicit, query optimization is eased considerably.

Array Algebra comprises the formal basis for the domain-independent array DBMS RasDaMan [17] vendored by Actived Knowledge GmbH[3]. The query language RasQL supports declarative array expressions embedded in standard SQL-92. The array query optimizer relies on about 150 algebraic rewrite rules on logical and physical level [21]. Streamlined storage management allows to distribute arrays across heterogeneous storage media. RasDaMan is being used, e.g., in the European Human Brain Database[4] for WWW-based access to 3-D human brain images.

Future work on the conceptual level will encompass domain–specific features such as dimension hierarchies for OLAP, including symbolic dimension handling instead of the pure numbering scheme used now, and vector/raster integration for geo applications. On the architectural level, extending RasQL functionality based on further benchmarking [17] will keep us busy for some time.

---

[3] See www.active-knowledge.de/

[4] see www.dhbr.neuro.ki.se/ECHBD/Database/

Acknowledgements

RasDaFolks – Andreas Dehmel, Paula Furtado, Roland Ritsch, and Norbert Widmann – form a group with outstanding ingenuity and team spirit; it needs such people to bring a system like RasDaMan into existence.

The RasDaMan project has been partially sponsored by the European Commission under grant no. 20073.

References

1. R. Kimball: *The Data Warehouse Toolkit.* John Wiley & Sons, 1996
2. R. Haskin, R. Lorie: *On Extending the Functions of a Relational Database System.* Proc. ACM SIGMOD, Orlando, USA, June 1982, pp. 207 - 212.
3. R. Agrawal, A. Gupta, S. Sarawagi: *Modeling Multidimensional Databases.* Proc. 13th ICDE, Birmingham, UK, April 1997, pp. 232 – 243.
4. J. Gray, A. Bosworth, A. Layman, H. Pirahesh: *Data Cube: A Relational Aggregation Operator Generalizing Group-By, Cross-Tabs, and Sub-Totals.* Technical Report MSR-TR-95-22, Microsoft Research, Advance Technology Division, Microsoft Corp., November 1995.
5. A. Bauer, W. Lehner: *The Cube-Query-Language for Multidimensional Statistical and Scientific Database Systems.* Proc. 5th DASFAA 1997, Melbourne, Australia, April 1997, pp. 263 - 272.
6. A. Shoshani: *Statistical Databases: Characteristics, Problems, and some Solutions.* Proc. VLDB 8, Mexico City, Mexico, September 1982, pp. 208 - 222.
7. A. Shoshani: *OLAP and Statistical Databases: Similarities and Differences.* Proc. PODS 16, Tucson, USA, May 1997, pp. 185 - 196.
8. E.F. Codd, S.B. Codd, C.T. Salley: *Providing Olap (On-Line Analytical Processing) to User-Analysts: An IT Mandate.* White paper, 1995, URL: www.arborsoft.com/papers/coddTOC.html
9. L. Cabibbo, R. Torlone: *A Logical Approach to Multidimensional Databases.* EDBT 1998.
10. C. Li and X.S. Wang: *A data model for supporting on-line analytical processing.* Proc. CIKM, Rockville, USA, November 1996, pp. 81 - 88.
11. Marc Gyssens, Laks, V.S. Lakshmanan: *A Foundation for Multi-Dimensional Databases.* Proc. VLDB, Athens, Greece, August 1997, pp. 106 - 115.
12. L. Libkin, R. Machlin, L. Wong: *A Query Language for Multidimensional Arrays: Design, Implementation, and Optimization Techniques.* Proc. ACM SIGMOD, Montreal, Canada, June 1996, pp. 228 – 239.
13. A. P. Marathe, K. Salem: *A Language for Manipulating Arrays.* Proc. VLDB, Athens, Greece, August 1997, pp. 46 – 55.
14. P. Buneman: *The Discrete Fourier Transform as a Database Query.* Technical Report MS-CIS-93-37, University of Pennsylvania, 1993.
15. P. Baumann: *On the Management of Multidimensional Discrete Data.* VLDB Journal 4(3)1994, Special Issue on Spatial Database Systems, pp. 401 – 444.
16. P. Baumann: *Language Support for Raster Image Manipulation in Databases.* Proc. Int. Workshop on Graphics Modeling and Visualization in Science & Technology, Darmstadt, Germany, April 1992.

17. N. Widmann, P. Baumann: Performance Evaluation of Multidimensional Array Storage Techniques in Databases. Proc. IDEAS, Montreal, Canada, June 1999 (accepted for publication)
18. G. Ritter, J. Wilson, J. Davidson: *Image Algebra: An Overview*. Computer Vision, Graphics, and Image Processing, 49(1)1994, pp. 297-336.
19. M. Stonebraker, D. Moore: *Object-Relational DBMSs: The Next Great Wave*. Morgan Kaufmann Publishers, 1996.
20. R.G.G. Cattell: *The Object Database Standard: ODMG-93*. Morgan Kaufmann Publishers, 1996.
21. R. Ritsch, P. Baumann: *Optimization and Evaluation of Array Queries*. RasDaMan Project Technical Report, FORWISS 1998.
22. M. Blaschka, C. Sapia, G. Höfling, B. Dinter: *Finding Your Way through Multidimensional Data Models*. Proc. Workshop on Data Warehouse Design and OLAP Technology DWDOT, Vienna, Austria, August 1998.
23. K.E. Iverson: *A Programming Language*. John Wiley & Sons, Inc., New York, 1962
24. J.A. Brown, H.P. Crowder: *APL2: Getting Started*. IBM Systems Journal, Vol. 30, No. 4, 1991, pp. 433 - 445
25. S. Vandenberg, D. DeWitt: Algebraic Support for Complex Objects with Arrays, Identity, and Inheritance. Proc. ACM SIGMOD, Denver, USA, May 1991, pp. 158 – 167.
26. A. Datta, H. Thomas: A Conceptual Model and an Algebra for Online-Analytical Processing in Data Warehouses. Proc. WITS 1997
27. W. Lehner: *Modeling Large Scale OLAP Scenarios*. Proc. 6th EDBT, Valencia, Spain, March 1998, pp. 153 - 167
28. P. Vassiliadis: *Modeling Multidimensional Databases, Cubes, and Cube Operations*. Proc. 10th SSDBM, Capri, Italy, July 1998

Dynamic Relationships and Their Propagation and Concurrency Semantics in Object-Oriented Databases

Amir Sapir and Ehud Gudes

Dept. of Mathematics and Computer Sciences, Ben-Gurion University of the Negev, Ben-Gurion Rd., Beer Sheva , ISRAEL

{amirsa , ehud}@cs.bgu.ac.il

Abstract. *Object-oriented databases has rich semantics, which enables the definition of various relationships among objects. Sharing levels and composition types necessitate the definition of whether, and to which extent, should a composed object propagate a message it receives, to its composing objects (propagation rules). Current solutions refer to a system with stable connections, so propagation values can be set at the design stage.*

Turning a compound object into a distributed collection of simpler ones, some of which are shared, necessitates defining exact protocols for transaction processing and concurrency control. The information system described contains complex relations, which vary on a daily basis. The paper examines the various update operations from relations creation point of view, and suggests an approach for defining these new relations and updating the propagation values dynamically. Thus, reflecting the changing nature of relations. KeyWords: Composite object , Message object, Propagation rules ,Dynamic relation creation .

1. Introduction

1.1 Object-Oriented Concepts

Object-orientation is an important modeling concept[2]. To be considered 'object oriented', a system has to fulfill several criteria. A basic paradigm is the notion of objects grouped into classes, which are themselves organized in sub-class hierarchies[18]. Such a system offers three basic relation types: Instantiation(Instance-of), Specialization(IS-A), Aggregation(Part-of), as described in [9].

In such a model, when an information unit (record, tuple, sub-object) can belong to more than one object, or when it has an independent behavior by its nature, the need arises to represent it as an object by itself, and make it a part of a complex object by a *composition relation* [1], [15], [6]. Kim[6] distinguishes between weak and composite references: Composite reference (*composite* in this paper) implies that the composing object is essentially a part of the main one it composes, may belong to a few other objects, but probably should not exist by itself. Weak reference (*reference* in this paper) means that the composing object exists by its own, the composed object does not own it, but merely accesses some information it contains.

The sharing possibilities and composition types necessitate the definition of two aspects: a. Whether, and to which extent, should a composed object propagate a message that it receives, to its composing objects - *propagation rules*. b. How to efficiently perform transactions.

One of the most relevant works on propagation is by Rumbaugh [15]. Rumbaugh proposed that: a) The decision as to the propagation step should be determined by the: Type of operation (copy, delete, save, print etc.), Type of relation (composition, reference), and the Class types. b) The possible propagation types: Propagate, Shallow, None and Inhibit. For each combination of an operation type and a relation between two objects there is a propagation value. Rumbaugh's work refers to a system with stable connections, so decision of propagation values can be made at the design stage. His ideas will be formalized in section 2.

When dealing with complex information systems, which evolve over time, the static approach of Rumbaugh may not be adequate. The need arises to determine propagation characteristics at the time a new relation is created. This property complicates the solutions to the previously mentioned problems. It requires adding new concepts and extending the algorithm.

The main contributions of this paper is the handling of propagation in dynamically evolving relations, handling concurrency and maintaining a relatively simple propagation algorithm by absorbing as much as possible of the changes in a *message object*.

1.2 Informal Description of the DA System

The information system that motivated the proposals of this paper, is that of the District Attorney office of the Negev region, Israel. This is a highly complex information system, which deals with several types of files as the main entity [Fig. 1]. Its complexity emerges not just because of the many attributes and mutual constraints among them, but mainly because of the complex and dynamic relations among objects. In order to simplify the examples only some of the main objects will be described, and a very small part of their attributes.

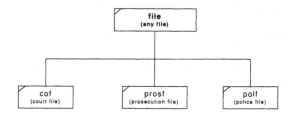

Fig. 1. The main DA system files.

A simplified explanation: After a crime is committed, a police file (POLF) is prepared, which contains information about the event, and the exhibits (EXH). If there is a suspect (SUS), with some evidence to his involvement in the crime, the file (possibly with other files concerning the same suspect) is handled to the DA office. A prosecution file (PROSF) is created. At that stage it is composed of : list of police files, list of suspects, and categorized by the list of offenses (OFF). Next stage is assigning a responsible prosecutor (PROAT) to it, who decides to prepare (an) accusation file(s) against some or all the suspects. Afterwards, much of the computer work is with the court files (COF), mainly updating and querying appearances (APP). The detailed relations are depicted in figure 2.

1.3 Organization and Motivation

In order to motivate our discussion of propagation rules, let us examine the operation Icopy. This operation is defined as duplicating a PROSecutionFile object from the main database to a private file, which belongs to a certain prosecutor who prepares her strategy on the case. Initiating Icopy does not imply copying everything that composes or is referenced by the original PROSecutionFile object. Rather it distinguishes between: Components that *should not be copied* because they were not an integral part of the original object (such as PROsecutingATtorney and OFFense, which are objects on their own right) or are part of the global database (like POLiceFile). Composing components that are currently at work and *should be copied* so that the prosecutor will perform her draft work on her private copy of that data. Some components which describe technical data (like list of secretaries who handled the file) and we expect the Icopy to skip them. The above behavior motivates the existence of multiple propagation types.

While doing so, the components may be involved in other operations, and lock conflicts may arise, even for small objects, because of the distributed nature of the model. We seek a solution that will guarantee correctness, will be efficient, and treat concurrency control mechanisms (lock/unlock) in a way that will resemble the way information processing operations are treated.

The rest of the paper is structured as follows. Section 2 contains basic definitions of composition types, propagation possibilities (attributes), and propagation criteria. It gives an example composition diagram with its propagation values. Section 3 introduces the basic propagation algorithm (based on [15]). It then demonstrates its application on the simplified PROSecutionFile object and suggests slight modifications. Section 4 describes the dynamic nature of relationships in the DA system through the Fjoin operation, regarding an operation as (eventually) a new relation with its attributes. It then suggests treatment of an operation not just as an action and a relation, but also as an object having attributes which influence its behavior. As a result, a much clearer algorithm is presented. Section 5 introduces the concurrency control problems in the model, the lock levels and treatment, modifications to system-wide structures and an algorithm. Section 6 summarizes this approach.

1.4 Other Directions

Work on dynamic creation of relationships among objects was done in other directions. An important one is Version Control. During schema evolution it might be required to maintain several versions of classes and / or objects, for various reasons (smooth incorporation of a new version, ability to cancel changes). The interested readers are referred to [5, ch. 5] for an introduction to the subject. Specific research works are described in [8] on version management for sets of modified objects, [4] on consistency maintenance, and [13] about sub-versions, to mention only a few.

Another important direction is that of Adaptive Programs (AP): An information system is described by: Class dictionary graphs and AP's. An AP is described by: An operation, Propagation patterns, wrapping code [10] , [11]. A class dictionary graph describes classes and relations between them. The operation is the 'main' instructions as to what type of calculations should be carried out. A propagation pattern is all the possible traversals between the start and end nodes, provided they obey the 'through nodes'. The wrapping code is the specific instructions that should be added to solve the particular task [12]. So, many programs can be produced from the same class dictionary graph, using a different or the same propagation pattern. The AP approach is directed mainly to retrieval tasks.

2. Basic Concepts and Data System

In this section we formalize Rumbaugh's [15] ideas: Basic relation types and formal propagation model (criteria and propagation types). Then the example classes / objects in our DA system are listed, together with some example operations. When referring to objects, we use M to denote a composed object and P as a composing one.

2.1 Basic Concepts of Propagation of Operations

As long as a compound object is considered to be a single instance of a class with aggregation relations to simpler classes, the usual data management operations are performed on the object as a whole. If an operation is to be performed on a particular aggregating component, the message is sent to the compound object (because its components cannot be addressed directly). The appropriate method of the compound object would be invoked. Then we might need variations on that method for other objects with such a component. Now, considering the parts to be independent objects, it is possible to send one standard message directly to the specific one. But usually we would like it to be performed on 'most' of the compound object. That can be achieved by sending it the message, and expecting it to propagate it appropriately. Whom to and to which extent? According to [15] this is determined by the: Type of operation, Type of relation and the class, as follows:

Type of Operation: Whether we want to copy, save, print, delete and so on, the main object. A *print* tends to be an operation which should be propagated, whereas for other operations propagation seems to be limited to some components only.

Type of Relation: Aggregation, Composition, Reference, as described in section 1.1. Generally aggregation causes propagation, Composition may or may not, and Reference leads to no propagation.

Classes involved: Which are the Main and Component classes and what is the semantics of the association between them? This makes it possible to refine the propagation value setting.

Rumbaugh[15] defines 5 propagation types: (full) propagation, shallow, none, inhibit, and error. This is an extension to previous works, which distinguished between deep propagation and none [2],[3].

Definition 1: Propagation types.

Propagate: The operation is performed on the composing element and relation.

Shallow: The operation is propagated only to the relation element.

None: The operation is not propagated at all.

Inhibit: The operation is not applied even to the receiving element, and no propagation occurs.

Error: The whole operation should be cancelled and all the composing objects (of the compound one) should retain their previous state.

In this paper we ignore the 'error' situation, and limit the 'inhibit' only to situations that produce an inhibit state, rather than as a propagation value. On the other hand, we introduce the 'must' and 'irrelevant' propagation values.

must: It is essential that the operation be performed on the component, as a part of performing the operation on the 'self' part of the composed one.

irrelevant: The operation can't fully propagate to the current object, so there is no meaning to any propagation attributes further on.

2.2 A Simplified DA Data System

Following is a set of data items of the DA system. It is simplified with respect to the types of objects mentioned and to the connections and limitations which exist practically. Also, only very few operations will be mentioned. We start with a table of propagation values for each of the combinations of relations between two objects, for each operation, followed by a PROSF figure. Then we briefly explain each operation.

Table 1. Propagation values for some combinations of relations and operations for the DA system. 'p' indicating full propagation, 's' shallow , 'n' none, '*' must, and '--' Irrelevant. They are stored within each object class, for each possible relation and function.

relation	Icopy	Ecopy	Print	Save	Del	Fjoin
$<M_{PROSF}, P_{PROSF\_ID}>$	*	*	*	*	*	*
$<M_{PROSF}, P_{POLF}>$	s	p	p	p	p	n
$<M_{POLF}, P_{POLF\_ID}>$	--	*	*	*	*	--
$<M_{POLF}, P_{OFF}>$	--	s	n	s	n	--
$<M_{POLF}, P_{EXH}>$	--	p	n	p	p	--
$<M_{EXH}, P_{EXH\_ID}>$	--	*	--	*	*	--
$<M_{EXH}, P_{EXHDSC}>$	--	*	--	p	p	--
$<M_{PROSF}, P_{COF}>$	p	p	p	p	p	p
$<M_{COF}, P_{COF\_ID}>$	*	*	*	*	*	*
$<M_{COF}, P_{OFF}>$	s	s	p	s	n	s
$<M_{COF}, P_{APP}>$	s	n	n	p	p	n
$<M_{PROSF}, P_{OFF}>$	s	s	p	s	n	s

And a typical PROSecution File can look like:

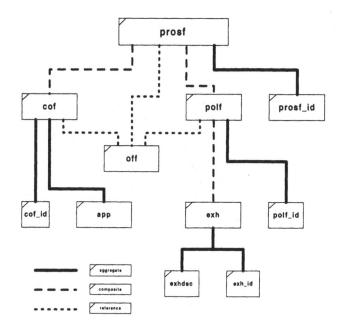

Fig. 2. Structure of a simplified PROSecutionFile

Where the example functions are:

Ecopy : Copies a PROSecutionFile object to a remote database, so whatever isn't global should be copied (except for 'unimportant' data).

Icopy : Copies a PROSecutionFile object to a private database in the same domain, so some information can be referenced instead of copied.

Print : Prints principal working data for the object.

Save : Saves the object and its components (data and / or references).

Del : Deletes the object and its components (unless an object participates in composing another object).

Fjoin : Regarding two DA files as one legal entity from now on. The operation is quite complex and will be described in detail in chapter 4.

3. Basic Propagation Algorithms

3.1 Building Blocks of Propagation

Formalizing Rumbaugh's ideas yields the *propagate1* algorithm. In order to present it, we define the following functions:

Next_Ref: Returns the ID of the next component of the compound object.

Get_Comp_Obj : Gets an object ID, returns a pointer to it.

Apply : The actual application of a specific operation on the *self* part.

Update_Ref : If a new object was created (by copy, version, etc.), updates reference between the current one and the new one.

Prop :   Gets an operation type and a class, returns the propagation
                          value from the receiving object's class to the class given as a
                          parameter, for that operation.
Example: $PROSF_1.prop(POLF_1.Type(),Ecopy) = 'p'$

Propagate1 is passed the operation as a parameter. It assumes pre-order processing
and does not handle the Inhibit situation. Its default propagation is *shallow*.

In *propagate1*, when an object receives the message, the operation is applied to its
integral parts, its first composing or referenced object is fetched, and we encounter the
main loop: Identifying the propagation type: propagate (designated as 5p), shallow
(5s) or none (5n). If a propagate is required, the composing object is sent the *propagate1* message, and each relation with each of the components of that object is examined for its propagation characteristic. Then, an Update_Ref message is sent, to handle (if necessary) changes of references / pointers. If it was shallow, only Update_Ref
(at most) is needed, and if none - no action is taken.

```
       Propagate1 (Operation OP)
       VAR   P_i : Object ;
             E_OBJ : Object ; /* E_OBJ ≡Effective object */
             R_i : Object_Reference ;
             ptype : Propagation_Type ;
             begin
{1}          E_OBJ := Self.Apply (OP) ;
{2}          R_i := Self.Next_Ref() ;
             while (R_i ≠ NULL) do
{3}              P_i := Self.Get_Comp_Obj(R_i) ;
{4}              ptype := Self.Prop(P_i.Type(), OP.Type()) ;
{5}              case ptype of
{5p}                 'p' :  P_i.Propagate1(OP) ;
                            E_OBJ.Update_Ref(R_i) ;
{5s}                 's' :  E_OBJ.Update_Ref(R_i) ;
{5n}                 'n' :  no action taken
                     otherwise :   E_OBJ.Update_Ref(R_i);
                 end case ;
{6}              R_i := Self.Next_Ref() ;
             end while;
{7}          return ;
       end ;
```

Propagate1: Basic propagation procedure.

3.2   Application of Propagate1 to the DA System

Figure 3 (to be read in parallel with figure 4) shows the application of Icopy, according to the propagation values of table 1. Propagation type is marked with the appropriate choice (5p means that a full propagate was chosen, 5s - shallow, 5n - none),
with an extension of 5p_b and 5p_e for beginning/end of a deeper level of composition, and underscores getting longer for each step down the composition tree.

propagate1 : Icopy:

{1}   PROSF$_2$:= (class PROSF).new ;

         PROSF$_2$.fill[1](I , PROSF$_1$.extract (I));

{2}   R$_i$:= ^POLF$_1$;

{3}   P$_i$:= POLF$_1$;

{4}   ptype := 's' ;

{5s}   PROSF$_2$.^POLF := PROSF$_1$.^POLF ;

{6}   R$_i$:= ^COF$_1$;

{3}   P$_i$:= COF$_1$;

{4}   ptype := 'p' ;

{5p_b} COF$_1$.Icopy ;

         Push[2] P$_i$, R$_i$ on stack

{1}   COF$_2$:= (class COF).new ;

              COF$_2$.fill(I,COF$_1$.extract(I)) ;

{2}   R$_i$:= ^OFF$_1$;

{3}   P$_i$:= OFF$_1$;

{4}   ptype := 's' ;

{5s}   COF$_2$.^OFF := COF$_1$.^OFF ;

{6}   R$_i$:= ^APP$_1$;

{3} {4} {5s} handling APP similar to OFF

{6}   R$_i$:= null ;

{7}   return

{5p_e} Pop P$_i$, R$_i$;

              PROSF$_2$.^COF$_2$:= COF$_2$.ident ;

{6} {3} {4} {5s} handling OFF similar to POLF

{6}   R$_i$:= null ;

{7}   return ;

Fig. 3. Applying *propagate1* to Icopy

3.3 Proper Component Processing

Two of the disadvantages of this algorithm are: it does not handle search order, and does not avoid multiple processing of the same component.

It seems that the choice between pre-order and post-order depends only on the operation: For *copy* pre-order is adequate, while *delete* should be performed as post-order. To handle this ordering, each operation is given an order value : 'pre' , 'post' or 'either'. 'either' means that the decision can be made based on other considerations, such as performance or logical representation (here pre-order is chosen). Example values are: <Icopy , pre> <Delete , post> <Save , either> <Print , pre>.

Propagate2 (which, for lack of space is not detailed here, but can be found on [17]), uses 'mark' and 'visited', to avoid processing the same node twice.

Mark :   The object has already been processed by the current operation.

Visited :   True if the object has been marked as visited.

---

[1] fill and extract are parts of Apply for Icopy, and perform as their names suggest.

[2] This results from the algorithm's recursive implementation.

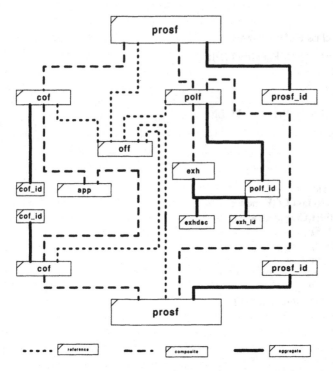

Fig. 4. Result of Icopy on PROSecutionFile

4 Relation Creating Operations and the Message (Operation) Object

The original motivation for Rumbaugh's algorithm was the handling of propagation for various types of objects and operations in relatively stable schemas. In some complex systems, relations between objects are added or changed often. This and other issues that should be considered during propagation motivates our idea to encapsulate operation-related decisions within 'message (operation) objects', thus simplifying the propagation algorithm.

4.1 Fjoin

One of the unique operations of the DA system is the Fjoin: A SUSpect is ACCused in committing several OFFenses on separate occasions, but wishes that only one procedure will be carried out against him. Fjoin maintains the following rules:

a. It is done on a per person basis. If the PROSecutionFile contains two ACCused persons, joining for one of them does not imply joining for the other one.

b. From the DA's point of view, it can be done only in two cases:

type 1 : Different PROSecutionFiles exist, but no COurtFile has been prepared yet. One PROSecutionFile will be regarded as the leading one, and only one COurtFile will be prepared.

type 2 : Different PROSecutionFiles and different COurtFiles exist. The ACCused may apply for an Fjoin, to reduce the overall punishment. The law agrees, provided that he has already been convicted.

The above operation seems specific to the DA application, but similar operations exist in other personnel related applications. The creation of new relations with their propagation properties is essential for semantically rich object-oriented databases.

4.2 Creation of Relation

After an Fjoin took place, we could settle for marking it by an indication and pointers, so that the system will be able to retrieve related information, and avoid irrational operations. But Fjoin has a deeper significance: it is a relation. We expect certain operations to be propagated from the leading PROSecutionFile to the joined ones. *Close*[3] should fully propagate, whereas *save* should not at all, and *print* only partially.

So, joining PROSecutionFile$_2$ to PROSecutionFile$_1$ involves the following steps:

a. Propagation of Fjoin, in parallel, to the components of the two files, according to the pairs <Fjoin , Relation> (in this case: only the COurtFiles are Fjoined). Then physical connection (pointers / relation objects as for other associations) would be established between the corresponding objects in a bottom-up manner.

b. Setting propagation values for existing operations on the new relation(s).

4.3 The Algorithm

Here we present *propagate3*, which incorporates creation of new relations. To achieve this goal, we define several new functions, and change the role of the effective object.

a. Create_New_Rel (Object OBJ , Object E_OBJ); Receives the two data objects involved, checks whether a new relation should be created between them (by an internal value of the receiving message object), and if so – calls a series of data-object methods to create the relation and set propagation attributes.

b.1. CreateRelation (Relation Rel , Object OBJ): Receives a relation type and an object, and creates the specified relation between the current object and the specified one, assuming leadership to the object which received the message.

b.2. Set_Prop(Object OBJ): Receives an object, identifies its type, and sets propagation attributes for that relation and each operation.

c. The Effective Object can have another possibility: a corresponding object that at first will be passed as a parameter, and then will require graph traversal of the corresponding object in accordance with the traversal of the original object.

The basic algorithm for creating new relations with their propagation values is quite straight-forward and will not be presented here. Instead we discuss a more general algorithm for the same purpose, which uses the concept of an *operation object*.

4.4   Building Blocks of the Operation Object

We propose to create an operation class, where each instance will be an operation. Its advantage is encapsulation of operation dependent decisions, as in *propagate3*. The encapsulated decisions are: *Order of Application* and whether to *create a new relation*.

---

[3] Another specific operation of the DA system. Usually propagated upward.

```
Propagate3(Operation OP , Object OBJ)
VAR  /*variable definitions as in propagate1 */
  begin
{1}   if not Self.visited() then
{2}       E_OBJ:= OP.Apply_Under_Cond(Self,'pre');
{3}       R_i := Self.Next_Ref() ;
          while (R_i ≠ NULL) do
{4}           P_i := Self.Get_Comp_Obj(R_i) ;
{5}           ptype := Self.Prop(P_i.Type(), OP.Type()) ;
{6}           case ptype of
{6p}              'p' :  P_i.Propagate3(OP , E_OBJ) ;
                         E_OBJ.Update_Ref(R_i) ;
{6s}              's' :  E_OBJ.Update_Ref(R_i) ;
{6n}              'n' :  no action taken
                  otherwise : E_OBJ.Update_Ref(R_i);
              end case ;
{7}           R_i := Self.Next_Ref() ;
          end while ;
{8}       E_OBJ:=OP.Apply_Under_Cond(Self,'post');
{9}       Self.mark() ;
{10}      OP.Create_New_Rel⁴(OBJ , E_OBJ) ;
{11}      return E_OBJ ;
      else   return  null_op ;   /* was processed */
  end ;
```

propagate3: prop' / rel' decisions in message object.

And an example message class can be:
class OPER {
    Attributes:
        op_name : string ;
        order   : (pre , post , either) ;
        newrel   : (true , false); <Create relation?>
        rel_of   : type of relation; <fully detailed in [17]>
        proptype : array [1..NumOfOPs] of ptypes ;
                   <attribute for each operation for the new relation>
    Methods:
        Apply_Under_Cond : <Applies 'apply' to object if order condition is satisfied>
        Create_New_Rel : <Creates, if needed, a relation between the involved objects>.
        Apply :   <Actual code to perform>
end;

Propagate3 can easily handle situations such as Fjoin, and the correct implementation of save / print on the joined files (see [17]). For lack of space, the methods Apply_Under_Cond and Create_New_Rel are not detailed here.

---

[4] Responsible for creating a new relation, as explained in 4.3 .

5. Incorporating Concurrency Control

Concurrency control (cc) is a well-investigated area, and we assume that the reader is familiar with the problems, properties, and principal solutions, as discussed in many books and articles, such as [5]. Incorporating it in our model was due to the mutual connection of compound-distributed objects and transactions: In our model, a simple operation turns to be a transaction, so existing solutions from cc field can be used. On the other hand, locking can be treated uniformly, by propagation rules.

5.1 Problem Domain

Proper transaction processing means that a transaction is performed as an atomic operation: either completely done, or cancelled with all its effect reset. If so, and the transactions bare the ACID properties, several problems can be avoided.

Transactions can be of long duration, nested, or distributed, and cc also deals with efficient ways to achieve the desired properties, to maximize throughput, mainly by exploiting parallelism. Known approaches are: Locking, Time-stamping, Versioning.

Basically, our solution is based on a variant of two-phase-locking (2PL). Existing protocols differ by the relationship between the beginning or end of the transaction and the lock phase, and the granularity (object size, lock exclusiveness). Recent protocols deal with locking in hierarchical structures, to solve technical lock problems in hierarchical data structures such as B-trees, or in conceptually hierarchical structures, such as a class and its members, when on-line schema modification is required. Such structures resemble, to a certain extent, the data model we present [16],[17].

When a compound object is made of separate smaller objects, an operation, which otherwise could be performed as an atomic one, turns to be a transaction: even if the actual read or write is to be done on a component, all the objects along the path from the compound object (the root) are involved. Further more: the actual sharing of objects in our model turns the object representation into a graph. This makes the 'usual' tree lock protocols inadequate. And in practice, the share level[5] can become quite high, which increases the probability of lock-conflicts. Another observation is that in a typical update operation, the objects that will be modified cannot be determined in advance. Locking them exclusively can lead to unnecessary performance degradation.

5.2 Solution Principles

The guidelines on which our solution is based were established by answering the following: a. How should a lock (unlock) be treated? b. Duration and 'perimeter' of the locked sub-graph. c. How should a transaction respond when encountering a locked item?

5.2.1 Lock / unlock treatment. In order to maintain consistent attitude, locking should be treated as the rest of the operations in the database: requiring a lock on (or removing it from) a compound object should be propagated to its components. One way is by establishing a 'lock object' and a propagation value for each relationship between a compound object and each of its components. But there are different levels of lock

---

[5] Which can be thought of as: how many complex objects share a certain component?

exclusiveness, and there is no need to propagate a lock to a component, if the operation for which the lock is required will not fully propagate to it. Another way is by considering locking to be a property of each operation.

The preferred solution is the second one: Locking is not a purpose by itself. It is intended to precede an operation, and it is more logical for an operation to know its locking requirement. And if the operation does not propagate, unlocking will not propagate naturally. Unlocking is done in the same cases as locking.

5.2.2 Lock duration and perimeter. Our locking protocol was basically a combination of conservative and strict 2PL. This assured[6] us that deadlock will not occur and, if a transaction fails, no cascading rollback will be necessary. The cost is three graph passes and long duration (processing doesn't start until all locks granted, and releasing them will be only after commit). But we gain finer granularity: common components (where a lock can cause several other transactions to wait), are usually connected by a reference relationship, and the operation will mostly be shallow propagated to it. So the lock level may be decreased or even no lock should propagate at all. The following procedure defines how and what lock should be set:

If the operation does not propagate	--	*Don't propagate the lock*
Else if the propagation is shallow	--	*Lock relation by lock level*
		Lock the component as shared
Else if the propagation is full	--	*Lock rel' and comp' by lock level*

Proc' 1: considerations for lock level and propagation.

5.2.3 Response on encountering a locked item. Assuming a transaction requires all its locks to be granted before the operation begins, how should it behave if encountered a locked[7] object? The following procedure describes the decision:

If another transaction waits to set a lock	--	*Don't wait*
Else if current transaction already locked some item	--	*Don'r wait*
Else	--	*Wait*

Proc' 2: transaction's response to a locked object.

Where a *'don't wait'* means removing the lock from the items that were already locked, and returning a failure code to the main propagation procedure. Note that this is not equivalent to rollback, since the transaction has not started yet.

Distinguishing between shared and exclusive locks increased the concurrency among transactions. Similarly, we propose an intermediate lock: intention to write (Int-exc). This refinement is suggested for the nature of update operations is that they incorporate many potential candidate data items for update, but eventually only one of them is really modified. In a typical data-entry process, the system cannot predict which data the user wishes to update, so the attitude will be:

---

[6] As we will see, it will later be replaced by a more relaxed locking protocol.
[7] Lock conflicts will be described shortly.

Table 2. lock grant

Current Requested	None	Shared	Int-exc	Exclusive
Shared	√	√	√	--
Int-exc	√	√	--	--
Exclusive	√	--	--	--

So a transaction which will not be greedy will be able to advance where a greedy one will be blocked. But while processing, it may be required to change the lock level for a certain item: to raise it in order to update or to lower it if it is evident that it will not update the item. The general idea is that increasing lock exclusiveness is approved provided that there is no lock conflict, whereas decreasing it is allowed unless the object has been actually modified, to make sure cascading rollback will not be necessary in case the current transaction will fail. A 'change of lock' table, the procedures to carry in case lock increase / decrease is required, and a semi-formal discussion and proof are given in [17].

5.3 Implementation Steps
Besides the principal changes that were explained above (lock levels, lock-grant, lock-modify and overall lock grant, and propagation decision), there are several procedural steps. They deal with splitting the tasks among the three categories of participants: *message objects, data objects, propagation algorithm.*

Each *message object* is added an attribute which states its lock demand. This could be one of: *none, shared, Int-exc, and Exclusive.* Int-exc is considered as an initial lock demand, and can be replaced by a more/less exclusive lock during run-time.

Data objects. For purpose of presentation of the algorithm, it is assumed that data objects maintain their lock status and queues, but other schemes are also possible.

Propagation is handled by 3 algorithms, which follow the same style: *Lock Propagation, Operation Propagation,* and *Release Propagation.* There is also a set of more technical functions to handle 'locking primitives'.

The additions to the data and message objects, the locking primitives, and motivation for our choice of access order are fully described in [17].

5.4 Protocol and Propagation Algorithms
To maintain consistent attitude, locking is treated as the rest of the operations in the database: requiring a lock on a compound object propagates to its components, and as much as possible of the added complexity should be resolved by the message object. The task carried out by the three propagation procedures, follows the next protocol:

One.   Propagate Lock to main object and its comp's
  1.   Lock main by lock level
  2.   Perform depth-first of lock propagation
       One.   If oper' propagated   – same with lock
       Two.   If oper' shallow propagates   – lock comp' object, do not prop'
              lock
       Three. If oper' does not propagate   – do nothing
Two.   If lock granted
       If oper' is pre-order - Perform oper' on the object
       In any case -- Perform depth-first of oper' prop'
              One.   If full propagation   --   propagate the oper', update rel'
                     object
              Two.   If shallow propagation   -- update relation object
              Three. If no propagation   – do nothing
       If oper' is post-order - Perform oper' on the object
c. In any case -   Release lock

```
      Propagate_Lock(Operation OP)
       VAR      /* variable definitions as in propagate1 */
          --> A_Locked_Item = false : common boolean;
       begin
{1}       if not Self.lock_visited() then /* by current trans' */
{2}       do  if not self.marked_for_lock then self.lock_mark
                                     else skip ;
              Lock_Res := 0;
{3}           if Lock_Table[OP.ltype , OBJ.ltype] then
{4}               Self.Lock(OP.lock_type) ;
                  A_Locked_Item := true;
{5}               Self.lock_unmark() ;
{6}               Rᵢ := Self.Next_Ref() ;
                  while (Rᵢ≠NULL) and (Lock_Res ≥ 0) do
{7}                   Pᵢ := Self.Get_Comp_Obj(Rᵢ) ;
{8}                   ptype := Self.Figure_Prop(Pᵢ.Type,OP.Type);
{9}                   case ptype of
{9a}                  'p' : Lock_Res := Pᵢ.Propagate_Lock(OP) ;
                            if (Lock_Res<0) then return Lock_Res;
{9b}                  's' : Lock_Res:=Pᵢ.Lock_No_Propagate(OP);
                            if (Lock_Res<0) then return Lock_Res;
{9c}                  'n' : no action taken
                      end case ;
{10}                  Rᵢ := Self.Next_Ref() ;
                  end while ;
{11}              return Lock_Performed;
{12}          else if (OBJ.lock_queue = NULL) then
{13}              if A_Locked_Item    then return Lock_Failed ;
{14}                                  else    OBJ.wait() ;
{15}          else
                  Self.lock_unmark() ;
{16}              return Lock_Failed ;
              end if ;
{17}      loop
```

```
{18}    elsereturn  null_op ;
   end ;
```

Another procedure, *Lock_No_Propagate*, does the same as *Propagate_lock*, but without recursion. This is necessary for situations in which the operation is shallow-propagated, but some reference to the composing object is required (for example: copy of a pointer to a shared object).

And the actual propagation algorithm is:

```
Propagate5(Operation OP , Object OBJ , int Lvl)
VAR    /* variable definitions as in propagate1 */
       EOBJ_P_i : Object ;   /* Current composing object */
       Lock_Res : int ;
begin
{1}    if (Level = 0) then      /* upmost level - lock */
{2}         if (Lock_Res:=OBJ.Propagate_Lock(OP.Type))<0 then
                 OBJ.Propagate_Release(OP) ;
            return Lock_Res ;        /* if locking failed */
       end if ;
       /* if locking succeeded - start processing */
{3}    if not Self.visited() then
{4}        Self.mark() ;
{5}        E_OBJ := OP.Apply_Under_Cond(Self , `pre') ;
{6}        R_i := Self.Next_Ref() ;
           while (R_i ≠ NULL) do
{7}             P_i := Self.Get_Comp_Obj(R_i) ;
{8}             ptype := Self.Figure_Prop(P_i.Type, OP.Type) ;
{9}             case ptype of
{9a1}           `p' :  EOBJ_P_i:=P_i.Propagate5(OP,E_OBJ,Lvl+1) ;
{9a2}                  E_OBJ.Update_Ref(R_i , EOBJ_P_i , OP) ;
{9b}            `s' :  E_OBJ.Update_Ref(R_i , EOBJ_P_i , OP) ;
{9c}            `n' :  no action taken
                end case ;
{10}            R_i := Self.Next_Ref;
           end while ;
{11}       E_OBJ := OP.Apply_Under_Cond(Self , `post') ;
{12}       OP.Create_New_Rel(OBJ , E_OBJ) ;
{13}       if Lvl > 0 then return E_OBJ ;
       else return  null_op ;       /* avoid Update_Ref */
       end if ;
{14}   if (Level = 0) then OBJ.Propagate_Release(OP);
end ;
```

propagate5: Transaction handling and lock propagation.

Releasing the lock is handled similarly, and will not be described here.

5.5 Correctness

Basically, being a most restrictive 2PL, ensured us that schedules are serializable, deadlock and cascading rollback are avoided. How does the ability to modify lock level affect these properties?

5.5.1 Serializability. There are two possible lock level increase: shared→int-exc and int-exc→exclusive. The minimal lock to begin with was shared, which means that no other transaction could actually update the object meanwhile. So if the increase is granted, the only transaction that can update the object is the current one, so serializability is preserved.

If the lock is not granted, then it will be granted eventually, or there is a deadlock (see below).

5.5.2 Cascading Rollback. Cascading rollback can occur when a transaction uses an uncommitted data of another transaction. The S2PL guarantees that all locks remain until commit. But allowing a transaction to decrease its lock level of an object can contradict the S2PL. Our approach was to benefit from lock level decreasing, as long as it does not contradict S2PL, as can be seen with the following M procedure:

If O was modified by T
   Do not approve decrease of lock level
else
   decrease lock level
   if lock level = shared
      signal waiting transactions
   else
      signal transactions waiting for shared lock
   end if
end if

Proc' M: decision whether to decrease lock level.

5.5.3 Deadlock Avoidance. Allowing a transaction to start based on moderate lock demand and then to increase it, may lead to deadlock. We decrease the probability of such a situation by the *access order* [17], and believe that the overall performance is improved, considering that concurrency increases. If deadlock does occur, there is a variety of methods to identify and resolve it, as described in [7].

6. Summary

This paper deals with schema evolution in dynamic object oriented systems. The first part of the paper reviews Rumbaugh's original work, refines it and presents a case-study of a legal application. A more general model is required when new relations are created, and new propagation values are needed.

For that purpose, a new class, OPER, is defined, where each operation is an instance. During the propagation process, the operation object receives a message to determine when it should be invoked, and whether it should create a new relation or disconnect an existing one. Some selected operations are given the capability to create a new relation between two objects. That requires, besides a flexible data structure, also a set of propagation values for that relation for each operation. Then the algorithm was generalized to include lock propagation, to ensure transaction consistency.

We observe then an operation as a three-fold phenomena: It starts as an operation, then as an object, and eventually (sometimes) as a relation. This multi-facet point of view reflects the complexity of schema evolution in dynamic object oriented systems.

References

[1]   E. Blake, S. Cook, "On including part hierarchies in OOPLs, with an implementation in Smalltalk", ECOOP87 Proc', p. 41-50, 1987.

[2]   B. Cox, "Object-Oriented programming", Addison-Wesley, 1986.

[3]   A. Goldberg, D. Robson, "Smalltalk-80: the language and its implementation", Addison-Wesley, 1983.

[4]   K. Gondow, T. Imaizumi, Y. Shinoda, T. Katayama, "Change Management and Consistency Maintenance in SDEs using OO Attribute Grammars", JSST Simp', p.77-94, 1993.

[5]   J. Grey, A. Reuter, "Transaction processing: concepts and techniques", Morgan Kaufmann, San Francisco, Calif., 1993.

[6]   W. Kim, "Introduction to object oriented databases", MIT press Cambridge, 1990.

[7]   N. Krivokapic, A. Kemper, E. Gudes, "Deadlock detection in distributed database systems – survey, a new algorithm, performance analysis", to appear.

[8]   E. Lippe, G. Florijn, "Implementation Techniques for Integral version Management", ECOOP91 Proc', p. 342-359, 1991.

[9]   M. Loomis, A. Shah, J. Rumbaugh, "An object modeling technique for conceptual design", ECOOP87 Proc' p. 192-202, 1987.

[10] K. J. Lieberher, I. Silva-Lepe, C. Xiao, "Adaptive OO Programming using Graph-Based Customization", Comm. ACM, vol. 37, num. 5, p. 94-101, May 1994.

[11] K. J. Lieberher, C. Xiao, "Object Oriented Software Evolution", IEEE Tran. on Soft. Engineering, vol. 19, n. 4, p. 313-343, 1993.

[12] L. Liu, R. Zicari, W. Hursch, K. J. Lieberher, "The Role of Polymorphic Reuse Mechanisms in Schema Evolution in an OODB", IEEE TKDE, vol.9, num. 1, p. 50-67.

[13] J. Plaice, W. Wadge, "A new Approach to Version Control", IEEE tran. on Software Eng', vol. 19, num. 3, p. 268-276, 1993.

[14] J. Rumbaugh , "Relations as semantic constructs in an OO language", ACM OOPSLA87 proc', p. 466-481, 1987.

[15] J. Rumbaugh , "Controlling propagation of operations using attributes on relations", ACM OOPSLA88 Proc' p. 285-296, 1988.

[16] A. Sapir, E. Gudes, "Dynamic relationships and their propagation attributes in OODB", DEXA98, p.967-974.

[17] A. Sapir, "Dynamic Relationships and their Propagation Attributes in OODB", Msc thesis.

[18] M. Stefik, D.G. Bobrow, "Object Oriented programming: Themes and variations", The AI magazine, vol. 6, num. 4, p. 40-62, 1986.

Tracking Moving Objects Using Database Technology in DOMINO

Ouri Wolfson[1], Prasad Sistla[1], Bo Xu[1], Jutai Zhou[1], Sam Chamberlain[2], Yelena Yesha[3], and Naphtali Rishe[4]

[1] University of Illinois at Chicago
851 S. Morgan St.
Chicago, IL 60608 USA
{wolfson,sistla,bxu,jzhou}@eecs.uic.edu
[2] Army Research Laboratories
Aberdeen Proving Ground, MD, USA
wildman@arl.mil
[3] Center of Excellence in Space Data and Information Sciences at NASA
Goddard Space Flight Center, Greenbelt, MD, USA
[4] Florida International University
Unversity Park, Miami, FL 33199, USA

1 Background

Consider a database that represents information about moving objects and their location. For example, for a database representing the location of taxi-cabs a typical query may be: retrieve the free cabs that are currently within 1 mile of 33 N. Michigan Ave., Chicago (to pick-up a customer); or for a trucking company database a typical query may be: retrieve the trucks that are currently within 1 mile of truck ABT312 (which needs assistance); or for a database representing the current location of objects in a battlefield a typical query may be: retrieve the friendly helicopters that are in a given region, or, retrieve the friendly helicopters that are expected to enter the region within the next 10 minutes. The queries may originate from the moving objects, or from stationary users. We will refer to applications with the above characteristics as moving-objects-database (MOD) applications, and to queries as the ones mentioned above as MOD queries.

In the military MOD applications arise in the context of the digital battlefield (see [1,2]), and in the civilian industry they arise in transportation systems. For example, Omnitracs developed by Qualcomm (see [3]) is a commercial system used by the transportation industry, which enables MOD functionality. It provides location management by connecting vehicles (e.g. trucks), via satellites, to company databases. The vehicles are equipped with a Global Positioning System (GPS), and they automatically and periodically report their location.

2 Research Issues

Currently, MOD applications are being developed in an ad hoc fashion. Database Management System (DBMS) technology provides a potential foundation upon which to develop MOD applications, however, DBMS's are currently not used for this purpose. The reason is that there is a critical set of capabilities that are needed by MOD applications and are lacking in existing DBMS's. The following is a discussion of the needed capabilities.

a) Location Modeling

Existing DBMS's are not well equipped to handle continuously changing data, such as the location of moving objects. The reason for this is that in databases, data is assumed to be constant unless it is explicitly modified. For example, if the salary field is 30K, then this salary is assumed to hold (i.e. 30K is returned in response to queries) until explicitly updated. Thus, in order to represent moving objects (e.g. vehicles) in a database and answer queries about their location, the vehicle's location has to be periodically updated and constant between updates. This case was analyzed in [10]. However, in our opinion this solution is unsatisfactory since either the location is updated very frequently (which would impose a serious performance overhead), or, the answer to queries is outdated. Furthermore, assuming that the location updates are generated by the moving objects themselves and transmitted via wireless networks, frequent updating would also impose a serious wireless bandwidth overhead.

b) Linguistic Issues

Generally, a query in MOD applications involves spatial objects (e.g. points, lines, regions, polygons) and temporal constraints. Consider for example the query: "Retrieve the objects that will intersect the polygon P within the next 3 minutes". This is a spatial and temporal range query. The spatial range is the polygon P, and the temporal range is the time interval between now and 3 minutes from now. Similarly, there are spatio-temporal join queries such as: "Retrieve the pairs of friendly and enemy aircraft that will come within 10 miles of each other, and the time when this will happen." Traditional query languages such as SQL are inadequate for expressing such queries. Although spatial and temporal languages have been studied in the database research community, the two types of languages have been studied independently, whereas for MOD databases they have to be integrated. Furthermore, spatial and temporal languages have been developed for data models that are inappropriate for MOD applications (due, for example, to the modeling problem mentioned above).

c) Indexing

Observe that the number of moving objects in the database may be very large (e.g., in big cities with millions of inhabitants). Thus, for performance considerations, in answering MOD queries we would like to avoid examining the location of each moving object in the database. In other words, we would like to index the location attribute. The problem with a straight-forward use of spatial indexing for this purpose is that the continuous change of the locations implies that the spatial index has to be continuously updated. This is clearly an unacceptable solution.

d) Uncertainty/Imprecision

The location of a moving object is inherently imprecise because, regardless of the policy used to update the database location of the object (i.e. the object-location stored in the database), the database location cannot always be identical to the actual location of the object. This inherent uncertainty has various implications for database modeling, querying, and indexing. For example, for range queries there can be two different kinds of answers, i.e. the set of objects that "may" satisfy the query, and the set that "must" satisfy the query. Thus, different semantics should be provided for queries. Another approach would be to compute the probability that an object satisfies the query. Although uncertainty in databases has been studied extensively, the new modeling and spatio-temporal capabilities needed for moving objects introduce the need to revisit existing solutions.

Additionally, existing approaches to deal with uncertainty assume that some uncertainty information is associated with the raw data stored in the database. How is this initial uncertainty obtained? For MOD applications the question becomes how to quantify the location uncertainty? How to quantify the tradeoff between the updating overhead and the uncertainty/imprecision penalty, and how frequently should a moving object update its location. How to handle the possibility that a moving object becomes disconnected and cannot send location updates?

3 The DOMINO Approach

Therefore, there is a critical set of capabilities that have to be integrated, adapted, and built on top of existing DBMS's in order to support moving objects databases. The objective of our Databases fOr MovINg Objects (DOMINO) project is to build an envelope containing these capabilities on top of existing DBMS's [6]. The key features of our approach are the following.

a) Dynamic Attributes

In our opinion, the key to overcoming the location modeling problem is to enable the DBMS to *predict* the future location of a moving object. Thus, when the moving object updates the database, it provides not only its current location, but its expected future locations. For example, if the DBMS knows the speed and the route of a moving object, then it can compute its location at any point in time without additional updates.

Thus, we proposed a data model called the Moving Objects Spatio-Temporal (or MOST for short) model (see [4] for a complete discussion). Its novelty is the concept of a dynamic attribute, i.e. an attribute whose value changes continuously as time progresses, without being explicitly updated. So, for example, the location of a vehicle is given by its dynamic attribute which consists of motion plan (e.g., north on route 481, at 60 miles/hour). In other words, we devise a higher level of data abstraction where an object's motion plan (rather than its location) is represented as an attribute of the object. Obviously the motion plan of an object can change (thus the dynamic attribute needs to be updated), but in most cases it does so less frequently than the location of the object. We devised mechanisms to incorporate dynamic attributes in existing data models and capabilities to be added to existing query processing systems to deal with dynamic attributes.

b) Spatial and Temporal Query Language

We introduced a query language called Future Temporal Logic (FTL) for query and trigger specifications in moving objects databases. The language is natural and intuitive to use in formulating MOD queries, and it is basically SQL augmented with temporal operators (e.g. SOMETIME-DURING, UNTIL, LATE) and spatial operators (e.g. INSIDE-REGION).

c) Indexing Dynamic Attributes

We propose the following paradigm for indexing dynamic attributes. The indexing problem is decomposed into two sub-problems; first is the geometric representation of a dynamic attribute value (i.e. a moving object's speed, initial location, and starting time) in multidimensional time-space, and second is the spatial indexing of the geometric representation. The geometric representation subproblem concerns the question: how to construct the multidimensional space, and how to map an object (more precisely, a dynamic attribute value) into a region (or a line, or a point) in that space, and how to map a query into another region in that space, so that the result of the query are the objects whose regions intersect the query region. The object region is updated only when the dynamic attribute is explicitly updated (e.g. when the speed of the object changes) rather than continuously. The spatial indexing subproblem concerns the question how to find the intersection-of-regions mentioned above in an efficient way. The latter subproblem can be solved by an existing spatial indexing method, but it is an open problem which method is most appropriate for a particular geometric representation and dynamic attribute values distribution. We have devised several solutions to the geometric representation subproblem (see [6]), and analyzed one in [12]. Another solution was analyzed in [11].

d) Uncertainty/Imprecision Management[1]

We extended our data model, query language, and indexing method to address the uncertainty problem. The data model was extended by enabling the provision

---

[1] See [5-9, 12] for a complete discussion of our approaches to this issue.

of an uncertainty interval in the dynamic attribute. More specifically, at any point in time the location of a moving object is a point in some uncertainty interval, and this interval is computable by the DBMS. Thus, the DBMS replies to a query requesting the location of a moving object m with the following answer A: "m is on route 698 at location (x,y), with an error (or deviation) of at most 2 miles". The bound b on the deviation (2 miles in the above answer) is provided by the moving object, i.e. the object commits to send a location update when the deviation reaches the bound. If the object m moves along a route, then at any point in time t, b and the value of the dynamic attribute at t define an uncertainty interval, i.e. a section of the road in which the moving object m can be at t.

The FTL language is also extended. We devised two extensions, a qualitative one and a quantitative one. In the qualitative extension, two kinds of semantics, namely *may* and *must* semantics, are incorporated, and the processing algorithms are adapted for these semantics ([4, 8]). The indexing method is also extended to enable the retrieval of both, moving objects that "must be" in a particular region, and moving objects that "may be" in it. For an example of the "may-must" semantics, consider the query: "Retrieve the objects that are in the polygon P". If the uncertainty intervals of moving objects 1 and 2 are given in Fig.1, then object 1 *may* satisfy the query, whereas object 2 *must* satisfy it. In the quantitative extension, the location of the moving object is a random variable, and the uncertainty interval, the network reliability and other factors are used to determine a probability density function for this variable. An algorithm was developed to associate with each object retrieved in response to a range query, the probability that the object satisfies the query ([6, 9]).

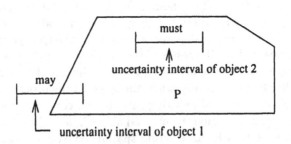

Fig. 1. *may* and *must* semantics

We also addressed the question of determining the uncertainty associated with a dynamic attribute, i.e. the bound b mentioned above. We proposed a cost based approach which captures the tradeoff between the update overhead and the imprecision. The location imprecision encompasses two related but different concepts, namely deviation and uncertainty. The deviation of a moving object m at a particular point in time t is the distance between m's actual location at time t, and its database location at time t. For the answer A above, the deviation is the distance between the actual location of m and (x,y). On the other hand, the uncertainty of a moving object m at a particular point in time t is the size of the interval in which the object can possibly be. For the answer A above, the uncertainty is 4 miles. The deviation has a cost (or penalty) in terms of incorrect decision making, and so does the uncertainty. The deviation (uncertainty) cost is proportional to the size of the deviation (uncertainty). The tradeoff between imprecision and update overhead is captured by the relative costs of an uncertainty-unit, a deviation-unit, and an update-overhead unit. Using the cost model we propose update policies that establish the uncertainty bound b in a way that minimizes the expected total cost. Furthermore, we propose an update policy that detects disconnection of the moving object at no additional cost.

4 The Demonstration

We will demonstrate the following features of Domino:

a) System Architecture

Our Domino system is the third in a three-layer architecture (see Fig.2). The first layer is an Object Relational DBMS. The database stores the information about each mobile unit, including its plan of motion. The second layer is a GIS that adds capabilities and user interface primitives for storing, querying, and manipulating geographic information. The third layer, Domino, adds temporal capabilities, capabilities of managing the uncertainty that is inherent in expected future motion plans, and a simulation testbed. Currently, Domino uses the Informix DBMS and the Arc-View GIS.

Fig. 2. System architecture

b) Motion Plan Specification

The motion plan of a mobile object is a sequence of way time points, (p_1,t_1), $(p_2,t_2),\ldots (p_n,t_n)$, indicating that the unit will be at geographic point p_1 at time

t_1, at geographic point p_2 (closer to the destination than p_1) at time t_2 (later than t_1), etc. The plan is interactively specified by the user on a GIS on a map. The mobile unit updates the database whenever the deviation from the plan exceeds a prespecified bound given in terms of distance or time. The update includes a revised plan and possibly a new bound on the deviation. Maintaining plan information enables queries pertaining to both, the current and future locations of mobile units, for example:

Q1 = Retrieve the mobile units that are expected to be in a given region R sometime during a given time interval I. (I may be a time interval that lies entirely in the future, i.e. after the time when Q is entered).

Also, queries may pertain to future arrival times, for example:

Q2 = Retrieve the mobile units that are expected to be late at their destination by more than one hour.

c) Spation-Temporal Capabilities

We will demonstrate the spatial and temporal primitives of the FTL query language and its answer-display screen. The primitives are given in graphical format, and they can be combined with textual SQL in a natural and intuitive way. For example, in the query Q1 above the region R may be drawn with a mouse on a real GIS map, and the time interval I may be specified on a graphical timeline. Then I and R can be incorporated in the textual part of an FTL query. Clearly, since FTL is an extension of SQL, the query can also include regular literals, e.g., WEIGHT > 5000. Information about the mobile units that satisfy the query is displayed in textual form, and the location of each such mobile unit is displayed as a point on the map.

d) Uncertainty

We will demonstrate the capabilities of the FTL query language and its answer-display screen in dealing with uncertainty. These include MAY and MUST semantics for queries. In other words, the query Q1 above can be specified with MAY or MUST semantics. Under the MAY semantics, an object will be retrieved if its uncertainty interval **intersects** the region R sometime during the interval I. Under the MUST semantics, an object will be retrieved if its uncertainty interval **is wholly contained in** the region R sometime during the interval I. The location of each mobile unit retrieved is displayed on the map, along with the uncertainty interval currently associated with the location.

e) Simulation Testbed

We will demonstrate a simulation testbed in which the performance of a moving objects database application can be evaluated. The input to the simulation system is a set of moving objects, their motion plans, their speed variations over time, the costs of deviation, the cost of uncertainty, the cost of communication, the wireless bandwidth distribution over the geographic area, and the location update policy used by each moving object. The objective is to determine the performance of MOD queries, as well as to answer questions such as: How many objects can be supported for an average imprecision that is bounded by x, and a wireless bandwidth allocated to location updates that is bounded by y? Or, given n moving objects and a bound of 10% on the imprecision, what percentage of the bandwidth is used for location updates?

References

1. Chamberlain, S.: Model-Based Battle Command: A Paradigm Whose Time Has Come. 1995 Symp. on C2 Research and Technology. (1995).
2. Chamberlain, S.: Automated Information Distribution in Bandwidth-Constrained Environments. 1994 IEEE MILCOM Conference Record. 2 (1994)
3. OmniTRACS: Communicating Without Limits. http://www.qualcomm.com/ProdTech/Omni/prodtech/omnisys.html.
4. Sistla, P., Wolfson, O., Chamberlain, S., Dao, S.: Modeling and Querying Moving Objects. Proceedings of the Thirteenth International Conference on Data Engineering (ICDE13), Birmingham, UK, Apr. 1997.
5. Wolfson, O., Chamberlain, S., Dao S., Jiang, L., Mendez, G.: Cost and Imprecision in Modeling the Position of Moving Objects. Proceedings of the Fourteenth International Conference on Data Engineering (ICDE14), Orlando, FL, Feb. 1998.
6. Wolfson, O., Xu, B., Chamberlain, S., Jiang, L.: Moving Objects Databases: Issues and Solutions. Proceedings of the 10th International Conference on Scientific and Statistical Database Management (SSDBM98), Capri, Italy, July 1-3, 1998, pp. 111-122.
7. Wolfson, O., Jiang, L., Sistla, P., Chamberlain, S., Rishe, N., Deng, M.: Databases for Tracking Mobile Units in Real Time. Springer-Verlag Proceedings of the Seventh International Conference on Database Theory (ICDT), Jerusalem, Israel, Jan. 10-12, 1999.
8. Sistla, P., Wolfson, O., Chamberlain, S., Dao, S.: Querying the Uncertain Position of Moving Objects. invited, appears as a chapter in the book *Temporal Databases: Research and Practice*, Etzion, O., Jajodia, S., Sripada, S., eds., Springer Verlag Lecture Notes in Computer Science number 1399, 1998, pp. 310-337.
9. Wolfson, O., Sistla, P., Chamberlain, S., Yesha, Y.: Updating and Querying Databases that Track Mobile Units. invited paper, to appear in a special issue of the Distributed and Parallel Databases Journal.
10. Pfoser, D., Jensen, C. S.: Capturing the Uncertainty of Moving-Object Representations. to appear, 6th Intl. Symposium on Spatial Databases (SSD'99), Hong Kong, July, 99.
11. Kollios, G., Gunopulos, D., Tsotras, V. J.: On Indexing Mobile Objects. to appear in PODS'99.
12. Tayeb, J., Ulusoy, O., Wolfson, O.: A Quadtree Based Dynamic Attribute Indexing Method. Computer Journal Vol. 41(3), 1998, pp. 185-200.

OLOG: A Deductive Object Database Language (Extended Abstract)

Mengchi Liu

Department of Computer Science, University of Regina
Regina, Saskatchewan, Canada S4S 0A2
mliu@cs.uregina.ca
http://www.cs.uregina.ca/~mliu

Abstract. Deductive object-oriented databases are intended to combine the best of the deductive and object-oriented approaches. However, some important object-oriented features are not properly supported in the existing proposals. This paper proposes a novel deductive language that supports important structurally object-oriented features such as object identity, complex objects, typing, classes, class hierarchies, multiple property inheritance with overriding, conflict-handling, and blocking, and schema definitions in a uniform framework. The language effectively integrates useful features in deductive and object-oriented database languages. The main novel feature is the logical semantics that cleanly accounts for those structurally object-oriented features that are missing in object-oriented database languages. Therefore it establishes a theoretical foundation for a practical deductive object-oriented database system for advanced database applications.

1 Introduction

In the past few years, a number of deductive object-oriented database languages have been proposed, such as O-logic [28], revised O-logic [17], F-logic [16], IQL [3], LOGRES [9], LLO [27], Noodle [30], Complex [14], CORAL++ [32], DLT [5], Gulog [12], Rock & Roll [6], ROL [22], DO2 [19], and ROL2 [20, 25].

The objective of deductive object-oriented databases is to combine the best of the deductive and object-oriented approaches, such as recursion, declarative querying, and a firm logical foundation from the deductive approach, and object identity, complex objects, typing, classes, class hierarchy, multiple property inheritance with overriding, conflict-handling and blocking, and schema definition from the object-oriented approach. However, the existing proposals fall into two kinds: languages with a logical semantics but only with limited object-oriented features such as revised O-logic, F-logic, and ROL, and languages with more object-oriented features but without a logical semantics such as IQL, Rock & Roll, CORAL++.

Non-monotonic multiple property inheritance is a fundamental feature of object-oriented database languages, such as O_2 [11] and Orion [18]. The user can explicitly redefine (override) the inherited attribute. For some applications, it is also important to be able to block the inheritance of attributes from super-classes (i.e., selective inheritance [18]). Besides, possible ambiguities may arise when an attribute name is defined in two or more superclasses, and the conflict should be handled properly. Unfortunately, multiple property inheritance with such overriding, conflict-handling and blocking capacity does not have a well-defined semantics even though it has been used in some object-oriented database languages. The main difficulty is that the inherited instances of a superclass may not be well-typed with respect to its type definition because of overriding, conflict and blocking. Most deductive object-oriented database languages, including revised O-logic, F-logic, only supports monotonic multiple property inheritance, which is not powerful enough. ROL has a semantics that accounts for multiple property inheritance with overriding but not conflict-handling and blocking in a limited context. Until now, a well-defined semantics for multiple property inheritance with overriding, conflict handling, and blocking in object-oriented databases is still missing from the literature.

Object identity is another fundamental feature of object-oriented databases. It is useful for supporting sharing and cyclicity [2, 3, 11]. In the object-oriented data model O_2, an object is a pair of object identifier (oid) and value. The value can be not only a tuple, but also a set, an atomic value, and even an image. In other words, an object identifier in O_2 can identify any kind of value. However, this important use of object identity is not directly supported in most deductive object-oriented database languages, including O-logic, revised O-logic, F-logic, Gulog, ROL, and ROL2, in which an object identifier can only directly identify a tuple. IQL is based on O_2 and is so far the only deductive object-oriented language that supports this use of object identity.

Another problem with existing languages is how to deal with object generation. In Datalog, we only have constants and facts that are used to represent real objects and their relationships. In O-logic, F-logic, and ILOG [15], skolem functions are used for generated object identifiers. Consider the following typical interesting_pair (ip) rule in revised O-logic (also in F-logic):

$$f(E, M) : ip[emp \rightarrow E, mgr \rightarrow M] :-$$
$$E : empl[name \rightarrow N, works \rightarrow D]$$
$$D : dept[mgr \rightarrow M : empl[name \rightarrow N]]$$

This rule generates object identifiers of the class ip of the form $f(E, M)$ with values E and M for corresponding attributes emp and mgr. Clearly, information about E and M is duplicated in the object identifier and the attribute values. As discussed in [17, 34], termination is still not guaranteed. The user has to properly define rules involving skolem functions in order to guarantee the termination of execution. For this reason, pure relation-based deductive approach is considered better in this regard [34]. Indeed, skolem functions are nothing more than relationships. Treating them as object identifiers is unnecessary and introduces redundancy. If relations are directly supported, we can avoid redundancy and guarantee termination. For example, we can represent the above rule equivalently as follows:

$$ip(emp : E, mgr : M) :\!-\ E : empl[name \rightarrow N, works \rightarrow D]$$
$$D : dept[mgr \rightarrow M : empl[name \rightarrow N]]$$

With both classes and relations, a DOOD language may become a super language for both deductive databases and object-oriented databases. IQL is in fact a language that supports both classes and relations. However, IQL suffers from the following problems.

First, the semantics of IQL is not logic-oriented as discussed in [7]. It uses variables that appear in the head of a rule but not in its body to create new object identifiers. Indeed, object identifiers can only be created in IQL in this way. As a result, it is quite cumbersome and procedural to actually use it to manipulate real databases in IQL. Let us see how to store the following two simple objects of the class *person* in IQL, where *adam, eve* are object identifiers:

$$(adam, [name : ``Adam", spouse : eve])$$
$$(eve, [name : ``Eve", spouse : adam])$$

First we need to declare two relations R_a and R_e of type $[l : person]$ for some l to hold object identifiers of the class *person* and two variables X, Y of class *person*. Then we use the following two rules to generate two object identifiers *adam* and *eve* respectively:

$$R_a(X) :\!-$$
$$R_e(Y) :\!-$$

Finally, we use IQL object identifier dereferencing mechanism to assign values to the corresponding objects:

$$\widehat{X} = [name : "Adam", spouse : Y] :\!-\ R_a(X), R_e(Y)$$
$$\widehat{Y} = [name : "Eve", spouse : X] :\!-\ R_a(X), R_e(Y)$$

Another problem with IQL is that its rules-based oid generation can lead to infinite loops. See [7] for details.

In this paper, we propose a novel deductive object-oriented database language called OLOG. OLOG is based on IQL and O_2. It overcomes the problems associated with IQL and supports important object-oriented features such as object identity, structured values, complex objects, typing, class hierarchies, multiple property inheritance with overriding, conflict handling, and blocking, and schema definition. Like IQL, it allows an object identifier to identify any kind of value. Besides, it effectively integrates useful features in other deductive languages, especially ROL [22] and Relationlog [24]. It has a logical semantics that cleanly accounts for all the structural features of object-oriented databases listed above. The objective of the paper is to establish a theoretical foundation for a practical DOOD system.

This paper is organized as follows. Section 2 introduces the syntax of OLOG. Section 3 presents the semantics of OLOG schema. Section 4 discusses Herbrand interpretations and models. Section 5 focuses on the bottom-up semantics of OLOG programs. Section 6 concludes the paper.

Due to space limitation, we omit the proofs of our results presented here.

2 Syntax of OLOG

We assume the existence of the following countably infinite and pairwise disjoint sets of atomic elements:

1. atomic type names $\mathcal{T} = \{none, integer, real, string, ...\}$;
2. relation names $\mathcal{R}$;
3. class names $\mathcal{C}$;
4. attribute labels $\mathcal{L}$ on which there is a total order $\leq_{\mathcal{L}}$;
5. atomic values $\mathcal{D}$;
6. object identifiers $\mathcal{O}$;
7. variables $\mathcal{V}$.

The set $\mathcal{D}$ is a union of the sets of all atomic values such as the set $\mathcal{I}$ of integers, the set $\mathcal{R}$ of real numbers, the set $\mathcal{S}$ of strings, etc. The total order on the set of attributes will be used in the semantics section only for technical reasons.

An OLOG database consists of two parts: a schema and a program. The schema contains the information about the structure of the database. The program contains information about objects in the database. First we define schema.

2.1 Schema

In this section, we define types, classes, direct subclass relationship, and schema.

Definition 1. The *types* are defined as follows

$$\tau = t \mid c \mid (l_1 : \tau, ..., l_k : \tau) \mid \{\tau\}$$

where τ is a type expression, t is an atomic type name, c is a class name, and $l_1, ..., l_k$ are attribute labels with $k \geq 0$.

Unlike IQL, we disallow union and intersection type. Instead, we directly support type inheritance via the subclass relationship.

Definition 2. Let c be a class name and τ a type. Then $c[\tau]$ is a *type definition* which declares that the class c has τ as its *directly defined type*. If τ is a tuple type, then c is called a *tuple* class; if τ is a set type, then c is called a *set* class; otherwise, c is called an *atomic* class.

A class may have subclasses, and a subclass may have more than one superclass in OLOG.

Definition 3. Let c and c' be class names. Then c *isa* c' is a *superclass definition* that declares c to be a *direct subclass* of c' and c' a *direct superclass* of c.

A subclass can inherit and override directly defined types from its direct and non-direct superclasses, and introduce a new type. We discuss them in the semantics section.

Definition 4. Let $c, c_1, ..., c_n$ be class names and τ a type with $n \geq 0$. Then a *class schema* is an expression of the form

$$class \ c \ isa \ c_1, ..., c_n \ [\ \tau \ ]$$

which stands for $c[\tau]$ and c *isa* c_1, ..., c *isa* c_n. When $\tau = ()$, we can simply use *class* c *isa* $c_1, ..., c_n$ instead.

Definition 5. A *relation schema* is an expression of the form

$$relation \ r(l_1 : \tau_1, ..., l_n : \tau_n)$$

where r is a relation name, $l_1, ..., l_n$ are attribute labels, and $\tau_1, ..., \tau_n$ are types with $n > 0$.

Definition 6. A *database schema* is a set of class and relation schemas that can be represented abstractly as a tuple $K = (C, isa, \sigma, R, \mu)$, where C is a finite set of class names; *isa* is a finite set of direct superclass definitions, which is in fact a binary relation over C; σ is a finite set of type definitions; R is a finite set of relation names; and μ is a finite set of relation schemas. If $c[\tau] \in \sigma$ then we note $\sigma(c) = \tau$.

2.2 Program

In this section, we define terms, values, atoms, objects, relation tuples, rules and programs of OLOG.

Definition 7. The *terms* are defined as follows:

1. a variable is either an *atomic value* term, an *oid* term, a *complete set* term, or a *tuple* term depending on the context;
2. an atomic value is an *atomic value* term;
3. an object identifier is an *oid* term;
4. if $T_1, ..., T_n, (n \geq 1)$ are terms and $l_1, ..., l_n$ are distinct attributes such that $l_i \leq_{\mathcal{L}} l_j$ for $i \leq j$, then $(l_1 : T_1, ..., l_n : T_n)$ is a *tuple* term;
5. if $T_1, ..., T_n, (n \geq 1)$ are terms, then $\langle T_1, ..., T_n \rangle$ is a *partial set* term;
6. if $T_1, ..., T_n, (n \geq 0)$ are terms not involving partial set terms, then $\{T_1, ..., T_n\}$ is a *complete set* term.

Partial set terms and complete set terms were first introduced in ROL [22] and later extended in Relationlog [24], which generalize the set treatment of Hilog [10], F-logic [16] and LDL [31]. and make the manipulation of sets convenient. They enable the user to encode the open and closed world assumption on sets directly in the program. See [26] for a detailed discussion.

A term is *ground* if it has no variables. A *tuple* is a ground tuple term. A *partial set* is a ground partial set term. A *complete set* is a ground complete set term.

A *value* is a ground term. A value is *compact* if it does not involve partial sets.

Definition 8. The *atoms* are defined as follows:

1. Let c be a class and O an oid term. Then $c\,O$ is an *oid assignment* atom.
2. Let O be an oid term and T a term. Then $O[T]$ is an *object* atom.
3. Let $c\,O$, $O[T]$ be atoms. Then $c\,O[T]$ is a *composite object* atom, while $c\,O$ and $O[T]$ are called its *constituent* atoms.
4. Let r be a relation name, $l_1, ..., l_n$ distinct attributes, $T_1, ..., T_n$ terms. Then $r(l_1 : T_1, ..., l_n : T_n)$ is a *relation* atom.

Note that our notion of relation atom actually generalizes the notion of atom of Datalog and Relationlog. As a result, OLOG subsumes them as special cases.

An atom is *ground* if it has no variables. An *oid assignment* is a ground oid assignment atom. An *object* is a ground object atom. An object is *compact* if it does not involve partial sets. A *relation tuple* is a ground relation atom. A relation tuple is *compact* if it does not involve partial sets.

Definition 9. A *rule* is an expression of the form

$$A :- L_1, ..., L_n$$

where the head A is an atom and the body $L_1, .., L_n$ with $n \geq 0$ is a sequence of atoms and the negation of atoms.

As usual, rules are required to be safe or covered as defined in [8, 35].

A *fact* is a safe rule with empty body.

The notion of stratification has been used in several logical languages to give semantics to programs involving negation and/or sets [1, 4, 8, 22, 24]. Normally, whether a program is stratified can be statically determined by using a dependency graph based on the defined symbols such as predicate, function or attribute symbols in the program. However in OLOG, we may have an atom which has no such symbol that we can use as a defined symbol, such as $O[Y]$ where O and Y are variables. Therefore, we cannot define stratification based on the syntax as usual. As in IQL, we let the OLOG programmer be responsible for any stratification of the program and organize the program into a sequence of subprograms explicitly.

A *subprogram* is a finite set of rules.

Definition 10. A *program* P is an expression of the form

$$P = P_1; P_2; ...; P_n$$

where $P_1, ..., P_n$ are subprograms with $n \geq 1$.

2.3 Databases

Definition 11. A *database* is a tuple $DB = (K, P)$ where K is a schema and P is a program.

Example 1. The following is a simple database in OLOG:

Schema
   class person[(age : integer,
                 parents : {person},
                 ancestors : {person},
                 trueAncs : {person})]

Program
   person pam [(age : 60)] :–
   person tom [(age : 65)] :–
   person sam [(age : 40, parents : {pam, tom})] :–
   person ann [(age : 20, parents : {sam})] :–
   $X[(ancestors : \langle Y \rangle)]$:– $X[(parents : \langle Y \rangle)]$
   $X[(ancestors : \langle Y \rangle)]$:– $X[(parents : \langle Z \rangle)], Z[(ancestors : \langle Y \rangle)]$
   $X[(trueAncs : \langle Y \rangle)]$:– $X[(ancestors : \langle Y \rangle)], \neg X[(parents : \langle Y \rangle)]$

Example 2. The following is another example of OLOG database which is based on an example used in [3]:

Schema
   class person[(name : string,
                  gender : string,
                  spouse : person,
                  children : personSet,
                  occupations : {string})]
   class personSet [{person}]
   relation family(husband : person,
                    wife : person,
                    children : {person})

Program
   person adam[(name :' Adam',
                 gender :' M',
                 spouse : eve,
                 children : aeChildren)]
   person eve   [(name :' Eve',
                   gender :' F',
                   spouse : adam,
                   children : aeChildren)]
   person cain [(name :' Cain',
                   occupations : {'Farmer',' Nomad',' Artisan'})]
   person abel [(name :' Abel',
                   occupations : {'Shepherd'}]

person seth[(*name* :' *Seth*',
                occupations : {}]

personSet aeChildren [{ *cain, abel, seth*}]

family(*husband* : H, *wife* : W, *children* : $\langle C \rangle$) :-
            H[(*gender* :' M', *spouse* : W, *children* : O)], O[$\langle C \rangle$]

In this database, there are a tuple class *person*, a set class *personSet*, and a relation *family*. The program has only one subprogram with one rule which specifies how to derive the relation *family* using objects in classes *person* and *personSet*.

Note that the object identifier *ae_chn* of the class *personSet* in the above example directly identifies a set so that *adam* and *eve* share. This fact can not be directly represented in all deductive object-oriented database language but IQL. However, to create such a fact in IQL is quite tedious and procedural as discussed in Section 1.

3 Semantics of OLOG Schema

In this section, we define the semantics of OLOG schema. Especially, we discuss how to deal with multiple property inheritance with overriding, conflict handling and blocking.

Given a schema $K = (C, isa, \sigma, R, \mu)$, we note isa^* the reflexive transitive closure of isa.

The isa relation is *well-defined* if there do not exist distinct classes c and c' such that $c \ isa^* \ c'$ and $c' \ isa^* \ c$.

Definition 12. A schema $K = (C, isa, \sigma, R, \mu)$ is *well-defined* iff the isa relation is well-defined.

For technical reasons, we define the function s to convert a type τ into a set of attribute and type pairs as follows:

$$s(\tau) = \begin{cases} \{l_1 : \tau_1, ..., l_n : \tau_n\} & \text{if } \tau = (l_1 : \tau_1, ..., l_n : \tau_n) \\ \{\} & \text{if } \tau \text{ is other than tuple type} \end{cases}$$

Similarly, we define the function t to convert a set of attribute and type pairs $s = \{l_1 : \tau_1, ..., l_n : \tau_n\}$ back into a tuple type based on the ordering on the sets of attributes in two steps as follows:

1. $s' = \{l : \tau \in s \mid$ if there does not exist $l : \tau' \in s$ such that $\tau \neq \tau'\} \cup$
   $\{l : none \mid$ if $l : \tau \in s$ and $l : \tau' \in s$ such that $\tau \neq \tau'\}$
2. Let $s' = \{l_1 : \tau_1, ..., l_m : \tau_m\}$. Then $t(s) = (l_1 : \tau_1, ..., l_m : \tau_m)$ where $l_i \leq_\mathcal{L} l_j$ for $0 \leq i \leq j \leq m$.

Note that if the set contains conflicting types for an attribute l, then we use $l : none$, which indicates the attribute is not defined by the notion of σ^* to be defined shortly.

We shall also use the functions t and s for tuple values in the same way in Section 5.

Let τ_1, τ_2 be tuple types. Then the *difference* of τ_1 and τ_2, denoted by $\tau_1 - \tau_2$, is defined as follows:

$$\tau_1 - \tau_2 = t(\{l : \tau \mid l : \tau \in s(\tau_1) \text{ and } \neg \exists \tau'(l : \tau' \in s(\tau_2))\})$$

We define the notion σ^+ to capture multiple property inheritance with overriding and conflict handling as follows:

1. if there does not exist a class c' such that c *isa* c' or c is other than tuple type, then $\sigma^+(c) = \sigma(c)$;
2. if c is a tuple type and c *isa* $c_1, ..., c_n$, then
   $$\sigma^+(c) = t(s(\sigma(c)) \cup s(\sigma^+(c_1) - \sigma(c)) \cup ... \cup s(\sigma^+(c_n) - \sigma(c)))$$

The first condition says if a class is the root of a hierarchy or is not a tuple class, then its properties are those directly defined on it. The second says that the properties directly defined on a class override the properties inherited from its superclasses.

Example 3. Consider the following example:

> $person\ [(age : integer, parents : \{person\})]$
> $french\ isa\ person\ [(id : string)]$
> $orphan\ isa\ person\ [(id : integer, parents : none)]$
> $french\_orphan\ isa\ french, orphan$

Based on the above definition, we have

> $\sigma^+(person) = (age : integer, parents : \{person\})$
> $\sigma^+(french) = (id : string, age : integer, parents : \{person\})$
> $\sigma^+(orphan) = (id : integer, age : integer, parents : none)$
> $\sigma^+(french\_orphan) = (id : none, age : integer, parents : none)$

Finally, we extend the notion σ^+ to σ^* to capture multiple property inheritance with overriding, conflict handling and blocking as follows:

$$\sigma^*(c) = t(\{l : \tau \mid l : \tau \in s(\sigma^+(c)) \text{ and } \tau \neq none\})$$

Continue with Example 3, we have

> $\sigma^*(person) = (age : integer, parents : \{person\})$
> $\sigma^*(french) = (id : string, age : integer, parents : \{person\})$
> $\sigma^*(orphan) = (id : integer, age : integer)$
> $\sigma^*(french\_orphan) = (age : integer)$

Therefore, for a tuple class to override an inherited attribute, we just need to introduce a new one for the class; for a tuple class to block the inheritance of an attribute l for itself and its subclasses, we just need to use $l : none$ in its directly defined type. If two superclasses have a conflicting attribute, then the subclass does not inherit it from either one as in C++ [33].

Definition 13. Let $K = (C, isa, \sigma, R, \mu)$ be a well-defined schema. Its semantics is given by isa^* and σ^*.

4 Interpretations and Models

In this section, we define the Herbrand universe, the Herbrand base, interpretations, and models of an OLOG program based on its schema.

The *Herbrand universe U* of values is the set of all ground terms.

Definition 14. Let $K = (C, isa, \sigma, R, \mu)$ be a schema. The *Herbrand base B_K* based on K is the set of all non-composite ground atoms which can be formed using elements in the universe U and class names in C and relation names in R.

The Herbrand base B_K can be partitioned into three sets: oid assignment base B_{K_A}, object base B_{K_O} and relation base B_{K_R} as follows:

1. $B_{K_A} = \{c\ o \in B_K\}$
2. $B_{K_O} = \{o[v] \in B_K\}$
3. $B_{K_R} = \{r(l_1 : t_1, ..., l_n : t_n) \in B_K\}$

Definition 15. Let $K = (C, isa, \sigma, R, \mu)$ be a schema. An *instance* of K is a tuple $I = (\pi, \Sigma, \Lambda)$, where $\pi \subseteq B_{K_A}$, $\Sigma \subseteq B_{K_O}$, and $\Lambda \subseteq B_{K_R}$. An instance $I = (\pi, \Sigma, \Lambda)$ of K is *compact* if each object or relation tuple $\psi \in \Sigma \cup \Lambda$ is compact. An instance $I = (\pi, \Sigma, \Lambda)$ of K has *unique oid assignment* if for each $c\ o \in \pi$, there does not exist c' such that $c'\ o \in \pi$ and $c \neq c'$. An instance $I = (\pi, \Sigma, \Lambda)$ is *consistent* if there is no pair of objects $o[v_1] \in \Sigma$ and $o[v_2] \in \Sigma$ such that $v_1 \neq v_2$.

Let $I = (\pi, \Sigma, \Lambda)$ be an instance of K. If $c\ o \in \pi$, then c is the *primary* class of o.

Let $I_1 = (\pi_1, \Sigma_1, \Lambda_1)$ and $I_2 = (\pi_2, \Sigma_2, \Lambda_2)$ be two instances of K. Then the union ($\sqcup$) of I_1 and I_2 is defined as $I_1 \sqcup I_2 = (\pi_1 \cup \pi_2, \Sigma_1 \cup \Sigma_2, \Lambda_1 \cup \Lambda_2)$.

Let $K = (C, isa, \sigma, R, \mu)$ be a schema and $I = (\pi, \Sigma, \Lambda)$ an instance of K with unique oid assignment. Then a value v is *well-typed* with respect to a type τ in I iff one of the following holds:

1. v is an atomic value and τ is an atomic type such that v is well-typed with respect to τ in the usual sense;
2. v is an object identifier o and τ is a class c and there exists c' such that $c'\ o \in \pi$ and $c'\ isa^*\ c$;

3. v is a tuple value $(l_1 : v_1, ..., l_n : v_n)$ and τ is tuple type $(l_1 : \tau_1, ..., l_n : \tau_n)$ such that v_i is well-typed w.r.t τ_i for $i \in [1, n]$;

4. v is a partial set value $\langle v_1, ..., v_n \rangle$ and τ is a set type $\{\tau\}$ such that v_i is well-typed w.r.t τ for $i \in [1, n]$;

5. v is a complete set value $\{v_1, ..., v_n\}$ and τ is a set type $\{\tau\}$ such that v_i is well-typed w.r.t τ for $i \in [1, n]$.

Definition 16. Let $K = (C, isa, \sigma, R, \mu)$ be a schema and $I = (\pi, \Sigma, \Lambda)$ an instance of K. Then an object $o[v] \in \Sigma$ is *well-typed* w.r.t K in I iff there exists a class definition $c[\tau] \in \sigma^*$ such that $c \, o \in \pi$ and v is well-typed w.r.t. τ in I. A relation tuple $r(l_1 : v_1, ..., l_n : v_n) \in \Lambda$ is *well-typed* w.r.t K in I iff there exists a relation schema $r(l_1 : \tau_1, ..., l_n : \tau_n) \in \mu$ such that v_i is well-typed w.r.t τ_i in I for each $i \in [1, n]$.

Note that we only require an object to be well-typed with respect to the type associated with its direct class. However, the identity of the object can belong to the superclasses of its direct class.

Let $I = (\pi, \Sigma, \Lambda)$ be an instance of the schema K. Then I is *well-typed* with respect to K iff each object $\psi \in \Sigma$ and each relation tuple in $\psi \in \Lambda$ are well-typed with respect to K in I.

Definition 17. Let K be a schema. An *interpretation* I based on K is an instance of K such that the following hold:

1. I is compact
2. I has unique oid assignment
3. I is consistent
4. I is well-typed

Before we define the notion of satisfaction, we introduce several auxiliary notions.

Definition 18. A *ground substitution* θ is a finite mapping from $\mathcal{V}$ to U. It is extended to terms, atoms and negated atoms as follows:

1. for a variable X, $\theta X = \theta(X)$
2. for an atomic value d, $\theta d = d$
3. for an object identifier o, $\theta o = o$
4. for a tuple term $(l_1 : T_1, ..., l_n : T_n)$,
   $\theta(l_1 : T_1, ..., l_n : T_n) = (l_1 : \theta T_1, ..., l_n : \theta T_n)$
5. for a partial set term $\langle T_1, ..., T_n \rangle$, $\theta \langle T_1, ..., T_n \rangle = \langle \theta T_1, ..., \theta T_n \rangle$
6. for a complete set term $\{T_1, ..., T_n\}$, $\theta \{T_1, ..., T_n\} = \{\theta T_1, ..., \theta T_n\}$
7. for an atom or the negation of an atom L, θL results from L by applying θ to every term in L.

In order to deal with partial sets that may appear in an object or a relation tuple, we introduce the following notion.

A value v is *part-of* a compact value v', denoted by $v \triangleleft v'$, iff

1. $v = v'$;
2. $v = (l_1 : v_1, ..., l_m : v_m)$ and $v' = (l_1 : v'_1, ..., l_n : v'_n)$ where $m \leq n$ such that $v_i \triangleleft v'_i$ for $i \in [1, m]$;
3. v is a partial set and for each $v_i \in v$ there exists $v'_i \in v'$ such that $v_i \triangleleft v'_i$.

Definition 19. Let K be a schema and $I = (\pi, \Sigma, \Lambda)$ an interpretation with respect to K. The notion of *satisfaction* (denoted by $\models$) and its negation (denoted by $\not\models$) are defined as follows:

1. $I \models c\, o$ iff $c\, o \in \pi$.
2. $I \models o[v]$ iff there exists $o[v'] \in \Sigma$ and $v \triangleleft v'$.
3. $I \models c\, o[v]$ iff $I \models c\, o$ and $I \models o[v]$.
4. $I \models r(l_1 : v_1, ..., l_n : v_n)$ iff there exists $r(l_1 : v'_1, ..., l_n : v'_n) \in \Lambda$ and $v_i \triangleleft v'_i$ for $i \in [1..n]$.
5. For the negation of a ground atom $B = \neg A$, $I \models B$ iff $I \not\models A$.
6. Let R be a rule of the form $A :- L_1, ..., L_n$. Then $I \models R$ iff for each ground substitution θ, $I \models \theta L_1, ..., I \models \theta L_n$ implies $I \models \theta A$.
7. For a program $P = P_1; ...; P_n$, $I \models P$ iff for each rule $R \in P_i$ for $i \in [1, n]$, $I \models r$.

Let $DB = (K, P)$ be a database. A *model* M of P is an interpretation w.r.t. K which satisfies P.

A partial order $\sqsubseteq$ on interpretations and models can be defined directly based on the orders introduced in [22, 24]. A model M of P is *minimal* iff for each model N of P, if $N \sqsubseteq M$ then $N = M$.

5 Bottom-Up Semantics

An OLOG program is a sequence of subprograms. We use fixpoint semantics for each subprogram. We show that for a program, if the model that can be computed using a sequence of fixpoint operators exists, then it is used as the intended semantics of the program.

Definition 20. Let P be a subprogram and I an interpretation w.r.t. K, the *one-step operator* T_P on I yields an instance $J = (\pi, \Sigma, \Lambda)$ of K, where

$$\pi = \{\theta B \mid A :- L_1, ..., L_n \in P, B \text{ is } A \text{ or is a constituent atom of } A,$$
$$\text{and there exists a ground substitution } \theta \text{ such that } \theta B \text{ is}$$
$$\text{an oid assignment and } I \models \theta L_1, ..., I \models \theta L_n\}$$

$$\Sigma = \{\theta B \mid A :- L_1, ..., L_n \in P, B \text{ is } A \text{ or is a constituent atom of } A,$$
$$\text{and there exists a ground substitution } \theta \text{ such that } \theta B \text{ is}$$
$$\text{an object and } I \models \theta L_1, ..., I \models \theta L_n\}$$

$$\Lambda = \{\theta A \mid A :- L_1, ..., L_n \in P, \text{ and there exists a ground substitution}$$
$$\theta \text{ such that } \theta A \text{ is a relation tuple and } I \models \theta L_1, ..., I \models \theta L_n\}$$

if $I \sqcup J$ has unique oid assignment and is well-typed w.r.t K; otherwise T_P is undefined.

Note that the notion of T_P incorporates unique oid assignment and typing constraints. However, $T_P(I)$ may not be compact or consistent.

Now we introduce the grouping operator G based on Relationlog [24]. It is used to group partial tuple and set information spread among objects and relation tuples into complete information. We first introduce the following auxiliary notion.

A set S of values is *compatible* iff for every pair $v, v' \in S$, one of the following holds:

1. $v = v'$;
2. $v = (l_1 : v_1, ..., l_n : v_n)$, $v' = (l_1 : v'_1, ..., l_n : v'_n)$, and v_i and v'_i are compatible for $i \in [1, n]$;
3. both v and v' are partial sets;
4. v is a partial set, v' is a complete set and $v \triangleleft v'$.

A set S of objects is *compatible* iff for every pair of objects $o[v], o'[v'] \in S$, $o = o'$.

A set S of relation tuples is *compatible* iff for every pair of relation tuples $r(l_1 : v_1, ..., l_n : v_n) \in S$ and $r(l_1 : v'_1, ..., l_n : v'_n) \in S$, v_i and v'_i are compatible for $i \in [1..n]$.

Let S be a set of relation tuples or objects and S' a compatible subset of S. Then S' is a *maximal* compatible set in S if there does not exist an element in $S - S'$ that is compatible with each element in S'.

Two tuples are disjoint if their attributes are disjoint. Let t_1 and t_2 be disjoint tuples. Then $t_1 \uplus t_2 = t(s(t_1) \cup s(t_2))$ where s and t are functions defined in Section 3.

Definition 21. The *grouping* operator G is defined on a set S of values recursively as follows:

1. $G(\{v\}) = v$ if v is compact.
2. Let S be a set of values with a compact value $v \in S$. Then $G(S) = v$ if for every $v' \in S$, $v' \triangleleft v$; otherwise $G(S)$ is undefined.
3. Let S be a set of partial sets. Then
$$G(S) = \{G(S'') \mid S'' = \{O \mid O \in S' \text{ and } S' \in S\} \text{ is a maximal compatible set and } G \text{ is defined on } S''\}$$
if G is defined on S''; otherwise G is undefined.
4. Let S be a compatible set of tuples. Then $G(S) = (l_1 : G(S_1), ..., l_n : G(S_n))$ if G is defined on S_i, where $S_i = \{v_i \mid (l_1 : v_1..., l_i : v_i, ..., l_n : v_n) \in S\}$ for $i \in [1..n]$; otherwise G is undefined.
5. Let S be a set of tuples that can be partitioned into pair-wise disjoint compatible sets $S_1, ..., S_n$. Then $G(S) = G(S_1) \uplus ... \uplus G(S_n)$.
6. In any other cases, G is undefined.

We extend G to a set S of objects or relation tuples as follows:

1. Let S be a compatible set of objects of the form $o[v]$. Then
$$G(S) = \{o[G(S')] \mid S' = \{v \mid o[v] \in S\}\}$$ if $G(S')$ is defined; otherwise $G(S)$ is undefined.

2. Let S be an arbitrary set of objects that can be partitioned into maximal compatible sets $S_1, ..., S_n$. Then $G(S) = G(S_1) \cup ... \cup G(S_n)$, if G is defined on S_i for $i \in [1..n]$. Otherwise, $G(S)$ is undefined.

3. Let S be a compatible set of relation tuples of the form $r(l_1 : v_1, ..., l_n : v_n)$. Then
$G(S) = \{r(l_1 : G(S_1), ..., l_n : G(S_n)) \mid S_i = \{v_i \mid r(..., l_i : v_i, ...)\}$ if $G(S_i)$ is defined for $i \in [1..n]$; otherwise $G(S)$ is undefined.

4. Let S be an arbitrary set of relation tuples that can be partitioned into maximal compatible sets $S_1, ..., S_n$. Then $G(S) = G(S_1) \cup ... \cup G(S_n)$, if G is defined on S_i for $i \in [1..n]$. Otherwise, $G(S)$ is undefined.

Finally, we extend G to an instance $I = (\pi, \Sigma, \Lambda)$ of the schema K such that $G(I) = (\pi, G(\Sigma), G(\Lambda))$.

Note that objects are grouped according to their identity.

Example 4. The following examples show how the grouping operator can be applied to values, objects and relation tuples:

$G(\{ann[(ancestors : \langle pam \rangle)],$
$\quad ann[(ancestors : \langle tom \rangle)],$
$\quad ann[(ancestors : \langle sam \rangle)],$
$\quad ann[(trueAncs : \langle pam \rangle)],$
$\quad ann[(trueAncs : \langle tom \rangle)]\})$
$= \{ann[G(\{(ancestors : \langle pam \rangle),$
$\quad\quad\quad\quad (ancestors : \langle tom \rangle),$
$\quad\quad\quad\quad (ancestors : \langle sam \rangle),$
$\quad\quad\quad\quad (trueAncs : \langle pam \rangle),$
$\quad\quad\quad\quad (trueAncs : \langle tom \rangle)\})]\}$
$= \{ann[G(\{(ancestors : \langle pam \rangle),$
$\quad\quad\quad\quad (ancestors : \langle tom \rangle),$
$\quad\quad\quad\quad (ancestors : \langle sam \rangle)\}) \uplus$
$\quad\quad\quad G(\{(trueAncs : \langle pam \rangle),$
$\quad\quad\quad\quad (trueAncs : \langle tom \rangle)\})]$
$= \{ann[(ancestors : \{pam, tom, sam\}) \uplus (trueAncs : \{pam, tom\})]\}$
$= \{ann[(ancestors : \{pam, tom, sam\}, trueAncs : \{pam, tom\})]\}$

$G(\{family(husband : adam, wife : eve, children : \langle cain \rangle),$
$\quad family(husband : adam, wife : eve, children : \langle abel \rangle),$
$\quad family(husband : adam, wife : eve, children : \langle seth \rangle)\}$
$= \{family(husband : adam, wife : eve, children : G(\{\langle cain \rangle, \langle abel \rangle, \langle seth \rangle\}))\}$
$= \{family(husband : adam, wife : eve, children : \{cain, abel, seth\})\}$

Proposition 1. Let I be an instance of the schema K. If $G(I)$ is defined, then $G(I)$ is an interpretation.

As in Relationlog [24], partial set terms in OLOG function in two different ways depending on whether they are in the head of rules or in the body of rules. When in the head, they are used to accumulate partial information for the corresponding complete sets. The conversion from partial sets to complete sets is done with the grouping operator G. When in the body, they are used to denote part of the corresponding complete sets. The conversion from complete sets to the corresponding partial sets is done by the part-of notion.

Definition 22. The powers of the operator T_P are defined using the grouping operator as follows:

$$T_P \uparrow 0(I) = I$$
$$T_P \uparrow n(I) = T_P(G(T_P \uparrow (n-1)(I))) \sqcup T_P \uparrow (n-1)(I) \qquad \text{if } G \text{ is defined}$$
$$T_P \uparrow \omega(I) = \sqcup_{n=0}^{\infty} T_P \uparrow n(I) \qquad \text{if } G \text{ is defined}$$

If G is not defined on $T_P \uparrow i(I)$, then $T_P \uparrow (i+1)(I)$ is undefined.

Definition 23. Let $T_{P_1}, ..., T_{P_n}$ be a sequence of operators. The *iterative powers* of the sequence are defined by

$$M_0 = \{\},$$
$$M_1 = G(T_{P_1} \uparrow \omega(M_0)) \qquad \text{if } G \text{ is defined}$$
$$M_2 = G(T_{P_2} \uparrow \omega(M_1)) \qquad \text{if } G \text{ is defined}$$
$$...$$
$$M_n = G(T_{P_n} \uparrow \omega(M_{n-1})) = M_P \qquad \text{if } G \text{ is defined}$$

Theorem 1. Let $P = P_1; ...; P_n$ be an OLOG program, $T_{P_1}, ..., T_{P_n}$ the corresponding one-step operators, and M_P evaluated as above. If M_P is defined, then it is a minimal model of P.

Definition 24. Given a program P, its *declarative semantics* is given by the model M_P if it exists.

6 Conclusion

In this paper, we have presented a practical deductive object-oriented database language OLOG. We have developed a Herbrand minimal model semantics that embodies in a natural and direct way the notions of object identity, structured values, complex objects, typing, class hierarchies, multiple property inheritance with overriding, conflict handling and blocking, and schema definition. Although OLOG is only a structurally object-oriented language, behaviorally object-oriented features such as methods and encapsulation can be introduced into OLOG in the way described in [23].

The prototype based on the OLOG language is currently under development at the University of Regina on top of the Relationlog system [21]. Most of coding has been finished. The system will soon be made available over the Internet for public access.

For a logic program with negation, the well-founded semantics [13] is now generally accepted as the standard semantics. However, we have found that such a semantics cannot be directly used for a language such as OLOG that supports both partial and complete set terms. If only partial set terms are supported, then its introduction to deductive object-oriented database languages is straightforward [29]. We would like to investigate this issue in our future research.

Acknowledgments

This work was supported by the Natural Sciences and Engineering Research Council of Canada.

References

1. S. Abiteboul and S. Grumbach. COL: A Logic-Based Language for Complex Objects. *ACM TODS*, 16(1):1–30, 1991.
2. S. Abiteboul and R. Hull. IFO: A Formal Semantic Database Model. *ACM Trans. on Database Systems*, 12(4):525–565, 1987.
3. S. Abiteboul and P.C. Kanellakis. Object Identity as a Query Language Primitive. In *Proceedings of the ACM SIGMOD International Conference on Management of Data*, pages 159–173, Portland, Oregon, 1989.
4. K.R. Apt, H.A. Blair, and A. Walker. Towards a theory of declarative knowledge. In J. Minker, editor, *Foundation of Deductive Databases and Logic Programming*, pages 89–148. Morgan Kaufmann Publishers, 1988.
5. R. Bal and H. Balsters. A Deductive and Typed Object-Oriented Language. In S. Ceri, K. Tanaka, and S. Tsur, editors, *Proceedings of the International Conference on Deductive and Object-Oriented Databases*, pages 340–359, Phoenix, Arizona, USA, 1993. Springer-Verlag LNCS 760.
6. M. L. Barja, A. A. A. Fernandes, N. W. Paton, M. H. Williams, A. Dinn, and A. I. Abdelmoty. Design and implementation of ROCK & ROLL: a deductive object-oriented database system. *Information Systems*, 20(3):185–211, 1995.
7. C. Beeri. A formal approach to object-oriented databases. *Data and Knowledge Engineering*, 5(2):353–382, 1990.
8. C. Beeri, S. Naqvi, O. Shmueli, and S. Tsur. Set Construction in a Logic Database Language. *J. Logic Programming*, 10(3,4):181–232, 1991.
9. F. Cacace, S. Ceri, S. Crepi-Reghizzi, L. Tanca, and R. Zicari. Integrating Object-Oriented Data Modelling with a Rule-Based Programming Paradigm. In *Proceedings of the ACM SIGMOD International Conference on Management of Data*, pages 225–236, 1990.
10. Q. Chen and W. Chu. HILOG: A High-Order Logic Programming Language for Non-1NF Deductive Databases. In W. Kim, J.M. Nicolas, and S. Nishio, editors, *Proceedings of the International Conference on Deductive and Object-Oriented Databases*, pages 431–452, Kyoto, Japan, 1989. North-Holland.
11. O. Deux and others. The Story of O_2. *IEEE Transactions on Knowledge and Data Engineering*, 2(1):91–108, 1990.
12. G. Dobbie and R. Topor. On the Declarative and Procedural Semantics of Deductive Object-Oriented Systems. *Journal of Intelligent Information System*, 4(2):193–219, 1995.
13. A. V. Gelder, K. A. Ross, and J. S. Schlipf. The Well-Founded Semantics for General Logic Programs. *Journal of ACM*, 38(3):620–650, 1991.

14. Sergio Greco, Nicola Leone, and Pasquale Rullo. COMPLEX: An Object-Oriented Logic Programming System. *IEEE Transactions on Knowledge and Data Engineering*, 4(4):344–359, 1992.

15. R. Hull and M. Yoshikawa. ILOG: Declarative Creation and Manipulation of Object Identifiers. In *Proceedings of the International Conference on Very Large Data Bases*, pages 455–468, Brisbane, Queensland, Australia, 1990. Morgan Kaufmann Publishers, Inc.

16. M. Kifer, G. Lausen, and J. Wu. Logical Foundations of Object-Oriented and Frame-Based Languages. *Journal of ACM*, 42(4):741–843, 1995.

17. M. Kifer and J. Wu. A Logic for Programming with Complex Objects. *J. Computer and System Sciences*, 47(1):77–120, 1993.

18. Won Kim. *Introduction to Object-Oriented Databases*. The MIT Press, 1990.

19. T.W. Ling and W.B.T. Lee. DO2: A Deductive Object-Oriented Database System. In *Proceedings of the 9th International Conference on Database and Expert System Applications (DEXA '98)*, pages 50–59, Vienna, Austria, 1998. Springer-Verlag LNCS 1460.

20. M. Liu and M. Guo. ROL2: A Real Deductive Object-Oriented Database Language. In *Proceedings of the 17th International Conference on Conceptual Modeling (ER '98)*, pages 302–315, Singapore, Nov. 16-19 1998. Springer-Verlag LNCS 1507.

21. M. Liu and R. Shan. The Design and Implementation of the Relationlog Deductive Database System. In *Proceedings of the 9th International Workshop on Database and Expert System Applications (DEXA Workshop '98)*, pages 856–863, Vienna, Austria, August 24-28 1998. IEEE-CS Press.

22. Mengchi Liu. ROL: A Deductive Object Base Language. *Information Systems*, 21(5):431 – 457, 1996.

23. Mengchi Liu. Incorporating Methods and Encapsulation into Deductive Object-Oriented Database Languages. In *Proceedings of the 9th International Conference on Database and Expert System Applications (DEXA '98)*, pages 892–902, Vienna, Austria, August 24-28 1998. Springer-Verlag LNCS 1460.

24. Mengchi Liu. Relationlog: A Typed Extension to Datalog with Sets and Tuples. *Journal of Logic Programming*, 36(3):271–299, 1998.

25. Mengchi Liu. Overview of the ROL2 Deductive Object-Oriented Database System. In *Proceedings of the 30th International Conference on Technology of Object-Oriented Languages & Systems (TOOLS USA '99)*, Santa Barbara, CA, USA, August 1-5 1999. IEEE-CS Press.

26. Mengchi Liu. Deductive Database Languages: Problems and Solutions. *To appear in ACM Computing Surveys*, 30(1), 1999. (45 pages).

27. Y. Lou and M. Ozsoyoglu. LLO: A Deductive Language with Methods and Method Inheritance. In *Proceedings of the ACM SIGMOD International Conference on Management of Data*, pages 198–207, Denver, Colorado, 1991.

28. D. Maier. A logic for objects. Technical Report CS/E-86-012, Oregon Graduate Center, Beaverton, Oregon, 1986.

29. W. May, B. Ludascher, and G. Lausen. Well-Founded Semantics for Deductive Object-Oriented Database Languages. In *Proceedings of the International Conference on Deductive and Object-Oriented Databases*, Switzerland, 1997. Springer-Verlag LNCS.

30. I.S. Mumick and K.A. Ross. Noodle: A Language for Declarative Querying in an Object-Oriented Database. In S. Ceri, K. Tanaka, and S. Tsur, editors, *Proceedings of the International Conference on Deductive and Object-Oriented Databases*, pages 360–378, Phoenix, Arizona, USA, 1993. Springer-Verlag LNCS 760.

31. Shamim Naqvi and Shalom Tsur. *A Logical Language for Data and Knowledge Bases*. Computer Science Press, 1989.

32. D. Srivastava, R. Ramakrishnan, D. Srivastava, and S. Sudarshan. CORAL++: Adding Object-Orientation to a Logic Database Language. In *Proceedings of the International Conference on Very Large Data Bases*, pages 158–170, Dublin, Ireland, 1993. Morgan Kaufmann Publishers, Inc.

33. Bjarne Stroustrup. *The C++ Programming Language*. Addison Wesley., 2 edition, 1991.

34. J. Ullman. A Comparison between Deductive and Object-Oriented Databases Systems. In C. Delobel, M. Kifer, and Y. Masunaga, editors, *Proceedings of the International Conference on Deductive and Object-Oriented Databases*, pages 263 – 277, Munich, Germany, 1991. Springer-Verlag LNCS 566.

35. J.D. Ullman. *Principles of Database and Knowledge-Base Systems*, volume 1. Computer Science Press, 1988.

Multiplex: A Formal Model for Multidatabases and Its Implementation

Amihai Motro

Department of Information and Software Engineering
George Mason University
Fairfax, VA 22030-4444
ami@gmu.edu
http://www.ise.gmu.edu/ ami

Abstract. The integration of information from multiple databases has been an enduring subject of research for over 20 years, and many different solutions have been attempted or proposed. Missing from this research has been a uniform framework. Usually, each solution develops its own ad-hoc framework, designed to address the particular aspects of the problem that are being attacked and the particular methodology that is being used. To address this situation, in this paper we define a formal model for multidatabases, which we call Multiplex. Multiplex is a simple extension of the relational model, which may serve as a uniform abstraction for many previous ad-hoc solutions. Multiplex is based on formal assumptions of integrability, which distinguish between scheme and instance reconcilability among independent databases. Multiplex supports database heterogeneity, and it provides several degrees of freedom that allow it to model actual situations encountered in multidatabase applications. In addition, in situations in which a single answer is not obtainable (either because the global query is not answerable, or there are multiple candidate answers), Multiplex defines approximative answers. Finally, Multiplex provides a practical platform for implementation. A prototype of such an implementation is described briefly.

1 Introduction

The integration of information from multiple databases has been an enduring subject of research for over 20 years. (Surveys of this area include [5, 7, 24, 31]; collections of articles on this topic include [17, 29, 16, 13]; recent workshops include [30, 12].) Indeed, while the solutions that have been advanced tended to reflect the research approaches prevailing at their time, the overall goal has remained mostly unchanged: to provide flexible and efficient access to information residing in a collection of distributed, heterogeneous and overlapping databases.[1]

A standard approach to this problem has been to integrate the independent databases by means of a comprehensive *global scheme* that models the information contained in the entire collection of databases (for example, [20, 33, 6,

---

[1] More generally, the problem may involve other kinds of information sources as well.

26]). This global scheme is fitted with a *mapping* that defines the elements of the global scheme in terms of elements of the schemes of the member databases. Algorithms are designed to interpret queries on the global scheme. Such *global queries* are translated (using the information captured in the mapping) to queries on the member databases; the individual answers are then combined to an answer to the global query. The global scheme and the scheme mapping constitute a *virtual database*; the main difference between a virtual database and a conventional database is that whereas a conventional database contains data, a virtual database points to other databases that contain the data. An important concern is that this query processing method be *transparent*; i.e., users need not be aware that the database they are accessing is virtual.

Much of the work in this area has been on the construction of global schemes. The main issue here is the resolution of *intensional inconsistencies* (semantic heterogeneity) among the member schemes (for example, [4, 14, 19]). Yet the complementary problem of *extensional inconsistencies* has received much less attention. This problem arises when alternative sources with overlapping information provide mutually inconsistent information, and requires methods for resolving such inconsistencies in global answers [1].

Inconsistencies result in multiple candidate answers; the dual problem also exists, in which a global query might have no answer at all. Such situations often occur when a member database becomes temporarily unavailable. In such cases, rather then reject the query altogether, it is desirable to *approximate* the global answer using whatever information that is available [9, 8].

Often missing from multidatabase research is a *uniform* framework; each solution formulates its own version of the problem, states its own assumptions, develops its own ad-hoc model, and proposes its own solutions. Often missing as well is a *formal* treatment of the subject, with precise formulation of all assumptions, definitions and algorithms.

In this paper we address these and other issues in a model and a system for multidatabases, which we call Multiplex. Several important features of the Multiplex model are elaborated below.

(1) **Extension of the relational model**. Multiplex extends the definition of relational schemes, queries and answers to an environment of multiple databases, and it provides a common ground for other definitions as they become necessary. The extension also retains the attractive *simplicity* of the relational model, with relatively few new concepts.

(2) **Formal assumptions of integrability**. Most integration methods have operated under tacit assumptions regarding the mutual consistency of the schemes and the instances of the underlying databases. Multiplex defines two kinds of inconsistency (intensional and extensional) and formulates two assumptions of integrability: the Scheme Consistency Assumption and the Instance Consistency Assumption. These explicit assumptions, which have been absent from previous work, provide an unambiguous framework, and help to classify other methods.

(3) **Full support for heterogeneity**. The simplicity and popularity of the relational model makes it an ideal integration model, and the integrated view

that Multiplex provides is indeed relational. Yet, there is no restriction on the underlying data models; the only requirement is that they communicate their results in tabular form. Consequently, the member databases in a Multiplex multidatabase may be relational, object-oriented, or, in general, stored in any software system that can respond to requests with tabulated answers.

(4) **Flexibility to model real-world situations**. The Multiplex model is distinguished by several *degrees of freedom* that allow it to model actual situations encountered in multidatabase applications. Specifically,

1. **Source unavailability**. Multiplex reflects the dynamics of multidatabase environments where member databases may become temporarily unavailable, and global queries might therefore be unanswerable in their entirety.
2. **Source inconsistency**. Multiplex accepts that requested information may be found in more than one database, and admits the possibility of inconsistency among these multiple versions.
3. **Ad-hoc integration**. Multiplex permits ad-hoc global schemes of limited scope, that cull from existing databases only the information relevant to a given application.

Intuitively, these degrees of freedom correspond to mappings (from the global scheme to the member schemes) that are *neither total, nor single-valued, nor surjective*. We note that earlier approaches to global scheme integration were based on often unrealistic assumptions that existing database schemes could be integrated completely and perfectly in a single global scheme (i.e., mappings that are total, surjective, and single-valued; sometimes even one-to-one). The complexity of existing databases quite often renders this approach unrealistic. The abovementioned degrees of freedom are therefore important, as they represent a significant departure from earlier approaches.

(5) **Approximative answers**. Because Multiplex mappings are not total, global queries may be *unanswerable*; because the mappings are not single-valued and because there is no assumption of mutual consistency among the member databases, global queries may have *several candidate answers*. In both these situations, Multiplex defines *approximative answers*. The overall concern is that when a single authoritative answer is unavailable, a multidatabase system should approximate the request as best as possible. For example, the best approximative answer to a query on the names, salaries, departments and locations of all employees, could be the names and departments of all employees, the salaries of some employees, and the locations for none of the employees. As another example, the best approximative answer to a query on the employees who earn over 50, could be the employees who earn over 40. Note that the former approximative answer was "less" than what was requested, whereas the latter was "more" than what was requested, corresponding to "below" and "above" approximations.

(6) **Quick adaptation to evolving environments**. Present data environments may be highly dynamic; for example, newly discovered data sources may need to be incorporated, the structure of existing data sources may change, or existing data sources may need to be deleted altogether. In Multiplex such changes are easy to effect. As we shall see, the integration consists of providing pairs of

equivalent views: a view on the global database ("the information needed"), and a view on a member database ("how it is materialized"). The complexity of these views can vary greatly: they could range from a complex calculation, to a statement that simply denotes the equivalence of two attribute names.

(7) **A practical platform for implementation**. Finally and most importantly, the Multiplex model is a practical platform for implementation. Hence, Multiplex is not only a formal model, but a practical system as well.

With respect to limitations, we note that Multiplex queries and mappings are based on conjunctive views with aggregate functions. Although a language based on conjunctive views and aggregate functions does not have the full power of the relational algebra or calculus, it is a powerful language nonetheless.

The recent explosion of on-line information sources on the Internet has increased the interest in this area significantly, with several systems that are roughly in the same class as Multiplex. These include SIMS [3], TSIMMIS [15], UniSQL [18], and the Information Manifold [2]. These systems are discussed later in this paper.

Section 2 defines the database concepts that will be used later. Section 3 discusses integrability, and defines multidatabases and multidatabase queries and answers. Section 4 extends the model to approximative answers. Section 5 describes the Multiplex prototype, Section 6 compares Multiplex to several other systems that share similar goals, and Section 7 concludes this paper with a brief summary and a discussion of further research issues.

2 Relational Databases

In this section we define the database concepts that will be used throughout this work. Our formalization of relational databases is mostly conventional.

2.1 Schemes and Instances, Views and Queries

Assume a finite set of attributes T, and for each attribute $A \in T$ assume a finite domain $dom(A)$, and assume a special value called *null* and denoted $-$, which is not in any of the domains. A *relation scheme* R is a sequence of attributes from T. A *tuple* t of a relation scheme $R = (A_1, \ldots, A_m)$ is an element of $dom(A_1) \cup \{-\} \times \cdots \times dom(A_m) \cup \{-\}$. A *relation instance* (or, simply, a *relation*) r of a relation scheme R is a finite set of tuples of R. A *database scheme* D is a set of relation schemes $\{R_1, \ldots, R_n\}$. A *database instance* d of the database scheme D is a set of relations $\{r_1, \ldots, r_n\}$, where r_i is a relation on the relation scheme R_i $(i = 1, \ldots, n)$. Finally, a *database* (D, d) is a combination of a database scheme D and a database instance d of the scheme D.

Let D be a database scheme. A *view* of D is an expression that defines (1) a new relation scheme V, and (2) for each instance d of D an instance v of V. v is called the *extension* of the view scheme V in the database instance d.

We shall assume that all views are of the family known as *conjunctive views* [34]. Although conjunctive views are a strict subset of the relational tuple calculus, they are a powerful subset, corresponding to the set of relational algebra expressions with the operations *Cartesian product*, *selection* and *projection* (where the selection predicates are conjunctive).

A *query* Q on a database scheme D is a view of D. The extension of Q in a database instance d of scheme D is called the *answer* to Q in the database instance d.

As an example, given the relation schemes $Emp = (Name, Salary, Dname)$ and $Dept = (Dname, Supervisor)$, a view Emp_sup may be defined by

$$project_{Name,Supervisor} \, select_{Emp.Dname=Dept.Dname} \, Emp \times Dept$$

The scheme of Emp_sup is $(Name, Supervisor)$.

2.2 View Operations

Given views V' and V of a database scheme D, V' is a *subview* of V, denoted $V' \sqsubseteq V$, if there exists a selection-projection view W of V, such that the schemes of V' and W are identical, and in every database instance d of D, the extensions of V' and W are identical. V is then a *superview* of V'

Note the difference between this definition of subview and the common definition of *contained view*, denoted $V' \subseteq V$, which is based on the containment of two sets of tuples. By restricting W to selection only, the concept of subview is reduced to contained view.

Assume that V' is a subview of V. The *enlargement* of V' to V is a view whose scheme is V, and for every database instance d of D, its extension is obtained by adding null values to the extension of V' in d in the attributes that are in V but not in V'.

Assume that V_1 and V_2 are subviews of V. The *subview union* of V_1 and V_2 *over* V, denoted $V_1 \sqcup V_2$, is the union of their enlargements to V. Assume that V_1 and V_2 are superviews of V. The *superview intersection* of V_1 and V_2 over V, denoted $V_1 \sqcap V_2$, is the intersection of their projections on V.[2]

When the definition of V may be assumed from the context, we shall call these operations simply the *subview union* and *superview intersection* of V_1 and V_2. Note that these operations generalize the union and intersection operations on views, which are commonly defined only for views that have the same scheme, because when V_1, V_2 and V all have the same scheme, these new operations are reduced to the common view operations. As we shall see, the subview union and the superview intersection will be used to provide *lower and upper bounds* of the view V.

Finally, views V_1 and V_2 of a database scheme D are *overlapping*, if there exists a view V of D, such that $V \sqsubseteq V_1$ and $V \sqsubseteq V_2$, and there exists some instance d of D in which the extension of V is non-empty.

---

[2] Note that it may be possible to *identify* separate tuples by using additional information that may be available, such as functional dependencies [25].

3 Multidatabases

We begin by defining derivative databases; i.e., databases derived from other databases. This notion is necessary to define equivalence between views of different databases, which in turn provides a method for expressing the commonality of two database schemes using scheme mappings. Scheme mappings are the basis for our definition of multidatabases. We then formulate the Scheme Consistency Assumption and the Instance Consistency Assumption. These assumptions lead to fundamental observations concerning the integrability of independent databases. We complete the description of the Multiplex multidatabase model by defining multidatabase queries.

3.1 Derivative Databases, View Equivalence and Scheme Mapping

Consider a database (D, d). Let D' be a database scheme whose relation schemes are views of the relation schemes of D. The database scheme D' is said to be *derived* from the database scheme D. Let d' be the database instance of D' which is the extension of the views D' in the database instance d. The database instance d' is said to be *derived* from the database instance d. Altogether, a database (D', d') is a *derivative* of a database (D, d), if its scheme D' is derived from the scheme D, and its instance d' is derived from the instance d.

In this paper we are not concerned with an effective procedure for determining whether one database is a derivative of another, a question that depends on the language for expressing views. For our purpose here, it is sufficient to note that a database may or may not be a derivative of another database.

Let (D_1, d_1) and (D_2, d_2) be two derivatives of a database (D, d). A view V_1 of D_1 and a view V_2 of D_2 are *equivalent*, if for every instance d of D the extension of V_1 in d_1 and the extension of V_2 in d_2 are identical. Intuitively, view equivalence allows us to substitute the answer to one query for an answer to another query, although these are different queries on different schemes.

Given two different database schemes, which are both derivatives of the same scheme (the "reference scheme"), we express their commonality by means of scheme mappings.

Assume two database schemes D_1 and D_2, which are both derivatives of a database scheme D. A *scheme mapping* (D_1, D_2) is a collection of view pairs $(V_{i,1}, V_{i,2})$ $(i = 1, \ldots, m)$, where each $V_{i,1}$ is a view of D_1, each $V_{i,2}$ is a view of D_2, and $V_{i,1}$ is equivalent to $V_{i,2}$.

As an example, the equivalence of attribute *Salary* of relation scheme *Emp* in database scheme D_1 and attribute *Sal* of relation scheme *Employee* in database scheme D_2 is indicated by the view pair

$$(project_{Salary} Emp, \ project_{Sal} Employee)$$

As another example, given the relation schemes *Emp* = *(Name, Title, Salary, Supervisor)* in database scheme D_1, and *Manager* = *(Ename, Level, Sal, Sup)* in database scheme D_2, the retrieval of the salaries of managers is performed differently in each database, as indicated by the view pair

$$(project_{Name,Salary} \, select_{Title=manager} \, Emp, \; project_{Ename,Sal} \, Manager)$$

From a practical point of view, note that the number of views in scheme mappings may be controlled, by mapping the "largest" views possible. The equivalence of their corresponding subviews may then be inferred.

3.2 Multidatabase

A *multidatabase* is

1. A scheme D.
2. A collection $(D_1, d_1), \ldots, (D_n, d_n)$ of databases.
3. A collection $(D, D_1), \ldots, (D, D_n)$ of scheme mappings.

The first item defines the scheme of a multidatabase, the second item defines the member databases in the multidatabase environment, and the third item defines a mapping from the multidatabase scheme to the schemes of the member databases.

The "instance" of a multidatabase consists of a collection of global view extensions that are available from the member databases. Specifically, the views in the first position of the scheme mappings specify the "contributed information" at the global level, and the views in the second position describe how these contributions are materialized.

As defined in Section 3.1, scheme mappings allow to substitute certain views in one database with equivalent views in another database. In a multidatabase, the former database is the global database, and the latter is a member database.

This definition may be considered a formalization of *virtual databases* defined in [26]. Scheme mapping may be considered an abstraction of different solutions that have been advanced to the task of relating global schemes to schemes of member databases (e.g., [20, 33, 6, 26]).

3.3 Integrability Assumptions

The purpose of multidatabases is to integrate information from several, independent databases. Of course, the problem of integration is trivial, unless the information sources are *inconsistent*: i.e., a portion of the real world is described differently by more than one source. Such inconsistencies fall into two categories: (1) *intensional inconsistencies*, and (2) *extensional inconsistencies*.

Intensional inconsistencies, often referred to as *semantic heterogeneity*, are defined as differences in *modeling*. For example, differences in relation schemes, or in the semantics of individual attributes (e.g., measurement units). Extensional inconsistencies surface only *after* all intensional inconsistencies have been resolved, at a point where the systems participating in a specific transaction may be assumed to have identical intensional representation for all overlapping information. At that point it is possible that two information sources would provide different answers to the same query.

We shall assume that there exists a single (hypothetical) database that represents the real world. This ideal database includes the usual components of scheme and instance. Its scheme is the perfect model, and its instance are the perfect data. We now formulate two assumptions. These assumptions are similar to the Universal Scheme Assumption and the Universal Instance Assumption [25], although their purpose here is quite different. These two assumptions are statements of the *integrability* of the given databases. They use the definition of derived databases in Section 3.1.

The Scheme Consistency Assumption (SCA). All database schemes are *derivatives* of the real world scheme. That is, every relation scheme is a view of the real world scheme. The meaning of this assumption is that the different ways in which reality is modeled are all correct; i.e., there are no *modeling errors*, only *modeling differences*. To put it in yet a different way, all intensional inconsistencies among the independent database models are reconcilable.

The Instance Consistency Assumption (ICA). All database instances are *derivatives* of the real world instance. That is, in each database instance, every relation instance is derived from the real world instance. The meaning of this assumption is that the information stored in databases is always correct; i.e., there are no factual *errors*, only different *representations* of the facts. In other words, all extensional inconsistencies among the independent database instances are reconcilable.

Although these assumptions have not been articulated before in the context of database integration, tacit assumptions have often been made. Most previous work on scheme integration has tacitly subscribed to the Scheme Consistency Assumption, and the different approaches to scheme integration are therefore implementations of specific techniques for reconciling modeling inconsistencies. With few exceptions in the areas of logic databases [32] and data fusion [1], most previous work on database integration has tacitly subscribed to the Instance Consistency Assumption as well, thus avoiding any possibility of data inconsistency.

The Multiplex model assumes that the Scheme Consistency Assumption *holds*, meaning that all differences among database schemes are reconcilable, and that the Instance Consistency Assumption *does not hold*, allowing the possibility of irreconcilable differences among database instances.

In other words, the member databases are all assumed to have schemes that are derivatives of a hypothetical real world database scheme; these schemes are related through the multidatabase scheme, which is yet another derivative of this perfect database scheme. But the member database instances are not assumed to be derivatives of the real world instance.

Clearly, without subscribing to the SCA, it is not possible to integrate a given set of databases. On the other hand, subscribing to the ICA would not reflect the reality of independently maintained databases.

3.4 Discussion

Our definition of multidatabases provides four important "degrees of freedom", which reflect the realities of multidatabase environments.

First, the mapping from D to the member schemes is not necessarily *total*; i.e., not all views of D are expressible in one of the member databases (and even if they are expressible, there is no guarantee that they are mapped). This models the dynamic situation of a multidatabase system, where some member databases might become temporarily unavailable. In such cases the corresponding mappings are "suspended", and some global queries might not be answerable in their entirety. Similarly, if an authorization mechanism is enforced, a user may not have permission to some views.

Second, the mapping is not necessarily *surjective*; i.e., the member databases may include views that are not expressible in D (and even if they are expressible, there is no guarantee that they are mapped). This models the pragmatism of multidatabases, which usually cull from existing databases only the information which is relevant to a specific set of applications. For example, a large database may share only one or two views with the multidatabase.

Third, the mapping is not necessarily *single-valued*; i.e., a view of D may be found in several member databases. This models the realistic situation, in which information is found in several overlapping databases, and provides a formal framework for dealing with multidatabase inconsistency. Recall that if we do not assume that the Instance Consistency Assumption holds, then we do not assume that the member instances are all derived from a single instance. Thus, the inclusion of view pairs (V, V_1) and (V, V_2) in two scheme mappings of a multidatabase does not imply that the extensions of V in the member databases are identical. Rather, it implies that they *should be* identical.

Fourth, while the definition assumes that the member databases adhere to the relational model defined here, they need not be relational, or even of the same data model. Recall that the only purpose of the views in the second position of the scheme mappings is to describe how the views in the first position are materialized. Therefore, the member databases need not be relational, and the views in the second position need not be relational expressions. The only requirement is that they compute tabular answers.

3.5 Multidatabase Queries

An essential part of the definition of a database model is its query language. The definition of a language must provide for syntax, as well as semantics; that is, one must define not only how queries are written, but also their extension in any database instance. In this section we consider multidatabase queries.

Syntactically, a multidatabase query is simply a query Q of the scheme D. Intuitively, the answer to a multidatabase query Q should be obtained by transforming it to an equivalent query of the views in the first position of the scheme mappings (the available information). These views would then be materialized (using the view definitions in the second position of the scheme mappings), and the translated query would be processed on these materialized views. Formally, the required transformation of Q is stated as follows.

Let $D = \{R_1, \ldots, R_n\}$ denote a database scheme, and let $M = \{V_1, \ldots, V_m\}$ denote a set of views of D. Translate a given query Q_D of the database scheme to an equivalent query Q_M of the view schemes.

However, a solution to this translation problem may not exist, or there could be multiple solutions. To observe that multiple solutions may exist, consider a database with a relation $R = (A, B, C)$ and views $V_1 = project_{A,B} R$ and $V_2 = project_{A,C} R$, and consider the query $Q = project_A R$. Q can be answered from both V_1 or V_2. To observe that a solution may not exist, consider a database with two relations $R = (A, B)$ and $S = (B, C)$, and one view $V = R \bowtie S$, and consider the query $Q = select_{A=a} R$. Clearly, Q cannot be answered from the view V, because the join would not necessarily include all of R's tuples.

This translation problem (for conjunctive queries and views) has been addressed by Larson and Yang [21,22], by Levy et al. [23] and by Brodsky and Motro [8]. We shall assume that a translation algorithm exists which is sound and complete; i.e., it computes all the correct translations that exist.

3.6 Multidatabase Answers

Assume a multidatabase with scheme D and mapped views M. The *answer* to a query Q on this multidatabase is the set of answers produced by a sound and complete translation algorithm. There are two possible cases:

1. When the translation algorithm produces more than one solution, these solutions may evaluate to different answers. Each such answer is a *candidate answer*. The answer to Q is the set of all candidate answers.[3]
2. When a solution to the translation problem does not exist, the answer to Q is the empty set of answers. This empty set of answers should be interpreted as *answer unavailable*.[4]

Of course, if we were to subscribe to the Instance Consistency Assumption, then all the solutions generated in the first case would be guaranteed to evaluate to the same answer, and the answer to Q would be this unique answer. In theory, this answer may be evaluated from an arbitrary solution to the translation problem. In practice, however, some realistic model of *cost* should be adopted, and the *cheapest* solution should be chosen. Note that under the Instance Consistency Assumption, it is possible that the translation algorithm will have no solutions. Hence, the possibilities under the ICA are one answer or no answer.

4 Approximative Answers

From a user perspective, each legitimate database query should evaluate to a single answer. The multidatabase answers defined in the previous section deviate from this ideal in two cases: when no answer is available, and when several

---

[3] Note that possibly none of these answers is consistent with the real world answer.
[4] Note the difference between an empty set of answers and an empty answer.

different answers are available. In either case, it is clear that a single *perfect* answer (i.e., an answer identical to the real world answer) cannot be determined from the multidatabase environment. At best, the system can provide an *approximation* of this elusive perfect answer. In this section, we extend the Multiplex model to handle these situations.

Intuitively, a global query cannot be translated to an equivalent query of the available views, because the mapping of the global scheme to the member schemes is not total; i.e., some information "promised" in the global scheme cannot be "delivered". The most common reason for this is that some member databases are not responding. But a similar situation would occur if some of the requested information cannot be delivered due to insufficient permissions, or due to some resource having been exhausted before the entire answer could be obtained (e.g., time, or some other cost measure). In situations where a query Q cannot be rewritten as an equivalent query of the available views, an issue of great importance is how well can Q be *approximated* using the available views; i.e., what is the best approximation of Q that can be evaluated from the views?

Intuitively, a global query is translatable to different equivalent queries over the available views, because the mapping of the global scheme to the member schemes is not single-valued; i.e., there exists a view of the global scheme that can be materialized in more than one way. This happens when two view pairs of the mapping have the *same* view in their first position. Obviously, for every translation that uses one view, there is an equivalent translation that uses the other view. More generally, it happens when two pairs have *overlapping* views in their first position, as this implies that the intersection view can be mapped in two different ways. The most common reason for such multivalued mappings is that the information resources have overlapping information. Unless the ICA holds, these different translations could evaluate to different answers. In situations where there are different ways to rewrite Q as an equivalent query of the available views, and they evaluate to different answers, an issue of great importance is whether any one specific answer should be *preferred* over the others, or how the answers could be *combined* into a single answer.

Our discussion of approximative answers is divided into two. First we assume that the ICA holds. Next we assume that the ICA does not hold. We begin with concepts that will be used in both situations.

4.1 Sound and Complete Answers

Recall our assumption of a (hypothetical) database that represents the real world perfectly. Under the Scheme Consistency Assumption (which is adopted in Multiplex) all database schemes are derivatives of this database, and without loss of generality we assume now that the scheme of the available database is *identical* to the real world model. Let (D, d_0) denote the real world database, and let (D, d) denote the actual database. Therefore, the database instance d is an *estimate* of the real database instance d_0.

Consider a query Q on the database scheme D. Let q denote its answer in the database instance d, and let q_0 denote its answer in the database instance

d_0; i.e., q_0 is the perfect answer, and q is its estimate from the actual database instance. Following [27], we say that q is a *sound* answer if $q \subseteq q_0$, and q is a *complete* answer if $q \supseteq q_0$. If q is both sound and complete then q has *integrity*.

Clearly, the perfect answer q_0 lies "between" any sound answer q_s and any complete answer q_c: $q_s \subseteq q_0 \subseteq q_c$. When the perfect answer cannot be computed from the available database, sound and complete answers serve as "below" and "above" *approximations*. Clearly, it is desirable to obtain the "largest" sound answer and the "smallest" complete answer. Together, these provide the tightest approximation for the perfect answer.

Consider a *subanswer* of Q (a subview *enlarged* with nulls to the scheme of Q). The elements of the subanswer are elements of q_0; hence the subanswer is a sound answer.[5] Consider a *superanswer* of Q (a superview *projected* on the scheme of Q). The elements of q_0 are elements of the supernaswer; hence the superanswer is a complete answer. Intuitively, combining subanswers and superanswers (through union and intersection) will provide us with the aforementioned "largest' sound answer and "smallest" complete answer.

However, when the ICA does not hold, inconsistencies among subanswers and superanswers are possible. For example, we may encounter a subanswer and a superanswer where the former is not contained in the latter (i.e., some elements of the subanswer are not in the superanswer).

It is possible to define models where such inconsistencies are resolved by preferring certain answers over others (based on known external properties of the answers). This version of Multiplex assumes that no such additional information is available, in effect accepting all answers, subanswers and superanswers as "equally good". Inconsistencies are then resolved on the basis of *voting*.

Sound answers establish that certain data are *included* in q_0; complete answers establish that certain data are *excluded* from q_0. Therefore, the soundness or completeness of an answer may be interpreted as a claim (a *vote*) on each element of the domain of the answer: a sound answer is a *yes* vote for its members, and a *maybe* vote for all its non-members. A complete answer is a *maybe* vote for its members and a *no* vote for all its non-members.

The assumption that all information is "equally good" is interpreted that each subanswer *claims* to be sound, each superanswer *claims* to be complete, and each answer *claims* to be both sound and complete. Our assumption that no additional information is available implies that all claims have the same likelihood of being correct; i.e., their individual votes have equal weights.

We now propose this three-valued operation to combine conflicting votes:

	yes	no	maybe
yes	yes	maybe	maybe
no	maybe	no	maybe
maybe	maybe	maybe	maybe

---

[5] We consider a tuple with null values to be sound if its non-null values match those of a tuple of q_0.

Briefly, according to this operation the final verdict is definite if and only if all votes are consistent. It is easy to verify that this operation is associative, and thus the order in which the candidate answers are considered is immaterial.

Consider an example with two answers q_1 and q_2. There are four subsets of the answer space that are treated homogeneously: $q_1 \cap q_2$, $q_1 - q_2$, $q_2 - q_1$, and $\overline{q_1 \cup q_2}$, . The subsets for which the vote is *yes* suggest a sound answer; the subsets for which the vote is not *no* suggest a complete answer. It is easy to verify that the elements in $q_1 \cap q_2$ have a *yes* vote, elements in $q_1 - q_2$ and in $q_2 - q_1$ have a *maybe* vote, and all other elements have a *no* vote. Hence, $q_1 \cap q_2$ is voted as a sound answer, and $q_1 \cup q_2$ is voted as a complete answer.

4.2 Approximation under the ICA

If we assume that the Instance Consistency Assumption holds, then the only possible anomaly are queries for which "full answers" (answers that respond to the entire query) are unavailable. We define "partial answers" (which the ICA would guarantee to be mutually consistent), and we show how they should be combined into *approximative answers*, consisting of the largest sound and the smallest complete answers.

Because the ICA holds, then every *subview* of Q that can be expressed with the available views would evaluate to a sound approximation of the answer to Q, and any *superview* of Q that can be expressed with the available views would evaluate to a complete approximation of the answer to Q.

As an example, assume the global scheme $Emp=(Ename,Salary,Department, Location)$ and the views

$$V_1 = project_{Ename,Salary} Emp$$
$$V_2 = project_{Ename,Salary} select_{Department=design} Emp$$
$$V_3 = project_{Ename,Department} Emp$$
$$V_4 = project_{Ename,Department} select_{Salary>40} Emp$$
$$V_5 = project_{Department,Location} Emp$$

and consider these two queries:

$$Q_1 = project_{Ename,Salary,Department,Location} Emp$$
$$Q_2 = project_{Ename,Department} select_{Salary>50 \wedge Location=midtown} Emp$$

Consider first Q_1. Normally, it would be answered by joining V_1, V_3 and V_5. Suppose that V_1 and V_5 are not available. By substituting V_2 for V_1, the system can provide the names and departments of *all* the employees, and the salaries of *some* of the employees, but locations for *none* of the employees. In effect, this information is the *union* of two *subviews* of Q_1.

Consider now Q_2. Normally, it would be answered by joining V_1, V_3 and V_5 and selecting $Location = midtown$ and $Salary > 50$. Suppose that V_1 is not available. By joining V_3 and V_5 and selecting $Location = midtown$ the system can provide the names and departments of the midtown employees. By itself, V_4 provides the names and departments of the employees who earn over 40. Each of these answers *contains* the requested answer. The *intersection* of these two *superviews* of Q_2 provides the requested information for the midtown employees who earn over 40, a set which is "close" to the answer.

Let $D = \{R_1, \ldots, R_n\}$ denote a database scheme, let $M = \{V_1, \ldots, V_m\}$ denote a set of views of D, and let Q be a query of D. A view V of M is a *maximal sound approximation* of Q using M, if $V \sqsubseteq Q$, and for every view V' of M: $V' \sqsubseteq Q \Rightarrow V' \sqsubseteq V$. A view V of M is a *minimal complete approximation* of Q using M, if $V \sqsupseteq Q$, and for every view V' of M: $V' \sqsupseteq Q \Rightarrow V' \sqsupseteq V$.

The following results follow from mathematical set theory. The maximal sound approximation of Q using M is the *union* of all the subviews of Q that are expressible with views of M: $\bigcup\{W_M \mid W_M \sqsubseteq Q\}$. The minimal complete approximation of Q using M is the *intersection* of all the superviews of Q that are expressible with views of M: $\bigcap\{W_M \mid W_M \sqsupseteq Q\}$.

Assume a multidatabase with scheme D and mapped views M. When a query Q on this multidatabase has no answer, the *approximate answer* to Q is the pair of maximal sound approximation and minimal complete approximation:

$$< \bigcup\{W_M \mid W_M \sqsubseteq Q\}, \bigcap\{W_M \mid W_M \sqsupseteq Q\} > \qquad (1)$$

Observe that, because the ICA holds, when Q is answerable in its entirety, this approximation converges to a single answer, as described in Section 3.6. Note that a minimal complete approximation is not guaranteed, because a query might have no superviews that can be expressed with the available views. Assume a database scheme with two relations R_1 and R_2 and one view $V_1 = R_1$, and consider the query $Q = R_2$. Clearly, Q cannot be expressed with the available views; moreover, there is no view of the available views that is a superview of Q. On the other hand, a maximal sound approximation is guaranteed because a subview (possibly empty) of a query always exists.

4.3 Approximation when the ICA Does Not Hold

Assume now that the Instance Consistency Assumption does not hold. In constructing an approximation for a query, we must consider both full answers and partial answers (subviews and superviews of the answer).

Let $D = \{R_1, \ldots, R_n\}$ denote a database scheme, let $M = \{V_1, \ldots, V_m\}$ denote a set of views of D, and let Q be a query of D. The result of the query translation algorithm is three sets of views:

1. $q_1, \ldots, q_k$ are the available answers,
2. $s_1, \ldots, s_m$ are the available subviews of the answer, and
3. $c_1, \ldots, c_n$ are the available superviews of the answer.

We assume that all these answers are *independent* of each other; that is, none of the translations are subviews of each other.

After the appropriate enlargements and projections, we have a total of $k + m + n$ answers that *vote* on the entire answer space. Every q_i votes *yes* on its members and *no* on all other elements; every s_i votes *yes* on its members, and *maybe* on all other elements; and every c_i votes *maybe* on its members and *no* on all other elements. Observe, however, that tuples may now be only partially specified (i.e., with null values). The question whether a tuple is a member of an answer is indeed whether a tuple *could* be a member of an answer.

The set of tuples for which the vote was unanimously *yes* is adopted as a sound estimate. The tuples for which the vote was not unanimously *no* is a adopted as a complete estimate:

$$< \{t \mid t \text{ has only } yes \text{ votes}\}, \{t \mid t \text{ does not have all } no \text{ votes}\} > \qquad (2)$$

Observe that these are now *estimates* of a sound lower bound and a complete upper bound: since the candidate answers and partial answers are not assumed to be sound or complete, the lower approximation is not guaranteed to be sound, and the upper approximation is not guaranteed to be complete.

Our assumption here is the most general: (1) that the ICA does not necessarily hold, and (2) that the translation algorithm delivers both full answers and partial answers (i.e., subviews and superviews). When more specific assumptions are made, this solution is simplified. First, if only full answers are considered, then these estimates are reduced, respectively, to the intersection and union of the full answers: $< \bigcap_{i=1}^{k} q_i, \bigcup_{i=1}^{k} q_i >$. Second, if the ICA holds, but only partial answers are available, then these estimates are reduced, respectively, to the subview union and the superview intersection defined in Formula (1). Finally, if the ICA holds, and a full answer is available, then these estimates converge to the simple answer defined at the end of Section 3.6.

The above estimates are aimed at maximizing soundness (the lower estimate) and completeness (the upper estimate). It is also possible to define answers "in between" these two. For example, the set of tuples for which at most one vote was not *yes*, the set of tuples for which at most two votes were not *yes*, and so on. This creates a sequence of containing answers that increase overall completeness while reducing overall soundness. It is then possible to provide the most sound answer which meets a user requirement on *minimal answer size*, or the largest answer which meets a user requirement on *minimal soundness*, and so on.

As mentioned earlier, when additional assumptions on the candidate answers can be made, more elaborate consolidation techniques may be developed. For example, instead of assuming that the alternative answers are of equal quality, we could assume that their individual quality measures are given, and adapt the voting scheme accordingly [28].

5 Implementation

As explained in the introduction, the Multiplex model is intended to provide both a formal foundation for research in multidatabases, and a practical architecture for a multidatabase system. Of course, actual implementations must consider additional details; yet the general principles of the Multiplex model would be upheld. In this respect it is similar to the relational model itself, whose

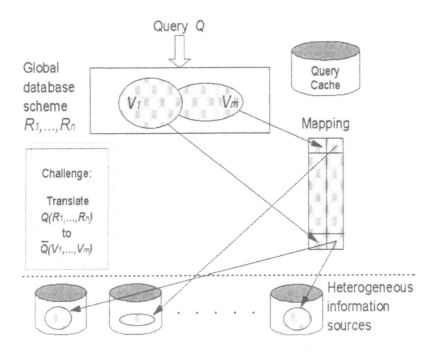

Fig. 1. A diagrammatic view of the Multiplex system.

formal definitions must be augmented with practical considerations in any implementation (e.g., optimization).

A prototype of the multidatabase model described in this paper has been implemented. A simple diagram of the system is shown in Figure 1.

The architecture and features of the Multiplex DBMS has six functional components: (1) user interface, (2) query parser, (3) query translator, (4) view retriever, (5) query optimizer, and (6) query processor, and it uses two sources of metadata: (1) a database scheme file, and (2) a database mapping file.

The user interface, the query parser, the query optimizer, the query processor, and the database scheme file are functionally similar to those of generic DBMS. There are two significant differences between a generic DBMS and Multiplex: (1) Multiplex does not have any relations; "instead" it has a scheme mapping file that matches views of the global scheme with views of the member databases. (2) Between the parsing and optimizing phases, which in a generic DBMS follow each other, the Multiplex query translator translates the global query to a query of the "available views", and the Multiplex view retriever obtains the necessary views from the member databases. The translated query is then optimized and processed in the retrieved views in the same way as in a generic DBMS. Indeed, Multiplex retrieves views into a commercial DBMS (Oracle), and then submits the translated query to be optimized and processed by this DBMS.

For brevity, we only mention here a few notable aspects of the Multiplex system.

1. Multiplex uses the HTTP protocol for communicating with the member databases. In other words, it is a World Wide Web application. The user interface is accessible via WWW browsers, and client databases are invoked by so-called "cgi scripts".
2. For its query translation, Multiplex uses the DRP software package [11], which has been modified and improved. For example, the translated query is modified further in an attempt to reduce transmission costs, using techniques known from distributed query optimization [10].
3. With respect to heterogeneity, presently, Multiplex can retrieve information from six kinds of sources: (1) relational (using Oracle), (2) object-oriented (using Ode), (3) simple files (using Unix shell scripts), and (4) Wide-area information services (WAIS, using SWISH 1.1 and WWWAIS 2.5) (5) spreadsheets (Microsoft Excell's HTML output), and (6) menu-based (the XLibris library retrieval system).
4. Multiplex answers (refer to Formula (2)) are presented, using color, as two relations: one contains the *sound estimate*, the other contains the tuples that augment the sound estimate to a *complete estimate* (i.e., the union of both relations is the complete estimate), and users are advised that the answer to their query is estimated to contain the first relation *plus* a subset of the second relation.
5. Multiplex extends the query language of conjunctive queries with *aggregate functions*. A language based on conjunctive queries with aggregation provides a fairly powerful querying tool.

Overall, the linkage between the global database and the contributing sources is rather quick, requiring only entering pairs of equivalent queries in the mapping file. The result is that new information sources may be "plugged-in" very quickly.

6 Comparison with Other Approaches

As mentioned in the introduction, there has been considerable work in the area of multidatabases. A comprehensive discussion of every project or product is beyond the scope of this paper. In this section we compare our model and system to four different works, representing fairly different approaches.

UniSQL [18] is an example of a multidatabase system based on a comprehensive mapping of its global database scheme to the component database schemes. UniSQL provides an exhaustive framework for handling schematic heterogeneity (i.e., intensional inconsistencies) among the participating databases. Its reliance on predefined, comprehensive mappings dictates that UniSQL may not be as suitable for ad-hoc integration, in which (1) relatively small portions of the component sources are of interest (their entire schemes possibly being irrelevant, unavailable or incomprehensible), and (2) component sources change frequently, with new sources being added and existing sources undergoing structural changes, or becoming altogether obsolete.

The TSIMMIS project [15] is an example of a system that is based on mediators and wrappers. *Mediators* [35] are software modules designed to deal with representation and abstraction problems that occur when trying to use data and knowledge resources. Mediators are understood to be active and knowledge-driven. *Wrappers* [35] are simpler software interfaces that allow a heterogeneous information sources to appear as if they conform to a uniform design or protocol. For example, a wrapper could be built to make a legacy database respond to a subset of SQL queries, as if it were a relational database. Multiplex makes fairly standard use of wrappers. With respect to mediators, a Multiplex query (a global view) may be considered a new "object". Its translation produces an ad-hoc "mediator", describing how the global object is to be constructed from the presently available sources. The advantage of such "dynamic mediation" are two: (1) Whereas with "static" mediators all integrated "objects' must be anticipated and predefined, in Multiplex an unlimited number of global objects may be defined spontaneously. (2) Static mediators need to be redefined whenever the available information sources change, whereas Multiplex only needs to have its mapping updated.

The approach of SIMS [3] to the integration problem is somewhat different. SIMS creates a *domain model* of the application domain, using a knowledge representation language to establish a fixed vocabulary describing objects in the domain, their attributes, and the relationships among them. Given a global query, SIMS identifies the sources of information that are required to answer the query and reformulates the query accordingly. SIMS is similar to Multiplex in that both do not rely on pre-programmed mediators, making the addition of new sources relatively simple. In both systems new sources have only to be *described* to the system. In SIMS, this description is in the knowledge representation language, using terms in the shared domain model; in Multiplex it is via pairs of equivalent views. Arguably, the SIMS descriptions are more demanding, but may allow the system to perform additional tasks. In contradistinction, Multiplex makes no claims of "intelligence"; it is a direct extension of relational model concepts, without the costs, risks, and possibly some benefits of a "knowledge-based" approach.

In many ways, the Information Manifold (IM) [2] is similar to SIMS. IM uses an object-relational model to integrate the various information sources, called *sites*. The individual sites are described and related to the global scheme, called the *world-view*, using the knowledge description language Classic. Like Multiplex, global query processing requires translation from the global set of relations to the set of available views. Like SIMS, and unlike Multiplex, the selection of relevant sites depends heavily on the quality of the site descriptions.

Finally, it should also be noted that none of these systems considers extensional inconsistencies ("too much data") and their handling of partial answers ("too little data") is fairly limited.

7 Conclusion

The Multiplex model that was described in this paper is both *formal* and *pragmatic*. It is a formal extension of the relational database model to multidatabases. This formalization reflects the important pragmatic issues encountered in actual multidatabase environments, and it can serve as the formal model behind many previous ad-hoc integration models that have already been designed.

The Multiplex model is also simple to implement, and when various pragmatic issues are addressed properly, it should prove to be highly practical. Towards this goal, we discuss several open issues and research directions.

Multidatabase design may be described as a mediation between the information needed (as expressed in the global database scheme) and the information available. The mediation process generates mappings that match information available (a view of some member database) with information needed (a view of the global scheme). An interesting issue that was not addressed in this paper is the *design* of the mapping. For example, a problem that might concern the designer is whether a present set of mapped views "covers" the global scheme. Formally, given a database scheme $D = \{R_1, \ldots, R_n\}$, does a set of views $M = \{V_1, \ldots, V_m\}$ guarantee that every query of D is expressible with M. Moreover, is it possible to characterize the queries that are not expressible, thus suggesting a view that would complement M?

As defined in this paper, both the relational model the Multiplex model do not include integrity constraints. We are currently extending Multiplex to include global integrity constraints. Like views, these constraints would be mapped to constraints that are defined and enforced in the member databases. Global integrity constraints would provide a means for pruning the set of candidate answers.

One of the unique features of Multiplex is that its approach to cross-source inconsistencies does not require user involvement, essentially providing approximations that are based on voting. Experience accumulated so far indicates that in many instances it is highly desirable to provide user control over the process of inconsistency resolution. Our current development efforts (informally dubbed Multiplex II) would provide comprehensive and flexible control of the process, by means of *conflict resolution strategies*. These strategies would consider *properties* of the data (such as quality, currentness, or cost) as well as their actual *values*. Users would be given options such as picking the highest quality data among the alternatives, or consolidating the alternatives by their average. The strategies for resolving conflicts would be stated as part of the multidatabase design.

Acknowledgment: This work was supported in part by ARPA grant, administered by the Office of Naval Research under Grants No. N0014-92-J-4038 and N0060-96-D-3202. The author is grateful to Philipp Anokhin, who developed the prototype described in Section 5, and to Igor Rakov, who implemented an earlier version of the system. Both also provided important comments on this paper. The author is also indebted to Alex Brodsky, for his many insightful comments and suggestions.

References

1. M.A. Abidi and R.C. Gonzalez, editors. *Data Fusion in Robotics and Machine Intelligence*. Academic Press, 1992.
2. A. Levy an D. Srivastava and T. Kirk. Data model and query evaluation in global information systems. *Journal of Intelligent Information Systems*, 5(2):121–143, Sep. 1995.
3. Y. Arens, C. A. Knoblock, and W.-M. Shen. Query reformulation for dynamic information integration. *Journal of Intelligent Information Systems*, 6(2/3):99–130, June 1996.
4. C. Batini, M. Lenzerini, and S. B. Navathe. A comparative analysis of methodologies for database schema integration. *Computing Surveys*, 18(4):323–364, Dec. 1986.
5. Y. Breitbart. Multidatabase interoperability. *SIGMOD Record*, 19(3):53–60, Sep. 1990.
6. Y. Breitbart, P. L. Olson, and G. R. Thompson. Database integration in a distributed heterogeneous database system. In *Proceedings of the IEEE Computer Society Second International Conference on Data Engineering*, pp. 301–310, 1986.
7. M. W. Bright, A. R. Hurson, and S. H. Pakzad. A taxonomy and current issues in multidatabase systems. *Computer*, 25(3):50–60, March 1992.
8. A. Brodsky and A. Motro. The problem of optimal approximations of queries using views and its applications. Technical Report ISSE-TR-95-104, Department of Information and Software Engineering, George Mason University, May 1995.
9. O. P. Buneman, S. Davidson, and A. Watters. Federated approximations for heterogeneous databases. *Data Engineering*, 3(2):27–34, Aug. 1989.
10. S. Ceri and G. Pelagatti. *Distributed Databases: Principles and Systems*. McGraw-Hill, 1984.
11. N. Coburn. *Derived Relation Prototype: User Guide*. Department of Computer Science, University of Waterloo, 1988.
12. P. Drew, R. King, D. McLeod, M. Rusinkiewicz, and A. Silberschatz. Report of the workshop on semantic heterogeneity and interoperation in multidatabase systems. *SIGMOD Record*, 22(3):47–56, Sep. 1993.
13. G. Wiederhold, editor. Special issue: Intelligent integration of information. *Journal of Intelligent Information Systems*, 6(2/3), June 1996.
14. D. Fang, J. Hammer, and D. McLeod. The identification and resolution of semantic heterogeneity in multidatabase systems. In *Proceedings of the First International Workshop on Interoperability in Multidatabase Systems*, pp. 136–143, 1991.
15. H. Garcia-Molina, Y. Papakonstantinou, D. Quass, A. Rajaraman, Y. Sagiv, J. Ullman, and J. Widom. The TSIMMIS approach to mediation: Data models and languages. In *Proceedings of the Second International Workshop on Next Generation Information Technologies and Systems*, pp. 185–193, 1995.
16. A. R. Hurson, M. W. Bright, and S. H. Pakzad, editors. *Multidatabase Systems: An Advanced Solution for Global Information Sharing*. IEEE Computer Society Press, 1994.
17. Y. Kambayashi, M. Rusinkiewicz, and A. Sheth, editors. *Proceedings of the First International Workshop on Research Issues on Data Engineering: Interoperability in Multidatabase Systems*, 1991.
18. W. Kim and J. Seo. Classifying schematic and data heterogeneity in multidatabase systems. *IEEE Computer*, 24(12):12–18, 1991.

19. R. Krishnamurthy, W. Litwin, and W. Kent. Interoperability of heterogeneous databases with semantic discrepancies. In *Proceedings of the First International Workshop on Interoperability in Multidatabase Systems*, pp. 144–151, 1991.

20. T. A. Landers and R. L. Rosenberg. An overview of Multibase. In H.J. Schneider, editor, *Distributed Databases*, North-Holland, 1982.

21. P.-A. Larson and H. Z. Yang. Computing queries from derived relations. In *Proceedings of the Eleventh International Conference on Very Large Data Bases*, pp. 259–269, 1985.

22. P.-A. Larson and H. Z. Yang. Computing queries from derived relations: Theoretical foundations. Technical Report CS-87-35, Department of Computer Science, University of Waterloo, Aug. 1987.

23. A. L. Levy, A. O. Mendelzon, Y. Sagiv, and D. Srivastava. Answering queries from views. In *Proceedings of the 14th Symposium on Principles of Database Systems*, pp. 95–104, 1995.

24. W. Litwin, L. Mark, and N. Roussopoulos. Interoperability of multiple autonomous databases. *Computing Surveys*, 22(3):267–293, Sep. 1990.

25. D. Maier. *The Theory of Relational Databases*. Computer Science Press, 1983.

26. A. Motro. Superviews: Virtual integration of multiple databases. *IEEE Transactions on Software Engineering*, SE-13(7):785–798, July 1987.

27. A. Motro. Integrity = validity + completeness. *ACM Transactions on Database Systems*, 14(4):480–502, Dec. 1989.

28. A. Motro and I Rakov. Not all answers are equally good: Estimating the quality of database answers. In *Flexible Query-Answering Systems*, pp. 1–21. Kluwer, 1997.

29. H.-J. Schek, A. Sheth, and B.D. Czejdo, editors. *Proceedings of the Third International Workshop on Research Issues on Data Engineering: Interoperability in Multidatabase Systems*, 1993.

30. P. Scheuermann, C. Yu, A. Elmagarmid, H. Garcia-Molina, F. Manola, D. McLeod, A. Rosenthal, and M. Templeton. Report on the workshop on heterogeneous database systems. *SIGMOD Record*, 19(4):23–31, Dec. 1990.

31. A. P. Sheth and J. A. Larson. Federated database systems for managing distributed, heterogeneous and autonomous databases. *Computing Surveys*, 22(3):183–236, Sep. 1990.

32. V. S. Subrahmanian. Amalgamating knowledge bases. *ACM Transactions on Database Systems*, 19(2):291–331, June 1994.

33. M. Templeton, D. Brill, S. K. Dao, E. Lund, P. Ward, A. L. P. Chen, and R. McGregor. Mermaid — a front-end to distributed heterogeneous databases. In *Proceedings of IEEE*, volume 75, number 5, pp. 695–708, May 1987.

34. J. D. Ullman. *Principles of Database Systems*. Computer Science Press, 1982.

35. G. Widerhold. Glossary: Intelligent integration of information. *Journal of Intelligent Information Systems*, 6(2/3):281–291, June 1996.

Temporal Active Rules

Mati Golani[1], and Opher Etzion[2]

[1]Information Systems Engineering Area
Faculty of Industrial Engineering and Management
Technion, Haifa, 32000, Israel
iemati@tx. technion.ac.il

[2]IBM - Haifa Research Lab
Matam, 31905, Haifa, Israel
opher@il.ibm.com

Abstract Many rule-base applications are required to support evolving behavior. This may be expressed using evolving rules. This paper describes a framework for the definition and use of temporal ECA rules. This framework supports: rule versions that may be simultaneously applicable, the selection of a rule among several alternatives, and flexible rules in decision support systems that employ hypothetical scenarios.

This paper presents and discusses several temporal models (transaction time model, valid time model and bi-temporal model) of rules, and their application to various types of databases. It presents an execution model that allows the system designer to select rules according to filters whenever different versions of rules may apply. This capability is vital for applications such as: rule evolution in an environment that allows retroactive update (E.g. tax system) and in decision support systems that manage hypothetical scenarios based on rules.

1. Introduction and Motivation

1.1   Introduction

The use of time in active databases has been materialized in previous works in several ways:

Temporal events are events that support some notion of time. Example: the Snoop system [1] supports temporal operators in composite events.

Temporal conditions are queries that may relate to time points in the past or the future, and require a temporal database, and a temporal query language,

Temporal actions are actions that modify data that is valid in the past or the future relative to the update point (these operations are known as retroactive or proactive actions).

Temporal events are applicable in temporal databases as well as non-temporal ones, however temporal conditions and actions are applicable only in the context of the temporal database area.

In this paper we describe an active database model with additional temporal functionality, by viewing the concept of an active (Event-Condition-Action) rule as a temporal entity. In analogous way to temporal data, rules are stored in the database

with temporal characteristics, and multiple versions of a rule may exist simultaneously.
The database itself may be non-temporal are of various temporal properties.

1.2 Motivation (by example)

In a tax payment system, the tax calculation formula has evolved over the years.

The Relevant action part of the tax rule for the year 1997 is *(R1, version-1997)*:

$$Tax: = 0.3 * Earning\text{-}Income + 0.25 * Other\text{-}Income \tag{1}$$

In the year 1998 the rule is updated to *(R1, version-1998)*:

$$Tax: = 0.45 * Income + 0.12 * Other\text{-}Income \tag{2}$$

A person wishes to make in 1999 a retroactive tax payment for the year 1997.
There can be several policies regarding this payment:
Payment according to *the rule that was valid in 1997 (R1, version-1997)*.
Payment according to *the current rule (R1, version-1998)*.
Using a grace period that allows the taxpayer to *choose among these rules*.

Current models do not allow flexibility in choosing applicable rules; thus current models cannot easily express this example. The support of this functionality in current active models requires to embed all the versions in a single rule using very complex conditions. Furthermore, in many cases a new version addition would require a manual update of existing rules.

The functionality provided by temporal rules can substantially reduce the development efforts of various types of applications, such as: tax systems, and other systems with evolving rules and retroactive updates of data are of that type. Rule-based scenario management is another example.

Our motivation is to construct a flexible system that allows using different versions of rules and choosing among them. The model presented in this paper is an extension of the regular temporal active database, by viewing rules as temporal entities. The model is flexible to dynamic changes of rules, while maintaining data integrity and supporting retroactive or proactive updates activation of rules.

1.3 The paper's structure

The paper is structured in the following way: Section 2 surveys related work, Section 3 discusses the various temporal models. Section 4 shows a comprehensive example, and Section 4 concludes the paper.

2. Related Work

We refer to related works in the areas of: temporal databases, schema versioning, temporal logic and simultaneous values.

2.1 Temporal databases

Temporal databases [2] is a discipline that gained a substantial interest during the last decade. In temporal databases, the concept of time is explicit in terms of logical model, indexes, query languages, and update capabilities.

We review some of its basic concepts [3], throughout this paper.
Chronon. A non-decomposable unit of time.
Time interval. The time between two chronons, such that if the time interval is defined as $[t_s, t_e)$ then t belongs to the time interval iff ts $\leq$ t < te.
Temporal element. A finite union of disjoint time intervals.
Valid time. The time when a fact is true in the modeled reality. It is represented as a time interval or a temporal element (the more general case).
Transaction time. The time when a fact becomes current at the database.

Temporal databases may support transaction time, valid time, or both (a bi-temporal model). Transaction time databases maintain versions of the data-items, each with its transaction time chronon. Valid time databases tag each data-item with its validity period. Bi-temporal database supports both features.

2.2 Schema versioning

Works on *schema versioning* in temporal or temporal active databases were focused on the versioning of meta-data entities. Some works used temporal schemata that support versioning along history [4], [5]. The work described in [6], supports a bi-temporal model of schema versioning, which there is an agent associated with each schema version. This agent manages the operations of this schema. An update operation that overlaps several schemata is executed by activating several agents that interact with one another.

2.3 Temporal logic

Many variations of temporal logic are used to model temporal databases.
[7] offers two temporal languages for the definition of temporal triggers: PTL and FTL. These languages meant to deal with the detection of temporal events using database timestamps with temporal operators: Since, Until, Nexttime, Eventually. The suggested model in [8] supports valid time and transaction time, and enables temporal actions.

2.4 Simultaneous Value Semantics (svs)

The paper [9] describes a bi-temporal database model in which simultaneous value (in the valid time sense) may exist simultaneously. The user may define a decision variable called SVS (simultaneous value semantics) to determine a selection policy.
The Possible values of SVS are:

Last. The selected value is the last value inserted (on the transaction time axis), which takes the standard assumption that the latest information is more accurate.

First. The selected value is the first value inserted (on the transaction time axis).

All. All the valid values are selected, and multiple answers are possible.

Single. Any mathematical combination (average, max, min) on the set of the valid values that returns a single scalar.

Subset. A subset of the valid values that is determined by a user-defined selection criterion. It should be noted that in [9], the simultaneous values apply only to data, and not to rules.

3   The Temporal Rule Models

3.1 General description

In this section we describe the various temporal models of active rules.
Figure 1 shows classification of cases according to the temporal characteristics of the rule model, and of the database model.

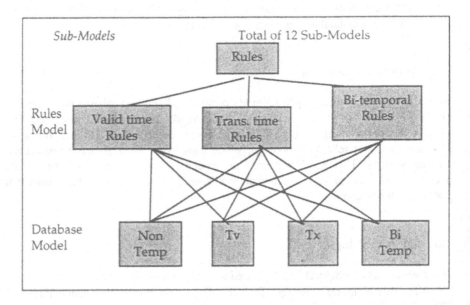

Figure 1. Available combination sub-models derived from temporal rule models & databases.

The rule-base is a temporal database that may be based on one of the three models, while the database may be either a non-temporal database, or support any of the three temporal models. Although the most general model is a bi-temporal model both in the database level and the rule-base level, it carries a substantial overhead that is not required by all applications.

Thus, different applications may require different combinations of rule and database temporal models. The supported rules are standard active ECA rules. In the sequel we discuss the different temporal rule models.

3.2. Rule activation

Regardless of the specific model, the activation of rule in run-time is specified with Two temporal variables:

Observation time. The chronon that reflects the database state from which the rule is applied. The observation time (defaults to: now), enables to activate rules during run-time from past versions of the database.
Reference time. A temporal element that specifies the validity time of the data, on which the rule should be applied.

3.3. The transaction time rule model

Structure. The transaction time rule model is an "append only" model, in the sense that new versions of rules are added, and the older version are kept in the system. In the case that multiple versions of the rules exist, the default action is to use the last version that was inserted into the database, however this is not true for every case. For example: in the tax formula example (Section 1.1) it is not necessarily true for retroactive updates. We can borrow most of the SVS values (first, last, all, subset) which have been defined for valid times, and translate it to transaction time terms. For each rule two values are associated with this rule, t_x designates transaction time, and t_e that represents the time in which a rule was logically erased from the database. The knowledge representation scheme for rules in this model is presented in Figure 2.

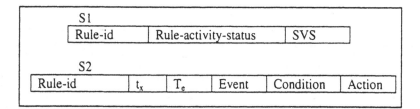

Figure 2. The basic schema for transaction time rule model

S1 includes non-temporal data about the rule, the "Rule-activity-status" attribute determines if the rule is active or inactive. S2 includes the different versions of the same rule. In a transaction time model, a rule is assumed to be valid from the time it is inserted to the database until the time it is erased from the database.

The rule activation process is, as follows:

When an event e_i which is part of rule r_i, is detected, the Rule-activity-status attribute of the rule r_i is checked to validate that it is active.

If it is active , then the candidate rule versions for execution are:

$$R' = \{ r_i \in S2: r_i.t_x < observation\_time \wedge r_i.t_e > observation\_time \} \qquad (3)$$

These candidates include all the rule versions that were inserted to the database before the observation time, and were not erased prior to the observation time.

From those candidates, the chosen rule version to be executed is selected according to the SVS value r_i.svs in S1.

$$R_x = \{ r' \in R': r'.t_x = SVS.(r'.t_x) \} \qquad (4)$$

The rules selection process is not dependent on the type of the database (i.e. the databases may be non-temporal, transaction time, valid time, and bi-temporal database).

When this model is implemented on a *transaction time database*, the data on which the rule is applied is the one with the most recent transaction time relative to the observation time.

Valid Time database and RAP. The combination of transaction time rule model with *valid time database* creates a possible ambiguity for the rule selection process, when the valid time of the updated data overlaps several versions of the rule.

Example:

The update of customer address triggers a rule. A retroactive update occurred from the Observation time = 1990, with the reference interval [1980-1985), and the update's input: 62 West Av.

The database S2 shown in Figure 3 contains the following versions : (The value ∞ in Te designates that the erase time has not been reported).

S2:

Version	Event	Cond	Action	Tx	te
1	Update address	C1	A1	1979	∞
2	Update address	C1	A2	1983	∞
3	Update address	C1	A3	1985	∞

Figure 3. A transaction time rule table

The visual temporal representation of this table's content is shown in figure 4. In current tools, we cannot define in a unique way what is the rule version that should be executed. Assume that the SVS value is "last". There are two possibilities:

- Activate version 1, because it is the last version that was inserted before the validity interval started;
- Activate version 2, because it is the last version that was inserted during the validity interval.

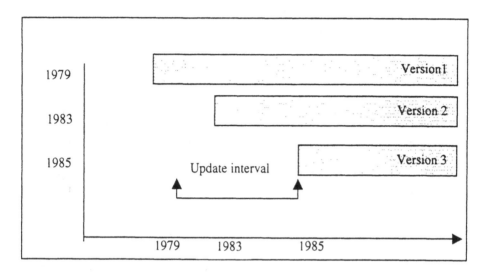

Figure 4. Visual description of temporal update

The policy whether to execute the two versions or one of them (and which one exactly) should be defined according to the required behavior in each specific application .

We can use the SVS value, however, the use of the SVS value may entail the triggering of several rules during the reference interval, even if we use singleton value of SVS such as: last. For example, if the SVS value in our example is **last**, then two rules are selected: version 1 for the interval [1980, 1983), and version 2 for the interval [1983, 1985). This may be undesirable, if the application requires consistent behavior throughout the reference interval.

This problem is solved by the addition of another decision variable called RAP (rule activation policy) to the schema S1. The modified schema S1 is presented in Figure 5.

S1			
Rule-id	Rule-activity-status	SVS	RAP

Figure 5. Modified Schema for S1

The RAP values are identical with the SVS values (first, last, all, subset), but there is a Semantic distinction between them.

SVS refers to all the rule versions that are applicable (inserted and not erased) at a specific chronon, and determines the selection policy from those versions. RAP refers to all the rule versions that are applicable in a specific time interval and defines the rules that should be executed (this is an additional filtering with respect to the SVS filtering).

In the above mentioned example, the valid versions are :
* version 1 for time interval [1979,1983);
* versions 1 and 2 for time interval [1983,1985).

For the first interval, the SVS value "last" is reflected by version 1. As for the second interval, the version 2 is chosen. If the RAP value is "last" as well, the second version is executed.

When the transaction time rule model is applied on a *bi-temporal database*, the values that are used within the rule definition are values the are valid at the reference interval. There is a subtle question of whether the value has been inserted before the start of its validity period, or later by a retroactive update.

If we would like to simulate the case in which the update occurred in the past, all the data items that were inserted into the database later than the observation time should be ignored:

$$\{\text{val: val}.t_x < \text{observation\_time} \land \text{val}.t_v \supseteq \text{observation\_time}\} \qquad (5)$$

If we would like to simulate the system's behavior at that time, but use the most updated data that is available to us, about that time, then the data that was inserted into the database later is also relevant:

$$\{\text{val: val}.t_v \supseteq \text{observation\_time}\} \qquad (6)$$

3.4 Valid time rules

The valid time model does not support multiple versions for the same chronon. Thus, rule versions are physically erased, if there exist newer versions that overlap all their validity period.

The behavior is similar to the transaction time rule case, the main difference is that the SVS variable is not required, since in any chronon there is only one valid version. RAP is still needed, because rules are applied on a reference time interval, and multiple rules can still be applicable for that interval.

If the valid time interval of the updated rule is not contained in the existing interval in S2, then at least one more instance of the rule is created in S2 will. All the other instances are updated such that their valid time interval does not overlap the new updated interval. versions.

Example: The existing rules are presented in Figure 6.

Version	Valid Time
Version 1	[1984, 1988)
Version 2	[1988, 1992)

Figure 6. The initial rules

A new version (Version 3) is inserted with valid time [1986,1990) in a valid time database, the updated table is shown in Figure 7.

Version	Valid Time
Version 1	[1984, 1986)
Version 3	[1986, 1990)
Version 2	[1990, 1992)

Figure 7. The updated rules

If the rule is activated with a reference time [1987, 1992) both version 2 and 3 are applicable and the rule version or versions according to the RAP value.

3.5 Bi-temporal rules

The bi-temporal database is unique in the sense that it can perform queries and updates of data in a certain period in time from another time point (also in the past).
In the context of rules, the bi-temporal model is useful for application of scenario analysis to perform hypothetical rule activations, such as: what would have been the results of applying the tax rule version that is valid in 1997, to the data that was inserted in 1995.

Since we are dealing with hypothetical updates, the updates should be performed on a replica.

Since it combines the properties of transaction time and valid time then the its behavior shares the property of both, as shown in the Figure 8:

Version	Transaction Time	Valid Time
Version 1	1983	[1984, 1988)
Version 2	1987	[1988, 1992)

Figure 8. The initial rules

A new version (Version 3) is inserted in 1989 with valid time [1986,1990) database, the updated table is shown in Figure 9.

Version	Transaction Time	Valid Time
Version 1	1983	[1984, 1988)
Version 2	1987	[1988,1992)
Version 3	1989	[1986,1990)

Figure 9. The updated rules

3.6 The language syntax

Rule insertion.

```
CREATE RULE   rule_name
ON event [ TO object]
WHERE condition
DO action
[VALID in [start,end)]
[USE rap_val]
[STATUS status]
```

Rule deletion.

```
DELETE RULE rule_name[(tvs)]
```

Rule activation status change.

```
ACTIVATE(rule_name)
DEACTIVATE(rule_name)
```

Rule modification.

```
UPDATE RULE   rule_name
[ON event [ TO object]]
[WHERE condition]
[DO action]
VALID in [start,end)
```

4. A Case Study

The objective of this example is to demonstrate different executions of rule versions at different times. Both the valid time or transaction time models can be used for that purpose. The major difference is that the transaction time model can execute rule versions from the time of their definition until deletion, in a continuous interval, while the valid time model is more flexible, and can use fragmented intervals for each version.

This example presents the resource allocation part of a project management system When a new project starts, the budget should be defined. The resource allocation is done concurrently with the employees' assignments, for more accurate evaluation of the project cost. The tax authorities approved amortization of allocated resources, so this amortization should be subtracted from the project cost. Until the year 1996 the deductible amortization for all electrical equipment was 20%/year. In 1997 it was increased to 33%/year for personal computing facilities.

The relevant relational structure:

Projects table

Project #
Start date
Budget
Expense
Manager

Assignments table

ID
Project #
Total hours

Resources table

Resource #
Model
Type
Cost
Amortized value

Resource assignments table

Resource #
Project #
TV

4.1 Defined rules:

```
CREATE RULE  amortization
ON insert  TO resource assignments AS RS
WHERE TRUE
DO update project expense(rs.project#, rs.resource#, 20%)
VALID in [1/1955,12/1996]
USE all
```

Updated version of the previous rule:

```
UPDATE RULE  amortization
ON insert  TO resource assignments AS rs
WHERE ( SELECT * FROM resources AS r  WHERE  r.type=!computer
AND r.resource # = rs.resource # )
DO update project expense(rs.project #, rs.resource #, 20%)
VALID in [1/1997, ∞)
```

A new rule that relates to personal computing facilities amortization:

```
CREATE RULE  amortization1
ON insert  TO resource assignments AS rs
WHERE ( SELECT * FROM resources AS r  WHERE  r.type=computer
AND r.resource # = rs.resource # )
DO update project expense(rs.project #, rs.resource #, 33%)
VALID in [1/1997, ∞)
USE all
```

4.2 Scenario:

Given the following projects:

Project #	start date	Budget	Expense	manager
500	1.1.95	1,000,000	0	123456
600	1.4.95	1,500,000	0	234567

Given the following resources:

Resource #	Model	Type	cost	Amortized val.
1	1995	Computer	2,000	0
2	1994	Video	300	0
3	1997	Computer	2,000	0

During the year 1995 the following assignments were done:

Resource #	Project #	Tv
1	500	[95,97]
2	500	[95,97]
3	600	[95,96]

In this event (insert to resource assignments), the rules: amortization and amortization1 are triggered. Since the RAP value of amortization is "all", all the rule versions that are valid in the data valid time, are executed.

The first assignment is valid during 95-97. The equipment type is "computer", so the updated version of amortization is not executed, and the original version which is valid for the relevant years 95-96 is executed with amortization rate of 20%/year. Amortization1 is executed as well for the year 97 with amortization rate of 33%/year.

The second assignment is valid during 95-97. Since the resource type is not "computer", both versions of amortization are executed: the original version for years 95-96, and the second one for year 97. Amortization1 is not executed since the resource type is not computer.

The third assignment is valid during 95-96. Since the resource type is "computer", the second version of amortization is not executed, but the first version with the relevant valid interval: [95-96], the amortization rate of 20%/year.

This example uses different amortization rates, thus a conceivable solution may be the use of temporal data (amortization rate) with the same rule each time. This is true if the ECA parts are the same and the only thing that changes is the evaluated data in those parts. If the action part is different, or the evaluated condition has been changed, a new version must be defined.

5 Conclusion

In this paper we have presented a new approach to "temporal rules". The suggested model enables retroactive and proactive rule version execution, by adding a new dimension to the rules.

The model supports simultaneous value semantics, so one can determine the desired rule version to be executed in a certain chronons out from the valid versions in that time. A new notion RAP (Rule Activation Policy) defines if a unified behavior is required over the reference interval, and determines the rule or rules to be executed.

The bi-temporal model supports scenario analysis, which enables execution of alternative rules.

Further research will extend the discussion to multiple context rules, in which, in addition to the time dimensions, other dimensions of space, multiple sources and others, are being used. This will be a natural, non-trivial, generalization of the model presented here.

References

1. Sharma Chakravarty, Deepak Mishra, Snoop : An Expressive Event Specification
   Language for Active Databases, *Data and Knowledge Engineering*, 13(3), October 1994.
2. R.. Snodgrass , I. Ahn. Temporal databases. *IEEE Computer, 19:35--42, Sep 1986.*
3. C. S. Jensen, C. E. Dyerson - The Consensus Glossary of Temporal Database Concepts - February 1998 version. In : O. Etzion, S. Jajodia, S. Sripada (eds) - *Temporal Databases: research and practice, Springer-Verlag, May 1998.*
4. Laine H. , Peltola E. , Grammatical Database Model, *information Systems*, Vol 4 pp. 257-267 ,1979.
5. Ariav G. : Temporally Oriented Data definitions : managing schema evolution in temporally oriented databases, *Data and Knowledge Engineering* Vol 6 pp. 451-467, 1991.
6. Avigdor Gal and Opher Etzion, A Multi-Agent Update Process in a Database with Temporal Data Dependencies and Schema Versioning *IEEE Transactions on Knowledge and Data Engineering.10(1), Feb 1998.*
7. A.P. Sistla and O. Wolfson, Temporal Triggers in Active Databases, *IEEE Transactions on Knowledge and Data Engineering* 7(3) pages 471-489 1995.
8. A.P. Sistla and O.Wolfson, Temporal Conditions and Integrity Constrains in Active Database Systems, *ARTDB* pages 122-141 1995.
9. O. Etzion, A. Gal , A. segev, Extended Update Functionality in Temporal Databases. In: O. Etzion, S. Jajodia, S. Sripada (eds) Temporal Databases, Research and Practice, Springer-Verlag. MAY 1998.

Cost-Effective Jukebox Storage via Hybrid File-Block Caching

Yitzhak Birk and Mark Mokryn

Technion – Israel Institute of Technology, Electrical Engineering Department,
Haifa 32000, Israel
{birk@ee, mark@psl}.technion.ac.il

Abstract. Caching jukeboxes combine the low media cost of CD and DVD with the higher performance of magnetic disk drives. We propose and evaluate the combination of aggressive file prefetching based on the a priori affinity among a file's blocks, with block-level usage tracking and removal. This apparently-inconsistent approach takes into account the usage time constants rather than merely the relative performance of two storage levels: the expected lifetime of a block in the large disk cache is long, rendering the fine-grain usage information much more meaningful than in higher levels of the memory hierarchy. Preliminary measurements carried out on our IntelliJuke prototype, along with comparative simulations, confirm the direct cost-performance benefits of our approach. One side benefit is increased effective mechanical reliability of the jukebox. Finally, this work motivates the support of sparse files on disk and illustrates the benefits of making additional information available to storage systems.

1 Introduction

Removable media such as CD-ROM, Digital Versatile Disc (DVD) and tape are attractive due to their physical portability, low media cost and high storage density. CD-ROM is currently the most widely used medium for software distribution, multimedia applications, encyclopedias, catalogs, and more. With the introduction of DVD, optical discs are approaching the storage capacities available on tape cartridges. Due to their immense popularity, this paper concentrates on effective storage techniques for a large number of optical discs, taking into account their common applications.

Organizations often possess many discs, which must be shared by many users. In such cases, manually swapping the discs in the drives is unrealistic. The viable storage options are: placing all the discs in drives, copying the data to magnetic drives, or using a robotic library (jukebox). In the latter case, a large number of discs share a small number of drives.

Table 1 depicts some basic parameters of the different options. We see that magnetic disks significantly outperform optical drives. Moreover, storing all the data on magnetic hard drives may be cheaper than using a "tower" of CDs. This advantage of magnetic disks is even more pronounced when CDs are not full to capacity, which is often the case. With DVD, however, copying all of the data to hard drives is not cost-effective at this time.

	Max Volume	$/MB	Mean Access Time	Transfer Rate (MB/sec)
Magnetic Disk	18 GB	0.05-0.15	12 ms	10-20
CD + Player	650 MB	≈ 0.15	100 ms	1.8-3.0
DVD + Player	17 GB	≈ 0.01	160 ms	1.3-2.7
Jukebox	100-600 discs	CD:$\approx$ 0.4-0.19 DVD:$\approx$ 0.001-0.07	3-20 sec for disc swap	2-4 player rate

Table 1. Basic parameters of disc storage options.

The remaining option is to use jukeboxes. One of the drawbacks of jukeboxes is the very long access time when the selected disc is not already in a drive. Jukebox manufacturers have attempted to reduce the disc swap time through the use of sophisticated mechanics. However, this has led to a tremendous increase in prices: high-capacity jukeboxes sell for $25-$125 per slot, depending mostly on robotic speed and reliability. High-capacity, low-performance audio jukeboxes, in contrast, sell for under $4 per slot. This is clearly a paradoxical situation: the original purpose of jukeboxes was to reduce system cost, yet a "high-performance" jukebox may be more expensive than a player per disc or storing all the data on magnetic hard drives, while offering inherently (much) worse performance. Thus, the only benefits of a jukebox are high volumetric density and low power consumption. Indeed, the beneficial use of jukeboxes is presently limited to infrequent, sparse access to very large amounts of data.

In view of the above, we have concluded that the path of optimizing robotic performance is a dead end. The main contribution of this paper is an approach that can make jukeboxes much more cost-effective, thereby extending their longevity and applicability. Our approach entails attaining different advantages through different means: low cost, high volumetric density and low power consumption (per unit data) will be provided by the jukebox, while high performance will be attained through the use of a cache on magnetic disks. To this end, we present a family of caching (fetching and replacement) policies that is uniquely suited to hierarchical storage systems for optical discs and their applications. These can be broadly described as hybrid file-block caching.

In addition to increasing performance, efficient caching would serve to dramatically reduce jukebox cost:

- Since media switches are responsible for most jukebox failures, and cache hits do not reach the jukebox, the mean time between failures for any given workload would be increased dramatically; alternatively, a far less reliable (and thus cheaper) jukebox would attain the same effective MTBF.
- The speed of the jukebox robotics would not be as important, so a slower one would suffice. This would dramatically reduce cost and possibly increase reliability.

We have embodied our ideas in IntelliJuke, a jukebox-based hierarchical storage management (HSM) system.

The remainder of this paper is organized as follows. In Section 2 we survey related work. In Section 3, we present our caching approach, and Section 4 describes IntelliJuke, our server prototype. Section 5 compares our caching scheme with traditional ones, and Section 6 offers concluding remarks along with directions for future research.

2 Related Work

In this section, we survey related work in several relevant areas: file-access patterns, file caching, block caching, distributed file systems, and jukeboxes.

2.1 File Access Patterns

Studies such as [1] and [2] have shown that a small fraction of files accounts for the vast majority of file accesses. [2] analyzed file accesses in several disparate environments over periods exceeding 150 days. On an average day, fewer than 5% of the files were referenced; of the files remaining at the end of any trace period, fewer than 30% were ever used. In addition, file accesses exhibited strong properties of temporal locality of reference. If a file was accessed on one day but not on the next, it had less than a 10% chance of being accessed on the third day. Moreover, it had only a 15%-45% chance of ever being accessed again! The above observations support the idea of hierarchical storage, whereby active data resides in fast magnetic disk and the vast majority of data resides in tertiary storage.

2.2 File-Caching HSMs

In such HSMs, the unit that is cached or removed is a file. The HSM sits above the file system in the hierarchy of system drivers (Figure 1), intercepts all file accesses, and carries out the caching operations. Implementation of file caching not as part as the operating system is complicated by the complexity and variability of file systems and their interfaces, which also makes porting difficult. Moreover, some operating systems do not support the insertion of third-party components above the file system. Until recently, this was the case with Microsoft's Windows NT. The main challenge with file caching, however, is dealing with cache objects of widely varying sizes.

In the systems analyzed in [2], 80% or more of the files were smaller than 32KB. However, over 50% of the data stored on disk belonged to files larger than 256KB. [3] and [4] showed that while most accesses are to small files, the majority of bytes transferred belong to relatively large files. These observations raise the open question of how to prioritize cached files: is it preferable to flush many small files or fewer large ones? At two opposite ends of the spectrum we have LRU, which flushes files based on their most recent access times, and the size-only algorithm, which flushes the largest file in the cache, striving to maximize the number of cached files. The

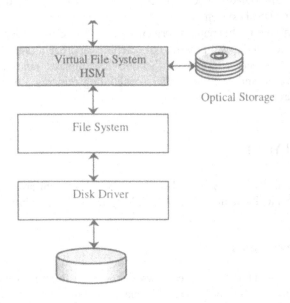

Fig. 1. HSM above the file system

Space-Time Product (STP) algorithm represents a compromise: it removes files with the highest value of *Size·Time*, where *Time* is the time since last reference. [5] and [6] found that for their respective traces, basing the caching priority on $Size·Time^{1.4}$ outperformed all the priority functions with which they compared it. See [7], [8] and [9] for additional file-caching algorithms.

2.3 Block-Caching HSMs

Figure 2 depicts a functional diagram of a block-caching HSM. The IBM Daisy HSM [10] is an example of such an implementation. Here, the hierarchical management software intercepts the user requests between the native file system driver and the actual disk access. One advantage of such a system is its simplicity: the interface to a disk system is much simpler than the interface to a file system. Also, virtual-disk HSMs are much more portable than virtual file system HSMs. In fact, it is even possible to place the HSM software on the disk interface card (e.g. SCSI card). Caching equal-sized objects also simplifies space management. Finally, virtual-disk HSMs work well with systems (such as databases) which operate on raw partitions. In these cases, there is no file system on top of which one can place HSM code.

The big disadvantage of virtual-disk HSMs is their lack of file knowledge. This makes prefetching a mostly capricious enterprise. Unknown file sizes make it impossible to know whether the data immediately following a requested block on the physical medium belongs to the same file. In read-write systems, file fragmentation

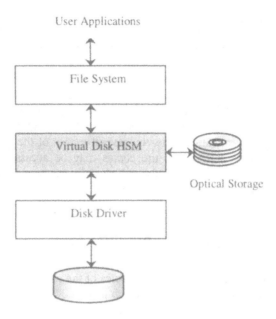

Fig. 2. HSM below file system

may moreover cause logically contiguous data to be scattered throughout the physical medium. Consequently, block-caching HSMs are very conservative in their prefetch sizes. (An aggressive prefetch policy for a block-caching system may fetch up to 64KB [11].) These issues make traditional block caching mostly unsuitable for hierarchical management of tertiary storage. Due to the long access times to tertiary storage devices, it is critical to perform large, effective prefetches to secondary storage.

2.4 Distributed File Systems

Caching is also employed by distributed file systems (DFSs) such as [12], [13], [14], and [15]. In a DFS, clients cache server-resident data in order to improve client performance and reduce network traffic and server load. An important aspect of DFS design is the cache coherency mechanism, since multiple clients may simultaneously cache identical objects. This is in contrast with hierarchical storage managers, which are typically centralized entities. Another major difference between DFSs and hierarchical storage is the much lower cache miss penalty seen in DFSs. Since the DFS miss penalty is measured in milliseconds, data prefetching takes on less importance, and most DFSs perform block caching with relatively modest prefetching.

2.5 Commercial Jukebox Servers

For information on commercial jukebox servers, see [16], [17], [18], and [19]. From the publicly available data on these systems, it appears that data caching has taken a backseat to considerations such as easy CD management, network accessibility, and archival support. Most commercial systems store on disk the entire directory structures of all the CDs. Most also permit the mirroring of selected CDs or files to hard disk in order to lessen the load on popular titles. Another approach to this end entails the use of replication, whereby several copies of the same disc are placed in multiple jukeboxes, and any of the copies may be accessed at any time. Some systems offer memory- or disk-caching of recently accessed blocks or files. Details of their implementations are for the most part not publicly available.

3 The Case for Hybrid File-Block Caching

In this section, we identify the characteristics of the elements of our storage system as well as interesting applications and access patterns. Based on those, we arrive at our caching approach. Unlike many discussions of hierarchical memory or storage systems, which focus on the relative performance of two adjacent layers while ignoring the absolute numbers, we do take those into account.

The miss penalty (jukebox access, possibly including waiting for a drive and switching media) is extremely high. The transfer rate, in contrast, is reasonable. Finally, the cache (magnetic hard drive) is not very expensive. In view of all this, effective prefetching is very important, and aggressive prefetching is viable. The best way to prefetch effectively is to use content-related information such as a priori affinity among blocks of data. The simplest example of this is blocks belonging to the same file. Another example is files that are known to be related, such as files with the same name and different suffixes. Such affinity information can also be supplied as hints or acquired in other ways. In any case, its exploitation precludes simple block prefetching and requires knowledge of the file-level information associated with a request.

The low cost of the cache not withstanding, large amounts of data are involved. Therefore, effective cache utilization is also important. Having done our best for prefetching (which is nonetheless still a speculative operation), we next turn our attention to the replacement policy. We begin by examining typical applications of jukeboxes, such as storing reference material.

Consider for example a popular library application, the Electronic Reference Library [20]. ERL provides browser-based network access to library indexes and catalogs, which are distributed on CDs. A large ERL library may hold tens or hundreds of CDs. A typical CD in the ERL system contains only a few files, and most of the data is found in files that are a few hundred megabytes in size. Clearly, these files are actually data structures that are accessed very sparsely. A similar situation exists in Microsoft's *Encarta95* encyclopedia: the Encarta disc contains many files, but most of the data is in three files, sized 79 MB, 144 MB, and 242 MB. Yet another similar example is the two-CD set of the journal *Software – Practice &*

Experience (SP&E) which contains papers from 1971 to 1990. The SP&E discs contain two huge files, sized 300 MB and 571 MB, along with several small files.

Since it is common to see huge files on CDs, especially on CDs containing reference material, and these files are moreover accessed sparsely, it is important to efficiently handle such files. Clearly, file caching does not do this. Given the justification for aggressive speculative prefetching, the solution called for is fine-grain usage tracking and eviction, e.g., at single-block granularity. However, so doing appears to be inconsistent with the rationale that led us to file-oriented prefetching. We next attempt to resolve this apparent inconsistency.

Since the cache (disk) is inexpensive and large, it is reasonable to design the system so that data can reside in the cache for many hours, possibly even days, after it has last been accessed, before it must be flushed. Considering the time frame of a user's activity and the findings of [2], the fact that a block has not been accessed throughout such a time interval provides a very strong indication (albeit not a guarantee) that it will not be accessed in the near future. We wish to stress that it is the consideration of the relevant time frame rather than relative performance which provides this insight. In fact, the same kind of argument would not hold for higher levels of the hierarchy, which are characterized by very short lifetimes, since one could rightfully argue that a block not accessed may very well have not **yet** been accessed.

Based on the foregoing observations and arguments, we believe that a hybrid policy is uniquely suitable for the caching situation considered in this paper. Such a policy would combine aggressive (pre)fetching based on a priori (or acquired) affinity information with fine-grained eviction based on a posteriori information (usage tracking). In the next section, we describe a prototype that implements such a policy.

4 The IntelliJuke Network-Attached HSM

The IntelliJuke jukebox server prototype was designed and constructed by the authors along with a team of students in the Parallel Systems Laboratory, and is presently operational. IntelliJuke was constructed in order to demonstrate our hybrid caching policies, permit the collection of traces from a live environment, and serve as a vehicle for further research into hybrid caching policies.

4.1 System Overview

IntelliJuke is implemented on a PC running Windows NT 4.0, and manages discs that are stored in a Kubik CDR-240 jukebox. The jukebox has 240 slots, and is presently equipped with two 12X CD-ROM drives. Disc exchange time is approximately 18 seconds.

IntelliJuke uses a large magnetic-disk cache and employs an aggressive prefetching strategy. To perform large prefetches effectively, the hierarchical storage manager is placed above the file system, thus implementing a virtual file system manager. Following a miss, IntelliJuke sequentially fetches the lesser of the entire file and 10MB. By placing IntelliJuke above the file system, it receives high-level information. This can be used for fetching related files, e.g., an executable and its accompanying help file. Usage tracking and eviction are carried out at single-block granularity. The replacement policy is presently an LRU approximation.

In order to flush individual blocks from a file, our scheme requires support for sparse files. Windows NT 4.0 does not provide this, but it does support file compression, which among its various techniques does not allocate disk space for all-zero blocks. The use of compression in order to flush blocks, in addition to a special mechanism that we had to implement in order to indicate on-disk blocks, incurs a performance penalty. Windows NT 5.0 will support sparse files, including the de-allocation of ranges and obtaining a list of allocated blocks within a range. In Unix, the "lseek" command may be used to seek beyond the end-of-file and thus create a sparse file, but this is not enough.

IntelliJuke is also equipped with a tracing facility that can log user requests and system responses for subsequent analysis. The traces can also be fed to simulations of various systems and caching schemes for comparison purposes.

4.2 Cache Structure

In order to maintain a relationship between a file and its cached blocks, we maintain a hash table that contains a node for each file, and link a file node to its cached blocks' metadata (see Figure 3). We decided to implement a coarse LRU replacement scheme, in which there are very few cache priority levels. For our purposes, implementing an exact LRU would be too expensive in both memory usage and time of execution. If file-to-block associations and cache priorities were to be maintained separately for every block, then in the worst case we could end up with four pointers for each cached block: a forward and back pointer to other cached blocks, and a couple of pointers to link a block with its file. This would also have an adverse effect on performance, since an access to each block could, in the worst case, result in pointer manipulation for every accessed block. Instead, we decided on the following structure: the cache metadata is arranged in several "age" buckets. Each bucket contains a doubly-linked list of bitmap nodes. Each such node indicates the on-disk blocks of a specific (file, age) combination. Note that a file F may have at most one node in any given bucket, but it may have nodes in multiple buckets. Pointers between bucket nodes and their corresponding file node correlate a file with its cache metadata, thereby permitting both block- and file-based cache management decisions.

Figure 3 depicts the structure of the cache metadata for a system with four age buckets. In this example, we see that file F, whose total size is 16 blocks, has blocks 0 through 3 on-disk. Blocks 0 and 1 reside in age 0, and blocks 2 and 3 are in age 3. File F does not have any on-disk blocks in ages 1 and 2. The memory cost for our bitmap is one bit per block. In addition, we have four pointers per bitmap. In the worst case, for a system configured with N age buckets, N bits represent a block, and there are $4N$ pointers per file. Since we intend on a small number of buckets, this is far cheaper than four times the number of file blocks, which would be the case with a strict LRU implementation. For a 4 GB disk cache, formatted at 1 KB per block and configured with four age buckets, the maximum bitmap cost is 4 MB, clearly a reasonable amount. In the worst possible case, we have 4 million files and eight pointers per file (three of them are null); the total cost of pointers is 128 MB, an amount that may be handled by a very large paging file. In practice, however, disk partitions are formatted for block sizes larger than 1 KB, with typical block sizes of 4 KB and 8 KB for large disk partitions, thus reducing the total overhead. Also, the vast majority of files are much larger than 1 KB in size, so the total pointer cost is lower by several orders of magnitude. In fact, we measured actual memory usage of only 2-4 MB when presenting 50 CDs with thousands of files, on a cache of 2 GB. The cache was formatted for 1KB blocks.

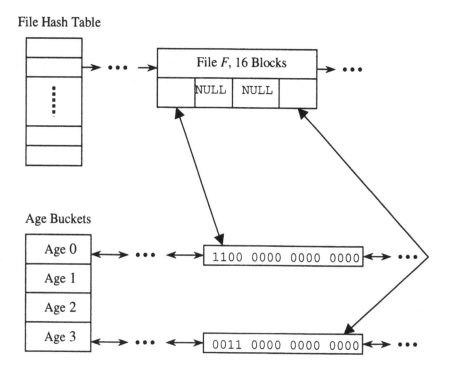

Fig. 3. Cache structure

When implementing an LRU replacement policy, we set the bits corresponding to the accessed blocks in the bucket node that is in the youngest age. If there are other bucket nodes for the accessed file, we make sure to unset their corresponding bits. Therefore, a given data block may not belong to more than one age. A bucket node that has no set bits is deleted.

Whenever the size (number of blocks) of the youngest-age bucket passes a given threshold, the system is aged. Aging entails two simple steps, and does not require copying:

1. Merge the bucket representing the oldest age into the bucket representing the second oldest age. The bucket representing the oldest age is now empty.

2. Rotate the age index. If A represents the number of ages, and bucket i represented an age j *(i.e. Age(i)=j),* then *Age(i)=(j+1)mod A.* The empty bucket that used to represent the oldest age now represents the youngest (age zero).

Whenever the amount of used disk space exceeds a high watermark, blocks residing in the oldest bucket are de-allocated until the amount of used disk space falls below a low watermark. If the bucket becomes empty in the process, step 2 of the aging algorithms is performed and a new, empty youngest bucket is created.

Our implementation allows us to prioritize cached data at will: for example, prefetched data can be placed in one of the older buckets. If the prefetched data is touched, it will naturally rise to the youngest age. This differential treatment would reduce the detrimental effect of an overly large prefetch. It must be stressed that we present a multi-level cache structure, which may serve as the basis for almost any file- or block-based cache management algorithm. For example, by reversing the cache priorities, we easily emulate MRU replacement. By adding a simple FIFO element, we may emulate the 2Q algorithm [8].

4.3 Deployment

IntelliJuke has been available to all users in the electrical engineering department at the Technion for several months, with over 50 CDs. The CDs contain approximately 20 GB in 60,000 files. Applications include games, conference proceedings, and encyclopedias. Over a certain period of eleven days, more than 530,000 reads were registered.

Presently, the system is being refined and will soon be ported to Windows NT 5.0, which should also improve performance due to the direct support for sparse files. Subsequently, it will serve as a platform for the collection of interesting traces and for experiments with variants of the hybrid caching approach.

5 Performance

We have written a simulation model of the IntelliJuke system using the Workbench event-driven simulation package (created by Scientific Engineering Software, Inc.). The model is linked with modified versions of the actual IntelliJuke code. The only modifications were the removal of all system calls, such as file accesses, semaphore operations, etc. Disk and CD access delays, as well as action dependencies (such as blocking reads when there are simultaneous misses to more CDs than the available number of drives), were simulated using the Workbench tools. For cache management, the simulator uses the modified IntelliJuke code. The simulator operates on actual IntelliJuke system traces. Each trace event indicates the file name, time of the event, and event type (e.g. open, close, read). Read events also include the starting offset and length.

Using the simulator, we can compare the effects of changing the cache size, caching algorithms, or various IntelliJuke system parameters. Thanks to the powerful statistics-gathering tools of Workbench, we can easily track system attributes such as miss rates and response time.

Our cache structure facilitates simulation of other caching policies. In order to simulate file caching, we always prefetch the entire file following a miss. A read access to a file always causes the entire file to be placed in age zero in the cache. Thus, for file caching, a file present in the cache is always allotted one bitmap. Block caching is characterized by very small prefetches. We emulate block caching in two ways. In one, we perform no prefetching and simply update the cache bitmaps according to the actual reads; in the other, we simulate "smart" block caching, in which we perform a "perfect" 64 KB prefetch following a miss, i.e., we fetch the next 64 KB of the file or until the end of the file, whichever is shorter. In reality, block caching rarely performs these large prefetches effectively, due to fragmentation and unknown file sizes. Still, these prefetches are far smaller than those performed by our hybrid caching scheme. The real performance of block caching probably lies somewhere between that of zero and 64 KB prefetching. We compared the performance of file and block caching with that of hybrid caching. Hybrid caching was simulated with both an upper limit of 10MB on prefetch size, and with prefetching of the entire file upon a miss (regardless of file size). The system was configured with four age buckets, ages zero to three. For hybrid caching, prefetched data was placed in age two, thus initially giving it a lower cache priority than user-requested data.

In order to demonstrate the effectiveness of hybrid file-block caching for applications that access large files, we compared the various algorithms using a trace of accesses to three CDs containing reference material. The CDs, described earlier, were *Encarta95* and the two-CD set of the journal *Software – Practice & Experience* (SP&E). The simulated jukebox contained a single drive.

5.1 Trace Characterization and Generation

Sparse file access is exemplified by the access pattern caused by browsing a ten-page article in SP&E. The access included navigating to a specific volume and issue, and browsing the article in its entirety. The accessed file is 300 MB in size. The access pattern included five chunks ranging in size from 3 KB to 8KB, all located within the first 8 MB of the file, probably corresponding to navigation through the table of contents. Following these accesses, we see accesses to a 640 KB chunk starting at a file offset of 75 MB, presumably the actual article. The accesses for this article touched approximately 0.2% of the entire file.

The access trace to the three CDs was obtained by simultaneous use of Encarta and SP&E over a period of three hours. Most accesses to Encarta were by jumping to related topics, starting with a general interest in medieval European history. Articles in SP&E were browsed based on keywords. Interesting articles were on occasion reread, while others were not always read in their entirety. There were 5087 read events over the three-hour period, totaling 73 MB from a working set of 33 MB.

5.2 Simulation Results

Figure 4 depicts the relative performance of the various caching algorithms as a function of cache size in a simulation run on this trace, starting with a cold cache. Simulated cache sizes ranged from 100 MB to 1.5 GB.

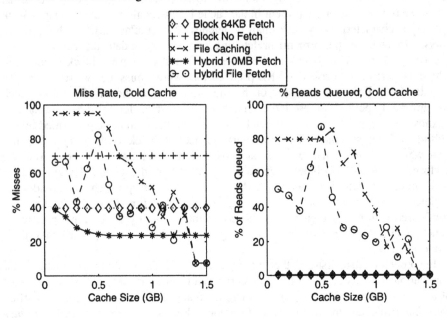

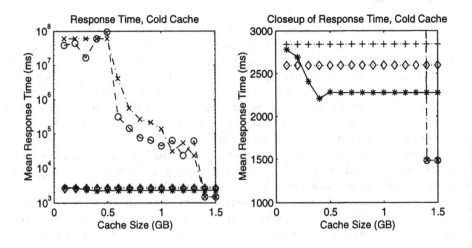

Fig. 4. Reference material trace, cold cache

The performance measure in the plots are miss rates, response times, and the percentage of read requests which are queued to the jukebox, i.e., they are misses to a disc that is not in a drive.

Since the accessed files are up to 500 MB in size, file-caching clearly requires at least that size in order to have a fighting chance. In fact, even the simulation of file caching was not able to operate below this size, and thus all the plot points up to and including 500 MB are artificial. They were included merely to overcome technical plotting problems. Of course it is unfair to expect file caching to operate on the smaller caches, but we wish to show that the other algorithms may operate successfully in this range. However, as we can see in the plots, even increasing the cache well beyond the largest possible file size did not allow file caching to perform reasonably. File caching performed miserably throughout the range, even when the cache was large enough to contain several of the huge files. Essentially, file caching was effective only when the cache was large enough to simultaneously contain all of the accessed files. In effect, for file caching to work in this scenario, the three CDs have to be copied almost in their entirety to the cache!

Since the access footprint is only 33 MB, large cache sizes had no effect on the performance of block caching. Block caching was stable throughout the tested range, with high miss rates due to the relatively small, if any, prefetch. Note that a 64 KB prefetch was able to bring the miss rate from 70% down to approximately 40%.

Hybrid file-block caching with a 10 MB prefetch provided the lowest miss rate by far. Hybrid file-block caching with a full file fetch provided mediocre to poor results, somewhere between the range of file caching and hybrid caching with a limited prefetch.

One must bear in mind that very aggressive prefetching may have several negative effects besides the possibility of filling the cache with unnecessary data. If a large prefetch is performed concurrently with requests to the disc directed at other files or to other regions of the same file, then those requests will suffer a long delay, and there is a possibility of the drive head thrashing. Most importantly, we must bear in mind that prefetching an entire 500 MB file from CD-ROM may take several minutes. This may have a strong negative effect for jukeboxes, since we may "lock" the disc in the drive unnecessarily for a very long time and cause requests for other discs to queue up. (Preemption is possible, but is extremely expensive in terms of lost drive work.) Thus, we see that file caching and hybrid caching with a full-file fetch have numerous queued requests when compared with the other algorithms, even at points at which they have lower miss rates. Their high number of queued reads leads to very poor average response times. We can see this phenomenon in Figure 4, wherein for caches greater than 700 MB, file caching and hybrid caching with a full-file fetch have lower miss rates than block caching, yet they have much longer response times.

Figure 5 depicts the results of the same simulation when run on a cache that was "warmed up" by simulating the same trace back-to-back. Thus, Figure 5 shows how well the various caching algorithms "remember" the previous accesses, as a function of cache size.

As we can see, block caching has the best memory, since it brings in very little, if any, superfluous data. Thus, after warming up the cache, block caching retains all relevant data in a very small cache. The other algorithms suffer due to the large prefetches, which bring in much data that is never accessed. Warming up the cache

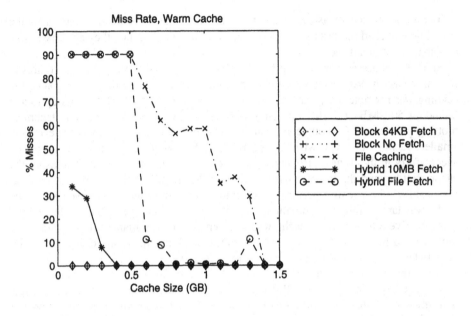

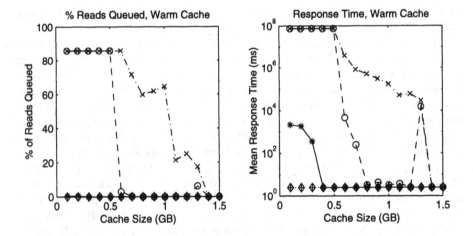

Fig. 5. Reference material trace, warm cache

for file caching has no positive effect, since it just continues to cycle large files in and out of the cache. Warming up the cache has a strong positive effect on hybrid caching, even when it performs a full file fetch. Clearly, its fine-grained block replacement policy allows hybrid caching to retain much of the relevant data in the cache. Warm-up of a cache of only 400 MB was enough for zero misses for hybrid caching with 10 MB prefetch. For hybrid caching with a full-file fetch, a cache of 600 MB sufficed to bring the miss rate down to a reasonable range.

The simulation results exhibit occasional non-monotonic behavior, as exemplified by the warm-cache plots for the hybrid scheme with a full file fetch at a cache size of 1.3 GB. This is apparently due to a combination of the small trace size and the merger of the two oldest buckets in the aging phase. The absence of such a phenomenon with the more moderate prefetches is a possible reinforcement to the intuition whereby one should restrict the prefetch size due to various detrimental effects and a diminishing return. Such phenomena are nonetheless unlikely to be visible in longer traces of systems with larger caches, which is really the more interesting case. (We had difficulty in generating heavy real-user load, and were consequently forced to use a small cache in order to have non-compulsory misses.)

If the simulation results are indicative of the relative performance of the different schemes in the case of concurrent accesses to numerous large files, the message is clear: file-caching would require a huge cache for reasonable performance; block caching would require a relatively small cache, but provides mediocre performance due to its limited prefetch. Therefore, hybrid file-block caching, preferably with an upper limit on prefetch size, emerges as the preferred approach for this environment.

6 Conclusions

This work was motivated by the frustration caused when trying to take advantage of the low cost of removable optical media in a shared-data environment. Even the willingness to sacrifice performance and use high-capacity jukeboxes did not help. This is due to the attempt by jukebox vendors to increase performance and reliability through mechanical means, which resulted in very high cost. Noting the futility of this direction, we decided to explore the merits of a hierarchical system in which the jukebox would be optimized for low cost and high volumetric density, whereas performance would be provided by caching data on a magnetic disk drive. The focus of the work was to understand the building blocks and the typical applications, and to then find the most suitable caching policy.

An examination of the characteristics of the various system components, the typical types of files residing on CDs and the way in which they are accessed has led us to the combination of aggressive file-oriented prefetching with fine-grain block-level usage tracking and eviction. The sensibility of this approach was reinforced by the observation that the lifetime of stale data in the cache is likely to be longer than the time frame of user accesses. Therefore, when the LRU order calls for the eviction of a "stale" block of an otherwise "active" file, the risk that it would be requested in the near future (resulting in a large miss penalty and consumption of precious jukebox resources) is very low. Note that in higher levels of the memory hierarchy, the confidence level would be much lower due to the shorter lifetime of a stale block (while the user's time frame is the same...). Our simulations subsequently confirmed the advantage of the resulting hybrid file-block caching architecture.

The IntelliJuke prototype is operational, and may soon be used in "production" environments, serving to collect interesting traces. Also, its cache architecture lends itself to simple modifications that permit implementation of a variety of caching policies. Future research will examine such policies and will extend the system to read/write media. Note that since our cache is inherently non-volatile, the caching of write data does not introduce a consistency problem.

In addition to increasing performance, maintaining a low miss rate obviates the need for highly reliable high-performance jukeboxes. This may help drop the price of jukeboxes by an order of magnitude while maintaining or even improving system performance and reliability relative to the present state. It may thus after all be possible to benefit from the low media cost in data-sharing environments.

This paper dealt with optical jukeboxes, but an examination of robotic tape libraries is also warranted. Since the similarities are clear as are some differences, the initial focus should be on characterization of "typical" applications.

Finally, two messages to operating-system designers: effective prefetching by a storage system is important, so higher-level information such as file names must be made available to it; also, system support for sparse files on disk is essential.

Acknowledgments. The contributions and product donations of EMC^2, Scientific Engineering Software and Microsoft are greatly appreciated. Also, the contributions of Uri Kareev, Eran Rosenberg, Eyal Zangi, Amnon Govrin and Ran Herzberg to the implementation of the IntelliJuke prototype [21] are gratefully acknowledged.

References

1. Smith, A.J., "Analysis of Long Term File Reference Patterns for Application to File Migration Algorithms," *IEEE Transactions on Software Engineering*, vol. 7 no. 4, 1981, pp. 403-417.
2. Gibson, T., Miller, E.L., Long, D., "Long-term File Activity and Inter-Reference Patterns," submitted to the CMG '98 Conference, December 1998, Anaheim, CA.
3. Baker, M.G., Hartman, J.H., Kupfer, M.D., Shirriff, K.W., and Ousterhout, J.K., "Measurements of a Distributed File System," *Proceedings of the 13th ACM Symposium on Operating Systems Principles*, 1991, pp. 198-212.
4. Ousterhout, J.K., Da Costa, H., Harrison, D., Kunze, J.A., Kupfer, M., and Thompson, J.G., "A Trace-Driven Analysis of the UNIX 4.2 BSD File System," *Proceedings of the 10th Symposium on Operating System Principles*, Orcas Island, WA, December 1985, pp. 15-24.
5. Smith, A.J., "Long Term File Migration: Development and Evaluation of Algorithms," *Communications of the ACM*, vol. 24 no. 8, 1981, pp. 521-532.
6. Strange, S., "Analysis of Long-Term Unix File Access Patterns for Application to Automatic File Migration Strategies," Technical Report UCB/CSD-92-700, Computer Science Division (EECS), University of California, Berkeley, CA, 1992.
7. Gibson, T., *Long-term File System Activity and the Efficacy of Automatic File Migration*, Computer Science Doctoral Dissertation, University of Maryland Baltimore County, May 1998.
8. Johnson, T., and Shasha, D., "2Q: A Low Overhead High Performance Buffer Management Replacement Algorithm," *Proceedings of the 20th Very Large Database (VLDB) Conference*, Santiago, Chile, 1994, pp. 439-450.

9. O'Neil, E.J., O'Neil, P.E., and Weikum, G., "The LRU-k Page Replacement Algorithm for Database Disk Buffering," *Proc. 1993 ACM SIGMOD International Conference on Management of Data*, 1993, pp. 297-306.
10. Menon, J., and Treiber, K., "Daisy: Virtual-disk Hierarchical Storage Manager," *SIGMETRICS Performance Evaluation Review*, vol. 25, no. 3, 1997, pp.37-44.
11. Rochberg, D., and Gibson, G., "Prefetching Over a Network: Early Experience with CTIP," *SIGMETRICS Performance Evaluation Review*, vol. 25, no. 3, 1997, pp. 29-36.
12. Howard, J.H., Kazar, M.L., Menees, S.G., Nichols, D.A., Satyanarayanan, M., Sidebotham, R.N., and West, M.J., "Scale and Performance in a Distributed File System," *ACM Transactions on Computer Systems*, vol. 6 no. 1, Feb. 1988, pp. 51-81.
13. Nelson, M.N., Welch, B.B., and Ousterhout, J.K., "Caching in the Sprite Network File System," *ACM Transactions on Computer Systems*, vol. 6 no. 1, Feb. 1988, pp.134-154.
14. Satyanarayanan, M., Kistler, J.J., Kumar, P., Okasaki, M.E., Siegel, E.H., and Steere, D.C. "Coda: A Highly Available File System for a Distributed Workstation Environment," *IEEE Transactions on Computers*, vol. 39, no. 4, Apr. 1990, pp. 447-459.
15. Sandberg, R., Goldberg, D., Kleiman, S., Walsh, D., and Lyon, B., "Design and Implementation of the Sun Network File System," *Proc. of the Summer 1985 USENIX*, June 1985, pp. 119-130.
16. Ixos Inc., web site: http://www.ixos.com
17. Ornetix Inc., web site: http://www.ornetix.com
18. SmartStorage Inc., web site: http://www.smartstorage.com
19. TenX Technology Inc., 100 Mbit Ethernet TenXpert CD-ROM File Server Reference Manual, P/N 25-079, April 1998.
20. SilverPlatter Information inc., ERL Administrator's Manual, September 1998.
21. Govrin, A.I., Herzberg, R., Kareev, U., Rosenberg, E., and Zangi, E., "IntelliJuke – A Smart Hierarchical Storage Server," Parallel Systems Lab Project Reports, Elec. Eng. Dept. Technion, Israel Institute of Technology, 1996.

Ontology-Driven Integration of Scientific Repositories[1]

Vassilis Christophides[1,2], Catherine Houstis[1,2], Spyros Lalis[1,2], and Hariklia Tsalapata[2]

[1]Department of Computer Science, University of Crete,
P.O. Box 1470, GR-71110 Heraklion, Greece
[2]Institute of Computer Science, Foundation for Research and Technology – Hellas,
P.O. Box 1385 Heraklion, Greece
{christop, houstis, lalis, htsalapa}@ics.forth.gr

Abstract. There is an increasing need to provide scientists and researchers as well as policy makers and the general public with value-added services integrating information spread over distributed heterogeneous repositories. In order to incorporate available data sets and scientific programs into a powerful information and computational system it is mandatory to identify and exploit their semantic relationship. For this purpose, we advocate an ontological framework that captures these relations and allows the inference of valid combinations of scientific resources for the production of new data. We show how a knowledge base that commits to an ontology can be used to generate workflows on demand for the multiplicity of resources known to the system. To validate our ideas, we are currently developing a prototype for the area of Coastal Zone Management.

1 Introduction

The rapid development of distributed computing infrastructures and the growth of the Internet and the WWW have revolutionized the management, processing, and dissemination of scientific information. Repositories that have traditionally evolved in isolation are now connected to global networks making their content available worldwide. In addition, with common data exchange formats [19], [25], [35], standard database access interfaces [27], [30], and emerging information mediation and brokering technologies (see middleware support in the context of I3 [26] and DLI [22]), data repositories can be accessed without knowledge of their internal syntax and storage structure. Furthermore, search engines [5], [18], [23] are enabling users to locate distributed resources by indexing appropriate metadata descriptions [14], [20], [24], [33]. Open communication architectures [4], [32], [34] provide support for language-independent remote invocation of legacy code thereby paving the way towards a globally distributed library of scientific programs. Finally, workflow management systems exist for coordinating and monitoring the execution of scientific

---

[1] This work was supported in part by the THETIS Project, EU Research on Telematics Programme, nr. F0069, URL: http://www.ics.forth.gr/pleiades/THETIS/thetis.html.

computations. The standardization and interoperability of workflow systems is pursued by the WMC [36].

This technology can be successfully used to address system, syntactic, and structural interoperability of distributed heterogeneous scientific repositories. However, interoperability at the semantic level remains a challenging issue [13]. Users still face the problem of identifying scientific resources that can be combined to produce new data. This is of key importance for providing widely diversified user groups with advanced, value-added information services.

In this paper we address the problem of producing meaningful combinations of available data sets and scientific programs to generate data needed for a particular task (e.g. environmental planning, forecasting). We advocate an ontological framework that captures domain and task specific knowledge in terms of concepts abstracting data sets, and relations between them abstracting implementations of physical models. We show how a Knowledge Base System (KBS) that commits to this ontology can infer valid combinations of scientific resources, alleviating the need to manually construct workflows. This process is dynamic, depending on the availability of data and programs. To validate our approach, we are currently developing a prototype for Coastal Zone Management [9].

The rest of the paper is organized as follows. Section 2 presents an example scenario regarding the generation of waste transport data for coastal areas. Section 3 introduces a corresponding application-specific ontology, provides its formal representation in a KBS, and illustrates the goal-driven generation of data production paths. In Section 4, a system architecture that employs this approach to integrate scientific repositories is sketched. Section 5 gives an overview of related work. Finally, Section 6 concludes and sets future research directions.

2 A Scenario for Coastal Zone Management

Environmental scientists and public institutions working on Coastal Zone Management (CZM) often need to extract and combine data from different scientific disciplines, such as marine biology, physical and chemical oceanography, geology, and engineering, stored in distributed repositories. Consider, for instance, the transport of waste in a particular coastal area given a pollution source. Local authorities could require this information to determine the best location for installing a waste pipeline.

This data is typically generated through a two-step process, involving the execution of two different programs (as shown in Fig. 1). First, Sea Circulation data is produced for the area of interest via an Ocean Circulation model that takes as input local Bathymetry and global (boundary) Current conditions. Then, Waste data is generated via a Waste Transport model that takes as input local Sea Circulation and Bathymetry data as well as the characteristics of the pollution source.

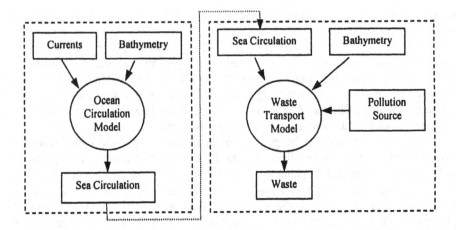

Fig. 1. Combination of data and programs for producing waste transport data. The production of *Sea Circulation* data is sketched on the *left* while the production of *Waste* data, which depends on the existence of *Sea Circulation* data, is given on the *right*.

Provided that the user has no knowledge of this information, the following actions are necessary to discover which productions can be used to obtain Waste data for a particular coastal area using the available resources:

1. Locate Waste data stored in the distributed repositories. This is typically done through a search engine that takes as input a few keywords and returns a list of relevant resource descriptions (metadata) available in the repositories.

2. Determine usability of search results. Due to the complexity of scientific metadata this requires a detailed inspection, as opposed to casual browsing, of the returned descriptions; the FGDC standard, for example, is several pages long.

3. If no Waste data that satisfies the user requirements is available (e.g. there is no data for the particular coastal area), locate programs capable of producing this data. Again, this involves a metadata search and examination of the returned program descriptions.

4. Having identified an appropriate program, i.e. a Waste Transport model, determine the required input. Ideally, this information is part of the program's metadata, else it must be acquired by contacting the creators of the program.

5. For each input, locate appropriate sources or determine ways to produce corresponding data sets. For instance, if Sea Circulation data is not available for the area of interest the possibility of producing it via an Ocean Circulation model must be pursued.

It becomes evident that manual discovery of combinations of data sets and programs that can lead to the production of desired data is tedious. It requires a rigorous investigation and understanding of metadata descriptions. This is difficult for a non-expert operating in a multidisciplinary environment. In addition, the user must keep track of interrelated searches to discover possible ways of producing data for a particular task. As shown in the above example, this can be hard to achieve even for a relatively simple scenario with merely a couple of intermediate computation steps.

Therefore, support for deriving valid combinations of data and programs in a straightforward way is invaluable, particularly for large information systems. To achieve this, we use a Knowledge Base System (KBS) that captures the expertise of scientists regarding the semantic relationships between scientific resources. This allows on-demand generation of data production paths without significant effort on the user's behalf.

3 Integration of Scientific Resources via a KBS

In the following, we present our approach by introducing an ontology along the lines of the Waste Transport scenario. Then, we show how this ontology can be captured in the form of rules stored in a KBS to support goal-driven generation of valid productions.

3.1 An Ontology for the Waste Transport Scenario

An ontology [7] describes concepts and relationships among them related to a particular domain, task, or application. Ontologies can be used to share knowledge about specific aspects of the real world between individual agents in an unambiguous way. Thus, as stressed in [13], capturing commonly agreed knowledge in terms of ontologies is a major step towards addressing semantic interoperability in information systems.

In Environmental Sciences, concepts such as Air, Water, Wave, and Waste give the intrinsic meaning of data and programs residing in the repositories. Associated with these concepts are several physical notions such as location, grid, or time that are encountered in the various geospatial and environmental metadata standards (e.g. FGDC, UDK). An ontological foundation of this knowledge provides a formal framework for inferring valid combinations of available scientific resources regarding concrete environmental problems, e.g. Waste Management.

Typical real-world applications yield an ontology that includes numerous intricately related concepts[2]. For the purposes of this paper, we consider merely a part of such an all-encompassing ontology where simplified CZM concepts are illustrated for the Waste Transport scenario (Fig. 2). Ontology concepts abstract data sets of environmental information. Relations between the concepts represent the programs employed to produce such data. As an example, Waste Transport models are viewed as functions mapping Sea Circulation and Bathymetry data onto Waste data; for simplicity, the characteristics of the pollution source are omitted. It must be pointed out that several different implementations of scientific models can be instances of the same abstract semantic relationship between concepts. For example, there may be two

---

[2] There is ongoing effort for the definition of an ontology in the area of Ocean Engineering at MIT [15].

programs implementing the Waste Transport Model relation, producing results with different precision or for different locations.

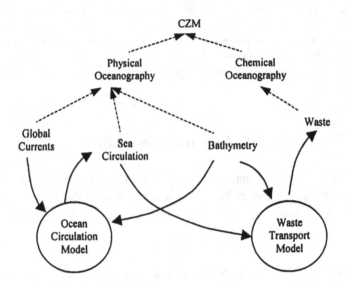

Fig. 2. A task-specific ontology for the Waste Transport application, introducing *Global Currents, Bathymetry, Sea Circulation,* and *Waste* concepts (data abstractions) that belong in wider thematic areas of CZM. These concepts are linked through *Ocean Circulation Model* and *Waste Transport Model* relations (program abstractions).

The semantics of this ontology are given by the interpretation of the various concepts and relations abstracting the underlying scientific resources. For this purpose, we follow an intentional definition of ontology notions using attributes such as location, grid resolution, etc, which describe the properties of scientific resources and are used to further specify the relations between them. From a logical viewpoint, the descriptions form a set of axiomatic rules, which are considered to be true independently of the actual content of the underlying repositories.

3.2 The Knowledge Base

In order to allow reasoning on the combination alternatives between data and programs we advocate a definition of the ontology notions in a KBS using Horn Clauses[3]. An ontology notion N is defined as a clause N(A1,A2,...,An), where A1, A2,..., An are it's attributes. Relations between concepts are expressed as rules of the form

---

[3] In this context, other knowledge representation and reasoning formalisms, like Description Logic [21], are less suited for handling arbitrary arity reasoning.

```
N(A1,A2,...,An):-
N1(A1,...,An),...,Nn(A1,...,An),Expr(A1,...,An)
```

where ":-" denotes implication and "," conjunction. The rule body includes program and data concepts Ni as well as constraints Expr, e.g. parameter restrictions, for deducing the notion appearing as a consequent in the rule head. Exactly one literal in the body describes the corresponding program notion. The rest of the literals stand for the description of input data required by that program.

According to this notation, the following clauses define the notions introduced in the above ontology (with considerably simplified attribute sets):

```
Bathymetry(Location,GridRes)
ExtCurrents(Location,GridRes)
SeaCirc(Location,GridRes)
Waste(Location,GridRes)
OceanCircModel(Location,GridRes)
WasteTranspModel(Location,GridRes)
```

In addition, the ontology relations shown in Fig. 2 are formalized using two rules:

```
R1:        SeaCirc(Location,GridRes)  :-
             OceanCircModel(Location,GridRes),
             ExtCurrents(Location,GridRes'),
             Bathymetry(Location,GridRes''),
             GridRes <= GridRes',
             GridRes <= GridRes''.


R2:        Waste(Location,GridRes)  :-
             WasteTranspModel(Location,GridRes),
             SeaCirc(Location,GridRes'),
             Bathymetry(Location,GridRes''),
             GridRes <= GridRes',
             GridRes <= GridRes''.
```

Rule R1 states that Sea Circulation data for a specific location and grid resolution can be derived from local Bathymetry and external Current data using an Ocean Circulation program. Similarly, rule R2 states that Waste data for a specific location and grid resolution can be produced by combining Sea Circulation with local Bathymetry data via a Waste Transport program.

Remark. In the above rules, "<=" denotes higher or equal grid resolution; for example $10m^3 <= 1m^2$ and $10m^2 <= 1m^3$.

Clauses without a body, called facts, are instances of abstract notions. Without loss of generality, in the following we use strings to denote attribute values. Locations are specified through symbolic names in place of geographical co-ordinates to enhance readability. For example, SeaCirc(HER, 10m3) stands for 3-D Sea Circulation for the area of Heraklion with a grid resolution of ten cubic meters. Similarly, WasteTranspModel(HER, 1m2) stands for a Waste Transport program that computes 2-D Waste data for the area of Heraklion with a grid resolution of one square meter.

Facts are either extensional, indicating available data sets or programs, or intentional, denoting data sets that can be generated through programs. Notably, there is no need to explicitly store facts in the KBS. Intentional facts are dynamically deduced through rules. Extensional facts can be constructed "on-the-fly" via a metadata search engine that locates the corresponding resources.

3.3 On-demand Generation of Data Production Paths

Given this formal representation of the ontology, requests for data productions translate into queries to the knowledge base. A query is a description of the desired resource in terms of an ontology concept. It must be satisfied through extensional or intentional facts, the latter being sub-queries requiring further expansion. This iterative matching process takes into account all possible combinations of rules and extensional facts. The result is a set of trees, whose nodes are intentional facts and leaves are extensional facts, embodying all valid production paths through which data for the queried concept can be generated.

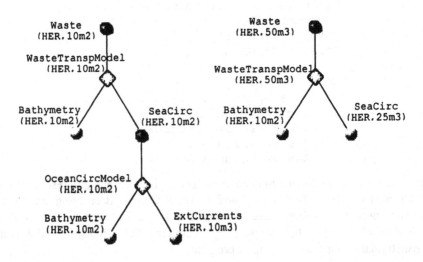

Fig. 3. Productions for *Waste* data, as presented to the user by a graphical user interface. Extensional facts are depicted in *light gray* while intentional facts, derived through rules, are depicted in *dark gray*. Program and data nodes appear as *squares* and *bullets* respectively.

Through a graphical user interface implemented on top of the KBS the user may explore valid data productions in a straightforward way. The GUI is responsible for forwarding user queries to the KBS, receiving and interpreting the resulting trees, and displaying this information.

To illustrate the on-demand generation of data production paths, let us assume that the following resources are available in the system repositories, expressed as extensional facts:

```
Bathymetry(HER,10m2)
ExtCurrents(HER,10m3)
OceanCircModel(HER,10m2)
SeaCirc(HER,25m3)
WasteTranspModel(HER,10m2)
WasteTranspModel(HER,50m3)
```

The user can inquire on the concept of Waste without restricting any attributes by posing the query Waste(X,Y). The result will be a graphical presentation of all productions for obtaining this data (as shown in Fig. 3). Two different production paths are possible for obtaining Waste data, for different sets of attributes: one for the area of Heraklion in 2-D with a 10m^2 resolution and one for the area of Heraklion in 3-D with a 50m^3 resolution. In the first production, the Sea Circulation data needed by the Waste Transport model must be computed via an Ocean Circulation model. In the second production, the required Sea Circulation data is already available.

The production trees depend on the attribute constraints posed by the user and on resource availability. For example, the addition of a repository containing an Ocean Circulation model for the computation of 3-D Sea Circulation data could result in further possible production trees, which would be displayed in subsequent queries. On the other hand, the user could request Waste data for a grid resolution of 50m^3, in which case only the production on the right of Fig. 3 would be generated. Similarly, the resolution attribute could be restricted to 10m^2 thereby resulting in the production on the left of Fig. 3.

4 Towards an Architecture for Integrated Scientific Repositories

We strongly believe that a KBS along the lines of this paper will be part of next-generation scientific information and experiment management systems. Specifically, we envision an advanced middleware architecture that seamlessly integrates Digital Library, Intelligent Information Integration, and Workflow technology. It is comprised of three main modules, the Metadata Search Engine, the Knowledge Base System, and the Workflow Runtime, which co-operate to provide the user with the desired functionality. The architecture is shown in Fig. 4. The functionality of each component is briefly described in the following.

The Metadata Search Engine is responsible for locating external resources, either data sets or programs. It may also retrieve complementary information stored in the repositories, e.g. user documentation on the available resources. The Search Engine accepts metadata queries on the properties of resources and returns a list of metadata descriptions and references. References point to repository wrappers, which provide an access and invocation interface to the underlying legacy systems where the data and programs reside.

The Knowledge Base System accepts queries regarding the availability of ontology concepts. It generates and returns the corresponding data productions based on the available resources and the constraints imposed by the ontology rules. These productions provide all the information that is needed to construct workflow specifications. The KBS regularly communicates with the Metadata Search Engine to update its extensional database.

The Workflow Runtime System monitors and coordinates the execution of workflows. It executes each intermediate step of a workflow specification, accessing data and invoking programs through the repository wrappers. Checkpoint and recovery techniques can be employed to enhance fault tolerance.

This architecture ensures the scalability and extensibility required in large, federated systems. It allows operationally autonomous and geographically dispersed organizations to selectively "export" their resources. Registering a new resource with the system requires merely supplying appropriate wrappers and metadata descriptions.

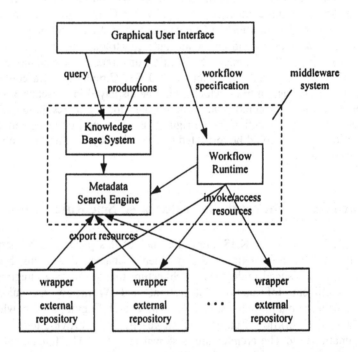

Fig. 4. A middleware architecture for distributed scientific repositories. The system consists of interoperable *Knowledge Base*, *Metadata Search*, and *Workflow Runtime* components.

To enhance performance and fault tolerance the Metadata Search Engine can be distributed across several machines. Also, several knowledge units adhering to different domains can be plugged into the Knowledge Base System to support a wide variety of applications and user groups.

We are currently developing a prototype system based on this architecture for the area of Coastal Zone Management [8]. Shortly, we hope to have a first version that will demonstrate the effectiveness of this design.

5. Related Work

Research on access and integration of heterogeneous information located over a number of distributed sources has attracted considerable attention during the past [22], [26], [28]. In this context, proposals have been presented for building global environmental systems [11]. Integration of scientific information has also benefited from workflow technology; while earlier focus was on business processes [1], workflow systems have recently been suggested as a powerful tool for scientific data management.

The Environmental Decision Support System (EDSS) [6] is a framework for the support of air quality modeling and management. Major physical and chemical phenomena are implemented as independent modules, which the user interconnects via a graphical interface. The selected modules are then obtained, compiled, linked, and executed automatically. Workflow and geospatial process management is explored in Geo-Opera [2], an extension of the Opera system [3] tailored for geographic and spatial modeling. Geo-Opera takes advantage of workflow technology to provide a fully distributed heterogeneous computing platform for managing complex geographic models. Another system that emphasizes management of scientific experiments is Zoo [10]. It uses Moose [16], an object oriented data model allowing computations to be described as graphs, and database functionality to control their execution. WASA [17] is a scientific application management environment, which uses IBM®'s FlowMark® [12], a business workflow management tool, to implement scientific processes. WASA supports dynamic replacement of a sub-workflow at run-time by another completely specified sub-workflow performing the same task.

In the above systems, workflows are explicitly specified. It is the user's responsibility to discover the availability of scientific resources and combine them into workflows. Once a workflow is defined it must be stored so that it can be retrieved at a later point in time. Also, for complex data productions it may be necessary to manually combine separate workflows. The efficiency of this approach greatly depends on the individual expertise of users.

Our approach can be viewed as a workflow generator. Rather than specifying workflows explicitly, a knowledge base committing to an environmental ontology is used to infer possible combinations between data and models automatically. Thus, it is possible even for non-experts to construct arbitrarily complex workflows. The effectiveness of the system is a direct function of the metadata design quality.

6. Conclusions

We have addressed the problem of determining combinations of available data and programs in the context of large-scale distributed scientific systems. We have proposed a Knowledge Base System that captures the semantic relations between data and programs, adhering to an application-specific ontology. Based on this information, the KBS dynamically deduces valid data production paths without user intervention. This support is particularly valuable in multidisciplinary applications.

It is important to further elaborate on the working paradigms of scientists to produce efficient combination rules that accurately capture the scope and restrictions of programs. Another challenging issue in this respect is to capture the knowledge of experts in metadata that could be used to create such production rules automatically.

An interesting extension, which can be easily implemented given the unification mechanism, is adding global constraints to the derivation of data production paths. This would also require appropriate metadata support. The user would then be able to pose restrictions regarding the total processing time or cost of data generation.

Finally, a distributed KBS consisting of a federation of logic modules embodying expertise in different scientific applications could be implemented. The KBS would distribute queries to the modules responsible for the specific concept domain. Interoperability could be achieved via standard protocols for exchanging queries and results [29], [31].

Acknowledgements

We would like to extend our thanks to the team from the Institute of Marine Biology of Crete consisting of George Triantafylou, Kaity Siakavara, George Petihakis, and Anika Polani for their discussions and sharing their knowledge on scientific models and data as they have appeared in our examples. We also thank Nickolas Patrikalakis for his valuable comments on earlier versions of this paper.

References

1. G. Alonso, D. Agrawal, A.El Abbadi, and C. Mohan, Functionality and Limitations of Current Workflow Management Systems. IEEE Expert Special Issue on Cooperative Information Systems, volume 1, number 3, 1997.
2. G. Alonso, H. Hagen, Geo-Opera: Workflow Concepts for Spatial Processes. Proceedings 5th Intl. Symposium on Spatial Databases (SSD '97), Berlin, Germany, June 1997.
3. G. Alonso, C. Hagen, H. Schek, M. Tresch, Towards a Platform for Distributed Application Development. 1997 NATO Advance Studies Institute (ASI). A. Dogac, L. Kalinichenko, T. Ozsu, A. Sheth (editors). August 12 -21, 1997, Istanbul, Turkey.
4. Object Management Group, The Common Object Request Broker: Architecture and Specification. Framingham, Mass., 1994. Revision 2.0.
5. C. Lagoze, E. Shaw, J.R. Davis, and D.B.Krafft, Dienst: Implementation Reference Manual. Cornell Computer Science Technical Report TR95-1514.

6. S. Fine and J. Ambrosiano, The Environmental Decision Support System: Overview and air quality application. Preprints, Symposium on Environmental Applications, January 28-February 2, Atlanta, GA, American Meteorological Society, 152-157, 1996. http://www.iceis.mcnc.org/pub_files/fine1996a.pdf
7. N. Guarino, Formal Ontology and Information Systems. In N. Guarino (ed.), Formal Ontology in Information Systems. Proceedings of the 1st International Conference, Trento, Italy, 6-8 June 1998. IOS Press.
8. C. Houstis, C. Nikolaou, S. Lalis, S. Kapidakis, V. Chrisophides, Open Scientific Data Repositories Architecture. Invited position paper, Invitational Workshop on Distributed Information, Computation and Process Management for Scientific and Engineering Environments proceedings, (edited by N. Patrikalakis), NSF sponsored, Washigton DC, May 15-16, 1998.
9. C. Houstis, C. Nikolaou, M. Marazakis, N. Patrikalakis, J. Sairamesh, A. Thomasic, THETIS: Design of a Data Repositories Collection and Data Visualization System for Coastal Zone management of the Mediterranean Sea. Invited publication, D-Lib magazine, The Magazine for Digital Library Research, November 1997. http://www.dlib.org/dlib/november97/thetis/11thetis.html
10. Y. Ioannidis, M. Linvy, S. Gupta, N. Ponnekanti, ZOO: A Desktop Experiment Management Environment. Proceedings of 22nd VLDB Conference Mumbai (Bombay), India, 1996.
11. A. Koschel, R. Kramer, R. Nikolai, W. Hagg,, and J. Wiesel, A Federation Architecture for an Environmental Information System incorporating GIS, the World Wide Web, and CORBA. Proceedings Third International Conference/Workshop on Integrating GIS and Environmental Modeling, National Center for Geographic Information and Analysis (NCGIA), Santa Fe, New Mexico, USA, January 1996.
12. F. Leymann, D. Roller, Business Process Management with FlowMark. Proceedings 39th IEEE Computer Society International Conference (CompCon), February 1994, pp230-233.
13. A. Seth, Changing Focus on Interoperability in Information Systems: From system, Syntax, Structure to Semantics. Interoperating Geographic Information Systems, M.F. GoodChild, M.J. Egenhofer, R. Fegeas, and C.A.Kottman (eds) Kluwer 1999.
14. O. Gunther, H. Lessing, and W. Swoboda, UDK: A European environmental data catalogue. Proceedings 3rd Int. Conf./Workshop on Integrating GIS and Environmental Modeling, National Center for Geographic Information and Analysis (NCGIA), Santa Fe, New Mexico, January 1996.
15. P.C. Wariyapola, S.L. Abrams, and N.M. Patrikalakis, Ontologies and Metadata for a Coastal Zone Management System. Technical Report (in preparation), MIT Ocean Engineering Design Laboratory, July 1998.
16. J. Wiener and Y. Ioannidis, A Moose and A Fox Can Aid Scientists with Data Management Problems, Proceedings 4th International Workshop on Database Programming Languages, New York, NY, August 1993, pp376-398.
17. Mathias Weske, Gottfried Vossen, Claudia Bauzer Medeiros, Scientific Workflow Management: WASA Architecture and Applications. Fachbericht Angewandte Mathematik und Informatik 03/96-I, Universität Münster, January 1996.

18. AltaVista. http://www.altavista.com
19. The CDF standard. http://nssdc.gsfc.nasa.gov/cdf
20. The Dublin Core. http://purl.org/metadata/dublin-core
21. Description Logics. http://dl.kr.org
22. The Digital Library Initiative. http://www.cise.nsf.gov/iis/dli_home.html
    Berkeley http://elib.cs.berkeley.edu
    Carnegie-Mellon http://informedia.cs.cmu.edu

Illinois http://dli.grainger.uiuc.edu
Michigan http://www.si.umich.edu/UMDL
Stanford http://www-diglib.stanford.edu
Santa Barbara http://alexandria.sdc.ucsb.edu
23. EnviroTech on-line. http://www.envirotech.org
24. Federal Geographic Data Committee, Content Standards for Digital Geospatial Metadata. March 1994. ftp://fgdc.er.usgs.gov
25. The HDF standard. http://hdf.ncsa.uiuc.edu
26. The Intelligent Integration of Information Initiative. http://mole.dc.isx.com/I3
  GARLIC http://www.almaden.ibm.com/cs/showtell/garlic
  TSIMMIS http://www-db.stanford.edu/tsimmis
  Information Manifold http://www.research.att.com/~levy/imhome.html
  SIMS http://www.isi.edu/sims
  InfoSleuth http://www.mcc.com:80/projects/infosleuth
  WebSemantics http://www.cs.toronto/~georgem/w5
27. The JDBC Data Access API. http://www.javasoft.com/products/jdbc/index.html
28. The Knowledge Sharing Effort. http://www-ksl.stanford.edu/knowledge-sharing
  Ontolingua http://www-ksl.stanford.edu/knowledge-sharing/ontolingua
  Mikrokosmos Ontology http://crl.nmsu.edu/users/mahesh/onto-intro-page.html
  Ontosaurus http://www.isi.edu/isd/ontosaurus.html
  Description Logic http://www.cs.rmit.edu.au/dl
  Knowledge Interchange Format http://logic.stanford.edu/kif/kif.html
29. The Knowledge Query Manipulation Language. http://www.csee.umbc.edu/kqml
30. Microsoft, Microsoft Odbc 3.0 Software Development Kit and Programmer's Reference. Microsoft Press, February 1997.
31. The Open Knowledge Base Connectivity. http://www.ai.sri.com/~okbc
32. A. Denning, OLE Controls Inside Out. Microsoft Press, 1995.
33. The Resource Description Framework. http://www.w3.org/Metadata/RDF
34. D. Curtis, Java, RMI and CORBA. http://www.omg.org/library/wpjava.htm
35. The Extensible Markup Language (XML) standard. http://www.w3.org/XML
36. The Workflow Management Coalition. http://www.aiai.ed.ac.uk/project/wfmc

Global Version Management for a Federated Turbine Design Environment[*]

Martin Schönhoff[1] and Markus Strässler[2]

[1] Department of Computer Science, University of Zurich, Switzerland,
mschoen@ifi.unizh.ch
[2] ABB Corporate Research Ltd., Baden–Dättwil, Switzerland,
straessl@ifi.unizh.ch

Abstract. Integrated engineering environments, based on federated database technology, are a means to control the integrity of and dependencies between product data created in many different engineering applications. Continuing the engineers' tradition of keeping different versions of drawings and documents, most engineering applications support the management of versions of a product and its parts. Consequently, federations in engineering environments should provide version management on their global layer in order to support homogeneous global access to versions from different local systems and to provide system-wide consistency of versioned data.

This paper identifies problems which are specific to global version management in a federated system. It then investigates and evaluates these problems and their solutions in the context of a turbine design environment. Finally, a generalisation of selected solutions for a wider range of application domains is discussed.

1 Introduction

The collection of all database objects and document files describing an industrial product (e.g., CAD drawings, 3D models, finite element analysis, fluid dynamic simulations) and its engineering and manufacturing process are considered as *product data*. This data is produced by many different heterogeneous engineering applications. Various versions of this product data are created while the design team is looking for the optimal solution. The precise tracking of the history of product data enables engineers to discover cases in which dependencies between data have been violated. This means that parts of the data are based on preconditions (e.g., based on other product data) which were later changed without adapting all depending data. Therefore, support of *versioning* is needed in modern engineering environments which integrate different applications, thus

---

[*] Work reported in this paper is executed within the project IDEE (Integration of Data in Engineering Environments). The project is part of the Swiss Priority Programme for Information and Communication Structures (SPP ICS, 1996–1999) sponsored by the Swiss National Science Foundation under project number 5003–045354. Additional information can be found at http://www.ifi.unizh.ch/dbtg/IDEE.

continuing the tradition of engineers, who manually traced versions of their designs on drawings and calculation documents.

In our IDEE project (Integration of Data in Engineering Environments) [SSD97], we integrate heterogeneous engineering applications into a tightly coupled database federation using an object-oriented global data model and operational integration. We apply federated database technology to build engineering environments of integrated product data. Thereby, imposed through the requirements of the engineering domain, versioning of design data and system-wide consistency of versions are our main goals.

A federated database system (FDBS) *with* version management offers additional functionality on its federation layer compared to an "unversioned" federation, e.g., the propagation of new local versions to the federation layer and an improved tracking of the current status of an ongoing engineering design project. This paper investigates requirements and concepts for version management on the global layer of a federated design environment for turbine development. Thereby, it focuses on the *integration* of basic versioning concepts like version histories or workspaces. It neither covers a concrete version model, common versioning problems like change propagation and notification (e.g., [Kat90]), nor mechanisms for transaction management, integrity control or access control.

The remainder of the paper is structured as follows. Section 2 presents our application scenario, and introduces version management concepts and federated database technology. Section 3 comprises the main part of the paper, namely the requirements on global version management which are specific to our environment as well as concepts to meet these requirements. Some of these concepts are generalised for a wider range of application domains in Sect. 4. Then we shortly introduce some related work in Sect. 5 before Sect. 6 concludes the paper.

2 Scenario and Terminology

The following simplified scenario introduces concepts and terminology needed in the industrial application of an integrated engineering environment. It reflects our experience in the gas and steam turbine development departments of ABB (Asea Brown Boveri), a global engineering group in power generation, transmission and distribution.

2.1 Initial Situation

As a practical example we take a look at the cooperation of aerodynamic specialists and mechanical integrity (MIT) engineers. Both groups of engineers use their specific calculation and simulation tools. The former design an aerodynamically optimal geometric shape of a turbine blade (consisting of an airfoil shape and a foot used to mount this blade into the turbine). The latter try to predict whether the design would last or would mechanically break due to stress overload.

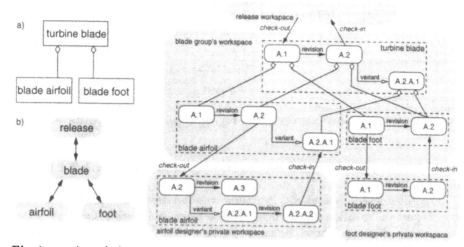

Fig. 1. Aero-design tool: (a) schema and (b) workspace hierarchy

Fig. 2. Versioning and revisioning of aerodynamic design data sets

The "Aero-design Tool" In this simplified example, a CAD "aero-design tool" is used to create the turbine blade which is an aggregation of a blade airfoil and a blade foot. Figure 1a shows this schema in UML (Unified Modelling Language [BJR98]) notation[1]. The tool supports a powerful version model, including a three-level *workspace* hierarchy (the relevant part is depicted in Fig. 1b).

Cooperation within the blade group is possible in their *group workspace*. A *check-out* (downward arrow) into his *private workspace* allows the airfoil designer to try out new versions of the design, which are inaccessible to others. The finished design is then *checked-in* (upward arrow) to the group workspace as a new version of the airfoil. Here, it can be combined with an appropriate blade foot to form a complete turbine blade. When the final design of the blade is reached, it is checked-in to the *release workspace*, where the data for the actual manufacturing of the design is stored. This process is shown in Fig. 2.

We call a versioned object that represents a real-world entity, e.g., a blade airfoil, a *design object* (depicted as a dashed box in Fig. 2). Its *versions* (or more exactly *version objects*) can further be differentiated as *variants* or *revisions*. A *revision* is a correction or an improvement of the preceding instance (called the *predecessor*). Thus revisions only generate linear *version histories*. For example, in Fig. 2, the blade airfoil's version A.3 in the airfoil designer's private workspace is a revision of version A.2. The existence of a revision implies that the preceding instance should not be used anymore. A *variant* is an alternative to its predecessor, i.e., there are still reasons to use the predecessor. For instance, variants are created to test the effect of design changes without affecting the rest of the design team which still uses the original variant. Variants generate branches in

---

[1] We omit association names and multiplicities for simplicity.

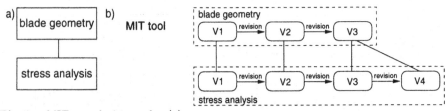

Fig. 3. MIT analysis tool: (a) schema and (b) workspace hierarchy

Fig. 4. Revisioning of MIT data sets

the version history which thus becomes a tree. In the example, A.2.A.1 is an alternative of A.2.

The aero-design system also supports *relationships* between objects, e.g., the "is-part-of" relationship between turbine blade and turbine airfoil. A *static* relationship always points to the same specific version, even if a new revision or variant of the referenced version is created. A *dynamic* relationship, on the other hand, points to a distinguished *current* version (e.g., the most recent version).

The "MIT Analysis Tool" The MIT analysis tool is used to create stress analysis data sets including boundary conditions, parameters and calculation routines. Each blade geometry (those parts of the aero-design's blade airfoil and blade foot data that are relevant for MIT analysis) is associated with a stress analysis data set. The tool does not support a workspace concept. The MIT tool's simple schema and workspace hierarchy are depicted in Fig. 3a and 3b, respectively. The stress analysis and blade geometry data sets are stored in separate files in a file system. Since the tool was written by the analysis engineers themselves, the files' data structures are available. A linear history of versions (i.e., only revisions) as shown in Fig. 4 is supported through the use of a simple file revisioning tool. Variants must be represented as new design objects.

It is obvious that an MIT stress calculation is no longer valid as soon as the geometric shapes which form the basis of the calculation have been changed. Without integrating the two systems, the designer of the basic shape has to notify the engineer calculating the mechanical integrity about design changes and send him the new data. Likewise, the MIT engineer must perform recalculations whenever he updates MIT parameters and must notify the aerodynamic designers of the results.

2.2 Integration through FDBMS

The main goals of the integration effort are to integrate objects from local systems with different versioning capabilities and to provide system-wide consistency of versions. Therefore, the global layer should provide homogeneous access to versions from different systems based on a powerful global version model. This especially means that the global version model should not be the least common denominator of the local models. System-wide consistency of versions

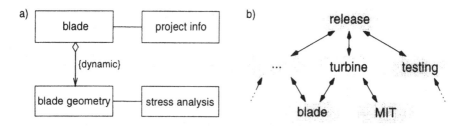

Fig. 5. Integrated system: (a) schema and (b) workspace hierarchy

comprises on one hand adequate mappings between versions on the global and the local layer (especially consistent predecessor/successor relationships), and on the other hand the propagation of new versions between local systems. Other integrity issues are outside the scope of this paper.

Our integrated system is based on an FDBS with a federated (*global*) schema (tightly coupled system [SL90]). A global schema is required to achieve a global view on data from *autonomous, heterogeneous* local systems (in our example, the aero-design and the MIT analysis tools). The integrated schema is shown in Fig. 5a. A blade has a blade geometry component, connected through a unidirectional, *dynamic* relationship. The blade and associated project info (cost, etc.) have no local counterparts and are thus stored globally. More characteristic for an FDBMS, the blade geometry and the related stress analysis objects are *virtually* integrated. That means these objects are globally represented only through their object identifiers. Their data is not materialised on the global layer. Instead, all accesses are mapped to the corresponding local operations. Since each stress analysis is only valid for the blade geometry it has been calculated for, their relationship is *static*.

Details of the aero-design tool's blade airfoil and blade foot data are not required on the global layer. The blade geometry data, however, must be propagated from the aero-design tool via the global layer to the MIT analysis tool. In the opposite direction, blade designers should receive the results of a stress analysis. However, autonomy of the aero-design tool forbids to add this data, or even just an attribute representing a "tested" status bit to the local schema.

Like the aero-design tool, the global version model supports a three-level workspace hierarchy (Fig. 5b), check-out, check-in (which creates new versions) and delete operations, and the distinction between revisions and variants. Note, however, that several members of the local blade and MIT groups can identify themselves as "the" global blade or MIT users, respectively. Thus the global workspaces on the private layer have effectively group access.

In the following sections, we make several (versioning-independent) assumptions about the *underlying FDBMS*. We assume that the FDBMS uses an object-oriented global data model, provides for object identification and mappings between global and local objects (i.e., their identifiers) and their (versioning-independent) relationships. The system also manages the propagation of newly created objects from the local to the global layer and vice versa. This step includes the detection of local changes.

3 Version Management in the Federated Turbine Design Environment

In this section, we first present the versioning-specific requirements on a federated turbine design environment which must be met to propagate versioning-relevant operations. Section 3.1 identifies the problem areas which have to be investigated. Afterwards, in Sect. 3.2, we look at the versioning-relevant operations and, based on the problem areas, identify the requirements to propagate these operations between the global and the local layer[2]. These requirements and their solutions for our example application domain are examined in detail in the following sections. Section 3.7 evaluates the solutions against our goals, the integration of versioning concepts and system-wide consistency of versions.

3.1 Problem Areas

The propagation of relevant changes from local systems to the global layer and vice versa is a fundamental characteristic of federated systems with a global schema. Relevant for version management are operations which *create*, *update* or *delete* version objects. Consequently, if such a *versioning-relevant operation* is executed on one layer of an FDBMS, the *source* layer, the result must be propagated to the other, the *destination* layer.

As an example, we examine the propagation of a newly created version from the aero-design tool to the global layer. This example presents the main problem areas of version propagation which we discuss later.

Let us assume that a new variant of a turbine blade is created through a check-in from the airfoil designer's private workspace to the group workspace of the aero-design tool (similar to the check-in of the blade airfoil version A.2.A.1 in Fig. 2). The first question to be answered is whether the new version needs to be propagated at all. In this example, it is reasonable to propagate the new version, because a design in the group workspace is not regarded to be as experimental as a design in a private workspace, hence the design should be tested through an MIT analysis such that structural defects can be detected as soon as possible. However, if a new version is created in the airfoil designer's private workspace, this operation is not propagated in order to protect the airfoil designer's private data and to avoid the proliferation of experimental designs which would trigger unnecessary MIT analysis work. We call this problem area *propagation selection*.

Once the new version has been selected for propagation, the underlying FDBMS's local-global user mapping facility is used to identify the global owner.

---

[2] *User* requirements (like access to different versions of a design object or the need to control and share access through a workspace concept) for the global layer of an FDBMS are not different to other systems. We thus do not need to treat them in this paper, see, e.g., [Kat90].

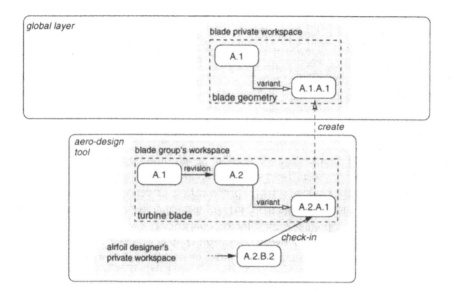

Fig. 6. Propagation of the creation of a new local version

Then, the next versioning-specific problem is to determine a suitable global workspace for the version. The FDBMS must provide a *workspace mapping* between the workspace hierarchy on the global layer and all local workspace hierarchies. In this example, it is obvious that the global **blade** private workspace is the counterpart to the aero-design tool's **blade** group workspace.

Version history mapping deals with the homogenisation of version history concepts. This is no real problem here because both, the global layer and the aero-design tool, support the same kind of version history, a tree with revisions and variants.

Several version history properties need to be identified for the new version: the global version history (i.e., the design object), the new version's predecessor and whether the new version is a revision or a variant of the predecessor. In our example, the new version becomes a direct variant of version A.1 on the global layer, because the local variant A.2, the new version's local predecessor, has not been propagated to the global layer[3]. Figure 6 depicts the result of this *version history identification*.

Finally, a *relationship mapping* is needed to map all relations which exist between the new global version and (versions of) other design objects from the local to the global layer. In our example, a global **blade geometry** is involved in two relationships. First, it is part of a global **blade**. Since a **blade** has no local counterpart, no mapping is required. Nevertheless, given that the blade design

---

[3] It is possible that the local turbine blade A.2 differs from A.1 in data that are not relevant for stress analysis. Given that a blade geometry is the subset of a turbine blade that *is* relevant for stress analysis (cf. Sect. 2.1), the blade geometry versions A.1 and A.2 are identical.

object is connected through a (unidirectional) *dynamic* relationship to the design object of the new **blade geometry** version (cf. Sect. 2.2), the global version system automatically updates this relationship to point to the new version. Note that this is a common version management feature and thus independent of integration aspects. Second, the new **blade geometry** version can also be associated with **stress analysis** data. This data cannot yet exist for a new **blade geometry**, hence this relationship is undefined.

We summarise the five federation-specific problem areas identified above:

Propagation Selection Not all versioning-relevant operations that are executed in a local system need to be propagated to the global layer and vice versa. There are both practical (proliferation of versions) and security reasons (for instance, versions from private workspaces should not be accessible elsewhere) to propagate only selected operations.

Workspace Mapping For every operation that is selected for propagation, a workspace on the destination layer must be determined to which the result of the operation can be propagated. Since local systems and the FDBMS usually apply different workspace concepts (number of levels, etc.), a mapping between local and global workspaces must be defined.

Version History Mapping The FDBMS must provide an integration of version history concepts such that global versions can be accessed homogeneously, even if they are based on data from local systems with different version history capabilities.

Version History Identification When new versions are propagated, several version history properties need to be identified for them before they can be placed on the destination layer, namely their version history (i.e., the design object), the new version's predecessor, and whether the new version is a revision or a variant of the predecessor.

Relationship Mapping Relationships of the new version with other design objects, e.g., static and dynamic aggregation relationships, must be mapped from the local to the global layer and vice versa.

3.2   Propagation of Versioning-Relevant Operations

Versioning-relevant operations (*create*, *update*, and *delete*) can be executed at the local or at the global layer[4]. Table 1 shows the resulting six cases with respect to the problem areas identified above. Note that some operations heavily depend on basic FDBMS functionality. In such cases, we also list these FDBMS services in the right column, for instance, the local-global object (identifier) mapping. The problem areas are printed in **boldface**.

In the following sections, we take a detailed look at these problem areas for both, local-to-global and global-to-local operation propagation.

---

[4] Global operations may not only be initiated by a global user, but also by the system itself, when it propagates an operation from one local system to the global layer. From the version management point of view, these operations can be treated as if they were initiated by a global user.

Operation	Description	Problem areas
local create	Decide whether the creation operation must be propagated, and if yes determine the global owner, determine the global workspace for the new object, map the local version history structures to the global ones, identify the new version's global design object (i.e., the version history), the new version's predecessor in the version history, and whether the new version is a revision or a variant of its predecessor, and establish or update versioning-specific global relationships.	**Propagation Selection** Local-Global User Mapping **Workspace Mapping Version History Mapping Version History Identification** **Relationship Mapping**
local update	Decide whether the update operation must be propagated, and if yes perform a global "in-place" update, or create a new global version.	**Propagation Selection** Unversioned Object Update see *local create*
local delete	Decide whether the delete operation must be propagated, and if yes delete the corresponding global version object.	**Propagation Selection** Local-global Object Mapping
global create	Decide whether the creation operation must be propagated, and if yes determine the local owner, determine the local workspace for the new object, map the global version history structures to the local ones, identify the new version's local design object (i.e., the version history), the new version's predecessor in the version history, and whether the new version is a revision or a variant of its predecessor, and establish or update versioning-specific local relationships.	**Propagation Selection** Local-Global User Mapping **Workspace Mapping Version History Mapping Version History Identification** **Relationship Mapping**
global update	Decide whether the update operation must be propagated, and if yes perform a local "in-place" update, or create a new local version.	**Propagation Selection** Unversioned Object Update see *global create*
global delete	Decide whether the delete operation must be propagated, and if yes delete the corresponding local version object.	**Propagation Selection** Global-local Object Mapping

Table 1. Problem areas during the propagation of versioning-relevant operations

3.3 Propagation Selection and Workspace Mapping

The requirements for propagation selection and workspace mapping are closely related. Therefore, we discuss them together.

In our scenario, the operations are *not* propagated from the global layer to the aero-design system. The reason is twofold. First, autonomy of the aero-design tool does not allow any additions to the local schema (cf. Sect. 2.1). Second, a complete blade cannot be propagated to the local layer, since the global blade geometry contains only some of the aero tool's data (cf. Sect. 2.2). Thus there is no data flow from the MIT tool via the global layer to the aero-design tool which notifies blade designers about a completed stress analysis; blade designers must actively check for the results of a stress analysis on the global layer. Alternatively, they may register to the global version model's change notification mechanism (e.g., via email).

In the opposite direction, *create*, *update* and *delete* operations are propagated from the aero-design tool's blade group and release workspaces to the global private blade and the turbine group workspaces, respectively.

For the MIT analysis tool, *delete* and *update* operations on a previously propagated local version are always propagated as well. For local *create* operations, however, it cannot be decided generally whether an operation should be propagated to the global layer or not. The decision depends on the "status" of the new version (e.g., experimental or finished) which cannot be retrieved from the local system, since it is implicit knowledge of the MIT specialist. Consequently, it is not possible to define a policy for *automated* propagation at integration time. Instead, local users must explicitly initiate the propagation (using a local application add-on) although such a mechanism is not transparent and violates local autonomy.

Similarly, the global workspace for the new local MIT version must also be determined through user interaction. The version may be placed into the global turbine group workspace if the MIT analysis results shall be visible to all turbine designers. Otherwise, if the results should be kept within the group of MIT engineers for further discussion, the version must be placed into the global MIT private workspace.

For global-to-local propagation, a suitable policy can be implemented at integration time. From both the turbine group workspace and the MIT private workspace the results of all three versioning-relevant operations are propagated to the MIT tool.

A summary of propagation selection and workspace mapping in our scenario is depicted in Fig. 7. A question mark "?" symbolises the need for user interaction.

3.4 Version History Mapping

Like the aero-design tool, the global layer of our design environment supports tree-like version histories. Both systems also use the same version labelling

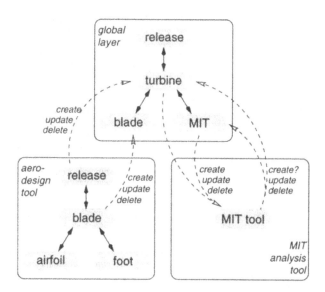

Fig. 7. Propagation selection and workspace mapping in the scenario

scheme. Mapping a version history between the aero-design tool (a turbine blade) and the global layer (a blade geometry) is thus straightforward.

The MIT analysis tool only supports a linear version history. While this can be easily mapped to the global layer, it is obvious that a tree-like global version history cannot be adequately mapped into a local linear version history. There are three possible solutions for this problem.

1. A global tree is mapped into a linear structure, e.g., ordered by creation time. However, the resulting loss of information can lead to inconsistent predecessor-successor relationships whenever a new version is created at either layer.

2. All branches of the global tree (i.e., all variants) are mapped to separate linear histories, which are only implicitly related (e.g., via comments) for the local users. This solution can also lead to consistency problems on either layer. On one hand, a new local "variant" cannot be automatically connected to the global history tree and, on the other hand, local designers may not realise that a new design object is in fact a variant of an existing design object.

3. The global version history is restricted to contain only revisions. Compared with a fully versionable history, this solution imposes a usability restriction for global users – they cannot create variants. If consistency cannot be guaranteed with one of the two other solutions, this is an acceptable price for a straightforward, consistent integration.

Solution 2 was selected for **blade geometry** objects for the following reasons:

– Solution 3 would have caused the same mapping problem (tree to linear history) for the propagation from the aero tool to the global layer.

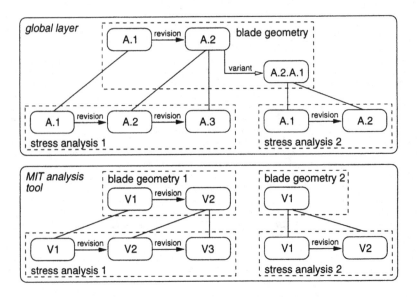

Fig. 8. Different global and local representation of version histories

- MIT analysts are used to represent variants as different design objects anyway (cf. Sect. 2.1).
- The global-to-local mapping is straightforward.
- The local-to-global mapping of revisions is straightforward. Propagating a new local design object will lead to a new global design object, which can be connected "by hand" as a variant to an existing global version history. Furthermore, the creation of a new blade geometry "variant" in the MIT tool (as a proposal to the aero-designers) is a rare event.

For stress analysis objects, solution 3 is applied:

- The mapping is straightforward in either direction.
- Applying solution 2 would have required to add almost all variants to the global history "by hand", since variants of stress analysis objects are mostly created in the MIT tool. Furthermore, the resulting lack of version history information on the global layer is acceptable, since this information can partly be derived from the tree of the associated blade geometry objects.

Figure 8 shows an example of the global and local representations of a blade geometry design object with associated stress analysis. Note that one can derive from the global blade geometry tree that the version A.1 of the global stress analysis 2 object is a variant of either the version A.2 or A.3 of stress analysis 1.

3.5 Version History Identification

Looking at the operations listed in Sect. 3.2, we note that the creation of a new version raises a number of version history identification issues which have to be treated during the propagation to the destination layer. We look at the creation of a new *local* version first.

Design Object The global design object (i.e., the version history) of the new version object must be determined. If the version object is the initial version of its history, a new global version history must be created. This implicitly creates a mapping between the local version and the new global object, because the FDBMS keeps a mapping between the local and the global version objects, while the global versioning mechanism keeps a mapping between a version history and its versions. These mappings allow to determine the global design object, because the *local* predecessor's global counterpart can always be identified[5].

Predecessor, Revision/Variant The predecessor (if applicable) of the new version must be identified within the version history. The new version must become either a revision or a variant of its predecessor.

The predecessor of a new revision created in the MIT tool is always the latest revision of the corresponding global design object. Thus, although not all local operations (especially no *deletes*) are propagated to the global layer, no inconsistent order of global revisions can occur.

A new version of a blade geometry cannot be propagated *automatically* from the aero-design tool to the global layer, for example, if there is no unique possible global predecessor. Such a situation is depicted in Fig. 9. An initial version A.1 of a blade geometry has been checked out from the global release workspace into the workspaces of the turbine and testing groups and was then revisioned in both of them[6]. According to the propagation selection policy described in Sect. 3.3, the new revisions have not been propagated to the aero-design system. Let a user who belongs to both the global turbine and testing group now create a new local version of the turbine blade in the local blade group workspace (dotted version in Fig. 9). This new version must be propagated as a blade geometry. However, the system is not able to determine the global predecessor of the new version automatically. It may be any global version shown in Fig. 9.

As a consequence, the propagation of a new version must be divided into two steps. Immediately after the local version has been created, all automated decisions are derived from policies fixed at integration time which are parametrised with run-time information. Later, the propagation is completed in interaction with a global user.

In the example of Fig. 9, the first step automatically determines the five possible predecessors and that the version is a revision on the local layer. In

---

[5] To be more precise, this is only true for versions which exist on both layers. In general, the mapping is only partial, e.g., because a local create may not have been propagated. However, if a local predecessor does not have a global counterpart, the first of the predecessor's global predecessors that can be mapped to the local system becomes the new version's predecessor.

[6] Note that, although both versions are *labelled* "A.2", they have been created independently of each other and *are not* identical. Each workspace has its own name space.

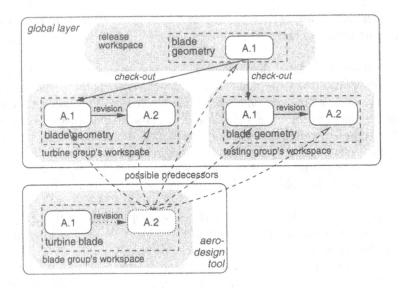

Fig. 9. More than one possible predecessor of a new global version

the second step, a global user, e.g., an engineer of the **turbine** group, completes the propagation. He chooses to place the new version in the **turbine** group's workspace. If he selects A.2 as predecessor, the new version will become revision A.3. Otherwise, with A.1 as the predecessor, the new version must become a variant A.1.A.1, because A.1 cannot have more than one revision.

The propagation of a new *global* version to the local layer is not a problem here. No global operations are propagated to the aero-design tool (cf. Sect. 3.3) and a predecessor in the MIT analysis tool can always be found. In the case that a revision should be propagated and the local predecessor already has a local revision which has not been propagated to the global layer, a new local design object must be created according to the version history mapping described in Sect. 3.4. Hence, the global revision is treated like a local variant.

Version history identification is trivial for *update* and *delete* operations (cf. Sect. 3.2), because all version(s) which are affected by one of these operations can be determined through the mapping between global and local objects which was defined when the versions were created.

3.6 Relationship Mapping

Relationships between design objects must be mapped from the local to the global layer and vice versa when the results of versioning-relevant operations are propagated. In our example, only the static relationship between **blade geometry** and **stress analysis** objects is relevant for relationship mapping. This relationship exists on both the global layer and in the MIT tool. Recall from the example in

Sect. 3.1 that the global relationship from a blade to its blade geometry is not relevant, because it is automatically updated through the global version system.

The mapping of relationships can be completely derived from the local-global object and version mappings. Let us consider the example of the creation of a new stress analysis object in the MIT tool, which is immediately associated with its blade geometry on the local layer. The relationship from the blade geometry to its new stress analysis can be resolved on the global layer in three steps:

1. The local counterpart of the global blade geometry is found using the local-global object and version mappings.
2. For the resulting object, the relationship to the stress analysis is traversed locally.
3. The local stress analysis is mapped to its global counterpart.

If either the blade geometry or the stress analysis object is not propagated to the global layer, step 1 or step 3 fails. If an object is propagated for which the relationship is locally undefined, step 2 fails. In these cases, the global relationship is undefined.

3.7 Evaluation

We have presented solutions to five problem areas of version propagation such that our integrated turbine design environment can support homogeneous global access to versions and system-wide consistency of versioned data – at least to a large extent.

Truly homogeneous access to global versions and straightforward version propagation can only be achieved if all local version histories are at least tree-like. In our example, we had to trade a straightforward propagation from the MIT tool to the global layer for the restriction that global stress analysis version histories can only be linear.

A two-step propagation of a new local version to the global layer, requiring user interaction, is not very appealing, but we have shown that it is unavoidable, because automated decisions about version history properties are sometimes not adequate and can cause consistency problems.

We were not able to achieve the propagation of MIT analysis data to the aero-design tool due to local autonomy. Instead, we still have to rely on a notification mechanism. For the MIT tool, on the other hand, reducing local autonomy was possible and we added a local mechanism for local-to-global version propagation selection. With this solution, the amount of MIT data to be propagated to the global layer (leading to considerable follow-up work) is considerably reduced compared with a solution which fully preserves autonomy.

4 Generalisation of Integration Concepts

Our discussion of the integration of local versioning mechanisms presented in the previous section is based on a concrete turbine design environment. This section shortly lists some important generalisations which must be considered for the integration of other local systems or in other application domains.

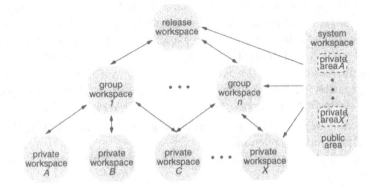

Fig. 10. The global workspace hierarchy and the system workspace

System Workspace The two-step propagation process which is required for version history identification can also be used to improve other mechanisms like the workspace, version and user mappings (for example, connecting a **blade geometry** variant created in the MIT tool to the global version tree, cf. Sect. 3.4). A *system workspace* that is orthogonal to the global workspace hierarchy (Fig. 10) can then be used to store new versions between the automated and the user-driven propagation step [SS98].

Versioning Usability Specifications Similar to the global **stress analysis** objects in our example, there are cases in which system-wide consistency of versions can only be guaranteed if some objects' global usability is restricted. From our experience, this leads to the following global *versioning usability specifications* [SSD97]. We distinguish (i) *fully versionable* objects (supporting revisions and variants, leading to a tree or a DAG), (ii) *revisionable* objects (linear histories) and (iii) *non-versionable* objects (only in-place updates are possible). This specifications allows the global versioning system to enforce the necessary restrictions for objects with "weak" versioning usability. It is hence not necessary to reduce the versioning capabilities of *all* global objects to the least common denominator of all local version models.

Propagation In our example, **stress analysis** objects are propagated from the MIT tool to the global layer and vice versa. We so far ignored that this can lead to "ping-pong" propagations of the same object between the two layers. In our case, this situation can be easily prevented by the integration system, because it always "knows" where a change originated. In general, cyclic propagations between several local systems (via the global layer) can occur.

Workspace Levels We already mentioned in Sect. 2.2 that the global private workspaces are in fact accessed by groups of users. Thus, in the general case, in which a global private workspace should only be accessed by a single "physical" user, at least four workspace levels are required.

5   Related Work

FDBMS have been a research topic for more than a decade now, version management models even since the 1950s [Tic94, preface]. Version management mechanisms that are suitable for engineering environments mostly have their roots in CAD systems (e.g., for VLSI design). [Kat90] is a good survey and proposes a unification of most mechanisms published until the late 1980s. Work since then includes, e.g., [KBG89, Sci94, RJ96]. Nevertheless, to the best of our knowledge, there are no publications about version management in FDBMS.

In industry, product data management (PDM) systems are a practical approach to version control over several applications. However, despite their name, these systems control documents, i.e., containers, rather than the data themselves. PDM systems are also inferior to FDBMS in many other aspect, most notably, transparent, homogeneous access to distributed, heterogeneous data.

A 5-level schema architecture [SL90] and an object-oriented global data model [SCG91] are generally accepted for most FDBMS [CEH+97]. [BNPS88] proposes operational integration to support a high degree of heterogeneity of the component systems. This is applied in [HD92] to introduce usability specifications to non-versioned object types such that even objects from component systems with weak object identification capabilities can be integrated. We adopted these approaches in the IDEE architecture, mainly because most engineering applications provide only poor support for their integration [SSD97].

6   Summary and Future Work

We have presented the requirements to provide version management on the global layer of an FDBMS in a turbine design environment and illustrated solutions to meet them. Finally, we sketched more general solutions which can be applied to other application domains as well.

We have shown that not all versioning-relevant operations need or can be propagated from the local to the global layer and vice versa. Therefore, a propagation selection is needed. Furthermore, suitable mappings between the global and local workspace concepts are required. However, we have illustrated that, in general, neither the propagation selection nor the workspace mapping can be fully automated for the creation of new versions in autonomous local systems. Hence, we recommended to split the local-to-global propagation of new versions in an automated and a user-driven step, because system-wide consistency of versions cannot be guaranteed with full automation.

We are currently working on the design and implementation of a global version model which comprises versioning usability specifications and a system workspace. Furthermore, we investigate how different versioning concepts can be mapped on each other. However, from the experiences of the simple example presented in this paper, we believe that it is unrealistic to strive for a universal solution due to the huge number of possible combinations of existing versioning concepts. Thus we will restrict ourselves to a few typical examples such that the lessons learned from these examples can be guidelines for concrete realisations.

Acknowledgements

We thank Klaus R. Dittrich and Dirk Jonscher for stimulating discussions and advice in the course of the IDEE project and on the preparation of this paper. We further thank the anonymous reviewers for their comments.

References

[BJR98]   G. Booch, I. Jacobson, and J. Rumbaugh. *The Unified Modeling Language User Guide*. Addison–Wesley Publishers, Reading, Mass., USA, 1998.

[BNPS88]   E. Bertino, M. Negri, G. Pelagatti, and L. Sbatella. The COMANDOS integration system: an object–oriented approach to the interconnection of heterogeneous applications. In *Proceedings of the Second International Workshop on Object–Oriented Database Systems (OODBS), Bad Münster am Stein–Ebernburg, Germany*, number 334 in Lecture Notes in Computer Science, pages 213–218. Springer-Verlag, September 1988.

[CEH⁺97]   S. Conrad, B. Eaglestone, W. Hasselbring, M. Roantree, F. Saltor, M. Schönhoff, M. Strässler, and M. Vermeer. Research issues in federated database systems. *SIGMOD Record*, 26(4):54–56, December 1997.

[HD92]   M. Härtig and K. R. Dittrich. An object–oriented integration framework for building heterogeneous database systems. In *Proceedings of the IFIP DS-5 Conference on Semantics in Interoperable Database Systems, Lorne, Australia*, pages 33–53, November 1992.

[Kat90]   R. H. Katz. Toward a unified framework for version modeling in engineering databases. *ACM Computing Surveys*, 22(4):375–408, December 1990.

[KBG89]   W. Kim, E. Bertino, and J. F. Garza. Composite object revisted. *SIGMOD Record*, 18(2):337–347, June 1989.

[RJ96]   R. Ramakrishnan and D. Janaki Ram. Modeling design versions. In *Proceedings of the 22nd International Conference on Very Large Databases (VLDB'96), Mumbai (Bombay), India*, pages 556–566, September 1996.

[SCG91]   F. Saltor, M. G. Castellanos, and M. García–Solaco. Suitability of data models as canonical models for federated databases. *SIGMOD Record*, 20(4):44–48, December 1991.

[Sci94]   E. Sciore. Versioning and configuration management in an object–oriented data model. *VLDB Journal*, 3:77–106, 1994.

[SL90]   A. P. Sheth and J. A. Larson. Federated database systems for managing distributed, heterogeneous, and autonomous databases. *ACM Computing Surveys*, 22(3):183–236, September 1990.

[SS98]   M. Schönhoff and M. Strässler. Issues of global version management in federated database systems for engineering environments. In *10th Workshop "Grundlagen von Datenbanken", Konstanz, Germany*, number 63 in Konstanzer Schriften in Mathematik und Informatik, pages 119–123, May 1998. Extended Abstract.

[SSD97]   M. Schönhoff, M. Strässler, and K. R. Dittrich. Data integration in engineering environments. In *Engineering Federated Database Systems (EFDBS'97) – Proceedings of the International CAiSE'97 Workshop, Barcelona, Spain*, Computer Science Preprint 6/1997, pages 45–56, University of Magdeburg, Germany, June 1997.

[Tic94]   W. F. Tichy, editor. *Configuration Management*. Wiley & Sons Ltd., Chicester, England, 1994.

From Object-Process Diagrams to a Natural Object-Process Language

Mor Peleg and Dov Dori

Faculty of Industrial Engineering and Management
Technion—Israel Institute of Technology
Haifa 32000, Israel
{mor, dori}@ie.technion.ac.il

Abstract. As the requirements for system analysis and design become more complex, the need for a natural, yet formal way of specifying system analysis findings and design decisions are becoming more pressing. We propose the Object-Process Language as a textual natural language means for systems specification that is complementary to the graphic description through Object-Process Diagrams.

1 Natural Languages and Graphic Representations of Systems

As the complexity of computer-based systems grows, precise and concise specification is in increasing demand, calling for new approaches of systems development. One very common and powerful modeling technique is simple prose, or natural language. Natural languages are very powerful because they are the result of thousands of years of evolution, during which humans who use them have developed the ability to make subtle observations and distinctions, such as those made in this sentence. However, natural languages are also frequently ambiguous and always linear, i.e., they must be read and spoken in a linear way – the "reading order". Systems in general and reactive systems in particular, feature things that exist or happen concurrently, making it difficult to model them with prose alone.

Formal textual languages based on logics and algebras are often used to specify complex dynamic systems [1]. Their formality makes it possible to verify desired system properties and check them for internal consistency. These languages are precise, amenable to verification and can potentially also serve as a basis for automatic conversion into executable code. Nevertheless, the task of specifying a system in logic is very difficult, and the resulting specification is hard to follow and understand by non-experts. Formal methods, notation and tools do not yet adequately support the development of large and complex systems [2]. Logics and algebras suffer from one more disadvantage; in addition to their being linear too, they are not intuitive and cannot be understood by non-experts. To demonstrate this, Fig. 1 presents specifications of the system requirement "Following the event of a repairman arriving at an elevator, the action Checking begins its execution within 1 minute" in three different logic languages.

The specification in Fig. 1(a) is done in Real-Time Logic (RTL) [3], the one in Fig. 1(b) is done in Metric Temporal Logic (MTL) [4], and that of Fig. 1(c) – in Timed Transition Models/Real Time Temporal Logics (TTM/RTTL) [5]. While some humans may understand a particular specification more than the other, it is evident from this small example that formal logic-based languages are far from being natural and intuitive, and therefore require a considerable amount of learning, training and adjustment that very few people would be willing to invest. In this work, we propose Object-Process Language (OPL) as a language that is both formal and intuitive, thereby catering to the need of humans on one hand and machines on the other hand. Fig. 1(d) presents the OPL specification of the same system requirement discussed above, which resembles a sentence in English.

$\forall x \, [@(\Omega \text{REPAIRMAN\_ARRIVED\_AT\_ELEVATOR}, x) \leq @(\uparrow \text{CHECKING}, x) \wedge @(\uparrow \text{CHECKING}, x) \leq @(\Omega \text{REPAIRMAN\_ARRIVED\_AT\_ELEVATOR}, x) + 1]$

Legend: Ω - event occurrence; $@$ - time of event occurrence; $\uparrow$ - beginning of an action;

(a)

Repairman_arrived_at_elevator $\rightarrow$ Eventually$_{\leq 1}$ checking

(b)

$\forall T \, [(\text{repairman\_arrived\_at\_elevator} \wedge t = T) \rightarrow \text{Eventually (checking} \wedge t = T+1)]$

(c)

Event RepairmanArrivedAtElevator[external] triggers Checking with a reaction time of (0, 1 m).

(d)

Fig. 1. Specification by logics vs. specification by OPL. (a) RTL; (b) MTL; (c) TTM/RTTL; and (d) OPL. All four specifications specify that following the event of a repairman arriving at an elevator, the action Checking begins its execution within 1 minute.

Diagrams are often invaluable for describing models of abstract things, especially complex systems. An accepted diagramming method has the potential of becoming a powerful modeling tool, provided that it really constitutes an unambiguous language, or a *visual formalism* [6]. A visual formalism is valuable if each symbol in the diagram has a defined semantics and the links among the symbols unambiguously convey some meaningful information that is clearly understood to those who are familiar with the formalism. Object-Process Diagrams (OPDs) provide such a concise visual formalism for specification of systems of all domains and complexity levels analyzed by the Object-Process Methodology (OPM) [7]. OPM is founded on an ontology that distinguishes between objects and processes as two types of things of basically equal status and importance in the specification of a system. The OPM model shows how objects interact with each other via processes such that both the structural and the procedural system aspects are adequately represented. OPM/T [8] is the extension of OPM that handles reactive and real-time systems by specifying system dynamics, including triggering events, guarding-conditions, temporal constraints and exception handling.

2 The Object-Process Language

The Object-Process Language is the textual, natural language-like equivalent of the graphical representation of the system being studied or developed through the OPD set. OPL is designed such that it is very close to English as a natural language, but with much more stringent and limited syntax. The similarity of OPL to natural language makes it readable and understandable to humans without the need to learn any programming or pseudo-code-like language. The system's OPL specification, resulting from an OPD set, is thus amenable to being checked by domain experts, who need not be software experts. While humans can also inspect diagrams, they are not expected to master all the OPD symbols and their semantics. The information provided in a natural language through OPL complements the graphic information and provides for a self-learning tool that can be consulted when in doubt as to the meaning of some graphic construct. Reviewing both the OPD set and is corresponding OPL sentence set decreases the likelihood of missing specification assertions.

This synergy between text and graphics is instrumental in closing the gap between the requirement specification, which is usually expressed in prose, and the actual system specification, resulting from the OPM analysis and design. The syntax of OPL is well defined and unambiguous. This eliminates the problem of the fuzziness of natural languages and provides a firm basis for automated implementation of executable code generation and database schema definition.

Through a detailed walkthrough of a simple case study, this paper presents and demonstrates the principles and syntax of the Object-Process Language, its equivalence to the graphic description done by Object-Process Diagrams and the production of OPL sentences with the OPL grammar.

3 The Elevator Checkup System

The Elevator Checkup and Repair is a simplified case study of a reactive system. The system requirement specification (SRS) document for this small example is listed in Fig. 2. Fig. 3 shows an OPD of the Elevator Checkup and Repair case study and its equivalent OPL text. The OPL text contains OPL sentences, which specify the system in Depth First Search (DFS) order. This ordering means, for example, that after listing the features of a thing T, we specify in detail the features and/or parts of each feature of T before moving on to specify the parts of T, if such parts exist.

> The elevator of a building has to be checked every two years. When the time for a checkup of the elevator arrives, the repairman is summoned. Within one minute of the repairman's arrival to check the elevator, the elevator is checked, and if necessary, repaired, so that it is again in a usable condition.

Fig. 2. The formal system requirement specification (SRS) document for the Elevator Checkup and Repair case study.

The top of the OPD of Fig. 3, as well as the first OPL sentence specify exactly what is understood naturally from reading it, namely the features that characterize Elevator: its object Status, and its two characterizing processes (methods, or services)

RepairmanCalling and **CheckingAndRepairing**. The "features" clause corresponds to the characterization symbol, denoted by the black triangle within a white triangle, as shown in the legend of Fig. 3.

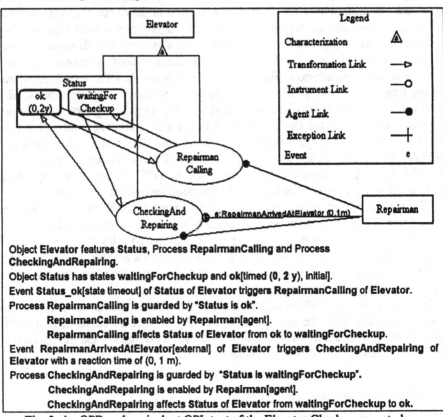

Object Elevator features Status, Process RepairmanCalling and Process CheckingAndRepairing.
Object Status has states waitingForCheckup and ok[timed (0, 2 y), initial].
Event Status_ok[state timeout] of Status of Elevator triggers RepairmanCalling of Elevator.
Process RepairmanCalling is guarded by "Status is ok".
　　RepairmanCalling is enabled by Repairman[agent].
　　RepairmanCalling affects Status of Elevator from ok to waitingForCheckup.
Event RepairmanArrivedAtElevator[external] of Elevator triggers CheckingAndRepairing of Elevator with a reaction time of (0, 1 m).
Process CheckingAndRepairing is guarded by "Status is waitingForCheckup".
　　CheckingAndRepairing is enabled by Repairman[agent].
　　CheckingAndRepairing affects Status of Elevator from waitingForCheckup to ok.

Fig. 3. An OPD and equivalent OPL text of the Elevator Checkup case study.

The following OPL sentences specify the details of the features of Elevator. The **Status** attribute of **Elevator** is specified as an object, which has two states: **waitingForCheckup** and **ok**. State **ok** is the initial state of **Status**, as can be seen in the OPD by its wider contour, and in the OPL sentence, by the use of the keyword initial. State **ok** is time constrained, meaning, in this case, that there is an upper time limit to being in that state.

The maximum time that can be spent in that state is two years (while the minimum time is zero). This is specified in the OPD as the interval (0, 2 year), written within state **ok** of object **Status**, which represents the duration constraint associated with this state. The analogous OPL sentence "Object **Status** has states **waitingForCheckup** and **ok**[[timed (0, 2 year), initial]." specifies these facts just as well.

Once **Status** has been in state **ok** for more than **2** years, a timeout event is triggered, which triggers the **RepairmanCalling** process. This timeout event is specified in the OPD by the Exception link emanating from state **ok** of **Status** to process **Repair-**

manCalling. It is also specified by the OPL sentence "Event Status_ok[state timeout] of Status of Elevator triggers RepairmanCalling of Elevator.".

The name of this event is Status_ok, which is a combination of the name of the state that is duration constrained (ok), preceded by the name of the object containing this state (Status). The event name is followed by the event type, which, in this case is [state timeout], and by the path that leads from state ok of object Status to its Root Object. The Root Object of an object B_1 is defined as an ancestor of B_1 that has no ancestors. In our example, the Root Object is Elevator.

The process RepairmanCalling can take place only if object Status, characterizing the same Elevator, is in state ok. This is specified by the fact that in the OPD, the transformation link (denoted as an arrow), emanates from this state toward the process RepairmanCalling. This same guarding condition is specified by the corresponding OPL sentence

Process RepairmanCalling is guarded by "Status is ok".

The process RepairmanCalling is enabled by the agent Repairman, who has to participate in the process. This is specified by the OPL-sentence "RepairmanCalling is enabled by Repairman[agent].".

The process RepairmanCalling, which characterizes Elevator, affects Status of that same Elevator. The effect is clearly expressed by the OPL-sentence "RepairmanCalling affects Status of Elevator from ok to waitingForCheckup.". In the OPD, it is reflected by the transformation link emanating from state ok of Status to process RepairmanCalling and the transformation link emanating from RepairmanCalling to state waitingFor-Checkup of Status. Note that the RepairmanCalling process is not only responsible for calling the Repairman but also for changing the state of the Elevator Status. In OPM, only processes change the state of an object. There are no direct transitions between object states in which no process is involved.

When Elevator is at state waitingForCheckup, it can respond to the external event marking the arrival of a Repairman at the Elevator. Within 1 minute, this external event triggers the CheckingAndRepairing process of Elevator. In the OPD this is specified by the agent link from Repairman to CheckingAndRepairing that has the letter e, for event, written inside the agent link circle, along which the label "e: Repairman Arrived at Elevator (0,1 m)" is written. The corresponding OPL sentence is

Event RepairmanArrivedAtElevator[external] of Elevator triggers CheckingAndRepairing of Elevator with a reaction time of (0, 1 m).

This sentence specifies the constraint on the reaction time elapsed from the occurrence of the event and the start of the execution of the process. This reaction time constraint is reflected in the OPD by the interval (0, 1 m) attached to the event link that connects the triggering object Repairman to the triggered process CheckingAndRepairing. The same constraint was specified by different logic languages in Fig. 1.

The OPL sentences

Process CheckingAndRepairing is guarded by "Status is waitingForCheckup".
CheckingAndRepairing is enabled by Repairman[agent].
CheckingAndRepairing affects Status from waitingForCheckup to ok.

specify that (a) the CheckingAndRepairing process can only take place if the object Status is in state waitingForCheckup; (b) CheckingAndRepairing is enabled by the agent

Repairman; and (c) CheckingAndRepairing affects Status by changing its state from waitingForCheckup to ok. The OPD of Fig. 3 expresses this graphically.

4 OPL Production Rules

The syntax of OPL is defined as a set of production rules through a context-free grammar [9] G_{OPL}. Like all context-free grammars, $G_{OPL} = \{S, P, \sigma, T\}$, where

S is the *Starting* symbol, from which all OPL sentences are produced;

P is the set of *Production rules*;

σ is the set of *Non-terminals;* and

T is the set of *Terminals.*

Due to lack of space, we cannot list the entire set of production rules. Instead, in Fig. 4, we provide a subset of rules that are used to produce the OPL sentence "Object Elevator features Status, Process RepairmanCalling and Process Checking." of Fig. 3 and show how this production is obtained using these rules.

A production rule (e.g., $A \rightarrow B$) consists of a non-terminal, called the *left side* of the production rule, an arrow, and a sequence of terminals and/or non-terminals called the *right side* of the production rule. Time New Roman Italics are used for representing non-terminals, or expressions, which can be decomposed into other non-terminals and/or terminals, by applying other production rules. Non-italics Arial font letters stand for terminal symbols, which are identifiers (e.g., the object-name Elevator) or reserved words (e.g., for). All OPL sentences use the Arial font. Identifiers (e.g., Elevator) are marked in bold, whereas reserved words are in regular font style. The non-terminal S is designated as the *start* symbol, from which all OPL-sentences are constructed. The '|' symbol represents the logical OR relation. It can be used to combine two production rules that have the same *left side* (e.g., the production rules $A \rightarrow B$ and $A \rightarrow c$ can be combined into the production $A \rightarrow B \mid c$).

The first OPL production rule, R1, specifies that an OPL sentence, produced from the initial symbol S, represents an Object expression, a Process expression, an Event expression or a Relationship expression (Relationship expression is not relevant to our example). R2 states that an object may be simple or complex. R3 states that a complex-object expression begins with the reserved word "Object", followed by the expression *object-statements*. R4 states that an *object-statements* expression can simply be an *object-statement* expression, or can be decomposed into an *object-statement* expression followed by an *object-statements* expression. R5 specifies that an *object-statement* expression can specify object features, parts, states, base class, or derived classes. Rules R6 and R7 are used to derive the *Object-names* expression. Rules R8 through R10 define an *Object-name* as a regular expression that begins by a *Capital Letter*, followed by a sequence of any number (* stands for 0 to many consecutive occurrences) of letters. Rules R11 through R14 specify how the *object-process-list* and *process-list* expressions are expanded.

Fig. 5 shows how the subset of production rules listed in Fig. 4 was used to derive the OPL sentence Object Elevator features Status, process RepairmanCalling and process Checking. The rule numbers are listed above the production rule arrows. To enhance readability, terminals in Fig. 5 are surrounded by frames, such that in the beginning no frame appears, and gradually they become larger and more frequent, until finally the entire sentence is surrounded by one frame.

(R1) *S* → *Object* | *Process* | *Event* | *Relationship*
(R2) *Object* → *simple-object* | *complex-object*
(R3) *complex-object* → Object *object-statements*
(R4) *object-statements* → *object-statement* | *object-statement object-statements*
(R5) *object-statement* → *Object-name* features *object-process-list*. |
  Object-name consists of *aggregate-list*. | *Object-name* has states *state-list* . |
  Object-name specializes *Object-names*. |*Object-name* generalizes *Object-names*.
(R6) *Object-names* → *Object-name* |
  Object-names-within-commas and *Object-name*
(R7) *Object-names-within-commas* → *Object-name* |
  Object-name, *Object-names-within-commas*
(R8) *Object-name* → *CapitalLetter (letter)**
(R9) *CapitalLetter* → **[A..Z]**   (R10) *letter* → **[a..z, A..Z]**
(R11) *object-process-list* → *Object-names* |
  Object-names-within-commas and Process *Process-name* |
  Object-names-within-commas, *process-list*
(R12) *Process-name* → *CapitalLetter (letter* | *digit)**
(R13) *process-list* → Process *Process-name* |
  process-names-with-commas and Process *Process-name*
(R14) *process-names-with-commas* → Process *Process-name* |
  process-names-with-commas , Process *Process-name*

Fig. 4. The subset of OPL production rules required to produce the OPL sentence Object Elevator features Status, Process RepairCalling and Process Checking.

5   Summary and Work in Progress

We have presented the principles of the Object-Process Language as the textual equivalent of the corresponding Object-Process Diagrams. We show how both the OPD and its OPL equivalent specify a system that is being analyzed. Although, for the sake of brevity, the example is simple, it does contain most of the elements required to model systems at any level of complexity, including reactive and real-time systems. The specification reader, when presented with both the graphic and the textual specification modes, enjoys the synergy of this combination. When in doubt as to the semantics of one mode, the other one can always be consulted, and so the two modes support and reinforce each other. The OPDs can, for example, be read in any sequence, and not just in the linear "reading order", which is helpful for presenting concurrent processes. Some people feel more comfortable with one representation while other – with the other.

The resulting OPL text is used for two major purposes: one is to provide a concise specification of the analyzed and designed system feedback to the prospective system customer, while the other is to automate the application generation, i.e., the executable code and database schema generation. Work in progress tackles these two tasks and we already have a working program for C++ code generation that is in line with [10] and database schema generation for relational, object-oriented and object-relational database types. The OPL compiler that generates C++ code creates full code, including a header file and a code file implementing object methods. It relies upon predefined modules that define, among others, classes of processes, states, events and an event queue. We are also improving the readability of OPL by eliminating non-natural elements like parentheses of various kinds.

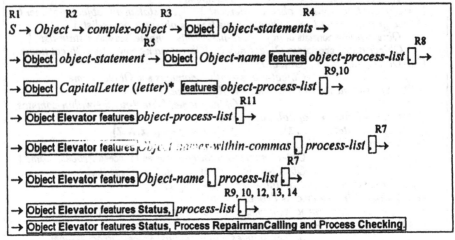

Fig. 5. Production of the OPL sentence "Object **Elevator** features **Status, Process RepairCalling and Process Checking**" by applying the OPL production rules listed in Fig. 4.

References

1. Ostroff, J.S. : Formal Methods for the Specification and Design of Real-Time Safety Critical Systems. The Journal of Systems and Software 18, 1, (1992) 33-60

2. Luqi and Goguen J.A.: Formal Methods: Promises and Problems. IEEE Software 1 (1997) 73-85

3. Jahanian, F. and Mok, A.: Safety Analysis of Timing Properties in Real-Time Systems. IEEE Transactions on Software Engineering Vol. SE-12, No. 9 (1986) 890-904

4. Koymans, R.: Specifying Message Passing and Time Critical Systems With Temporal Logic. Lecture Notes in Computer Science, Vol. 651. Springer-Verlag , Berlin Heidelberg New York (1992)

5. Ostroff, J.L., and Wonham, W.M.: A Framework for Real-Time Discrete Event Control. IEEE Transactions on Automatic Control, 35, 4. (1990) 386-397.

6. Harel, D.: Statecharts: a Visual Formalism for Complex Systems. Science of Computer Programming (1987) 231-274.

7. Dori D.: Object-Process Analysis: Maintaining the Balance between System Structure and Behavior. Journal of Logic and Computation. 5, 2 (1995) 227-249.

8. Peleg, M. and Dori, D.: Extending the Object-Process Methodology to Handle Real-Time Systems. Journal of Object-Oriented Programming 11, 8, (1999) 53-58.

9. Aho, A.V., Sethi, R. and Ullman, J.D.: Compilers/Principles, Techniques, and Tools, Addison-Wesley, 1986.

10. Dori, D. and Goodman, M.: From Object-Process Analysis to Object-Process Design, Annals of Software Engineering, Vol. 2: Object-Oriented Software Engineering: Foundations and Techniques (1996) 25-20.

eColabra

An Enterprise Collaboration & Reuse Environment

Orit Edelstein, Avi Yaeli, Gabi Zodik

IBM Haifa Research Lab

MATAM, Haifa 31905, Israel

{ orit, aviy, gabi }@vnet.ibm.com

Abstract. In this paper we present a new methodology to achieve reuse and knowledge sharing, by applying **information retrieval** techniques to OO resources while exploiting the OO language semantics and characteristics. We present a methodology that can cut down costs not only of development and maintenance but also reduce the *"time to market"*. Unlike traditional reuse processes/infrastructures, we show that applying our methodology requires extremely low investment, leading to a **Win Win solution**. This is achieved by our environment based on autonomous tools that require no support while implementing our approach. We further describe novel techniques to combine free text and attribute based searches and show how they improve search precision. In addition eColabra server collects valuable statistics which can serve as the organization's knowledge management infrastructure.

1   Introduction

The ability to develop new applications (in particular Web-based applications) in a short time is crucial to the success of software companies that need to compete aggressively in today's market. Considering the fact that software technologies emerge very fast, change on a daily basis, this becomes an even more complicated task. For this reason it is vital to share and reuse the knowledge and the programming experience gained inside development organizations in an efficient and productive manner.

Previous attempts have been made at solving the reuse problem. Most solutions rely on radical changes to the developer's programming habits, software engineering processes and software architectures [Griss 97]. Organizations have to establish a reuse infrastructure including a component library where developers have to register their code in specific ways. These attempts have failed in most cases mainly because of the additional overhead which these solutions introduced and because of the additional cost required during the development of reusable components and the maintenance of the component's libraries.

Other projects, such as jCentral [Watson 97] [jCentral 98], attempted to create a global network reuse environment, on the WWW. These projects were focused on the Java language only and assumed that Java programmers share their code on HTTP servers. The later assumption is still valid, however these days we find more and more Java developers inside our organizations, something that was not true two or three years ago. Under this observation, we should first exhaust the knowledge and the reuse of source code inside our organization before seeking it outside on the web. In addition inside the organization's intranet we no longer seek for information on HTTP servers only, but our main target for information gathering is from any shared file system. The advantages are obvious, no royalty is required, the quality of the code is according to the organization's standards, and it can lead to reduction in the cost of code maintenance by sharing the same class library. These are the main reasons that have driven us to establish eColabra, an enterprise collaboration and reuse environment

eColabra supports a large variety of programming languages in addition to Java. eColabra already supports Java, C++, C, OO-COBOL, and COBOL, moreover the same ideas apply to structured documents as well, our system already supports structured and free text searching through HTML and XML documents.

We believe that within the enterprise, code reuse can and should be achieved in more ways than the traditional black box reuse. We perceive **knowledge sharing** as an additional important way of reuse, and in particular the reuse of specific programming knowledge and reuse of design and design patterns.

With eColabra one can **automatically** assemble a repository, with a simple classification scheme that does not require manual registration or quality control, while providing advanced retrieval and visualization mechanisms so as to facilitate the locating and integration of reusable code resources. We have embodied our approach into, eColabra, a **costless** environment for enterprise collaboration & reuse that we describe below.

2   eColabra - The Proposed Solution

We have developed an environment for reuse, *eColabra*, by building upon previous attempts at solving the reuse problem that were based on applying **information retrieval** techniques to software components in general [Frakes & Nejmeh 87] [Maarek et al. 91], or to OO classes [Helm & Maarek 91] [jCentral 98], and applying them to a large variety of programming languages and structured documents in order to create one large reusable repository. We take advantage of highly precise information retrieval indexing [IMT 98] methods and graph visualization techniques (e.g., [Maarek et al. 97] [Zernik & Zodik 97]) in order to customize reuse during the two basic stages of reuse, the classification stage, by using a language (programming language) specific indexing and classification scheme when adding selected resources to the repository, and at the retrieval stage, by displaying the reuse candidates in a meaningful and novel way.

In addition the system includes annotation and notification services. The notification service releases developers from the burden of following the eColabra repository for updates, instead eColabra will provide automatic notification on registered items.

Annotation are feedback collected by eColabra from developers. Once the repository will include a sufficient amount of annotations, the users will be able to specify more detailed queries that can take advantage of this additional information encapsulated inside these annotations.

2.1 Reuse Categories

We consider many additional aspects of code reuse, compared with traditional reuse which focused mainly on Black Box reuse. However, one must consider another major benefit of code reuse, namely *"time to market"*. The time to market will be reduced no matter which of the following reuse methods is being used, although the maintenance and development costs may not be reduced in all cases. However, in many situations the economic advantage of being first in the market can have tremendous impact on the future of the organization in general and create opportunities for much higher profits to the company.

We have classified the various reuse types into the following 6 categories. We have done so in order to emphasize the different potential cost savings between the various reuse methods.

Starting at the top with the best case, i.e. reuse of code and design with frameworks.

- **Frameworks** - reusing code and design

- **Black box reuse** - using the module (class, component) or a class library as is.

- **Collaborated modules and component sharing** - a module being productively maintained by one team and used by several teams.

- **White box reuse** - browsing through the code in order to reuse pieces of it while making local changes.

- **Learn by example** - see how others have implemented or used a class, method, event, or new undocumented features in order to learn from other's experience.

- **Knowledge sharing** - browse or search the enterprise's code resources to find out what has been and is being developed by other teams.

All of the above reuse categories can be achieved while using our tool. However its major contribution is in promoting reuse of the last four categories. Our methodology is focused on knowledge sharing and not on the software process that leads to reusable components and frameworks as traditional reuse methodologies provide.

2.2 An Economic View on Reuse

The two main reasons that lead organizations to try to accomplish reuse are: first the benefits of cutting down development and maintenance costs and second to shorten the time to market of their products. Essentially if one takes a closer look at all the various reasons that drive reuse, one will notice that they are all rooted in economic reasons, mainly in order to improve company's profits.

Naturally the obvious question is the profitability of the entire process and investment, as it is with any project. The answer to this question is not trivial and in many cases impossible to resolve, mainly because these projects have to be measured for long periods while technologies change very fast and require new investments. In addition, the benefit of reuse is very hard to measure.

Our approach to overcome this open question is to provide a solution that involves almost no cost at all. Moreover, compared to costs that organizations have to invest these days in setting up a traditional reuse environment this amount is neglectable. We achieve this goal by providing an automatic tool that can handle all the activities. Based on this fact we state that our strategy is a **Win Win solution**, as the organization using our tool can only gain from the reuse and cannot loose. Even if the high level of black box reuse is not achieved and only more simple cases of reuse happen, they can only raise the company's profit by reducing development and maintenance costs, and more important, the *"time to market"* can be reduced significantly even by these so called lower level reuse categories. This in turn can become a significant factor for companies profits and in their role in the market place.

2.3 eColabra Architecture

The eColabra architecture consists of two main modules, presented in fig 1 and fig 2: information gathering and run time. During the information gathering phase, resources are discovered/crawled, analyzed and stored in a searchable database. During the run time phase, analyzed information is retrieved from the database and results are delivered to the client in a client-server model over the Web via the HTTP protocol.

2.3.1 Information Gathering Architecture

The information gathering module is responsible to collect the raw resource data, analyze it, and then store it in a database. After the analyzed resources have been stored in the database the textual information is indexed, by making use of IBM Intelligent Text Miner [IMT 98]. The time spent in this phase grows linearly with the amount and types of resources that have to be analyzed, it is performed off-line.

Information Gathering Architecture

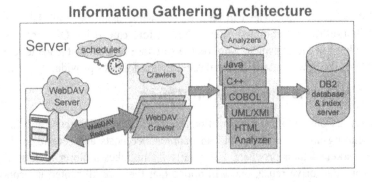

Fig. 1. The information gathering architecture.

2.3.2   Run Time Architecture

The serve/run time architecture is designed as a 3-tier client-server model over the Web, using the HTTP protocol. The client is accessing eColabra HTTP server using a standard browser, filling in forms (in the HTML version) or the various fields in an Applet (in the Applet interface). The outcome of both interfaces is a POST request sent to the server. The client's requests are received by the server and are processed and invoked against the DB2 database server. The query results obtained from the database are further processed by the result processor, formatted and sent back to the client in XML format. The client Applet receives the XML response and presents the results, in case of HTML clients, the XSL [XML 98] processor (on the client browser) will be used with the suitable stylesheet in order to present the XML result.

Run Time Architecture

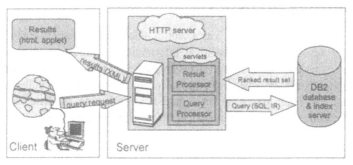

Fig. 2. The run time architecture.

2.4   Search & Retrieval

eColabra provides two kinds of search options *"simple search"* and *"power search"*. In the power search forms, the user is able to query on language specific source attributes. For example, in the Java power search form, the user will be able to ask questions like *"search for all classes that implement method add() and are subclass of Hashtable and include the following free text 'capable to handle large sets of data'"*. The type of searchable attributes varies from one programming language to another, however the OO languages will naturally share many common attributes.

We enable the user to mix attribute-based queries with free text queries. We believe that this feature will enable the users of eColabra to express more precisely their needs and thus the system will be able to provide more precise results. Previous works have based their solution either solely on free text searches [Helm & Maarek 91] or provided attribute based searches only.

This new and important feature, introduces additional complexities. The free text query is a relevance oriented query while the attribute based query is a boolean oriented query. This problem, of mixing different types of queries is known in the literature and some solutions have been suggested [Fagin 98]. In our current implementation we have implemented an algorithm that does an intersection between these two domains. We however, intend to implement Fagin's algorithm and continue research in this field. Another solution we plan to implement for solving this problem is by defining weights for each of the attributes. Then we perform a weighted union on all the records in the database that include at least one of the attributes or obtained a none zero rank in the free text query.

In the context of personalization, we consider to maintain a user profile, in which we will save, among other parameters, the weights of the various attributes as they have been adjusted along the time by each individual user.

2.5   Repository Statistics

One of the additional benefits of eColabra as a central place that developers contact in order to search for resources is the statistical information accumulated over time. Based on our past experience with such systems in particular with jCentral [jCentral 98] we can describe the characteristics and types of information we plan to collect and the conclusion one can reach based on these statistics. Following are listed a few examples that demonstrate the kind of statistical information that we plan to collect with eColabra:

1. Reuse statistics

2. Organization/project design, implementation and usage characteristics based on implementation. These include: (a) design characteristics, for example we can find out how deep are project hierarchies, or what is the average number of inherited classes, the typical/average number of overridden methods, typical number of virtual methods. (b) implementation characteristics include code size, what external packages or libraries are being used, average number of methods per class, average number of classes in a project, etc.

3. User query statistics, this includes a wide range of information regarding the various types and content of queries. For example one could find out what content is most frequently searched for and on what source type it is applied.

3   Conclusions

In this paper we have presented a new methodology to achieve reuse and knowledge sharing, by applying information retrieval techniques to OO resources while exploiting the OO language semantics and characteristics. We have described several novel techniques to combine free text and attribute based searches, used during query composition time and while processing the result sets.

We have demonstrated how by using our methodology one can cut down costs not only of development and maintenance but also reduce the *"time to market"*. Unlike traditional reuse processes/infrastructures, we have shown that applying our methodology requires almost no investment, leading to a **Win Win solution**. This is achieved by our methodology and environment that is based on autonomous tools which requires very low support while implementing our approach.

In addition we plan to exploit eColabra server to collect valuable statistics, both organization's usage patterns and resource assets. We shall further investigate how to exploit this data in particular how it can serve to manage organization's knowledge, which much of it is embodied in it's code resources.

In the near future we plan to investigate new/additional indexing schemes, enable browsing by categories, add additional source/document analyzers and support new novel integration tools to enhance further reuse from within IDEs.

4   Acknowledgments

We express our appreciation to Ron Pinter for his contribution to this project and for all the previous works that have established the ground for this work. We would like to thank Yoelle Maarek and Pnina Vortman for their contribution in past activities that have enabled this project, and David Bernstein for his support through all the stages of this activity.

5   References

[DB2 98] : http://www.software.ibm.com/data/DB2/

[DOM 98] : http://www.w3.org/DOM/

[ECOOP 97] Gabi Zodik, Yardena Peres, Jerry W. Malcolm, Pnina Vortman *"A Framework Registration Language"*, 11th European Conference on Object-Oriented Programming 1997.

[Fagin 98] Ron Fagin, Yoelle Maarek, *"Allowing users to weight search terms"*, IBM Research Report RJ 10108, March 1998.

[Frakes & Nejmeh 87] W. B. Frakes and B. A. Nejmeh. *"Software reuse through information retrieval"*. In the Proceedings of the 20th Annual HICSS, pages 530-535, Kona, HI, January 1987.

[Frakes 97] W. B. Frakes, personal communication, August 97.

[Gamma] Erich Gamma, Richard Helm, Ralph Johnson, and John Vlissides, *"Design Patterns Elements of Reusable Object-Oriented Software"*, Addison-Wesley, ISBN 0-201-63361-2

[Griss 97] Ivar Jacobson, Martin Griss, Patrik Jonsson, *"Software Reuse, Architecture, Process and Organization for Business Succcess"*, ACM press and Addison Wesley Longman, ISBN 0-201-92476-5

[Grouper 98] : http://zhadum.cs.washington.edu/zamir/cluster.html

[Hawaii 99] S. Teng, Q. Lu, M. Eichstaedt, D. Ford, T. Lehman, *"Collaborative Web Crawling: Information Gathering/Processing over Internet"*, Hawaii International Conference on System Sciences, January 1999.

[Helm & Maarek 91] Richard Helm and Yoelle S. Maarek. *"Integrating Information Retrieval and Domain Specific Approaches for Browsing and Retrieval in Object-Oriented Class Libraries"*, In the Proceedings of OOPSLA'91, Las Vegas, 1991.

[jCentral 98] Qi Lu, Reiner Kraft, Matthias Eichstaedt, Gabi Zodik, Daniel Ford, Ron Pinter, Dirk Nicol, *"jCentral: Search the Web for Java"*, WWW8.

[IMT 98] : Intelligent Miner for Text, http://www.software.ibm.com/data/iminer/fortext/

[Maarek et al. 91] Y.S. Maarek, D.M. Berry and G.E. Kaiser, *"An Information Retrieval Approach for Automatically Constructing Software Libraries"*, in Transactions on Software Engineering, 17:8, August 1991.

[Maarek et al. 97] *"WebCutter: A System for Dynamic and Tailorable Site Mapping"*, Yoelle S. Maarek , Michal Jacovi, Menachem Shtalhaim , Sigalit Ur, Dror Zernik and Israel Z. Ben Shaul , Computer Networks and ISDN Systems, Elsevier Science, to appear. Also In the proceedings of the 6th WWW Conference, Santa-Clara, CA, April 1997.

[Oren Z. 98] Oren Zamir, Oren Etzioni, *"Web Document Clustering: A Feasibility Demonstration"*, In proceedings of the 19th ACM SIIR' 98, pages 46-54, 1998.

[Research 97] *"Information on the Fast Track"*, IBM Research Magazine, Vol. 35, No. 3, pp 18-21, 1997

[StrField 97] Reiner Kraft, Qi Lu, Ron Pinter: *"System for Creating Structured Fields on Electronic Forms"*, 1997, US-Patent

[Watson 97] Joshua Dobies, Dan Ford, Reiner Kraft, Pete Lazarus, Qi Lu, Ron Pinter, Orit Edelstein, Yoelle Maarek, Fang Min, Pnina Vortman, Gabi Zodik, *"Java Central: An Internet Java Resource Center"*, The 1997 IBM T.J. Watson Research Java Conference.

[XML 98] : http://www.w3.org/XML/ , http://www.w3.org/TR/WD-xsl

[Zernik & Zodik 97] Dror Zernik and Gabi Zodik, *"A graph management framework for 3D visualization"*, IBM Object Technology 97.

Workflow Management in the Internet Age

C. Mohan

INRIA (Rocquencourt, France) and
The IBM Research Center at Almaden (San Jose, USA)
Email: mohan@wanda.inria.fr, mohan@almaden.ibm.com

In the last few years, workflow management has become a hot topic in the research community and in the commercial arena. Workflow systems hold the promise of facilitating the efficient everyday operation of many enterprises and work environments. Workflow management is multidisciplinary in nature encompasses many aspects of computing: database management, distributed systems, messaging, transaction management, mobile computing, collaboration, business process modelling, integration of legacy and new applications, document management, etc.

Many academic and industrial research projects have been underway for a while. Numerous products are currently in use. The capabilities of these products are being enhanced in significant ways. Standardization efforts are in progress under the auspices of the Workflow Management Coalition and OMG.

As has happened in the RDBMS area with respect to some topics, in the workflow area also some of the important real-life problems faced by customers and product developers are not being tackled by researchers. Based on my experience founding and leading the Exotica workflow project at IBM Research, and my close collaboration with the IBM FlowMark (now called MQSeries Workflow) and Lotus Notes product groups, in this talk I will discuss the issues relating to contemporary workflow management systems. I will also elaborate on various directions for research and potential future extensions to the design and modelling of workflow management systems.

A Component-Based Workflow System with Dynamic Modifications*

Pinar Koksal   Ibrahim Cingil   Asuman Dogac

Software Research and Development Center
Department of Computer Engineering
Middle East Technical University (METU)
06531 Ankara Turkiye
asuman@srdc.metu.edu.tr

Abstract. Adapting to changes in its environment dynamically is a very important aspect of workflow systems. In this paper, we propose a component-based workflow system architecture specifically designed for this purpose. To allow for easy modification of workflow instances, an instance is designed as an object that contains all the necessary data and control information as well as its execution history. This feature facilitates to dynamically modify the process definition on instance basis at run time. The system is designed to consist of functional components like, Basic Enactment Service, History Manager, Workflow Monitoring Tool, Dynamic Modification Tool, etc. The clients of the system are coded as network-transportable applets written in Java so that the end user can activate workflow system components by connecting to the Workflow Domain Manager over the Internet. In this paper we also present a workflow process definition language $FLOW_{DL}$, its graphical representation $FLOW_{GRAPH}$ and a workflow process modification language $FLOW_{ML}$ and illustrate how the modification process is handled.

1   Introduction

A workflow is defined as a collection of processing steps (activities) organized to accomplish some business processes. An activity can be performed by one or more software systems or machines, by a person or a team, or a combination of these. In addition to collection of activities, a workflow defines the order of activity invocations or condition(s) under which activities must be invoked (i.e. control flow) and data-flow between these activities. Activities within a workflow can themselves again be a workflow.

It is widely recognized that one of the basic characteristics that workflow system should provide is flexibility. In a fast-changing environment, companies need to constantly refine their processes in order to effectively meet the constraints

---

* This work is partially being supported by Middle East Technical University, the Graduate School of Natural and Applied Sciences, Project Number: AFP-97-07.02.08 and by the Scientific and Technical Research Council of Turkey, Project Number: 197E038.

and opportunities proposed by new technology, new market requirements, and new laws. Furthermore, in particular in the first execution of a process, unplanned situations not considered in the design could urge for a modification of the workflow definition [4].

Change in business processes can arise due to three main reasons [22]: *Process Improvement,* which involves performing the same business process with increased efficiency, e.g., organizational restructuring. *Process Innovation,* which involves performing the business process in a radically different way. *Process Adaptation,* which involves adapting the process for unforeseen change, e.g. passing of a new law or handling a special case in student admission.

One of the most challenging issues in the modification of workflows is the management of executions started with the old workflow model. Simple solutions, such as letting the processes finish according to the old model or aborting them, are often inconvenient or impossible to be applied, depending on the notification of the change and the nature of the workflow.

In this paper, we propose a component-based workflow system architecture specifically designed for adapting the business processes to changes in its environment dynamically. We also present a workflow process definition language $FLOW_{DL}$, its graphical representation $FLOW_{GRAPH}$ and a workflow process modification language $FLOW_{ML}$. Afterwards we illustrate how the modification process is handled.

The paper is organized as follows: In Section 2, related work is presented. Section 3 provides the system architecture, namely $FLOW_{DL}$, $FLOW_{GRAPH}$ and component-based workflow architecture. Handling dynamic modifications is described in Section 4. The syntax of $FLOW_{ML}$ and an example are also provided in this section. Finally, the paper is concluded with Section 5.

2 Related Work

[4] focuses on workflow modifications involving the flow structure, i.e., the definition of the sequence in which activities should be executed within a process. They propose a complete, minimal and consistent set of primitives that allow generic modification of a workflow, preserving syntactical correctness criteria both when they are applied to a static workflow description and to dynamic workflow instances. Then a taxonomy of policies to manage evolution of running instances when the corresponding workflow schema is modified, is introduced.

Three main policies have been devised to manage workflow instance evolution:

- *Abort:* All workflow instances of old schema are aborted.
- *Flush:* All existing instances terminate following the old schema. When all instances are finished, new instances can start following the new schema.
- *Progressive:* Different decisions for different instances are taken, according to instance's state or its history. Multiple schema versions may exist at the same time. It is the workflow administrator that should analyze running

instances of old workflow schema, and for each of them, define which policy should be applied.

In [17], Liu et.al. propose a handover policy specification language. A handover policy is specified to migrate current running instances of a workflow model to the new workflow model. When a handover policy is applied to an evolution of a workflow model, the running instances may be executing at any task of the old specification. Therefore, different instances may require different handover strategies. A handover policy is defined by a set of handover statements. Three handover aspects of a running instance are described in each handover statement: current position, history and action to be taken. Three actions are supported: rollback, change-over and go-ahead.

In [19], [20], a formal foundation for the support of dynamic structural changes of running workflow instances is presented. Based upon a formal workflow model, ADEPT, a complete and minimal set of change operations, ADEPT-$_{flex}$ is defined. ADEPT$_{flex}$ comprises operations for inserting tasks as well as whole task blocks into a workflow graph, for deleting them, for fast forwarding the progress of a workflow by skipping tasks, for jumping to currently inactive parts of a workflow graph, for serializing tasks that were previously allowed to run in parallel, and for the dynamic iteration and the dynamic rollback of a workflow respectively of a workflow region.

The structural changes are managed differently according to whether an applied change must be preserved until the completion of the workflow (permanent change), or whether it is only of temporary nature (temporary change). If it is a temporary change, then the change should be undone at the next iteration.

In [21], the authors use the clinical application domain to explain and to elaborate the functionality needed to support dynamic workflow changes in an advanced application environment using ADEPT$_{flex}$. In [19] and [20], they have only considered the adhoc changes, that do not affect the original workflow template. However in [21], issues related to the adaptations in the definition of a workflow type are also addressed and migrating the running workflow instances from the old template to the new one is discussed.

[10] presents a formal definition of a dynamic change, and a mathematical approach to its analysis. They use a Petri net formalism to analyze structural change within workflow procedures. Two types of dynamic changes are defined: *immediate*, i.e., changes done on a region take effect immediately, and *quasi-immediate*, i.e., both the old and the new change regions are maintained in the new region. Quasi-immediate change ensures that tokens already in the old change region will finish their progression in the old region.

In [12], changes are differentiated at four different levels: structure level, task level, resource level and system level. Structure level changes affect the interdependencies and sequences of tasks, task level changes are concerned with modifications of individual tasks, resource level changes are concerned with changes of workflow resources, and system level changes refer to adjustments of a concrete execution environment. The authors claim that this separation is very useful for allocating responsibility and controlling change right.

The authors also mention about two popular approaches concerning the adaptation of workflow models; meta-model approach and open-point approach. Meta-model approaches utilize meta-models to determine the structures and types of constituent components of workflow models. A set of primitives is usually defined with which change operations can be performed to a workflow model or even a certain model instance. Open-point approaches set up special points in a workflow model, where adaptation can be made. The concept of adaptation is often generalized, including provision of multiple choices for users, binding of certain resources at runtime, or provision of an open interface through which the late-modeling can be made. A major deficiency of open-point approaches is that they have difficulties to deal with certain structural changes. The approach that have been discussed in [12], supports both the meta-model and open-point approaches.

In [22], the following classes of change for workflows are identified:

- *Flush:* All current instances are allowed to complete according to the old process model.
- *Abort:* An ongoing workflow could be deliberately aborted when the process model is changed.
- *Migrate:* The change affects all current and new instances.
- *Adapt:* This class of change includes cases of errors and exceptions, where the process model does not change, but some instances have to be treated differently because of some exceptional and unforeseen circumstances.
- *Build:* Building of a new process is also a class of process change. The difference is that the starting point is not a detailed pre-existing model, but an elementary description.

The authors in [22], differentiate between two aspects of the workflow model: The *build time* aspect relates to the semantics of the process, and is captured by the process model. The *run time* aspect relates to process instances, and is handled by the process execution model. Then a simple formalization of a workflow, as a directed acyclic graph, is introduced by giving the necessary definitions formally.

After the workflow model is described, a three-phase methodology for dynamic modification is proposed which consists of defining, conforming to and effectuating the modification.

In [18], a family of activity-split and activity-join operations with a notion of validity are described. The Transactional Activity composition Model (TAM) as a concrete underlying environment for the specification of workflows with well defined semantics, is adopted, since TAM has a simple and effective facility feature to allow activity designers to specify the behavioral composition of complex activities and a wide variety of activity interaction dependencies declaratively and incrementally. In the paper, first, basics for activity restructuring operations are described on the TAM. Afterwards, two groups of activity restructuring operations, namely *activity-split* and *activity-join* operations, to allow users or applications to dynamically modify the set of concurrent activities while they are in progress are introduced.

In [14], first, the requirements of workflow evolution are identified. The different propagation strategies of workflow schema changes to their workflow instances that have to be provided by a WFMS are given:

- *Lazy propagation:* A workflow schema is changed without any impact on currently enacting instances. The new workflow schema version becomes only relevant for all new workflow instances.
- *Eager propagation:* Workflow schema changes are propagated immediately to all workflow instances of the changed workflow definition.
- *Selective propagation:* Workflow schema changes are propagated immediately to a selected set of workflow instances of the changed workflow definition.
- *Local modifications and upward propagation:* The propagation is applied to exactly one workflow instance in order to locally customize the workflow structure for a special case or to locally adjust it. This strategy is also useful in the case of processes which cannot be planned completely in advance.
- *Merging:* When changes have to be applied to different workflow variants, some mechanisms are required which support merging of different workflow specifications.

The process modeling, described in [14], is based on object-oriented modeling techniques. Workflow schema and workflow instance elements are modeled as first level objects and their relationships are explicitly maintained. The workflow schema and instance elements are tightly integrated. Workflow schema changes immediately affect all instances since the workflow engine will schedule the task according to the changed schema. To support lazy and selective propagation as well as local modifications of a workflow instance, the schema versioning is used.

3 Component-Based Workflow System Architecture: METUFlow$_2$

3.1 METUFlow$_2$ Process Definition Language: FLOW$_{DL}$

METUFlow$_2$ has a block structured specification language, namely METUFlow$_2$ Process Definition Language (FLOW$_{DL}$). FLOW$_{DL}$ describes the tasks involved in a business process and the execution and data dependencies between these tasks. FLOW$_{DL}$ has also a graphical user interface developed through Java which allows defining a workflow process by accessing METUFlow$_2$ from any computer that has a Web browser [25]. This feature of METUFlow$_2$ makes it possible to support mobile users.

The WfMC have identified a set of six primitives with which to describe flows and hence construct a workflow specification [13]. With these primitives it is possible to model any workflow that is likely to occur. These primitives are: sequential, AND-split, AND-join, OR-split, OR-join and repeatable task. These primitives are all supported by FLOW$_{DL}$ through its block types. FLOW$_{DL}$ contains eight types of blocks, namely, serial, and_parallel, or_parallel, xor_parallel, for_each, contingency, conditional and iterative blocks. Of the above block types,

```
DEFINE_PROCESS OrderProcessing()
  ...
  GetOrder(OUT productNo, OUT quantity, OUT dueDate, OUT orderNo,
           OUT customerInfo)
  EnterOrderInfo(IN productNo, IN quantity, IN dueDate, IN orderNo)
  CheckBillofMaterial(IN productNo, OUT partList)
  PAR_AND (part = FOR EACH partList)
    SERIAL
        DetermineRawMaterial(IN part.No, IN part.Quantity, OUT rawMaterial,
                             OUT required)
        CheckStock(IN rawMaterial, IN required, OUT missing)
        IF (missing > 0) THEN
           VendorOrder(IN rawMaterial, IN missing)
        WithdrawFromStock(IN rawMaterial, IN required)
        GetProcessPlan(IN part.No, OUT processPlan, OUT noofSteps)
        i:=0
        WHILE (i < noofSteps)
           Assign(IN processPlan[i].cellId, IN orderNo, IN part.No,
                  IN part.Quantity, IN rawMaterial, IN required)
        END_WHILE
    END_SERIAL
  END_PAR_AND
  AssembleProduct(IN productNo)
  ...
  Billing(IN orderNo, IN productNo, IN quantity, IN customerInfo)
  ...
END_PROCESS
```

Fig. 1. Order Processing Example

serial block implements the sequential primitive. And_parallel block models the
AND-split and AND-join primitives. AND-split, OR-join pair is modeled by
or_parallel block. Conditional block corresponds to OR-split and OR-join primitives. Finally, repeatable task primitive is supported by the iterative block.

A workflow process is defined as a collection of blocks, tasks and subpro-
cesses. A task is the simplest unit of execution. Processes and tasks have input
and output parameters corresponding to workflow relevant data to communicate with other processes and tasks. The term *activity* is used to refer to a block,
a task or a (sub)process. Blocks differ from tasks and processes in that they
are conceptual activities which are used only to specify the ordering and the
dependencies between activities.

An order processing example in a highly automated manufacturing enterprise is provided using $FLOW_{DL}$ [3], [8], [11], [15], [16]. An incoming customer
request causes a product order to be created and inserted into an order entry database by *GetOrder* and *EnterOrderInfo* activities respectively (Figure 1).
The next step is to determine required parts to assemble the ordered product
by *CheckBillofMaterial* activity. A part is the physical object which is fabricated
in the manufacturing system. For each part, *DetermineRawMaterial* activity
is executed to find out the raw materials required to manufacture that part,

and a *CheckStock* activity is initiated afterwards to check stock database for the availability of these raw materials. If the required amounts of these raw materials do not exist in the stock, they should be ordered from the external vendors through *VendorOrder*. After all missing raw materials are obtained, required raw materials to fabricate the part is withdrawn from the stock to be sent to the manufacturing cells. This is accomplished by *WithdrawFromStock* activity by decrementing the available amount of the withdrawn raw material (i.e., $quantity(m)$) in the stock database. The required steps to manufacture a part, and the manufacturing cells where these steps are performed are obtained as a result of *GetProcessPlan*. Actual manufacturing activity is initiated by assigning the work to the corresponding cells for each step in *Assign*. Finally, manufactured parts are assembled to form the product that the customer had ordered by the activity *AssembleProduct*. Further downstream activities include a billing activity. *Billing* is responsible for collecting bills of ordered products. *VendorOrder*, *GetProcessPlan* and *Billing* are also workflow processes which should be defined in the same manner as *OrderProcessing*.

In METUFlow$_2$, there are five types of tasks. These are TRANSACTIONAL, NON-TRANSACTIONAL, NON-TRANSACTIONAL with CHECKPOINT, USER and 2PC_TRANSACTIONAL activities. USER activities are in fact NON-TRANSACTIONAL activities. They are specified separately in order to be used by the worklist manager which handles the user-involved activities.

These activity types may have some attributes such as CRITICAL, NON-VITAL and CRITICAL_NON_VITAL. Critical activities can not be compensated and the failure of a non-vital activity is ignored [7], [5]. Besides these attributes, activities can also have some properties like retriable, compensatable, and undoable. A retriable activity restarts execution depending on some condition when it fails. Compensation is used in undoing the visible effects of activities after they are committed. Effects of an undoable activity can be removed depending on some condition in case of failures.

The block structured nature of FLOW$_{DL}$ prevents cyclic definitions and unreachable states. The further advantages brought by this language are summarized in [8].

3.2 Graphical Representation of the FLOW$_{DL}$: FLOW$_{GRAPH}$

METUFlow$_2$ system has graphical tools to define a new process definition, to modify the definition dynamically and to monitor the state of the instances, described in detail in the next section. The same graphical representation, called FLOW$_{GRAPH}$, is used at these tools. In FLOW$_{GRAPH}$, each block has a *begin* and *end nodes*. For the AND_PARALLEL, OR_PARALLEL, XOR_PARALLEL and IF blocks, the join node is the *end node*. However SERIAL, CONTINGENCY, WHILE, FOR_EACH blocks have their own *end nodes*. The representation of the blocks in FLOW$_{GRAPH}$ can be seen in Figure 2.

In Figure 2, circles represent the activities. If the activity is a subprocess, it is shown with a thicker circle. Also note that, since a process definition has

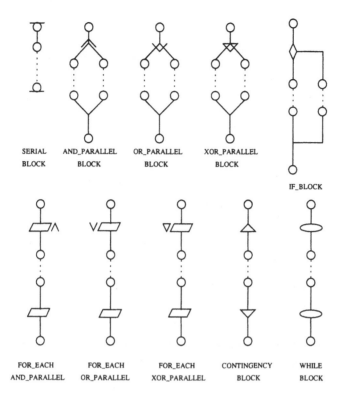

SERIAL   AND_PARALLEL   OR_PARALLEL   XOR_PARALLEL
BLOCK   BLOCK   BLOCK   BLOCK

IF_BLOCK

FOR_EACH   FOR_EACH   FOR_EACH   CONTINGENCY   WHILE
AND_PARALLEL   OR_PARALLEL   XOR_PARALLEL   BLOCK   BLOCK

Fig. 2. The representation of the blocks in FLOW$_{GRAPH}$

SERIAL_BLOCK characteristics although not defined explicitly, the begin and end of a process are shown similar to that of SERIAL_BLOCK.

The graphical representation of the order processing example, described in Section 3.1 is given in Figure 3.

3.3 Component-Based Architecture

We have designed a workflow system architecture based on Internet and CORBA with the following features:

- Each process instance is a CORBA object that contains all the necessary data and control information as well as its execution history. This feature makes it possible to dynamically modify the process definition on the instance basis at run time, and to migrate the object in the network to provide load balancing. It should be noted that with this architecture, a site failure affects only the process instances running on that site.
- The system is designed to consist of functional components containing but not restricted to: Basic Enactment Service, User Worklist Manager, Workflow Monitor, Workflow History Manager, Dynamic Modification Tool, Process Definitions Library Manager, Reliable Message Queue Manager, and

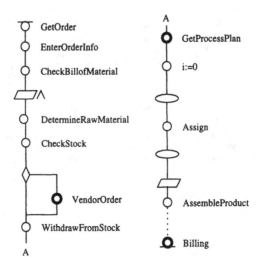

Fig. 3. The representation of the order processing example in FLOW$_{GRAPH}$

Workflow Domain Manager. This component-based architecture makes it possible to incorporate the functionality and thus the complexity only when it is actually needed at run time by a process instance by downloading only the necessary components which results in effective usage of system and network resources. It is also possible to add new components or maintain and upgrade the existing components of the system incrementally without effecting the other parts of the system. The component-based architecture facilitates the replication to a great extent. Each site can download its own copy of component server; also the Workflow Domain Manager can be replicated at each site as a Site Manager. This provides for availability and prevents network overhead.

The clients of the system are coded as network-transportable applets written in Java so that the end user can acquire workflow components from the Workflow Domain Manager over the network. Thus it is not necessary to have the software pre-installed on the user machine. This promotes user mobility further as well as easy maintenance of the system components which can be upgraded transparently on the server side.

There are four basic components of the METUFlow$_2$ system architecture shown in Figure 4, as presented in the following:

1. *Component-Server Repository:* The components of the system are implemented as CORBA objects that are invoked by Java applets. The Component-Server Repository contains these applets. The Java applets are downloaded to the client machine when a user through a Web browser accesses the Workflow Domain Manager and asks for a specific service. Thereon the Java applets interact with the user and direct the user requests to the appropriate

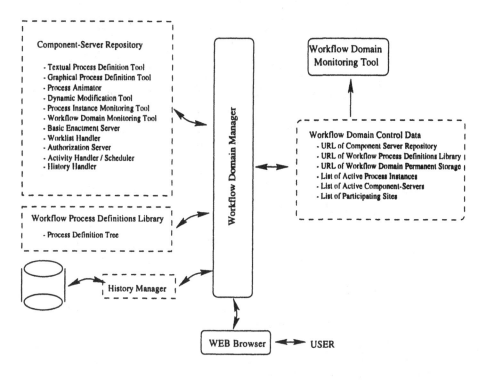

Fig. 4. Basic components of the METUFlow₂ Architecture

CORBA objects. Some of the components of our system are listed in the following:

- *Workflow Process Definition Tool;* to define new workflow processes.
- *Workflow Dynamic Modification Tool;* to modify previously defined workflow processes that are stored in the Workflow Process Definition Library and/or a particular workflow process instance.
- *Workflow Process Instance (WPI) Monitoring Tool;* to trace workflow process instances that have been initiated and extract run-time information about the current execution status of an instance.
- *Monitoring and Measurement Tool;* to collect and measure process enactment data needed to improve subsequent process enactment iterations as well as documenting what actions actually occurred in what order.
- *Enactment History Capture and Replay;* to simulate the re-enactment of a process graphically in order to more readily observe process state transitions or to intuitively detect possible process enactment anomalies.

2. *Workflow Process Definitions Library:* Workflow definitions (i.e. process templates), organizational role definitions, participant-role assignments are durably stored in this library. Only Workflow Specification Tool and Dynamic

Modification Tool inserts or updates workflow process templates in this library. This library is maintained by the WFMS Library Manager.

Different workflow schema versions have to be managed and different propagation strategies of workflow schema changes to their workflow instances have to be provided by a WFMS in order to flexibly support the migration from one business process to an improved one, to support alternative workflows for process variants, and to support adhoc changes of a workflow [14]. When the workflow definition is modified permanently, the versions of workflow definitions are stored, since:

- In some cases, it may be necessary to recover to the old workflow definition. For example, when it is observed that the new definition performs worse than the old definition.
- It may be desired that more than one version of definitions are active at the same time. That is, some instances are created from one version, and some others from a different version of the definition.

In the METUFlow$_2$ architecture, to handle the versioning of definitions, a *definition tree* is kept to provide the administrator the flexibility of modifying a definition several times. During the modification, the administrator selects one version, default being the last one. Thus new instances are created from the default definition, if the version number of workflow definition is not identified explicitly during the instance creation.

3. *History Manager:* The History Manager handles the database that stores the information about workflow process instances which have been enacted to completion to provide history related information to its clients (e.g. for data mining purposes). It should be noted that the history of active process intances are stored in the process instance object.

4. *Workflow Domain Manager:* The Domain Manager is the Web server of the system. All clients access to the Domain Manager via their Web browsers and in response to their authorized service requests, the Domain Manager downloads appropriate Java applets to the client which then handles subsequent requests of the same client for that particular service which is provided by a component server. If the client needs a different WFMS service, the Domain Manager is then accessed again via the Web browser and another Java applet is downloaded. The Domain Manager keeps runtime information such as list of active process instances, active component servers, list of participating sites, etc. for domain monitoring purposes.

The run-time system despite having a central control on a process instance basis, brings out all the benefits of highly distributed environments. Each WPI may execute at a different site. Component-Server Repository, Workflow Definition Library, Workflow Domain Control Data and Workflow Domain Manager may all be replicated for better performance and availability. Each participating site may have its own replication of Workflow Domain Manager as the Site Manager. Since no prior installation of any WFMS software is required on the client side the system is highly dynamic and thus any component-server implementation may be upgraded at the server side without needing any changes on the client side. In addition a site failure can be overcome simply by migrating the instances to be executed on that site to another site/other sites. Detailed work on the component-based workflow system architecture can be found in [6].

4 Handling Dynamic Modifications in METUFlow$_2$

The set of running instances of a workflow definition can be called as *instance domain*. The modifications can be applied to none of the instances, to a single instance, to a set of instances, or to all of the instances of the *instance domain* depending on the modification that has been done and what the modification administrator, who has granted to make modifications on workflow definitions, defines as the domain that the modifications are applied. For example, a modification can be applied on the instances which have passed a particular point on the execution flow or a modification can not be applied to some of the instances since they have passed the critical point. The administrator can indicate the domain on which the modifications are applied. If the domain is not given, the modification is applied to all of the instances.

The changes can be classified in two groups, as permanent and temporary changes:

- For permanent changes, the workflow definition is changed permanently, so that the new instances are created from the new definition by default. The running instances may also be selectively migrated to the new definition.
- For temporary changes, the modification is only applied to the running instances, but not to the workflow definition. For example, there may be some user activities which are assigned to the users by adding the activity to their worklists, in the workflow definition. If a user is absent temporarily, because of illness for example, her/his activities can be assigned to another user who takes the responsibility of the activities of the absent user.

In our system, dynamic modification of an instance and/or a workflow definition template can be initiated in two ways: either by a user or by means of a special activity specified in the process definition as explained in the following:

- A user via her/his Web browser may access the Workflow Domain Manager and download the Dynamic Modification Tool which helps the administrator make necessary changes on the workflow definition and/or the running instances. Modifications on the workflow definition can only be done by authorized users.

  Dynamic Modification Tool asks the Authorization Server about the modification grant of the user whether the user can modify the definition, or not. Three different grants can be given to the users according to their roles by the Authorization Server:

  - *modify-permanently;* given to the users, like system administrator, to modify the workflow definition template and/or some/all of the process instances in the instance domain.

- *modify-temporarily-all;* given to the users to modify some/all of the instances in the instance domain temporarily. These users, who have this type of grant, can not modify the workflow definition template.
- *modify-temporarily-own;* given to the users to modify only the instances that they are the owners. These users also can not modify the workflow definition template.

If the user has taken any one of the modification grants, s/he chooses a workflow definition to update. The information about definitions can be obtained from Workflow Process Definition Library through Workflow Domain Manager and the set of running instances can be obtained from the Workflow Domain Control Data of the Workflow Domain Manager.

– Workflow process definition may contain a special activity called Workflow Process Modification Activity (WPMA) that (when executed) automatically invokes the WPI Dynamic Modification Tool on behalf of a user so that the user can modify the process instance. The WPMA handles instance-specific differences of the process definition when necessary. Each specification of the WPMA activity results in a separate modification of the instance. A WPMA initiated modification may not affect other instances of the same workflow process or the workflow definition template.

After the modification process is initiated by any one of the ways described above, the workflow definition is represented graphically using the $FLOW_{GRAPH}$.

The user can make the following modifications on this graphical definition using the Dynamic Modification Tool:

– A new activity can be defined, and inserted in the workflow definition.
– New control dependencies can be given, or they can be changed.
– Conditions can be updated or a new one can be given.
– The values of workflow relevant data can be modified.
– Block types can be updated.
– A user or a role, assigned to a user activity, can be changed.
– Activities can be deleted.

In addition to these modifications and augmentations, the domain can be specified to identify the instances that the modifications are to be applied, along with the type of modification, whether permanent or temporary.

After all of the necessary information are gathered from the user, by going through both the old and the new workflow definitions, the modification region is determined. A *modification region* contains the minimum part of the definition that includes all the modifications, that is, starts with the first modified activity and ends with the last one. An example is given in Figure 5.

If the modification is to be applied to the running instances, the modification region is checked for the critical points, if there are any in the workflow definition. If the modification region is after the critical points in the execution flow, then all the instances of this definition can be adapted to the new definition. However if a critical point is after the modification region, execution states of the instances

```
P1() {                          P1() {
    T1;                             T1;
    T2;                             T2;
    AND_PARALLEL {                  T6;             ---
        T3;                         AND_PARALLEL {   |
        T4;                             T3;          | Modification
    }                                   T4;          | Region
    T5;                             }                |
}                                   T7;             ---
                                    T5;
                                }
```

Fig. 5. A Modification Region Example

should be checked. If their executions have passed the critical point and the critical activity needs to be compensated to migrate the running instance to the new definition, then the modification should be rejected for these instances. If the critical point has not been executed yet, then the modification can be applied to these instances.

The instances that the modification can be applied, are grouped according to their execution states:

- The instances whose execution states has not reached to the modification region yet, are directly adapted to the new definition.
- If the first activity of the modification region is running then this activity is aborted, and these instances can continue their executions from the new workflow definition.
- If the execution is either running in the modification region or has passed the region, then the execution of these instances are held on. The activities until the beginning of the modification region are rolled back according to a compensation strategy. Afterwards their execution can continue using the new schema. For an activity (if it is not a critical activity), if a compensation activity is not given, this means that there is no need to compensate this activity during recovery. Also note that, critical activities can not be recovered, therefore they do not have compensation activities.

Dynamic Workflows which have no pre-specified process definition can be handled with another special activity called Dynamic Workflow Special Activity (DWSA) that automatically invokes the Dynamic Modification Tool on behalf of a user so that the user can specify the next activity to be executed. A dynamic workflow process definition initially includes only one activity, the DWSA. When this process is initiated, the DWSA invokes the Dynamic Modification Tool and awaits the user to specify activities to be executed. When the user specifies the next activity or activities, another DWSA is appended automatically such that after the user-specified next activity(s) is executed, the DWSA will be invoked again. The DWSA will not be appended only if the user explicitly indicates that no more activities are to be specified in which case the termination of DWSA will indicate the termination of the process instance. In this way a workflow process can interactively be defined on-the-fly by a user and it is saved in the Workflow Process Definition Library if the user specifies so at the terminating DWSA.

4.1 METUFlow$_2$ Modification Language: FLOW$_{\mathrm{ML}}$

The user who has a grant to modify a workflow definition or its running instances, should provide:

- an action, the modification that should be made. The user can provide this information using our modification language, FLOW$_{ML}$ as:

```
{ ADD | MODIFY | DELETE } { PROCESS <processname> |
                            TASK <taskname> |
                            BLOCK <blkname> |
                            CONDITION AT <activityname> |
                            WRD <wrdname> | USER AT <activityname> |
                            ROLE AT <activityname> } [AS <new defn> ]
```

- a place, where the modification is applied, can be given using FLOW$_{ML}$ as:

```
[ AFTER { <activityname> | <blkname> } | BEFORE { <activityname> |
  <blkname> } | IN { <activityname> | <blkname> } ]
```

- a domain that includes the instances to which the modification is applied, by providing the object references or the execution states of the instances. This information can be given using FLOW$_{ML}$ as:

```
DOMAIN [ALL | NONE] <processname>
[ WHICH OBJ_REF <comparison_op> objref |
  BEFORE { <activityname> | <blkname> } STARTS |
  AFTER { <activityname> | <blkname> } COMMITS |
  AT { <activityname> | <blkname> } EXECUTING ]
```

- the type of the modification, permanent or temporary, can be given as:

```
[PERMANENTLY | TEMPORARILY]
```

More than one modification statements can be combined with **AND** connector.

The user can use either our modification language, FLOW$_{ML}$, or graphical dynamic modification tool to specify the modifications or additions.

After the modification of the processes, the modified process definition is checked for the following:

- If a new activity is defined, its input parameters are checked whether they have been defined or not, before the activity.
- Task, block and process names that appear in the "place" or "domain" part of the FLOW$_{ML}$ are checked whether they exist in the old definition or not.
- For DELETE and MODIFY statements, the validity of task names, block names, conditions, role names, user names and wrd names are checked.
- For DELETE statements, it is checked that whether the deletion affects the input and output parameters of other activities.

4.2 An Example

The manufacturer may decide to modify their billing process as requesting some percentage of the total payment in advance before the manufacturing steps have started. Therefore a new *"RequestPayment"* activity may be added after the activity *"EnterOrderInfo"*. Additional changes should be handled at the *Billing* subprocess also. In METUFlow$_2$, these modifications can be defined either graphically by using the Dynamic Modification Tool, or textually by FLOW$_{ML}$. The FLOW$_{ML}$ statements for these modifications are as follows:

```
ADD TASK RequestPayment (IN int orderNo, IN int productNo,
                         IN int quantity, IN custumerStruct customerInfo,
                         OUT double amountPaid)
AFTER EnterOrderInfo
AND
MODIFY PROCESS Billing
AS Billing (IN int orderNo, IN int productNo, IN int quantity,
            IN custumerStruct customerInfo, IN double amountPaid)
AND
MODIFY TASK Payment
AS Payment (IN int orderNo, IN int productNo, IN int quantity,
            IN custumerStruct customerInfo, OUT double amount,
            OUT int paymentStatus, IN double amountPaid)
DOMAIN ALL OrderProcessing
PERMANENTLY;
```

First FLOW$_{ML}$ statement adds a new activity *"RequestPayment"* after the activity *"EnterOrderInfo"*. Second and third statements add a new *IN* parameter to the *"Billing"* subprocess and the *"Payment"* task respectively. The *"RequestPayment"* task should be written and the operation logic of the *"Payment"* task should also be changed accordingly. However from a workflow point of view, a WFMS does not have the responsibility of providing these changes. This modification is applied to all of the instances of the process *"OrderProcessing"* and the definition of the process is also modified permanently. This means that a new version of the definition is created and stored in the Process Definitions Library.

5 Conclusion and Future Work

Business processes need to be constantly refined in order to effectively meet the constraints and opportunities proposed by new technology, new market requirements, and new laws. Workflow Management Systems, which are used for the development of business applications, should provide the facilities to manage the dynamic modification of running instances to the modified definition. The component-based architecture that we propose in this paper facilitates dynamic modification on an instance basis and avoids process template modification problems by keeping the process definition for each instance separately. After The user provides the modifications to the process definition either by using FLOW$_{ML}$ or by using graphical modification tool, the Dynamic Modification Tool determines on instance basis how the migration of instances to the new definition can be handled, and without any further user interaction, the instances are migrated.

During the migration of the running instances to the new process definition, sometimes the need may arise to rollback some of the committed tasks using compensation tasks. In many situations there is no need to compensate all of the tasks, since the modification region has not affected all of them. Therefore during roll-back operation, the Modification Tool determines which tasks to be compensated according to the modification region. To make this automatic, the dependence between the tasks should be determined automatically. Our work on determining task interdependencies according to the data and control flow between them still continues.

References

1. N. Adam, V. Atluri, W. K. Huang; "Modeling and Analysis of Workflows Using Petri Nets", Journal of Intelligent Information Systems, Special Issue on Workflow and Process Management, Volume 10, Issue 2, March 1998.
2. G. Alonso, and H. J. Schek; "Research Issues in Large Workflow Management Systems", Proc. of NFS Workshop on Workflow and Process Automation in Information Systems: State-of-the-Art and Future Directions, Edited-by A. Sheth, Athens, Georgia, May 1996.
3. I. B. Arpinar, S. (Nural) Arpinar, U. Halici, and A. Dogac; "Correctness of Workflows in the Presence of Concurrency", Intl. Conf. on Next Generation Info. Tech. and Sys., Israel, July 1997.
4. F. Casati, S. Ceri, B. Pernici, G. Pozzi, "Workflow Evolution", Data and Knowledge Engineering, Volume 24, Issue 3, pp. 211-238, January 1998.
5. Q. Chen, U. Dayal, "A Transactional Nested Process Management System", Proc. of the 12th Intl. Conf. on Data Engineering, New Orleans, Louisiana, USA, February 1996.
6. I. Cingil, A. Dogac, "A Component-based System Architecture for Adaptable Workflow Systems", Technical Report 98-2, Software Research and Development Center, Dept. of Computer Engineering, Middle East Technical University, 1998.
7. U. Dayal, M. Hsu, R. Ladin, "A Transaction Model for Long-running Activities", Proc. of the 17th Intl. Conf. on Very Large Databases, pages 113-122, September 1991.

8. A. Dogac, E. Gokkoca, S. Arpinar, P. Koksal, I. Cingil, I. B. Arpinar, N. Tatbul, P. Karagoz, U. Halici, M. Altinel, "Design and Implementation of a Distributed Workflow Management System: METUFlow", In: [9].

9. A. Dogac, L. Kalinichenko, M. T. Ozsu, and A. Sheth (eds.), "Advances in Workflow Management Systems and Interoperability", Springer Verlag, 1998.

10. C. Ellis, K. Keddara, and G. Rozenberg, "Dynamic Change Within Workflow Systems", Proc. of the ACM Conf. on Organizational Computing Systems, 1995.

11. E. Gokkoca, M. Altinel, I. Cingil, N. Tatbul, P. Koksal, A. Dogac, "Design and Implementation of a Distributed Workflow Enactment Service", Proc. of Intl. Conf. on Cooperative Information Systems, Charleston, USA, June 1997.

12. Y. Han, A. Sheth, "On Adaptive Workflow Modeling", 4th Intl. Conf. on Information Systems Analysis and Synthesis, Orlando, Florida, July 1998.

13. D. Hollinsworth, "The Workflow Reference Model", Technical Report TC00-1003, Workflow Management Coalition, December 1996. Accessible via: http://www.aiai.ed.ac.uk/WfMC/.

14. G. Joeris, O. Herzog, "Managing Evolving Workflow Specifications", 3rd Intl. Conf. on Cooperative Information Systems, COOPIS'98, New York, August 1998.

15. P. Karagoz, S. Arpinar, P. Koksal, N. Tatbul, E. Gokkoca, and A. Dogac, "Task Handling in Workflow Management Systems", Intl. Workshop on Issues and Applications of Database Technology, Berlin, June 1998.

16. P. Koksal, S. Arpinar, and A. Dogac, "Workflow History Management", ACM Sigmod Record, Vol. 27, No. 1, March 1998.

17. C. Liu, M. E. Orlowska, H. Li, "Automating Handover in Dynamic Workflow Environments", CAiSE 1998, pp. 139-157.

18. L. Liu, C. Pu, "Methodical Restructuring of Complex Workflow Activities", Intl. Conf. on Data Engineering, ICDE '98, 1998.

19. M. Reichert, P. Dadam, "A Framework for Dynamic Changes in Workflow Management Systems", in Proc. of DEXA'97, September 1997, Toulouse, France.

20. M. Reichert, P. Dadam, "ADEPT_flex-Supporting Dynamic Changes of Workflows Without Loosing Control", in Journal of Intelligent Information Systems (JIIS), Special Issue on Workflow and Process Management, Volume 10, Issue 2, March 1998.

21. M. Reichert, C. Hensinger, P. Dadam, "Dynamic Workflow Changes in Clinical Application Environments", in Proc. of EDBT-Workshop, 1998.

22. S. W. Sadiq, M. E. Orlowska, "On Dynamic Modification of Workflows", Technical Report, July 1998.

23. A. Sheth, D. Georgakopoulos, S. Joosten, M. Rusinkiewicz, W. Scacchi, J. Wileden, A. Wolf, Report from the NSF workshop on workflow and process automation in information systems, in ACM SIGMOD Record, 25(3):55-67, December 1996.

24. A. Sheth, K. Kochut, "Workflow Applications to Research Agenda: Scalable and Dynamic Work Coordination and Collaboration Systems", in [9].

25. E. Turanalp, "Design and Implementation of a Graphical Workflow Definition Tool", Master Thesis, Department of Computer Engineering, Middle East Technical University, Ankara, Turkiye, 1997.

A Temporal Reasoning Approach to Model Workflow Activities

Nihan Kesim Çiçekli

Department of Computer Engineering, METU, Ankara, Turkey
nihan@ceng.metu.edu.tr

Abstract. A logical framework for modeling workflow activities is presented. A simplified form of Kowalski and Sergot's Event Calculus is introduced as a basis for tackling the problem and it is extended first with a convention for representing causal laws, and then to include higher-order persistence and potential events. The proposed framework maintains a representation of the dynamic world being modeled on the basis of user supplied axioms about preconditions and effects of events and the initial state of the world. The net effect is that a workflow specification can be made at a higher level of abstraction. A logic programming approach to the computational problem is adopted and a logic program presented which is efficient yet retains many of the logical properties of the set of Event Calculus axioms.

1 Introduction

A workflow process is defined as a collection of processing steps (activities) organized to accomplish some business process. An activity can be performed by different processing entities. An activity defines some work to be done and can be specified in a number of ways, including a textual description in a file or a form or a computer program. A processing entity that performs the activity may be a person or a software system.

Two problems need to be addressed, in general, in order to automate a workflow. The first is the specification of a workflow: detailing the activities that must be carried out, and defining the execution sequence of the activities. The second problem is the execution of the workflow, which must be done while providing the safeguards of traditional database systems related to computation correctness, data integrity and durability.

At any time during the execution, the state of a workflow consists of the collection of states of the workflow's constituent activities, and the states of all variables in the workflow specification. The coordination of activities can be specified either statically or dynamically. In a static specification, the activities and dependencies among them are defined before the execution of the workflow begins. The dependencies among the activities may be simple since each task has to be completed before the next begins. Thus in this strategy all possible activities in a workflow and their dependencies are known in advance, but only those activities whose preconditions are satisfied are executed. The preconditions can be defined through some dependency rules, such as "activity a_i cannot start until activity a_j has ended" or "activity a_i can start if activity a_j returns a value 25", etc.

An example of dynamic scheduling of activities is an electronic-mail routing system. The next activity to be scheduled for a given mail message depends on what the destination address of the message is, and on which intermediate routers are functioning.

In this paper we deal with the problem of specification of workflows where the coordination of activities can be defined statically. This can be realized through different types of methods[6]: script languages, net-based methods, logic-based methods, algebraic methods and event-condition-action rules. We argue that the specification of workflow processes can be enhanced by integrating them with temporal databases and/or with temporal logic programming systems. Addition of a temporal dimension to workflows can enhance their facilities in different ways. It will provide mechanisms for storing and querying the history of all processes. This may serve the need for querying some piece of information in the process history. Or it may serve the need for mining the history of the workflow to analyze and assess the efficiency, accuracy and the timeliness of the processes.

In this paper we investigate the ways in which the event calculus can be used as a basis for the specification of a workflow enhanced with temporal reasoning. The event calculus, developed by Kowalski and Sergot [4], provides a framework for temporal reasoning by employing the classical first-order predicate logic. We show a modified version of the event calculus through the introduction of causal laws (or discontinuous events). We demonstrate how the extended version of the event calculus can be used in the modeling of workflows so that it is possible to ask queries like which activities follow which ones, or when they did/will happen, and also the state of the system can be derived at any time in the past or future.

The rest of the paper is organized as follows. Section 2 introduces a simplified version of the event calculus. The causality relation is discussed in Section 3. In Section 4, the modeling of a workflow process using the event calculus is described with an example. Section 5 discusses the computational problems and proposes a logic program to solve the inefficiency problems. We conclude the paper by summarizing the features of the proposed system in section 6.

2   The Event Calculus

The original event calculus[4] and its descendants[3] provided a framework for reasoning about time based on events and properties. Events initiate or terminate properties. An event has a unique time instant associated with it, whereas properties are associated with a number of time periods (or intervals) over which they hold. In this paper we will use a simplified version of the event calculus given by Kowalski and Sergot in [4]. Only the following clauses are necessary:

holds_at(P, T) if
      happens(E, T1) and T1 < T and
      initiates(E, P) and
      not broken(P, T1, T).

broken(P, T1, T2) if
      happens(E', T') and
      terminates(E', P) and T1 ≤ T' and T' < T2.

The predicate *holds_at(P, T)* represents that property P holds at time T. The predicate *happens(E, T)* represents that the event E occurs at time T. The times are ordered by the usual comparative operators. The formula *initiates(E, P)* represents that the event E initiates a period of time during which the property P holds, and *terminates(E, P)* represents that the event E terminates any ongoing period during which property P holds. The *not* operator is interpreted as negation-as-failure. The use of negation-as-failure gives a form of default persistence. The formula *broken(P, T1, T2)* represents that the property P ceases to hold at some time between $T1$ and $T2$ due to an event which terminates it.

The problem domain is captured by a set of initiates and terminates clauses. For example blocks and their places can be described by the following clauses. The term *on(X, Y)* names the property that block X is on top of block Y or at location Y; and the term *clear(X)* names the property that block or location X has nothing on top of it. The term *move(X, Y)* names the event of moving X onto block or location Y.

initiates(move(X, Y), on(X, Y))
initiates(move(X, Y), clear(Z)) if
      happens(move(X, Y),T) and
      holds_at(on(X, Z),T) and Z ≠ Y

A particular course of events to represent that a block a was moved to location x and then to location y can be written as:

happens(move(a, x), t_1).
happens(move(a, y), t_2).

where t_1 is less than t_2.

These axioms can be used deductively to predict the locations of blocks at different times by querying the system with the *holds_at* predicate.

In the event calculus events have a general notation. They can be represented with simple terms as given in the example, or they can be represented as a set of binary predicates if the event description needs to be more informative. For instance, the event of moving the block a onto x can also be represented as

happens(e₁, t₁).
act(e₁, move).
block(e₁, a).
destination(e₁, x).

The main intended application of the event calculus is the representation of events in database updates and discourse representation. The approach is closely related to McCarthy's situation calculus [5] and Allen's interval temporal logic [1]. The granularity of events depends on the application domain. An event may correspond to a simple action like updating a single record or to a more complex action like processing a product in a manufacturing system. The granularity depends on the level of abstraction.

3 The Causality Relation

We want to use the event calculus in the specification of a workflow process. A workflow process contains a collection of activities and the order of activity invocations or conditions under which activities must be invoked (i.e. control flow) and also data flow between the activities. In the event calculus framework, events will denote the start and end time points of activities. The state of the workflow will be described by the properties. In other words events will specify the control flow and the effects of the events are used to describe the data flow within the workflow.

In the simplified form of the event calculus above, like the original Kowalski and Sergot formalism, it is not clear how to represent that a certain type of event invariably follows a certain other type of event, or that a certain type of event occurs when some property holds. We will need to be able to do this to model workflow processes.

In [8], Shanahan extends the original event calculus and presents a convention for representing causal laws. In order to state that an event occurs depending on another event or a property one can write clauses of the form

$$happens(f(E_1), T) \; if \; happens(E_1, T_1) \; and \; Q_1 \ldots Q_n$$

The skolem function $f(E_1)$ names an event caused by E_1. The function name f identifies the type of the event.

Suppose, for example, that we want to represent a law that states whenever an alarm is set at time t, it goes off at time $t + n$. The following axioms will be sufficient for this.

happens(go-off(E), Tn) if
    happens(E, T) and act(E, set_alarm) and
    Tn is T + n

The inference of the causality relation from typical statements about it can be quite difficult. This is because statements can refer to the past as well as the future of causing events. The latter happens when delays occur between causes and effects and during these delays, conditions arise which preclude expected effects from occurring. For example, an event of an aircraft taking off towards a radar at time t causes an event of detection by that radar at time t+20 provided:

    a) an event of its being instructed to fly low has not occurred before t.

    b) an event of its changing course does not occur between t and t + 20.

> *happens(detects(A, R), T+20) if*
>   *happens(flies_towards(A, R), T),*
>   *not happens(told_to_fly_low(A, X), T1) and T < T1 < T+ 20 and*
>   *not happens(changes_course(A, Y), T2) and T < T2 < T + 20*

4 Modeling Activities in the Event Calculus

This section presents the event calculus as a first-order formalism for the specification of workflow processes. Once the event occurrences till time t are known, the state of the system can be computed at any point of time until t. Thus modeling can be regarded as the computation of event occurrences.

We illustrate the idea by using an example of a flexible manufacturing system (FMS) [7]. Modern manufacturing systems are complex organizations consisting of several functional subsystems such as processing, tooling, inventory, and ordering, each performing different activities to achieve overall production goal. In the following we provide the specification of a workflow in an assembly line at the processing subsystem.

An FMS can produce a wide range of manufacturing units in a highly flexible manner by retooling and changing setups of its machines. To describe how an FMS works, it is assumed that it assembles a certain line of products, such as different kinds of toasters. It is also assumed that the initial part of an assembly is brought into the system through a load-unload station. It is then carried among various manufacturing units, called cells., where assembly processes take place. For example, one cell can be responsible for making the outer body of a toaster, another for installing its heating elements, another for assembling knobs on its front panel and so on. A special vehicle, called and automatic guidance vehicle (AGV), carries incomplete assemblies among the various cells. When the assembly process is completed, the finished units are brought by AGVs back to the station, where they are removed from the FMS system.

The state of such an FMS system can be defined with the predicates presented in Figure 1. The predicates *next, process_time* and *travel* are rigid, that is, they do not change over time. The other predicates are time-dependent. It is assumed that a cell never processes the same assembly twice. Figure 2 presents the possible events occurring in an FMS system.

dock(AGV, C) :	a vehicle AGV is docked at a cell C.
on(ASM, AGV) :	an assembly ASM is loaded on a vehicle AGV.
empty(AGV) :	a vehicle AGV is empty.
idle(C) :	a cell C is idle, i.e. does not process any assembly.
moving(AGV, C) :	an AGV is moving to cell C.
occupied(C, ASM) :	a cell is occupied by some assembly ASM.
processed(ASM, C) :	an assembly has been processed by a cell C.
next(C1, C2) :	after the operation in cell C1, the next assembly operation is done in cell C2.
travel(C1, C2, T) :	it takes T units of time for an AGV to travel from cell $C1$ to $C2$.
process_time(C, T) :	it takes T units of time to perform an operation in cell C.

Fig. 1. Predicates describing the state of an FMS system

move(AGV, C) :	move a vehicle AGV to a cell C.
arrives(AGV, C) :	a vehicle AGV arrives at a cell C.
load(AGV, ASM, C) :	load an AGV with an assembly at a cell C.
unload(AGV, ASM, C) :	transfer an assembly from an AGV to a cell C.
start_process(C, ASM) :	a cell C starts processing an assembly.
finish_process(C, ASM) :	a cell C finishes processing an assembly.

Fig. 2. Possible events occurring in the FMS system

Examples of several clauses, partially describing the behavior of an FMS, are presented as follows:

R1: If an AGV starts moving to the next cell, it arrives there at a time determined by the relation *travel*.

> *happens(arrives(AGV, C), T) if*
> *happens(move(AGV, C), T_o) and next(C_1, C) and*
> *travel(C_1, C, T_d) and T is $T_o + T_d$*

R2: If an AGV has arrived at a cell then dock it at that cell.

> *inititates(arrives(AGV, C), dock(AGV, C)).*
> *terminates(arrives(AGV, C), moving(AGV, C)).*

R3: If an AGV arrives at a cell with an assembly loaded on it and no other assembly is in that cell, then transfer the assembly from the AGV into the cell. Let it stay there for the time period determined by the relation *process_time*.

$$happens(unload(AGV, ASM, C), T) \ if$$
$$happens(arrives(AGV, C), T) \ and$$
$$holds\_at(on(ASM, AGV), T) \ and$$
$$holds\_at(idle(C, T)$$

$$happens(finish\_process(C, ASM), T) \ if$$
$$happens(unload(AGV, ASM, C), T_1) \ and$$
$$process\_time(C, T_p) \ and$$
$$T \ is \ T_1 + T_p$$

R4: If an operation on an assembly is finished by the cell, and an empty AGV is docked at the cell, then load the AGV with the assembly at that cell and move the AGV to the next cell.

$$happens(load(AGV, ASM, C), T) \ if$$
$$happens(finish\_process(C, ASM), T) \ and$$
$$holds\_at(dock(AGV, C), T) \ and$$
$$holds\_at(empty(AGV), T)$$

$$happens(move(AGV, C_2), T) \ if$$
$$next(C_1, C_2) \ and$$
$$happens(load(AGV, ASM, C_1), T)$$

These rules describe the processes and their effects within the example workflow . In order to start the execution of the workflow, it is necessary to specify the initial state of the system.

5 The Computational Problem

In this section we discuss the computational aspects of the logical description given above. The theory can be implemented in several different ways. One approach is to use a general-purpose theorem prover directly with the event calculus. Since the axioms presented are all Horn clauses, they can be used more or less directly with a Prolog. However as they stand, the general structure of the search space that would be explored by SLDNF resolution is riddled with non-terminating loops and redundancy. For example consider the execution of the query $holds\_at(dock(AGV, C), t_1)$. A direct translation of the axioms into a Prolog program will cause an infinite loop, because the definition of $holds\_at$ includes calls to $happens$ and that in turn includes calls to $holds\_at$.

These problems may be overcome in several ways. For instance, a different sort of theorem prover could be used, or we could rewrite the axioms so that they are more suitable for SLDNF resolution (but perhaps less declarative), or we could abandon theorem proving altogether and write an appropriate algorithm for a procedural language. We prefer rewriting the axioms since it has the advantage that the result is still an expression of a logic problem. We will still have the "interface" of the theory as the predicates *happens, holds_at, initiates,* and *terminates.*

The major reason of the problem of getting infinite loops is that, in the execution of holds_at, after finding a relevant event, all events (past or possible future events) must be searched again in order to show that there is no other event affecting the established relation. This is because of the negation in the formulation of holds_at. Therefore we must restrict the search space in such a way that only the past relevant events (i.e. events which have occurred) should be searched.

In order to achieve this we have to consider the causality of events. The current formulation does not consider the event occurrence order at all. We can rewrite the clauses so that a Prolog interpreter can proceed forwards in time from the earliest known event, maintaining a list of ongoing events. If we know which events occur after which events, given the initial event(s), we can compute the entire history. We proceed roughly in a bottom-up manner: we compute what events the initial events cause in the history, then compute what events these cause in the history, and so on.

Let E_0 be the initial event for the system. Assume that E_0 has occurred. A history of the system is defined to be a sequence of events starting at E_0. Intuitively it contains all of the events whose occurrence is required by the occurrence of the initial event and the causality rules, and only these events. More than one sequence can be a history. This happens when concurrent events occur. In other words when an event causes more than one event to occur we can reason about concurrent events in the same fashion.

In the following logic program, the predicate *generate_events(EL)* is used to generate a list of all events occurring in the system. The program uses the higher order predicate *findall(happens(E, T), P(E, T), EL)* which holds when *EL* is a list of all the terms *happens(E, T)* such that *P(E, T)*. In order to specify the causality relation between the possible events, the predicate *follows(E_1, T_1, E_2, T_d, EL)* is introduced. This predicate denotes that event E_2 follows event E_1 that happened at time T_1, with a time difference T_d. With these clauses, a Prolog interpreter proceeds forwards in time from the earliest event, maintaining a list of all occurred events.

```
generate_events(EL) if
    findall(happens(E, T), first_event(E, T), InitialList),
    update_event_list(InitialList, InitialList, EL).


update_event_list([], ActualEL, ActualEL).
update_event_list(EL, CurrentEL, ActualEL) if
    EL = [happens(E, T) | Rest],
    findall(happens(E1, T1), new_events(E, T, E1, T1, ActualEL), NewEvents),
    append(CurrentEL, NewEvents, CurrentNL),
    append(Rest, NewEvents, NewRest),
    update_event_list(NewRest, CurrentNL, ActualEL).


new_events(E,T,E1,T1,EL) if
    follows(E, T, E1, Td, EL),
    T1 is T+Td.
```

The predicate *first_event(E, T)* holds when *E* is an initial event to occur at time *T*. The predicate *new_events(E, T, E1, T1, EL)* holds when *E1* is an event which occurs at time *T1* after the event *E* at time *T*. The predicate *follows* finds event *E1* by considering the list *EL* of all events which occurred before time *T*.

The specification of the predicate *follows* depends on the application domain. We can illustrate the use of it by considering the FMS example again. In that domain we can write the following to replace the clauses for the predicate *happens* (see previous rules R1, R2 and R3):

> *follows(move(Agv, C), T, arrives(Agv, C), Td, EL) if*
>   *next(P, C),*
>   *travel(P, C, Td).*
>
> *follows(arrives(Agv, C), T, unload(Agv, Asm, C), 0, EL) if*
>   *holds_at*(on(Asm, Agv), T, EL),*
>   *holds_at*(idle(C), T, EL).*
>
> *follows(unload(Agv, Asm, C), T, finish_process(C, Asm), Td, EL) if*
>   *process_time(C, Td).*
>
> *follows(finish_process(C, Asm), T, load(Agv, Asm, C), 0, EL) if*
>   *holds_at*(dock(Agv, C), T, EL),*
>   *holds_at*(empty(Agv), T, EL).*
>
> *follows(load(Agv, Asm, C1), T, move(Agv, C), 0, EL) if*
>   *next(C1, C).*

We will have an additional clause for events following a *load* operation. With this clause we represent concurrent events which happen after loading an assembly onto a vehicle at a cell. In addition to *move* event, *unload* event may also follow the *load* event since there may be other vehicles with other assemblies waiting for that cell. So we write:

> *follows(load(Agv, Asm, C1),T, unload(Agv1, Asm1, C1), 0, EL) if*
>   *holds_at*(dock(Agv1, C1), T, EL),*
>   *Agv1 ≠ Agv,*
>   *holds_at*(on(Asm1, Agv1), T, EL).*

In the presented program, the predicate *holds_at** is to be replaced with the predicate *holds_at*. The definition of this new clause is slightly different :

> *holds_at*(P, T, EL) if*
>   *initiates(Ev, P),*
>   *member(happens(Ev, T1), EL), T1 ≤ T,*
>   *not broken*(P, T1, T, EL).*

$broken^*(P, T1, T2, EL)$ if
$terminates(Ev, P)$,
$member(happens(Ev, T), EL)$,
$T1 \leq T < T2$.

Instead of searching all events, the new definition searches only the past events which are known to have occurred already (i.e. *member* relation checks the elements of the list *EL*).

These new axioms can be directly translated into a Prolog program. After all the events in the system are generated, it is possible to ask queries of the form

$? - holds\_at^*(P, t_1)$.

to find out the state of the system at any time after the given initial event.

6   Conclusion

We have demonstrated how the event calculus might be extended to describe the specification and execution of a workflow process. The event calculus as presented exhibits three conceptual differences over the proposed formalisms.

First of all, it is purely declarative. Programs in most traditional formalisms usually contain side-effect causing operations such as event scheduling (insertion) and unscheduling (deletion) upon an event queue. We are able to compute event occurrences without any use of event queues, scheduling or unscheduling.

Second, there is no explicit state. Traditional programs keep past object states explicitly as a collection of tuples (P, V, T) each meaning that the value of state parameter P is V at time T. In the event calculus however only the sequence of events are retained instead of explicit states. The state at any time can be derived using the axioms of the event calculus.

Finally, a general definition of event is introduced. An event can be any real world event that occurs when a proposition becomes true. A wide range of happenings can be regarded as events and thus different domains can be modeled in a similar fashion.

References

[1] Allen J. F., *Towards a General Theory of Action and Time*, Artificial Intelligence, volume 23, p123, 1984.
[2] Dogac A. and others, Advances in Workflow Management Systems and Interoperability, Springer-Verlag, 1998.
[3] Evans C. and Shanahan M., The Event Calculus. EQUATOR working document, 4th Revised Version, Logic Programming Group, Imperial College, June 1989.
[4] Kowalski R. A. and Sergot M., A Logic-Based Calculus of Events, New Generation Computing, volume 4, p267, 1986.

[5] McCarthy J. and Hayes P. J., Some Philosophical Problems from the Standpoint of Artificial Intelligence, Machine Intelligence, 4, ed. Michie D. and Meltzer B., Edinburgh University Press, 1969.

[6] Muth P. and others, Enterprise-wide Workflow Management based on State and Activity Charts, in [2].

[7] Ranky P.G., Computer Integrated Manufacturing, Chapters 6-8, Prentice-Hall, 1986.

[8] Shanahan M., A Simple Logical Framework for Prediction Problems, Technical Report, Logic Programming Group, Imperial College, November 1988.

Dynamic Configuration and Enforcement of Access Control for Mobile Components

Yoad Gidron[1,2], Israel Ben-Shaul[1], and Yariv Aridor[2]

[1] Technion - Israel Institute of Technology, Electrical Engineering department,
Haifa, Israel
{yoad@tx, issy@ee}@technion.ac.il
[2] IBM, Haifa Research Laboratory, Haifa, Israel
yariv@il.ibm.com

Abstract. Dynamic execution layout is the capability to (re)map at runtime the logical components of a distributed application onto physical hosts. From the resource management perspective, this paradigm raises three challenges: dynamic matching of available and required resources by providers and consumers, respectively; instance-level permission setting and enforcement; and access control over migrating resources. The proposed model employs a pairwise negotiation mechanism that enables to query resource availability and agree on a "contract", along with an enforcement mechanism that extends Java 1.2 and allows mobile components to fulfill their contracts despite their potential relocation.

1   Introduction

Wide area computing enables the deployment of distributed applications over a large number of geographically distant hosts. In such a setting, hosts are typically heterogeneous, ranging from small palmtop devices to full-blown workstations, and they are interconnected by heterogeneous networks with different bandwidth, reliability and general quality of service.

The large and non-uniform deployment space implies that the designer is unlikely to know in advance how to structure the application in a way that best leverages the available infrastructure. Furthermore, the dynamic nature of such global environments implies that even assumptions that are made at deployment time regarding the underlying physical infrastructure are unlikely to hold throughout the lifetime of the (possibly long running) application. Thus, a static mapping of the logical components of an application onto a set of physical hosts — termed the layout of the application — is undesirable and likely to decrease its scalability.

An alternative approach is then to consider *dynamic layout* [1]. With dynamic layout, components of the application can be relocated at run-time, without making any changes to the source code. For example, a component C_1 may be moved from site A to B in order to decrease the load on A; or, C_1 may need to exchange large amounts of data with C_2, which resides at B, but the network connection between A and B has deteriorated; or, A might be getting disconnected, and C_1 "jumps" to B in order to continue its execution; etc.

As a concrete example, consider an application that runs on a handheld PC and needs to access frequently a large remote database. The device is typically connected with a low-bandwidth, high-latency, and high-cost network connection, thus minimizing traffic over this connection is clearly desirable. By sending the (lightweight) component to the remote server, the component can continuously query the database with high bandwidth, returning only the (short) result to the client over the low-bandwidth connection.

From the perspective of access to resources, dynamic layout introduces new challenges. First, since the same component may execute in different hosts during its lifetime or across executions, there should be a *dynamic mechanism for establishing access control* between components. This mechanism should check: 1. whether the hosting site has sufficient resources, both in terms of type (e.g., does the the hosting laptop has a disk ?) and volume (e.g., can the host reserve 50 MB disk space for the component ?); and 2. whether the hosting site allows the visiting component to use the amount of resources it requests. The global scope means that a host might not know in advance what are the potential components that will be deployed to it, and the component and target host might each be administered by a different authority. This suggests a *negotiation*-based access control mechanism. Second, the model needs to be integrated with dynamic layout. In particular, it should support logical security policies that hold despite physical relocation of components. Third, the access control mechanism needs to distinguish between instances of components, as opposed to component classes. The distinction is important because components migrate with their state, and because different instances of the same component class might belong to different owners [2].

In the rest of this paper we present a resource management model that addresses the above challenges, and its implementation in FARGO, a Java based environment for dynamically relocatable distributed applications. Section 2 presents an overview of FARGO, Section 3 describes the resource management model, Section 4 discusses the enforcement of the model in FARGO, and Section 5 concludes the paper.

2 FarGo Overview

The FARGO system [1,3] presents a novel programming model that supports dynamic layout. Since the emphasis is on components that are part of a larger application (as opposed to typical "mobile-agents" that are often autonomous applications), component relocation preserves the validity of incoming and outgoing component references, in addition to the internal state of the component. Thus, FARGO inter-component references can dynamically stretch (i.e., become remote) and shrink (become local), unlike traditional references, which are fixed at design time to be either local or remote. On top of this basic capability, FARGO provides two unique layers:

1. The references that interconnect components (or complets, in FARGO terminology; we will use these terms interchangeably) can be associated with semantics that govern co- and re-location of the source and target complets. Hence, complet references drive and constrain the component mapping process. For example, a Pull reference from complet A to complet B implies that whenever A relocates, it "pulls" B along to the same host. Hence, A and B are guaranteed to always be co-located. Such a relationship should be used, for example, when the complets exchange large amounts of data, interact frequently, or cannot tolerate partial failure. Another example is a Stamp reference, which, upon movement of the source, doesn't pull the target complet along but instead looks up and connects to a local complet with the same type as the original target complet. This reference is useful for modeling relationships between mobile and stationary complets (e.g., moving to a new site and connecting to a local printer). FARGO defines an extensible set of such references, each with different (re)location semantics, and the runtime ensures the validity of the references by automating derived relocations and by restricting illegal relocations that would break the semantics of the references. Technically, this is achieved by implementing a complet reference as a set of first class objects (generated by the FARGO compiler), which are subject to program manipulation like any other object, and thus enable flexibility in controlling the relationships.

2. A monitoring facility is available to applications for making judicious relocation decisions. An application (or external administrator, see below) can request FARGO to monitor various system or application parameters, and register for events that indicate certain (threshold) parameter values. When such events occur, the requesting complet is notified, and can react, e.g., by relocation. In addition to the monitoring API, FARGO provides an event-based scripting language that can be used outside the application, possibly after it was designed and even after deployment. Finally, a graphical monitoring tool can be used by human administrators to analyze and manually control complet relocation.

The FARGO system consists of a set of distributed *core* objects. Cores are uniquely identified objects that provide system support for mobilizing and interconnecting software components across machines. In particular, they implement the access control mechanism.

3 A Resource Management Model

The basic entity in the model is a *resource*. A resource is a component that provides state and functionality to be utilized by other components. Resources are divided into two basic categories: system resources and application resources. System resources are controlled by the local core, and are by definition stationary (non-movable), representing hardware devices (e.g. disk) or logical system objects (e.g. socket). In contrast, application resources are software components, they are potentially mobile and are managed by their applications.

The distinction between system and application resources brings up the issue of *ownership*. Each resource has a specific owner: system resources are owned by the core, and application resources are owned by an application.

The owner controls the resource and has special permissions including setting a policy and moving the resource (if it is mobile). The owner of a resource is termed a *provider*, while the owner of component that uses a resource is termed a *consumer*. Clearly, a provider can also be a consumer of another provider.

A complet, and the core in which the complet currently resides, may each be owned by a different autonomous authority, and therefore their objectives and/or resource requirements can be in conflict. Thus, a fundamental aspect of our model is that granting access to a specific resource requires *negotiation* between the provider of the resource and the consumer, with a successful negotiation leading to an agreement on the allowed access and use of the resource. Each resource can be associated with *Permissions*, which define what actions the consumer is allowed to perform on a resource that is owned by the provider and under what limitations. Such agreements protect the provider against unauthorized access and unlimited consumption of its resources. It should be noted that negotiation ranges from a simple "one-iteration" session whereby the provider checks whether the requested usage is allowed and returns a boolean value, to applying sophisticated policies by each entity in order to maximize their gain (i.e., permissions) involving multiple iterations (e.g., as in Kasbah [4]). The negotiation mechanism, shown in more detail below, is policy-independent. The advantage of negotiation-based allocation and access control is that it enables to agree on the type of service and on the volume based on the needs of the application and on the current resource availability and general state of the host. For example, consider a mobile server that requires disk space for storing data. The more disk space it gets, the more clients it can serve. When this server migrates to a new host it can negotiate on the amount of disk space that it will get and configure the number of clients according to this quota. Alternatively it can negotiate with multiple hosts and migrate to the host that offers the most resources. Another advantage of negotiation-based agreement is that it enables a consumer to make better relocation decisions, since the outcome of the negotiation determines what part of the application (if any) should be migrated. For example, consider again an application that uses the disk. When this application needs to migrate to a new diskless host (e.g., a palmtop), it may leave behind the disk-accessor component, and refer to it remotely from the new site.

3.1 Negotiation

The negotiation process is described in Figure 1. It involves exactly two participants, one provider and one consumer. The consumer is always a complet, but the provider can be either a core (for system resources) or a complet (for application resources). The actual negotiation takes place between peer *negotiators*, which are lightweight objects that operate on behalf of their participants. The provider's negotiator is initialized with a policy that determines the range of permissions that can be given to each consumer. A policy need not be specified

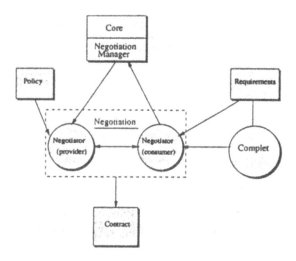

Fig. 1. Negotiation Process

for each complet, however, and a default policy is applied with a lack of a specific one.

Figure 2 shows a sample FARGO policy file with two permissions that are granted to a complet that is owned by user "jack" and that was originally created at dsg.technion.ac.il. The first permission is to read and write from/to the disk with a limit of 30,000 bytes, and the second permission is to perform select and update on an SQL server with a limit of 3 queries.

```
grant ownedBy "jack" instanceBase
      "fargo://dsg.technion.ac.il/core" {
  permission fargo.resources.DiskPermission *
    "read,write" "maxQuantity=30000";
  permission fargo.resources.CompletPermission
    "SQLServer" "select,update" "maxQueries=3";
};
```

Fig. 2. Policy File

The consumer's negotiator is initialized with a policy that specifies the resources that are needed by the application, and the required quantities/characteristics. The requirements of the consumer are analogous to requirements that are given in conventional software installations. A sample FARGO requirements file is given in Figure 3, showing two requirements: a disk space with minimal quantity of 20,000 bytes, and a requirement for access to an SQL server for up to 5 queries.

```
request {
  permission fargo.resources.DiskPermission *
    "read,write" "minQuantity=20000";
  permission fargo.resources.CompletPermission
    "SQLServer" "select" "numQueries=5";
};
```

Fig. 3. Requirements File

The negotiation protocol flows as follows. First, the consumer's negotiator is sent to the core of the provider. Conceptually, the negotiators could be remote to each other, but practically, since negotiation is expected to consist of many iterations, our design requires them to be co-located so as to minimize the latency in their communication. When the consumer's negotiator arrives to the core, it contacts the local negotiation manager, which is a built-in service of every core. The negotiation manager examines the requirements of the negotiator and tries to find a suitable provider, i.e., a complet that can provide the required service. If a provider is found, a negotiator complet implementing the provider's policy is created. At this point the negotiation "channel" is established, and negotiation proceeds in the form of exchanging offers that include suggested permissions. The goal is to reach a set of permissions that are acceptable by both the provider and the consumer. Each permission refers to a specific resource and can include several actions and consumption limits. Each consumption limit can be changed separately from offer to offer. When one negotiator accepts an offer of the other negotiator, the permission in this offer becomes part of the final agreement. If one of the negotiators quits the negotiation or the negotiation process lasts too long, the negotiation process fails.

3.2 Contracts

The outcome of a successful negotiation is a *contract* — a set of permissions that are granted by the provider to the consumer. A contract extend the notion of a lease that is a grant of access over a time period [5]. The contract specifies the permissions that are granted, possibly under some consumption limitations and always limited by time. When the provider is the core, the contract includes permissions for system resources like disk, threads and sockets, and when the provider is a complet, the contract includes permissions for accessing the particular complet (instance) only.

a contract need not necessarily be signed with a single consumer. Instead, it can be signed with a group of consumers that can be categorized by their codebase, code signer, origin core and/or owner. Thus, one complet can (re)use a contract that was signed by another complet.

An important design issue is with respect to the meaning of a contract, i.e., what does it promise to its participants. In that respect, we distinguish between two types of contracts: *loose* and *binding*. The difference between loose and binding contracts is somewhat analogous to the difference between soft and hard real-time. That is, a loose contract specifies what a consumer is allowed to do, but does not guarantee that the consumer will indeed be able to take advantage of everything it is allowed to do. The provider makes a best effort to provide the requested resources, but cannot ensure that they will be available. In contrast, a binding contract ensures that the resources will be available when needed, which means that these resources need to be reserved at contract time and kept reserved as long as the consumer complet is active. Implementation of binding contracts is both complicated and potentially resource-wasteful. Moreover, just like with real time systems, in many cases it is impossible to provide hard binding contract, since it requires full and exclusive control over the resources. At the very least it requires accessibility at the operating system level. This could be partly achieved if the JVM of the core was the only process in the system but is not feasible in the general case. Another problem with binding contracts stems from the fact that some contracts may have dependency relationships between them. Often a complet must use system resources in order to provide services to consumers. In this situation a contract in which a complet is the provider could depend on a contract between this complet and its local core. These dependencies imply that in order to fulfill a contract, it should be possible to inspect and compute the transitive closure of contract-dependencies, which can be very complex. It also implies that the complet must sign a contract with the core before it can sign contracts with any consumers, and a provider complet that serves other complets cannot move to a new core before it signs a contract with this core. To date, we support only loose contracts, although in some special cases they can effectively be binding.

4 Enforcement in FarGo

The main challenge of the implementation was the provision of complet-level access control without changing the Java virtual machine. But first, one has to be convinced that the existing Java security model is not sufficient. The security model of Java has been significantly evolved since it was first introduced. The original security model (JDK 1.0), known as the *sandbox* model, provided a very restricted environment in which untrusted code could run. The next version (JDK 1.1) introduced the concept of signed applets, where a correctly signed applet is treated as a trusted code, if the signature is recognized as trusted by the end system that receives the applet. The security model of the latest version, 1.2., is much more flexible, allowing to specify security policies that determine which permissions will be given to code that is identified by its source, i.e. where it was loaded from and by which author (identified by a digital signature).

However, Java security fails to meet the demands of dynamically relocatable components. Specifically, the Java security policy is defined statically, and maps permissions (e.g. what actions upon local resources are allowed) to classes, but cannot distinguish between several instances of the same class. This is sufficient for applets where the instances are always created locally, but not for mobile objects that can arrive from different places and have different *owners*. Permissions are also defined globally per a virtual machine and there is no notion of a per-component policy, which would enable to protect the (mobile) component itself, as opposed to only protecting the host. Thus, the FARGO security model was implemented on top of Java 1.2 security model [6], but extended it to support the missing features that re required by our model.

Enforcement support had to address the following requirements:

- Authentication of complet instances.
- Interception of method invocations between complets and between a complet and a core.
- Enforcement of consumption limits.

The authentication process is based on the public key authentication model [7] that is provided by Java. Unlike Java applets, however, for which only their code source is authenticated, in case of a complet, the *instance source* must be authenticated as well. The instance source includes the identity of the owner (creator) and the core in which the complet was instantiated. This information is attached to the complet upon its creation.

In the Java security model, a policy of a class defines the permissions that should be applied to its methods. FARGO extends Java permissions, allowing consumption limits (e.g. time limit) in addition to allowed actions. Another extension concerns the scope of the permissions. While Java security model supports policies only on a codebase (the URL from which the class was loaded) and signature basic, FARGO allows policies to be maintained on a per object basis, in order to comply with the support for mobile components (see section 1). Thus, each complet is associated with a policy that moves along with the complet. Notice, however, that inside a complet, the interaction of (local) objects still complies with the conventional security rules. In order to protect access to system resources from objects that are not part of any complet (i.e., by "regular" java objects), the core has a policy that controls access to system resources, which is enforced by the security manager.

4.1 Complet Access Control

The implementation of access control for complets takes advantage of the FARGO architecture. In this architecture, complets are never called directly as plain Java objects. Instead, a reference to a complet is implemented as a stub that delegates the calls to the actual complet. The enforcement of access to complets is done by using *hidden capabilities* [8]. A capability is a token that allows its holder to perform some operations on a specific complet. Verification of hidden capabilities is performed transparently by the underlying system (typically the operating system). The advantages of using capabilities over the conventional access-control lists, is that the implementation of a complet does not include explicit calls to the security manager as required in plain Java objects, and the security check is more efficient because there is no need to resolve the permissions in each invocation.

The security mechanism is activated when a new complet reference is requested in order to set the proper capabilities in the stub corresponding to that reference. In FARGO, a complet reference can be obtained in three possible ways: (1) instantiating a new complet; (2) performing lookup by name ; (3) receiving a reference from another complet. In all these cases a new stub is created. The first case is different in the sense that the instantiator has full permissions on the new complet that is created. In the other two cases the identity of the requester is checked and a resolution of the permissions is done. If a valid contract exists (i.e., either a contract which was previously signed by that complet, or one which is shared by its code-base or owner), the permissions are derived from it. Otherwise, the default policy of the provider complet determines the permissions. Finally, the capabilities are encapsulated inside the generated complet stub. These capabilities are digitally signed to prevent users from tampering them, and are later on passed by the reference in each invocation. The ability to intercept method invocations that are done through complet references, allows the security mechanism to perform a fast check on the capability (i.e. verify signature) and prevent the invocation if necessary.

4.2 Core Access Control

Access to the core and to local resources is enforced by a special implementation of Java's SecurityManager class. This security differs from the standard Java security manager in two aspects. First, the Java stack that is used for determination of protection domains is on a class level basis. FARGO security manager must know which complet instance did the invocation and is not interested in the classes on the stack. Therefore, a special stack is maintained that tracks only the invocation between the complets. The FARGO security manager uses this stack to determine the identity of the current complet and apply the appropriate permissions. Second, FARGO security manager can enforce both standard permissions and FARGO permissions that include in addition to actions, consumption limits. Hence, the existence of a permission is not enough to allow access and the security manager must also check that the invoker did not exceed the given limits.

5 Conclusions

This paper presents a model of resource management in the context of dynamic layout of mobile components. This model, based on negotiations between consumer components and and provider components offering services, allows:

- Efficient dynamic layout of components based on knowledge they can have on remote resources they require, prior to traveling.
- *Dynamic* and advanced control on consumption of resources.

The model is being applied and implemented in the FARGO mobile component system.

6 Acknowledgments

This work is supported by the Israeli Ministry of Science, Basic Infrastructure Fund, Project 9762.

We would like to thank the developers of the FARGO project, Ophir Holder and Hovav Gazit, for their contribution to this work.

References

1. O. Holder, I. Ben-Shaul, and H. Gazit, "Dynamic layout of distributed applications in FarGo", in *Proceedings of the 21th Internationsl Conference on Software Engineering*, Los Angenes, CA, May 1999, To Appear.
2. D. Milojicic, G. Agha, P. Bernadat, D. Chauhan, S. Guday, N. Jamali, and D. Lambright, "Case studies in security and resource management for mobile objects", in *Proceedings of the ECOOP 4th Workshop on Mobile Object Systems: Secure Internet Mobile Computations*, Belgium, July 1998, pp. 191–205.
3. O. Holder, I. Ben-Shaul, and H. Gazit, "System support for dynamic layout of distributed applications", in *Proceedings of the 19th International Conference on Distributed Computing Systems (ICDCS '99)*, Austin, TX, May 1999, To appear.
4. A. Chavez and P. Maes, "Kasbah: An agent marketplace for buying and selling goods", in *Proceedings of the 1st International Conference on the Practical Applications of Intelligent Agents and Multi-Agent technology*, 1996.
5. J. Waldo, "Jini architecture overview", 1998, Available at: http://www.sun.com/jini/whitepapers/.
6. L. Gong, M. Muller, H. Prafullchandra, and R. Schemers, "Going beyond the sandbox: An overview of the new security architecture in the java development kit 1.2", in *Proceedings of the USENIX Symposium on Internet Technologies and Systems*, December 1997.
7. R. L. Rivest, A. Shamir, and L. Adelman, "A method for obtaining digital signatures and public-key cryptosystems", *Communications of the ACM*, February 1978.
8. D. Hagimont, J. Mossiere, X. Rousset de Pina, and F. Saunier, "Hidden software capabilites", in *Proceedings of the 16th International Conference on Distributed Computing Systems (ICDCS '96)*, Hong Kong, May 1996, pp. 282–289.

The MY VIEW Project: A Data Warehousing Approach to Personalized Digital Libraries

Jens E. Wolff and Armin B. Cremers

Institut für Informatik III, Universität Bonn,
Römerstr. 164, 53117 Bonn, Germany

{jw,abc}@informatik.uni-bonn.de

Abstract. The MYVIEW project aims at the integration of both structured and unstructured bibliographic information from a diversity of heterogeneous Internet repositories like electronic journals and traditional libraries. Based on the user's individual information need MYVIEW maintains a personalized warehouse for bibliographic data in a unified scheme, which is locally available for browsing, ad hoc queries and analysis. This paper gives an overview of the project, emphasizes research issues and describes the current state of the implementation.

1 Introduction

The recent development in multimedia technology and the growth of the World Wide Web will have profound influence on libraries of the future. Besides traditional libraries offering their bibliographic data on the Web, many research projects in the USA (Digital Library Initiative[1]), UK (eLib Project[2]), Germany (Global Info[3]) and other countries (see [18]) have invested in digital library development. Nevertheless, however libraries will look like and whatever information they will provide in the end, the general problem for the user remains the same: how to query distributed repositories of knowledge efficiently and effectively with regard to her personal information need.

The vision behind MYVIEW is that of a personalized information space, tailored to its user's information need offering efficient query evaluation and customized result presentation, with browsing facilities (eg authorship or citation networks), ad hoc analysis and sophisticated ranking techniques (eg weighted search terms, best-match retrieval) and with the integration of all kinds of "libraries".

In the following we will discuss the concepts of the MYVIEW system which supports the maintenance of a personalized collection of bibliographic data[4]

---

[1] http://www.dli2.nsf.gov

[2] http://www.ukoln.ac.uk/services/elib/

[3] http://www.global-info.org

[4] Bibliographic data are metadata consisting of title, author, publisher and year, for instance, and possibly a link to the electronic version of the corresponding document.

about "documents". It locates resources and gathers information from multiple heterogeneous distributed information sources containing bibliographic data as there are digital libraries, traditional library catalogues, pure text archives (eg FTP Server for Technical Reports) and semi-structured WWW pages (eg catalogues of publishing houses or electronic journals).

The rest of this paper is organized as follows. Section 2 provides an overview of the goals and concepts of the MYVIEW project. A detailed description of the system is given in Sec. 3. Implementation aspects are outlined in Sec. 4. In Sec. 5 we comment on other work that is closely related to MYVIEW. Finally, Sec. 6 concludes and points out directions for future work.

2 Goals and Concepts

The MYVIEW project aims at supporting the user-friendly definition, generation and maintenance of collections of bibliographic data records which are relevant to a user's individual information need.

The system gathers catalogue information from a multitude of heterogeneous information servers. It presents them in a unified view and supports direct on-line reorganization, browsing and selection as specified by the user. MYVIEW's goal is the shift from data-centered to user-centered information access, as observed by Watters and Shepherd [38].

To support the above mentioned new functionalities, MYVIEW transforms the gathered bibliographic data records into a uniform scheme and stores them in a personal database. In the database community this approach has recently become popular as *data warehousing* (see [14, 40]). Efficient data retrieval and query post processing on the local warehouse can thus be realized.

To justify the use of the term warehouse in our scenario consider the issues discussed in [40]:

> "The topic of data warehousing encompasses architectures, algorithms, and tools for bringing together selected data from multiple databases or other information servers into a single repository, called a *data warehouse*, suitable for direct querying or analysis."

MYVIEW retrieves potential relevant information from different sources in advance, based on the specification of the user's information need. Data are stored in a personal database and queries are exclusively evaluated against this single repository without accessing the original sources. The advantages of this redundant storage of bibliographic data are obvious: efficient and rapid query processing, lower net load in the long run, uniform scheme, customizable searching and ranking, annotating, and managing historical information. Of course, the drawbacks of redundancy and missing up-to-dateness have to be considered. But in our application the amount of necessary storage is reasonably modest and the topicality can be achieved by periodical updates of small portions in spare hours.

Even if the primary use of data warehouses is in the commercial segment for decision support, the term warehouse for MYVIEW's local database is used on account of the affinity to the above mentioned characteristics.

The principle architecture of the MYVIEW system is sketched in Fig. 1.

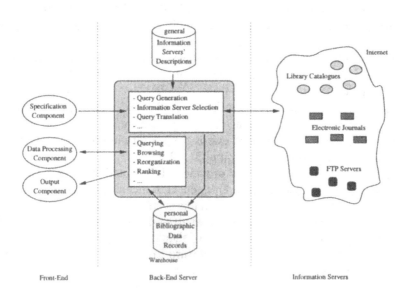

Fig. 1. MYVIEW architecture

2.1 Front-End

The customizable front-end components (see Fig. 1 left-hand side) embody the interface to the user.

- The *specification component* allows the user to specify her individual information need.[5] Identifying the personal information need as the central motivation behind MYVIEW, supporting its gratification efficiently is the logical consequence. In general retrieval tools of traditional libraries support only restricted functionalities and simple exact-match queries (Boolean retrieval model). Sophisticated query languages and best-match evaluation (vector space retrieval model) overcoming this lack are rarely supported by their interfaces.

  The standardized Z39.50 protocol [32], for instance, is widely used by traditional libraries and catalogue centers for supporting information retrieval services. Although many functionalities are defined in the standard, only

---

[5] Beside content related specifications other selection criteria concerning the information servers themselves have to be taken into account. We are currently working on automated resource selection integrating additional criteria like costs, language, and electronic availability.

a few are actually provided by every Z39.50 server, typically linking query terms by Boolean operators and counting the result size of a query.

It is generally accepted in the information retrieval community that Boolean retrieval is insufficient [7] and yields the worst retrieval quality in comparison with other retrieval models. Therefore MYVIEW has to support functionality going beyond the existing services. So, bridging the gap between individual user-specific information needs and simple queries for information servers is a basic but heavy duty that must be mastered.

The description of the possibly complex information need is of essential significance. As the formulation of the specification itself should be user-friendly and simple MYVIEW allows the user to define her information need by just entering a set of keywords and keyword phrases. This approach naturally raises the problem of mapping the intended meaning of a term set on the restricted query capabilities of existing repository interfaces. A detailed discussion of this aspect can be found in [42, 43].

- The *data processing component* provides all the functionalities to explore the personal local warehouse data. Our goal is to include, for instance, querying, browsing and ad hoc reorganization like sorting or formatting. Furthermore analyzing procedures (eg statistical analysis), annotations and the definition of views (ie subsets of the warehouse) should be supported. A view may, for example, be defined by all the literature from a certain database research group together with a list of title keywords. An ad hoc query may select documents about some topic which are accessible electronically (ie which have an URL).

  Functionalities for the management of the warehouse data are also provided like adding, deleting and updating bibliographic data. The underlying storage management system is interchangeable and not restricted to a special type. For example SGML/XML[6] files, the Lore DBMS [30] or other suitable systems can be used to manage the semi-structured information.

- The *output component* for instance, presents the query results to the user, displays browsing hierarchies and exports bibliographic data for further usage in different settings.

2.2 Back-End

The tasks of the back-end server are to gather bibliographic data from a multitude of heterogeneous information servers on the Internet and fill the local warehouse in accordance with the user specification. That means selecting suitable information servers, translating queries, loading results, transforming and storing them in the warehouse. This process – following Wiederhold's idea of a mediator architecture [41] – is done automatically and does not require any modifications on server side (information provider).

To let MYVIEW select the appropriate bibliographic data repositories and interact properly with them some general knowledge is required about these servers

---

[6] http://www.oasis-open.org/cover/sgml-xml.html

like access methods (ie whether a search engine is provided or the Z39.50 protocol supported), data formats (eg a certain HTML layout, BibTEX, MARC[7](Machine-Readable Cataloguing)) and so on. It is also essential to know which kind of information each server offers. All these general descriptive information are stored in a database.

2.3 Information Servers

The information servers are distributed over the whole Internet acting as bibliographic data repositories. Among these heterogeneous servers different types can be identified which reveal the complexity of the whole information gathering process.

Traditional libraries maintain large catalogues which are generated in a very disciplined way according to sophisticated rules like AACR2 (Anglo-American Cataloguing Rules) and represented in standardized formats like MARC and its derivatives. These libraries are increasingly becoming accessible via the WWW.

Bibliographic data as provided by libraries are at the one extreme. At the other extreme we have an FTP server without any additional information. Here the only information provided by the server are filenames and nothing else.

There may be reasonable forms of metadata in between these extremes. The Dublin Core for instance (see [39]) consists of a restricted set of 15 attributes (much smaller than in complex systems like USMARC) which should encourage the authors to describe their documents by themselves, but their use is optional.

Semi-structured WWW pages offered by electronic journals, for example, can also be seen as bibliographic data repositories, but this is a completely different case once more: In general, they do not provide the data in accordance with some generally accepted predefined scheme. When using XML in the future the information exchange will hopefully become much easier.

Nevertheless, all the above mentioned repositories should be accessible via MYVIEW.

3 MYVIEW System

The two main tasks of the system are building the warehouse and exploring it. In the following we will discuss both jobs and end with some remarks on customization.

3.1 Building the Warehouse

The process of building the warehouse according to user's defined criteria incorporates all the steps from specifying the information need, selecting appropriate resources, translating queries, querying internet repositories, transforming query results and storing the retrieved bibliographic data records. For reasons of space, we discuss only some of these aspects in this paper.

---

[7] http://lcweb.loc.gov/marc/

Specifying Information Needs. The specification of the individual information need is the initial task of constructing the warehouse. In the current implementation, MYVIEW allows only the use of simple nested Boolean queries with operators AND and OR, such as `database AND (relational OR deductive)` to initiate the gathering process. Since the result set is not presented to the user directly but stored in the local warehouse for further explorations, the original query may be "generous" in some way.

However, the uncertainty in formulating a vague information need, particularly at the beginning of the work, should not be underestimated. Therefore we investigated in [43] a different approach. Users should be able to specify their interests in a simple and comfortable way. Building on experiences gained by the information retrieval community, we propose sets of weighted terms and best-match retrieval for this purpose. However, many on-line library catalogues and WWW gateways provide only a Boolean interface (exact-match retrieval). We have therefore to tackle the problem of mapping a set of weighted terms to an appropriate collection of Boolean queries, considering the restrictions of local warehouse resources and the generated net load.

In [43] we define the mapping problem and optimal solutions in exact terms. We develop two heuristic algorithms for the weighted and unweighted case and discuss some important implementation aspects.

Querying Internet Repositories. MYVIEW gathers bibliographic data from heterogeneous information servers. Since the properties of the servers are sometimes quite similar, we assign different classes to the query components (wrappers) to reuse subcomponents. Currently MYVIEW supports the following three classes of information servers:

- Z39.50: This class encapsulates servers offering database access via the standardized Z39.50 protocol. The only individually needed information are the host name, the port address and a few other parameter. These data are dynamically loaded from external files. New Z39.50 servers can thus be added very easily by extending these files.
- WWW gateways: This general class incorporates servers with WWW access, ie all those offering a fill-out form and returning results as HTML pages. Since the provided search engines and the layout of the result pages are extremely varying every such server is handled by a separate program. Adding a new server results in writing a new piece of code, compiling it and linking it to the system.
- Semi-structured documents: This class encapsulates servers presenting their information in semi-structured HTML pages, such as electronic journals or technical report collections without search engines. In difference to the above classes no explicit querying is needed. The bibliographic data are extracted directly from the HTML pages by using a rule-based layout description language. The rule sets for the different servers are stored in external files and are interpreted during the extraction process. Once again, new servers can easily be added to MYVIEW.

There are, of course, other approaches for extracting and transforming semi-structured data (see [4, 5, 9, 25]). Our language was inspired by the pattern matching approach of Hammer et al. [24] and the extension of attribute grammars proposed by Abiteboul et al. [2]. The requirements of being simple, flexible, robust and that the layout structure should not influence the final storage structure motivated us to develop our own method. It is not an all purpose language and not as powerful as other approaches, but it is suitable for our application and easier to use. For a detailed description we refer to [26].

The query components realize the functionalities for collecting and transforming bibliographic data from different information servers. Since the individual steps are independent (uniform interfaces provided) the query components can be divided into subcomponents, which can be reused and combined. The correct combination of the subcomponents for each class is the task of the back-end server.

To query the heterogeneous information servers their individual characteristics have to be considered. Therefore a description of their features is indispensable. The necessary information are stored in an external file, the so-called *General Information Servers' Descriptions*. The metadata about the information servers can be divided into three categories:

- Information, that are absolutely necessary for identifying and contacting the server (eg name, query component class).
- Information, that describe the properties of the server (eg query language, result format).
- Information, that support the automatic resource selection of relevant servers (eg content description, word distribution, language).

A detailed consideration of the maintained attributes can be found in [36].

The task of describing query capabilities or general features of data sources has already been considered in different efforts. The STARTS protocol [21] (see Sec. 5) defines two formats for resource description and content characterization. It is partly integrated in our scheme. Other approaches like [33] consider rewriting techniques based on capability descriptions to take advantage of all the query power of the different sources. As a first step, we have focused on Boolean queries, because they are at least supported by most information providers. Using not all possible query capabilities is compensated by the retrieval facilities of the warehouse.

Storing Bibliographic Data. The retrieved query results have to be transformed from their heterogeneous formats into a uniform scheme to enable efficient data retrieval and processing. There are a diversity of formats for describing, storing and exchanging bibliographic information. When analyzing the demands of MyVIEW we considered many of them, for instance MARC (library exchange format) [15], BibTEX (LATEX bibliography format) [20], SOIF (Harvest)

[10], RFC 1807 (NCSTRL) [27], Dublin Core [39], RDF (Resource Description Framework) [31], MCF (Meta Content Framework) [12], Semantic Header [16] and TEI (Text Encoding Initiative) [6].

Basically all formats are more or less suitable for our warehouse scheme. Only the expense for modifications varies in order to meet our requirements. Every format was developed with a special application domain in mind (eg MARC for cataloguing in libraries, BibTEX for maintaining bibliographies in LaTEX) resulting in a special attribute set. But extending these sets lead to incompatibilities (eg RFC1807 has a fixed scheme) or makes it much more difficult to process them (eg repetition of the same attribute in SOIF or attribute hierarchies in "flat" formats like BibTEX). The SGML based formats like TEI, RDF, and MCF are very flexible, but too complex or not finally released.

In the end, we decided to define a new format for the MyView warehouse to meet all our demands. This approach should not be mistaken for a proposal of a new format. It is just for internal use. It comprises the common attributes of the previously mentioned formats, especially BibTEX, RFC1807 and Dublin Core, and partly represents the complexity of MARC by using a fine-grained structure of title and keyword attributes. The format is based on SGML to take advantage of its internationally standardization, flexibility and widespread use (many tools and applications). It uses only basic features to achieve compatibility to XML. For reasons of space we skip the detailed discussion of the maintained attributes (see DTD in [36]). Instead, to convey an impression of the stored information in the warehouse format and the underlying tree structure we present an example:

```
<!DOCTYPE metarec SYSTEM "metarec.dtd">
<metarec>
  <record>
    <sys>
      <source>test.bib</source>
      <srcid>rijsbergen79:inf</srcid>
      <add-date>
        <year>1998</year>
        <month>January</month>
        <day>13</day>
      </add-date>
    </sys>
    <names>
      <author>
        <name>van Rijsbergen, C.J.</name>
      </author>
      <publisher>
        <name>Butterworth</name>
        <address>London</address>
      </publisher>
    </names>
    <phys>
      <ident>
        <isbn>0-408-70929-4</isbn>
      </ident>
      <pub-date>
        <year>1979</year>
      </pub-date>
      <edition>2nd</edition>
      <type>book</type>
    </phys>
    <desc>
      <titles>
        <title>Information Retrieval</title>
      </titles>
    </desc>
  </record>
</metarec>
```

The information of a bibliographic data record is divided into five sections:

<sys> – information about the data provider
<names> – information about persons and organizations
<phys> – information describing the formal/technical properties
<desc> – information describing the content
<unknown> – information that can not be mapped or transformed, but should be available (not present in the example)

There is, of course, a great need for standardization to simplify the information exchange on the Web, as the many discussions about metadata formats show. But there will be still a great discrepancy between different objectives tied up with different demands (eg cataloguing information in libraries in extensive formats like MARC following sophisticated rules and a minimalistic set of 15 attributes in Dublin Core for describing networked documents). Therefore the explicit collection of metadata in non-uniform schemes will go on in the future. The only thing to pay attention to is a common basis and the chance for a simple transformation like in MYVIEW.

3.2 Exploring the Warehouse

After the local warehouse is filled with potential relevant bibliographic data the user can explore the gathered information.[8] By now, we have implemented a Boolean query engine and an interface to a Lore DBMS. Browsing facilities are in preparation.

Boolean Queries. One possibility of querying the warehouse is the use of a WWW based interface for submitting Boolean queries (see Fig. 2). On the left-hand side attribute names or path expressions can be specified. The corresponding search strings are entered into the fields on the right-hand side. The search terms can be connected using the Boolean operators AND and OR. Furthermore the user can select case sensitive or insensitive processing.

The query depicted in Fig. 2 searches for all documents about logic which are accessible electronically. This is achieved by forcing the string "logic" to appear in an attribute "below" the node DESC (eg TITLE or ABSTRACT) and by checking whether the attribute URL exists. The query language is inspired by the subtree model proposed by Lowe et al. [28]. A discussion of this language and its features is beyond the scope of this article (see [26]).

Lorel Queries. As a proof-of-concept for the interchangeability of the underlying storage management system, we have implemented an interface to the Lore DBMS [30]. In addition the user can take advantage of the supported query capabilities of the Lorel query language (see [3]), assuming she is familiar with Lorel or OQL.

The following query, for instance, searches for all document titles containing the string "logic" in the attribute TITLE when knowing just the root node and the attribute name:

```
select T
from METAREC.#.TITLE T
where T grep "logic";
```

---

[8] The process of retrieving data from different sources may take some time. The user should not expect the system to establish the warehouse within a few minutes. Ideally, the process should be carried out over night.

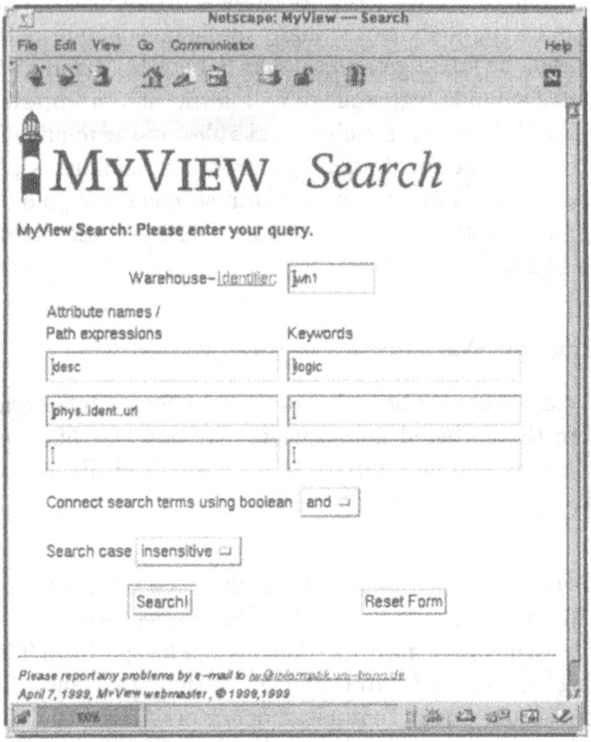

Fig. 2. Query form for searching

The above mentioned query (Sec. 3.2) for selecting all data records containing the string "logic" below the node DESC and having an URL entry looks like this:

```
select T,U
from METAREC.RECORD.DESC.# T,
     METAREC.RECORD.PHYS.IDENT.URL U
where T grep "logic"
and exists(METAREC.RECORD.PHYS.IDENT.URL);
```

To "discover" the structure of the underlying data, one can ask for all paths from the root node METAREC to the leaves named NAME:

```
select distinct path-of(P)
from METAREC.#@P.NAME;
```

One would obtain:

```
RECORD.NAMES.AUTHOR
RECORD.NAMES.CORPAUTHOR
RECORD.NAMES.EDITOR
RECORD.NAMES.PUBLISHER
RECORD.NAMES.CONTRIBUTOR
```

These are only some simple examples for the use of Lorel. Other more complex queries can be constructed.

3.3 Customization

The integration of information providers is done manually by an administrator (one day possibly customized by the user). It is intentionally not our goal to automate this process as the quality assurance should be up to an expert.

So far, we discussed the idea of MYVIEW in the context of a single individual information system. But the same method can be applied in shared environments like project groups, departments or the like, where people with the same interests are working together. In such cases it pays off to have one central internal administrator. She maintains the information servers for common use that individual users wanted to be added. Sharing the same system enables the participants to search for information in the common warehouse and benefit from previously collected data. This results in faster response time and avoidance of redundant searches. The union of individual users with nearly the same focus of interest in fact is desirable to achieve a high synergetic effect in the long run: everyone knows different valuable information servers resulting in a highly relevant server collection for the common information need.

4 Implementation

The previous sections described the conceptual architecture of the MYVIEW system. We now outline some implementation aspects.

4.1 Component Architecture

Let us begin with the back-end server. Figure 3 illustrates its structure and the connection of the separate components. The shaded areas represent the interfaces to the user (front-end) and to the Internet resources (information servers).

The WWW server (Apache[9]) establishes the contact to the user by presenting HTML pages (server data) for specifying the information need, managing and querying the warehouse and displaying query results. Additional server programs (CGI scripts) are necessary to add supplementary data to the HTML pages dynamically.

The construction of the warehouse is done as described in Sec. 3.1. The query components are divided into the three subcomponents query translation, server communication and query result transformation, which are supplied with metadata from the general information servers' descriptions.

The exploration of the warehouse is again realized through a WWW interface in combination with additional tools (sgrep, see Sec. 4.4).

---

[9] http://www.apache.org/

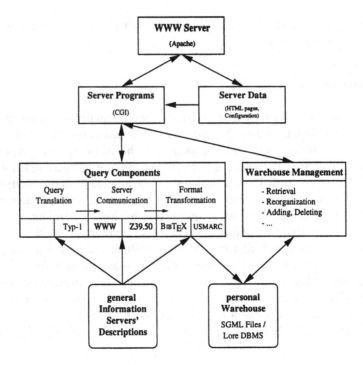

Fig. 3. Component architecture of the back-end server

4.2 Integrated Information Servers

At present the integrated information servers are[10]

- libraries offering a Z39.50 interface (Library of Congress Server, Bell Labs Server, On-line Computing Library Center (OCLC) Test Server),
- on-line catalogues with WWW gateway (The Collection of Computer Science Bibliographies[11]), and
- semi-structured WWW pages without search engine (Technical Report Server University Bonn[12], Journal of AI Research[13], Logic Journal of the IGPL[14], The Computer Journal[14], Journal of Logic and Computation[14]).

To implement the Z39.50 protocol we made use of an Application Programming Interface (API) used in a german library network project (DBV-OSI II). The queries are transformed in Typ-1 format with the Bib-1 attribute set. The query results are converted from USMARC into the internal warehouse format.

---

[10] This is an ongoing process, of course; we expect a fully-operational system to have many more information servers.

[11] http://liinwww.ira.uka.de/bibliography/

[12] http://www.informatik.uni-bonn.de/III/forschung/publikationen/tr/

[13] http://www.cs.washington.edu/research/jair/

[14] http://www.oup.co.uk/igpl/ or http://.../comjnl/ or http://.../logcom/

The communication with the WWW gateway is realized by constructing an appropriate HTTP-Request and by extracting the results from the corresponding HTTP pages. Due to lack of space we do not discuss these issues and the implementation of the query functionalities for the semi-structured WWW pages, but refer the reader to [26].

4.3 Layer Model

When bibliographic data are collected from internet repositories, they are transformed into the uniform MYVIEW scheme. This scheme should not be mistaken for conventional database schemes. The structure of bibliographic data records is irregular [37]: Some may have an abstract, a reference to conference proceedings or a journal volume, other do not. The record structure is implicit: Single items must be identified in raw data as different as BIBTEX and MARC. Bibliographic data records thus have features typical of *semi-structured data* as defined by Abiteboul [1].

Graphs and trees have proved to be suitable for representing semi-structured data (see [13]). A tree representation of data records is at the heart of the MYVIEW system. Each data record is represented by a tree with labeled internal and external nodes. Labels of internal nodes denote record components (author, title, ...), whereas labels of external nodes carry the values (eg an author's name). In our (as yet) simplified model all values are of type string.

This conceptual data model links the physical data storage with the interface layer. The interface layer is responsible for the transmission of data from internet repositories. Data are transformed into their internal tree representation which is then passed to the physical layer for persistent storage. This layered architecture enables us to experiment with different storage mechanisms as SGML/XML files and the Lore DBMS.

Furthermore, the conceptual data model forms the basis for user queries. The user may search for documents which contain some given keywords. But he can also require these keywords to occur only in certain leaves of the tree which are specified by their ancestor nodes. We picked up this issue in Sec. 3.2.

4.4 Warehouse Management

So far, we have implemented only a few retrieval functionalities (see Sec. 3.2: Boolean queries, Lorel queries). The Boolean queries are translated into sgrep[15] commands operating on an SGML file representation of the warehouse data.

sgrep (structured grep) is a tool for searching text documents. The search is based on text regions, which can be defined by constant strings or start and end tags (like in SGML). An sgrep query consists of region expressions and can for example check, whether one region includes another region.

An sgrep command for a query which searches for documents containing the string "sgml" in the title, looks like this

---

[15] http://www.cs.helsinki.fi/~jjaakkol/sgrep.html

```
sgrep -i 'NAMED_ELEMS(record) containing (NAMED_ELEMS(title) containing
                         ((''sgml'')))'.
```

The option -i is for switching to case insensitive search and NAMED_ELEMS(X) is a macro for defining a region enclosed with start and end tags for X.

The Lorel queries are evaluated directly through Lore (the Lore API could be used instead). The underlying Database is constructed by transforming the warehouse format into the Object Exchange Model (OEM) used in Lore.

5 Related Work

In recent years many efforts have been made in digital library projects and Internet information retrieval tools to provide functionalities like search, storage, access, and organization. In the following we describe some of the proposed approaches and compare them with MYVIEW.

Existing search engines (AltaVista[16], InfoSeek[17]) and resource discovery tools (see [11]) are impressively powerful what concerns the keyword-driven discovery of Internet resources. But they do not integrate the millions of document descriptions of traditional library catalogues. Web-based interfaces to libraries[18] on the other hand will in most cases support only simple queries and each offers a different user interface. In-between these two extremes meta search engines (MetaCrawler [35], SavvySearch[19]) and networked literature collections (NCSTRL[20]) overcome the latter interface diversity, but problems remain: predefined search space not configurable by the user, restricted retrieval capabilities.

The Harvest system [10] is an integrated set of customizable tools for gathering information from diverse Internet repositories and their subsequent effective use. The architecture enables the construction of topic-specific content indexes (broker), but the definition of a personalized view is not supported directly. As stated in [29], the original goal of having enough Harvest brokers for most purposes and leading the users by querying a central registry (Harvest Server Registry) to the right broker has never been reached. Furthermore some types of information repositories cannot be handled, such as traditional library catalogues.

The Search Broker[21] [29] is a search tool combining two search phases into one regular search. In a first phase the search is after the right database, whereas in a second phase the selected database is queried for relevant information. This idea grew out of the Harvest project. User input is a list of keywords with the first being a subject identifier followed by the actual query. When asking for just

---

[16] http://www.altavista.com/

[17] http://www.infoseek.go.com/

[18] http://www.lights.com/webcats/

[19] http://www.savvysearch.com/

[20] http://www.ncstrl.org/

[21] You can find the homepage at http://sb.cs.arizona.edu/sb/, but the system is no longer maintained.

one keyword the internal subject list is queried and information about it and all its related subjects is given for further usage. Usually, the response of a regular search is not modified and just appended to an introduction describing and referencing the source search engine. So, no further processing of the result sets is done leaving the work to the user. This is one of the differences to MYVIEW. We are in the line with the Search Broker and many other meta search engines what concerns the usage of available search engines on the web. But our approach also integrates different information providers and explicitly stores and maintains the gathered information.

The TSIMMIS system [19] integrates data from multiple heterogeneous sources and provides users with seamless integrated views of the data. It translates a user query on an integrated view into a set of source queries and postprocessing steps that compute the answer to the user query from the results of the source queries. The explicit view definitions and the view expansions by the mediators are the precondition for query evaluation and as such the central key to the underlying information. An automated resource selection has not to be done in TSIMMIS at the expense of predefining the views. The MYVIEW system pursues a different path. Instead of describing the properties of the information repositories extensively, it only needs some general metadata to connect to the information server and query their repositories. Naturally, the querying on the local warehouse has still to be done. The heterogeneity of the data sources in TSIMMIS is handled by using the semi-structured data model OEM (Object Exchange Model).

A system which aims at integrating distributed Internet resources and uses word-frequency information for their selection is *GlOSS* [23]. It focuses on the identification of relevant text databases for a given query and uses the word-frequencies to estimate the result sizes of the query. The hard problem of modeling a user's information need is not tackled in *GlOSS*. The generalized version *gGlOSS* [22] also deals with vector-space databases and queries, but at the expense of additionally required statistical information about the databases.

The *Stanford Proposal for Internet Metasearching* STARTS[22] tries to facilitate the three main tasks a metasearcher has to perform: the selection of the best source, the evaluation of the queries at these sources, and the result merging. The group effort of more than ten companies and organizations, coordinated by Stanford's Digital Libraries Project leads to a protocol definition for Internet retrieval and search [21]. Unfortunately, as far as we know, STARTS is only used in Stanford's own InfoBus [34] - a prototype infrastructure to extend the current Internet protocols. We would really appreciate the realization of the STARTS proposal, but we believe that the active support of information providers like libraries or publishing houses is the exception in real life applications.[23] That is the reason why we do not wait for the providers to do something, but describe the resources on our own in MYVIEW.

---

[22] http://www-db.stanford.edu/~gravano/starts_home.html

[23] The involvement in such projects may be motivated by the hope of taking some advantage (image cultivation or in financial ways), when the taken approach reveals to be widely accepted.

Beside the Lore DBMS mentioned above other approaches have been made for combining structured documents with database technology. Böhm et al. [8] describe declarative and navigational access mechanisms in HyperStorM, building on a configurable database-internal representation of documents. Avoiding the parsing of a DTD to speed up operations may be worthwhile to consider in the future.

We strongly believe that our approach is an improvement and has the potential to be a significant step forward. A user can use the default settings and participate in the benefits of the system. Under the prerequisite of investing some time at the beginning for customization (adding servers that has a relevance to the personal information need or, as a first guess, selecting some of those already known to the system) the query results will be of even higher quality. This may not be very surprising, but a lot of systems do not even give the end users a chance in controlling its behaviour.

6 Conclusions and Future Work

The MYVIEW project comprises a diversity of research issues in the area of digital libraries, networked information retrieval and internet information systems. For instance, the resource discovery problem, the collection fusion problem and the metadata discussion have to be considered. We know, that one system or even one model is not capable of solving all the problems, but we have shown how such an approach may look like and how we believe to realize some aspects of it. Our proposal combines fully automatic parts (query generation and submission) and manual parts (adding information providers, defining the information need) to support the user in time-consuming and monotonous tasks, but leave the responsibility to him in mission critical details.

In this paper we presented the present state of the MYVIEW system, a warehouse for bibliographic data which is locally available for browsing, ad hoc queries, re-arrangements and analysis. The global architecture was sketched and the current implementation described. At the moment we are working mainly on the automated resource selection of the information repositories and investigate in suitable query languages and user interfaces for the warehouse exploration. Furthermore, we have to examine how we can take advantage of the recent XML developments.

We have discussed the MYVIEW concept in the domain of searching for literature, but the principle design decisions and the architecture are of general interest for a number of other application domains. We strongly believe that the MYVIEW approach is a worthwhile step in the right direction.

7 Acknowledgements

We are grateful to Jürgen Kalinski, Annette Langer, Jan Stohner and all the others involved in the MYVIEW project for many fruitful discussions and the contributions they made.

References

1. Abiteboul, S. Querying semi-structured data. In *Proc. of the 6th Int. Conf. on Database Theory (ICDT)*, LNCS 1186, 1–18. Springer, 1997.
2. Abiteboul, S., S. Cluet, V. Christophides, T. Milo, G. Moerkotte, and J. Siméon. Querying documents in object databases. *Int. J. on Digit. Libr.*, 1(1):5–19, 1997.
3. Abiteboul, S., D. Quass, J. McHugh, J. Widom, and J. Wiener. The Lorel Query Language for Semistructured Data. *Int. J. on Digit. Libr.*, 1(1):68–88, 1997.
4. Atzeni, P., G. Mecca, and P. Merialdo. Semistructured and structured data in the web: Going back and forth. *SIGMOD Record*, 26(4):16–23, 1997.
5. Atzeni, P., G. Mecca, and P. Merialdo. To weave the web. In *Proc. of the 23th Int. Conference on Very Large Data Bases (VLDB)*, 206–215. 1997.
6. Barnard, D. and N. Ide. The Text Encoding Initiative: Flexible and Extensible Document Encoding. *J. of the Am. Soc. for Information Sci.*, 48(7):622–628, 1997.
7. Belkin, N. J. and B. W. Croft. Retrieval techniques. *Annual Review of Information Science and Technology*, 22:109–145, 1987.
8. Böhm, K., K. Aberer, E. Neuhold, and X. Yang. Structured Document Storage and Refined Declarative and Navigational Access Mechanisms in HyperStorM. *VLDB Journal*, 6(4):296–311, 1997.
9. Bonhomme, S. and C. Roisin. Interactively Restructuring HTML Documents. In *Proc. of the 5th Int. WWW Conf.*, 1996.
10. Bowman, M., P. Danzig, D. Hardy, U. Manber, and M. Schwartz. The Harvest Information Discovery and Access System. In *Proc. of the 2nd Int. WWW Conf.*, 763–771, 1994.
11. Bowman, M., P. Danzig, U. Manber, and M. Schwartz. Scalable Internet Resource Discovery: Research Problems and Approaches. *CACM*, 37(8):98–107, 1994.
12. Bray, T. and R. V. Guha. A MCF Tutorial, 1997.
13. Buneman, P. Semistructured Data. In *Proc. of the 16th ACM Symp. on Principles of Database Systems (PODS)*, 117–121. 1997.
14. Chaudhuri, S. and U. Dayal. An Overview of Data Warehousing and OLAP Technology. *SIGMOD Record*, 26(1):65–74, 1997.
15. Delsey, T. The Evolution of MARC Formats. In *The Future of Communication Formats*, International Conference, Canada, 1996.
16. Desai, B. C. Supporting Discovery in Virtual Libraries. *Journal of the American Society for Information Science*, 48(3):190–204, 1997.
17. Dogac, A., M. T. Ozsu, and O. Ulusoy, eds. *Current Trends in Data Management Technology*. Idea Group Publishing, Hershey, USA, 1999.
18. Fox, E. A. and G. Marchionini. Toward a worldwide Digital Library. *CACM*, 41(4):29–32, 1998.
19. García-Molina, H., Y. Papakonstantinou, D. Quass, A. Rajaraman, Y. Sagiv, J. Ullman, V. Vassalos, and J. Widom. The TSIMMIS approach to mediation: Data models and Languages. *J. of Intelligent Information Systems*, 8(2):117–132, 1997.
20. Goossens, M., F. Mittelbach, and A. Samarin. *The LATEX Companion*. 1994.
21. Gravano, L., C.-C. K. Chang, H. García-Molina, and A. Paepcke. STARTS: Stanford Proposal for Internet Meta-Searching. In *Proc. of the 1997 ACM SIGMOD Int. Conference on Management of Data*, 207–218. 1997.
22. Gravano, L. and H. García-Molina. Generalizing GlOSS to vector-space databases and broker hierarchies. In *Proc. of the 21th Int. Conf. on Very Large Data Bases (VLDB)*, 78–89. 1995.

23. Gravano, L., H. García-Molina, and A. Tomasic. The efficacy of GlOSS for the text database discovery problem. Tech. Rep. STAN-CS-TN-93-2, Stanford University, 1993.

24. Hammer, J., H. García-Molina, J. Cho, R. Aranha, and A. Crespo. Extracting semistructured information from the web. In *Workshop on the Management of Semistructured Data*, 1997.

25. Document Style Semantics and Specification Language (DSSSL), 1996.

26. Langer, A. *Extraktion von halbstrukturierten Daten im personalisierten Literaturkatalog* MYVIEW. Master's thesis, Inst. f. Inf. III, Univ. Bonn, 1998. in German.

27. Lasher, R. and D. Cohen. A Format for Bibliographic Records. Request for Comment (RFC) 1807, 1995.

28. Lowe, B., J. Zobel, and R. Sacks-Davis. A formal model for databases of structured text. In *Proc. of the 4th Int. Conf. on Database Systems for Advanced Applications*, vol. 5, 449–456. 1995.

29. Manber, U. and P. A. Bigot. The Search Broker. In *First Usenix Symp. on Internet Technologies and Systems, Monterey, CA*. 1997.

30. McHugh, J., S. Abiteboul, R. Goldman, D. Quass, and J. Widom. Lore: A database management system for semistructured data. *SIGMOD Record*, 26(3):54–66, 1997.

31. Miller, E. An introduction to the resource description framework. *d-lib Mag*, 1998.

32. National Information Standards Organization. Information Retrieval (Z39.50): Application Service Definition and Protocol Specification. NISO Press, 1995.

33. Papakonstantinou, Y., A. Gupta, and L. Haas. Capabilities-based query rewriting in mediator systems. In *Proc. of the Int. Conf. on Parallel and Distributed Information Systems*. 1996.

34. Röscheisen, M., M. Baldonado, C. Chang, L. Gravano, S. Ketchpel, and A. Paepcke. The Stanford InfoBus and Its Service Layers: Augmenting the Internet with Higher-Level Information Management Protocols. In *Digital Libraries in Computer Science: The MeDoc Approach*, LNCS 1392, 213–230. Springer, 1998.

35. Selberg, E. and O. Etzioni. Multi-Engine Search and Comparison using the MetaCrawler. In *Proc. of the 4th Int. WWW Conf.*, 195–208. 1995.

36. Stohner, J. *Sammlung von Metainformationen im personalisierten Literaturkatalog* MYVIEW. Master's thesis, Inst. f. Inf. III, Univ. Bonn, 1998. in German.

37. Suciu, D. Semistructured Data and XML. In *Proc. of the Int. Conf. on Foundations of Data Organization*. 1998.

38. Watters, C. and M. A. Shepherd. Shifting the information paradigm from data-centered to user-centered. *Information Processing & Management*, 30(4):455–471, 1994.

39. Weibel, S. and J. Hakala. DC-5: The Helsinki Metadata Workshop. *D-Lib Magazine*, 1998.

40. Widom, J. Research Problems in Data Warehousing. In *Proc. of the 4th Int. Conf. on Information and Knowledge Management*, 25–30. 1995.

41. Wiederhold, G. Mediators in the architecture of future information systems. *IEEE Computer*, 38–49, 1992.

42. Wolff, J. and J. Kalinski. The MYVIEW System: Tackling the Interface Problem. Tech. Rep. IAI-TR-97-5, Institut für Informatik III, Universität Bonn, 1997.

43. Wolff, J. and J. Kalinski. Mining Library Catalogues: Best-Match Retrieval based on Exact-Match Interfaces. In *Proc. of the Int. Workshop on Issues and Applications of Database Technology (IADT'98)*. 1998. Also appeared in [17].

Integrating Data Mining with Relational DBMS: A Tightly-Coupled Approach

Svetlozar Nestorov[1] and Shalom Tsur[2*]

[1] Department of Computer Science, Stanford University,
Stanford, CA 94305, USA
evtimov@db.stanford.edu
http://www-db.stanford.edu/people/evtimov.html
[2] Surromed, Inc.
Palo Alto, CA 94303, USA
tsur@surromed.com

Abstract. Data mining is rapidly finding its way into mainstream computing. The development of generic methods such as itemset counting has opened the area to academic inquiry and has resulted in a large harvest of research results. While the mined datasets are often in relational format, most mining systems do not use relational DBMS. Thus, they miss the opportunity to leverage the database technology developed in the last couple of decades.

In this paper, we propose a data mining architecture, based on the query flock framework, that is tightly-coupled with RDBMS. To achieve optimal performance we transform a complex data mining query into a sequence of simpler queries that can be executed efficiently at the DBMS. We present a class of levelwise algorithms that generate such transformations for a large class of data mining queries. We also present some experimental results that validate the viability of our approach.

1 Introduction

Data mining — the application of methods to analyze very large volumes of data so as to infer new knowledge — is rapidly finding its way into mainstream computing and becoming commonplace in such environments as finance and retail, in which large volumes of cash register data are routinely analyzed for user buying patterns of goods, shopping habits of individual users, efficiency of marketing strategies for services and other information. The development of generic methods such as itemset counting and the derivation of association rules [1,3] has opened the area to academic inquiry and has resulted in a large harvest of research results.

From an architectural perspective, the common way of implementing a data mining task is to perform it using a special purpose algorithm which typically analyzes the data by performing multiple sequential passes over a data file. The

---

* This work was done while the author was affiliated with Research and Development Lab, Hitachi America, Ltd., Santa Clara, California, USA.

performance measure is usually the number of passes required to conclude the analysis. There are obvious advantages in integrating a database system in this process. In addition to such controlling parameters as support and confidence levels, the user has an additional degree of freedom in the choice of the data set to be analyzed, which can be generated as the result of a query. Furthermore, the well understood methods for query optimization, built into the DBMS, can be utilized without further development. While the potential benefits of an integrated data-mining/DBMS system are easy to perceive, there is a performance issue that requires consideration: can we achieve a comparable, or at least an acceptable level of performance from these integrated methods when compared to the special-purpose external methods? This question was previously examined in a more narrow context of association rules and a particular DBMS in [7] and [2]. Section 2 of this paper elaborates on the general architectural choices available and their comparison.

The idea of flocks [11] was presented as a framework for performing complex data analysis tasks on relational database systems. The method consists of a generator of candidate query parameter settings and their concomitant queries, and a filter which passes only those results that meet the specified condition. The canonical example for flocks is itemset counting. An earlier paper [8] has addressed the query optimization problems that arise when existing query optimizers are used in the context of flocks. Various means of pushing aggregate conditions down into the query execution plan were examined and a new logical operator *group-select* was defined to improve the flock execution optimization plan.

The emphasis of this paper is on the relationship between the system architecture and the flock execution plan. The choices involved are not independent: different optimization plans may result in the execution of the flock either internally, by optimizing the order of introduction of selection and grouping criteria on the underlying relations or externally, by means of auxiliary relations. Section 3 of this paper introduces the idea of auxiliary relations and their use in flocks execution. Section 4 elaborates on the generation of query flock plans. Section 5 reports on some experimental results applying these methods and choices to a large database of health-care data. In section 6 we conclude this paper.

2 Architecture

There are three different ways in which data mining systems use relational DBMS. They may not use a database at all, be loosely coupled, or be tightly coupled. We have chosen the tightly-coupled approach that does (almost) all of the data processing at the database. Before we justify our choice, we discuss the major advantages and drawback of the the other two approaches.

Most current data mining systems do not use a relational DBMS. Instead they provide their own memory and storage management. This approach has its advantages and disadvantages. The main advantage is the ability to fine-tune the memory management algorithms with respect to the specific data mining task.

Thus, the data mining systems can achieve optimal performance. The downside of this database-less approach is the lost opportunity to leverage the existing relational database technology developed in the last couple of decades. Indeed, conventional DBMS provide various extra features, apart from good memory management, that can greatly benefit the data mining process. For example, the recovery and logging mechanisms, provided by most DBMS, can make the results of long computations durable. Furthermore, concurrency control can allow many different users to utilize the same copy of the data and run data mining queries simultaneously.

Some data mining systems use a DBMS but only to store and retrieve the data. This loosely-coupled approach does not use the querying capability provided by the database which constitutes both its main advantage and disadvantage. Since the data processing is done by specialized algorithms their performance can be optimized. On the other hand, there is still the requirement for at least temporary storage of the data once it leaves the database. Therefore, this approach also does not use the full services offered by the DBMS.

The tightly-coupled approach, in contrast, takes full advantage of the database technology. The data are stored in the database and all query processing is done locally (at the database). The downside of this approach is the limitations of the current query optimizers. In was shown in [10] that performance suffers greatly if we leave the data mining queries entirely in the hands of the current query optimizers. Therefore, we need to perform some optimizations *before* we send the queries to the database, taking into account the capabilities of the current optimizers. To achieve this we introduce an *external optimizer* that sits on top of the DBMS. The external optimizer effectively breaks a complex data mining query into a sequence of smaller queries that can be executed efficiently at the database. This architecture is shown in Fig. 1.

The external optimizer can be a part of larger system for formulating data mining queries such as query flocks. The communication between this system and the database can be carried out in ODBC or JDBC.

3 Framework

3.1 Query Flocks

The query flock framework [11] generalizes the *a-priori trick* [1] for a larger class of problems. Informally, a query flock is a generate-and-test system, in which a family of queries that are identical except for the values of one or more *parameters* are asked simultaneously. The answers to these queries are filtered and those that pass the filter test enable their parameters to become part of the answer to the query flock. The setting for a query flock system is:

- A language to express the parameterized queries.
- A language to express the filter condition about the results of a query.

Given these two languages we can specify a query flock by designating:

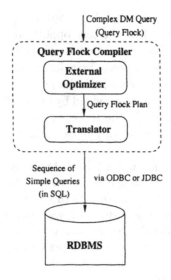

Fig. 1. Tightly-coupled integration of data mining and DBMS.

- One or more predicates that represent data stored as relations.
- A set of *parameters* whose names always begin with $.
- A *query* expressed in the chosen query language, using the parameters as constants.
- A *filter condition* that the result of the query must satisfy in order for a given assignment of values to the parameters to be acceptable.

The meaning of a query flock is a set of tuples that represent "acceptable" assignments of values for the parameters. We determine the acceptable parameter assignments by, in principle, trying all such assignments in the query, evaluating the query, and checking whether the results pass the filter condition.

In this paper, we will describe query flocks using conjunctive queries [4], augmented with arithmetics, as a query language and an SQL-like notation for the filter condition. The following example illustrates the query flock idea and our notation:

Example 1. Consider a relation diagnoses(Patient,Disease) that contains information about patients at some hospital and the diseases with which they have been diagnosed. Each patient may have more than one disease. Suppose we are interested in pairs of diseases such that there are least 200 different patients diagnosed with this pair. We can write this question as a query flock in the following way:

QUERY:

```
answer(P) :- diagnoses(P,$D1) AND diagnoses(P,$D2)
             AND $D1 < $D2
```

FILTER:

```
COUNT(answer) >= 200
```

First, let us examine the query part. For a given pair of diseases ($D1 and $D2) the **answer** relation contains all patients diagnosed with the pair. The last predicate ($D1 < $D2) insures that the result contains only pairs of different diseases and does not contain a pair and its reverse. The filter part expresses the condition that there should be at least 200 such patients. Thus, any pair ($D1,$D2) that is in the result of the query flock must have at least 200 patients diagnosed with it.

Another way to think about the meaning of the query flock is the following. Suppose we have all possible disease values. Then, we substitute $D1 and $D2 with all possible pairs and check if the filter condition is satisfied for the query part. Only those values for which the result of the query part passes the test will be in the query flock result. Thus, the result of the query flock is a relation of pairs of diseases; an example relation is shown in Table 1.

Table 1. Example query flock result.

$D1	$D2
anaphylaxis	rhinitis
ankylosing spondylitis	osteoporosis
bi-polar disorder	insomnia

3.2 Auxiliary Relations

Auxiliary relations are a central concept in the query flock framework. An auxiliary relation is a relation over a subset of the parameters of a query flock and contains candidate values for the given subset of parameters. The main property of auxiliary relations is that all parameter values that satisfy the filter condition are contained in the auxiliary relations. In other words, any value that is not in an auxiliary relation is guaranteed not satisfy the filter condition. Throughout the examples in this paper we only consider filter conditions of the form $COUNT(ans) >= X$. However, our results and algorithms are valid for a larger class of filter conditions called *monotone* in [11] or *anti-monotone* in [9]. For this class of filter conditions, the auxiliary relations can be defined with subset of the goals in the query part of the query flock. For a concrete example, consider the query flock from Example 1:

Example 2. An auxiliary relation *ok_d1* for parameter $D1 can be defined as the result of the following query flock:

QUERY:

```
ans(P) :- Diagnoses(P,$D1)
```

FILTER:

    COUNT(ans) >= 200

The result of this flock consists of all diseases such that for each disease there are at least 200 patients diagnosed with it. Consider a pair of diseases such that there are at least 200 patients diagnosed with the pair. Then, both diseases must appear in the above result. Thus, the auxiliary relation is a superset of the result of the original query flock.

3.3 Query Flock Plans

Intuitively, a query flock plan represents the transformation of a complex query flock into a sequence of simpler steps. This sequence of simpler steps represent the way a query flock is executed at the underlying RDBMS. In principal, we can translate any query flock directly in SQL and then execute it at the RDBMS. However, due to limitations of the current query optimizers, such an implementation will be very slow and inefficient. Thus, using query flock plans we can effectively pre-optimize complex mining queries and then feed the sequence of smaller, simpler queries to the query optimizer at the DBMS.

A query flock plan is a (partially ordered) sequence of operations of the following 3 types:

Type 1 Materialization of an auxiliary relation
Type 2 Reduction of a base relation
Type 3 Computation of the final result

The last operation of any query flock plan is always of type 3 and is also the only one of type 3.

Materialization of an auxiliary relation: This type of operation is actually a query flock that is meant to be executed directly at the RDBMS. The query part of this query flock is formed by choosing a safe subquery [12] of the original query. The filter condition is the same as in the original query flock. Of course, there are many different ways to choose a safe subquery for a given subset of the parameters. We investigate several ways to choose safe subqueries according to some rule-based heuristics later in the paper. This type of operation is translated into an SQL query with aggregation and filter condition.

For an example of a step of type 1, recall the query flock that materializes an auxiliary relation for $D1 from Example 2.

QUERY:

    ans(P) :- Diagnoses(P,$D1)

FILTER:

    COUNT(ans) >= 200

This materialization step can be translated directly into SQL as follows:

```
(1) ok_d1(Disease) AS
    SELECT Disease
    FROM diagnoses
    GROUP BY Disease
    HAVING COUNT(Patient) >= 200
```

Reduction of a base relation: This type of operation is a semijoin of a base relation with one or more previously materialized auxiliary relations. The result replaces the original base relation. In general, when a base relation is reduced we have a choice between several reducers. Later in this paper, we describes how to choose "good" reducers.

For an example of a step of type 2, consider the materialized auxiliary relation ok_d1. Using ok_d1 we can reduce the base relation **diagnoses** as follows:

QUERY:

```
    diagnoses_1(P) :- diagnoses(P,$D1) AND ok_d1($D1)
```

This can be translated directly into SQL as follows:

```
(2) diagnoses_1(Patient,Disease) AS
    SELECT b.Patient, b.Disease
    FROM diagnoses b, ok_d1 r
    WHERE b.Disease = r.Disease
```

Computation of the final result: The last step of every query flock plan is a computation of the final result. This step is essentially a query flock with a query part formed by the reduced base relations from the original query flock. The filter is the same as in the original query flock.

4   Algorithms

In this section we present algorithms that generate *efficient* query flock plans. Recall that in our tightly-coupled mining architecture these plans are meant to be translated in SQL and then executed directly at the underlying RDBMS. Thus, we call a query flock plan *efficient* if its execution at the RDBMS is efficient. There are two main approaches to evaluate the efficiency of a given query plan: cost-based and rule-based. A cost-based approach involves developing an appropriate cost model and methods for gathering and using statistics. In contrast, a rule-based approach relies on heuristics based on general principles, such as applying filter conditions as early as possible. In this paper, we focus on the rule-based approach to generating efficient query flock plans. The development of a cost-based approach is a topic of a future paper.

The presentation of our rule-based algorithms is organized as follows. First, we describe a general nondeterministic algorithm that can generate all possible query flock plans under the framework described in Section 3.3. The balance of this section is devoted to the development of appropriate heuristics, and the intuition behind them, that make the nondeterministic parts of the general algorithm deterministic. At the end of this section we discuss the limitations of conventional query optimizers and show how the query flock plans generated by our algorithm overcome these limitations.

4.1   General Nondeterministic Algorithm

The general nondeterministic algorithm can produce any query flock plan in our framework. Recall that a valid plan consists of a sequence of steps of types 1 and 2 followed by a final step of type 3. One can also think of the plan as being a sequence of two alternating phases: materialization of auxiliary relations and reduction of base relations. In the materialization phase we choose what auxiliary relations to materialize one by one. Then we move to the reduction phase or, if no new auxiliary relations have been materialized, to the computation of the final result. In the reduction phase we choose the base relations to reduce one by one and then go back to the materialization phase.

Before we described the nondeterministic algorithm in details we introduce the following two helper functions.

MaterializeAuxRel(Params, Definition) takes a subset of the parameters of the original query flock and a subset of the base relations. This subset forms the body of the safe subquery defining an auxiliary relation for the given parameters. The function assigns a unique name to the materialized auxiliary relation and produces a step of type 1.

ReduceBaseRel(BaseRel, Reducer) takes a base relation and a set of auxiliary relations. This set forms the reducer for the given base relation. The function assigns a unique name to the reduced base relation and produces a step of type 2.

We also assume the existence of functions *add* and *replace*, with their usual meanings, for sets and the function *append* for ordered sets. The nondeterministic algorithm is shown in Fig. 2

The number of query flock plans that this nondeterministic algorithm can generate is rather large. Infact, with no additional restrictions, the number of syntactically different query flock plans that can be produced by Algorithm 1 is infinite. Even if we restrict the algorithm to materializing only one auxiliary relation for a given subset of parameters, the number of query flock plans is more than double exponential in the size of the original query. Thus, we have to choose a subspace that will be tractable and also contains query flock plans that work well empirically. To do so effectively we need to answer several questions about the space of potential query flock plans. We have denoted these questions in Algorithm 1 with (Q1) – (Q5).

(Q1) How to sequence the steps of type 1 and 2?
(Q2) What auxiliary relations to materialize?
(Q3) What definition to choose for a given auxiliary relation?

```
Algorithm 1
    Input:  Query flock QF
            Parameters – set of parameters of QF
            Predicates – set of predicates in the body of the query part of QF
    Output:  Query flock plan QFPlan
    // Initialization
        BaseRels = Predicates
        AuxRels = ∅
        QFPlan = ∅
    // Iterative Generation of Query Flock Plan
        while(true) do
(Q1)        choose NextStepType from {MATERIALIZE, REDUCE, FINAL}
            case NextStepType:
            MATERIALIZE: // Materialization of Auxiliary Relation
(Q2)            choose subset S of Parameters
(Q3)            choose subset D of BaseRels
                Step = MaterializeAuxRel(S, D)
                QFPlan.append(Step)
                AuxRels.add(Step.ResultRel)
            REDUCE: // Reduction of Base Relation
(Q4)            choose element B from BaseRels
(Q5)            choose subset R of AuxRels
                Step = ReduceBaseRel(B, R)
                QFPlan.append(Step)
                BaseRels.replace(B, Step.ResultRel)
            FINAL: // Computation of Final Result
                Step = MaterializeAuxRel(Parameters, BaseRels)
                QFPlan.append(Step)
                return QFPlan
            end case
        end while
```

Fig. 2. General nondeterministic algorithm.

(Q4) What base relations to reduce?

(Q5) What reducer to choose for a given base relation?

There are two main approaches to answering **(Q1)** – **(Q5)**. The first one involves using a cost model similar to the one used by the query optimizer within the RDBMS. The second approach is to use rule-based optimizations. As we noted earlier, in this paper we focus on the second approach.

In order to illustrate Algorithm 1, consider the following example query flock, that was first introduced in [11].

Example 3. Consider the following four relations from a medical database about patients and their symptoms, diagnoses, and treatments.

diagnoses(Patient, Disease) The patient is diagnosed with the disease.
exhibits(Patient, Symptom) The patient exhibits the symptom.
treatment(Patient, Medicine) The patient is treated with the medicine.
causes(Disease, Symptom) The disease causes the symptom.

We are interested in finding side effects of medicine, i.e., finding pairs of medicines $M and symptoms $S such that there are at least 20 patients taking the medicine and exhibiting the symptom but their diseases do not cause the symptoms. The question can be expressed as a query flock as follows:

QUERY:

```
ans(P) :- exhibits(P,$S) AND
          treatment(P,$M) AND
          diagnoses(P,D) AND
          NOT causes(D,$S)
```

FILTER:

```
COUNT(ans) >= 20
```

One possible query flock plan that can be generated by Algorithm 1 for the above query flock is shown in Table 2. This plan consists of a step of type 1 followed by two steps of type 2 and ending with the final step of type 3. The first step materializes an auxiliary relation ok_s($S) for parameter $S. The next two step reduce the base relations causes(D,$S) and exhibits(P,$S) by joining them with ok_s($S). The last step computes the final result, relation res($M,$S), using the reduced base relations.

Table 2. Example of a query flock plan produced by Algorithm 1.

Step	Type	Result	QUERY	FILTER
(1)	1	ok_s($S)	ans_1(P) :- exhibits(P,$S)	COUNT(ans_1) >= 20
(2)	2	c_1(D,$S)	c_1(D,$S) :- causes(D,$S) AND ok_s($S)	-
(3)	2	e_1(P,$S)	e_1(P,$S) :- exhibits(P,$S) AND ok_s($S)	-
(4)	3	res($M,$S)	ans(P) :- e_1(P,$S) AND treatment(P,$M) AND diagnoses(P,D) AND NOT c_1(D,$S)	COUNT(ans) >= 20

4.2 Levelwise Heuristic

First, we address the question how to sequence the steps of types 1 and 2 ((Q1)) along with the questions what auxiliary relations to materialize ((Q2)) and what base relations to reduce ((Q4)). The levelwise heuristic that we propose is loosely fashioned after the highly successful a-priori trick [1]. The idea is to materialize the auxiliary relations for all parameter subsets of size up to and including k in a levelwise manner reducing base relations after each level is materialized. So, starting at level 1, we materializing an auxiliary relations for every parameter. Then we reduce the base relations with the materialized auxiliary relations. At level 2, we materialize the auxiliary relations for all pairs of parameters, and so on. The general levelwise algorithm is formally described in Fig. 3.

Algorithm 2

    Input: Query flock QF; K – max level

            $Parameters$ – set of parameters of QF

            $Predicates$ – set of predicates in the body of the query part of QF

    Output: Query flock plan $QFPlan$

    // Initialization

        $BaseRels = Predicates$

        $QFPlan = \emptyset$

    // Levelwise Generation of Query Flock Plan

        for $i = 1$ to K do

            $AuxRels_i = \emptyset$

        // Materialization of Auxiliary Relations

            for all $S \subset Parameters$ with $\mid S \mid = i$ do

(Q3)   choose subset D of $BaseRels$

                $Step = MaterializeAuxRel(S, D)$

                $QFPlan.append(Step)$

                $AuxRels_i.add(Step.ResultRel)$

            end for

        // Reduction of Base Relations

            for all $B \in BaseRels$

(Q5)   choose subset R of $AuxRels_i$

                $Step = ReduceBaseRel(B, R)$

                $QFPlan.append(Step)$

                $BaseRels.replace(B, Step.ResultRel)$

            end for

        end for

    // Computation of Final Result

        $Step = MaterializeAuxRel(Parameters, BaseRels)$

        $QFPlan.append(Step)$

        return $QFPlan$

Fig. 3. General levelwise algorithm.

The levelwise heuristic has also some important implications on the choice of definitions of auxiliary relations and the choice of reducer for base relations discussed in the next two section.

4.3 Choosing Definitions of Auxiliary Relations

When choosing definitions of auxliary relations ((Q3)) there are two main approaches single and group. In the single approach, we choose a definition for a single auxiliary relation without regard to any other choices. In the group approach, in contrast, we choose definitions for several auxiliary relations at the same time. Thus, we can exploit existing symmetries among the parameters or equivalences among syntactically different definitions. Regardless of the particular approach we only consider definitions that form *minimal* safe subquesies, not involving a cartesian product. The subquesies are minimal in a sense that eliminating any subgoal will either make the subquery unsafe or will turn it into a cartesian product.

The already chosen levelwise heuristic dictates the use of the group approach in our algorithm. We can take advantage of the fact that we are choosing definitions for all auxiliary relations for a given level *simultaneously*. Thus, it is rather straightforward to use symmetries among parameters and equivalences among subqueries to choose the smallest the number of definitions that cover all auxliary relations. We refer to this strategy as the *least-cover* heuristic.

4.4 Choosing Reducers of Base Relations

When choosing a reducer for a given base relation we can employ two strategies. The first strategy is to semijoin it with the join of all auxliary relations that have parameters in common with the base relation. The second strategy is to semijoin it with all auxiliary relations that only have parameters appearing in the given base relation. With the second strategy we minimize the number of relations in the reduction joins while keeping the selectivity as high as possible. Again the use of the levelwise heuristic dictates our strategy choice. At the end of each level we have materialized auxiliary relations for all parameter subsets of the given size. Thus, the first strategy yields unnecessarily large reducers for every base relation at almost every level. Therefore, in our algorithm, we employ the second strategy.

4.5 K-Levelwise Deterministic Algorithm

Choosing the least-cover heuristic for (Q3) and the strategy outlined in Section 4.4 for (Q5) we finalize our algorithm that generates query flock plans. The formal description of the k-levelwise deterministic algorithm is shown in Fig.3.

Algorithm 3
  Input: Query flock QF; K – max level
        $Parameters$ – set of parameters of QF
        $Predicates$ – set of predicates in the body of the query part of QF
  Output: Query flock plan $QFPlan$
  `// Initialization`
    $BaseRels = Predicates; QFPlan = \emptyset$
  `// Levelwise Generation of Query Flock Plan, up to level K`
    for $i = 1$ to K do
      $AuxRels_i = \emptyset; MinDefs_i = \emptyset$
      `// find all minimal definitions of auxiliary relations`
      for all $S \subset Parameters$ with $\mid S \mid = i$ do
        $MinDefs_i.add(GetMinDefs(S, BaseRels))$
      end for
      `// choose least cover of minimal definitions`
      $Cover_i = GetLeastCover(MinDefs_i)$
      `// for each definition in the cover add corresponding`
      `// auxiliary realtions for all covered parameter subsets`
      for all $\langle Def, CoveredParamSets \rangle \in Cover_i$ do
        for all $S \in CoveredParamSets$ do
          $Step = MaterializeAuxRel(S, Def)$
          $AuxRels_i.add(Step.ResultRel)$
        end for
        `// materialize the shared definition only once`
        $QFPlan.append(Step)$
      end for
      `// Reduction of Base Relations`
      for all $B \in BaseRels$ do
        $R = \emptyset$
        `// choose reducer for base relation`
        for all $A \in AuxRels_i$ do
          if $GetParams(A) \subset GetParams(B)$ then
            $R.add(A)$
        end for
        $Step = ReduceBaseRel(B, R)$
        $QFPlan.append(Step)$
        $BaseRels.replace(B, Step.ResultRel)$
      end for
    end for
  `// Computation of Final Result`
    $Step = MaterializeAuxRel(Parameters, BaseRels)$
    $QFPlan.append(Step)$
    return $QFPlan$

Fig. 4. K-Levelwise deterministic algorithm.

The k-levelwise deterministic algorithm uses the following three helper functions.

GetMinDefs(Params,Preds) takes a set of parameters and a set a of predicates (query). The function returns a tuple where the first element is the set of parameters and the second element is the set of all minimal definitions (subqueries) for the auxiliary relation for the given set of parameters.

GetLeastCover(Set of (Params,Defs)) takes a set of tuples composed of a set of parameters and a set of definitions. The function returns the smallest set of definitions that covers all sets of parameters using equivalences among syntactically different definitions.

GetParams(Pred) takes a predicate and returns the set of parameters that appear in the given predicate.

The query flock plan produced by Algorithm 3 with $k = 1$ for the query flock from Example 3 is shown in Table 3.

Table 3. Query flock plan produced by Algorithm 3 with $K = 1$.

Step	Type	Result	QUERY	FILTER
(1)	1	ok_s($S)	ans_1(P) :- exhibits(P,$S)	COUNT(ans_1) >= 20
(2)	1	ok_m($M)	ans_2(P) :- treatment(P,$M)	COUNT(ans_2) >= 20
(3)	2	c_1(D,$S)	c_1(D,$S) :- causes(D,$S) AND ok_s($S)	-
(4)	2	e_1(P,$S)	e_1(P,$S) :- exhibits(P,$S) AND ok_s($S)	-
(5)	2	t_1(P,$M)	t_1(P,$M) :- treatment(P,$M) AND ok_m($M)	-
(6)	3	res($M,$S)	ans(P) :- e_1(P,$S) AND t_1(P,$M) AND diagnoses(P,D) AND NOT c_1(D,$S)	COUNT(ans) >= 20

4.6 Comparison with Conventional Query Optimizers

Recall that we use query flock plans to insure the efficient execution of query flocks at the underlying RDBMS. The shortcomings, with respect to query flocks, of conventional query optimizers are the fixed shape (left-deep trees) of their query plans and the fact that aggregation is usually done last. Query flock plans rectify these problems by using reduction of base relations to circumvent the shape of the query plan and auxiliary relations to use aggregation on partial results as early as possible

The problem of including aggregation in query optimization is studied in [13,6,5]. In these papers, aggregation is pushed down, (or sometimes up), the query plan tree. The key difference with our work is that we use aggregation on a subset of the original query and the result is used to reduce the size of intermediate steps. Eventually the aggregation must be performed again but we have gained efficiency by having much smaller intermediate results.

5 Experiments

Our experiments are based on real-life health-care data. Below we describe a representative problem and the performance results.

Consider a relation `Diagnoses(PatientID,StayCode,Diagnose)` that contains the diagnoses information for patients during their stays at some hospital. Another relation, `Observe(PatientID,StayCode)`, contains the pairs of `PatientID` and `StayCode` for patients that are kept for observations for less than 24 hours. The rest of the patients are admitted to the hospital. Consider the following problem.

Find all pairs of diagnoses such that:

1. There are at least N patients diagnosed with the pair of diagnoses
2. At least one of them is an observation patient

We can express this problem naturally as a query flock:

QUERY:

```
ans(P,S) :- Diagnoses(P,S,$D1) AND
            Diagnoses(P,S,$D2) AND
            Diagnoses(Q,T,$D1) AND
            Diagnoses(Q,T,$D2) AND
            Observe(Q,T) AND
            $D1 < $D2
```

FILTER:

```
COUNT(ans) >= N
```

This problem is important to the hospital management because the reimbursement procedures and amounts for admitted and observation patients are different. Thus, management would like to identify some exceptions to the general trends, find their causes, and investigate them further for possible malpractice or fraud.

The `Diagnoses` relation contains more than 100,000 tuples, while the `Observe` relation contains about 8,000 tuples. We compared the performance of the 1-levelwise and 2-levelwise algorithms as well as the direct approach where the query flock is directly translated into SQL. We used a standard installation of ORACLE 8.0 running under Windows NT. The results are shown in Fig. 5.

For this dataset, the 2-levelwise algorithm outperforms the 1-levelwise algorithm more than 3 times. This result is somewhat surprising because the two

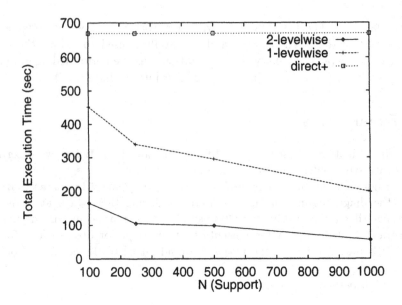

Fig. 5. Performance results on health-care data.

parameters $D1 and $D2 are symmetric (excluding the inequality) and thus, only one relation is materialized at level 1. However, the reduced base relation **Diagnoses** after level 1 is still rather large and the computation of the final result at this stage is much slower than materializing the auxiliary relation for the pair of parameters.

As expected, both algorithms perform much better than the direct approach where we translate the query flock directly in SQL. Infact, the actual translation did not finish executing in a reasonable amount of time. Thus, we had to augment the direct translation, hence *direct+*, with a preliminary step where we joined the **Observe** and **Diagnoses** relations. This step had the effect of reducing the size of the relations for two of the four **Diagnoses** predicates and eliminating the **Observe** predicate.

6 Conclusions

In this paper, we presented a tightly-coupled approach to integrating data mining and relational DBMS. We based our approach on the query flock framework where complex mining queries expressed as flocks are transformed into a query flock plan that consists of simpler queries. These queries can be optimized effectively by the query optimizer in the RDBMS. Thus, using query flock plans, we can execute complex mining queries efficiently in the RDBMS. We presented a class of levelwise algorithms for generating query flock plans. We also reported on some performance results that validate the effectiveness of our approach.

We are currently investigating cost-based optimization algorithms that interact with the internal optimizer of the RDBMS. Query flock plans produced by such algorithms could be even more efficient than the plans produced by rule-based algorithms. Our future work includes combining the rule-based and cost-based approaches to achieve optimal performance.

Acknowledgment: The authors would like to thank prof. Jeffrey Ullman for many discussions on the topic of query flocks.

References

1. R. Agrawal, T. Imilienski, and A. Swami. Mining association rules between sets of items in large databases. In *Proceedings of ACM SIGMOD International Conference on Management of Data*, pages 207–216, May 1993.
2. R. Agrawal and K. Shim. Developing tightly-coupled applications on ibm db2/cs relational database system: Methodology and experience. Research report, IBM Almaden Research Center.
3. R. Agrawal and R. Srikant. Fast algorithms for mining association rules. In *Proceedings of the 20th International Conference on Very Large Data Bases*, pages 487–499, Santiago, Chile, September 1994.
4. A. Chandra and P. Merlin. Optimal implementation of conjunctive queries in relational databases. In *Proceedings of 9th Annual ACM Symposium on the Theory of Computing*, pages 77–90.
5. S. Chaudhuri and K. Shim. Including group-by in query optimization. In *Proceedings of the 20st International Conference on Very Large Data Bases*, pages 354–366, Santiago, Chile, September 1994.
6. S. Chaudhuri and K. Shim. Optimizing queries with aggregate views. In *Proceedings of the 5th International Conference on Extending Database Technology*, pages 167–182, Avignon, France, March 1996.
7. H. Houtsma and A. Swami. Set-oriented mining of association rules. In *Proceedings of International Conference on Data Engineering*, pages 25–33, Taipei, Taiwan, March 1995.
8. S. Nestorov and S. Tsur. Efficient implementation of query flocks. Technical report, Research and Development Lab, Hitachi America, Ltd., Santa Clara, California, September 1998.
9. R. Ng, L. Lakshmanan, J. Han, and A. Pang. Exploratory mining and pruning optimizations of constrained associations rules. In *Proceedings of ACM SIGMOD International Conference on Management of Data*, pages 13–24, Seattle, Washington, June 1998.
10. S. Sarawagi, S. Thomas, and R. Agrawal. Integrating association rule mining with relational database systems: Alternatives and implications. In *Proceedings of ACM SIGMOD International Conference on Management of Data*, pages 343–354, Seattle, Washington, June 1998.
11. S. Tsur, J. Ullman, C. Clifton, S. Abiteboul, R. Motwani, S. Nestorov, and A. Rosenthal. Query flocks: a generalization of association-rule mining. In *Proceedings of ACM SIGMOD International Conference on Management of Data*, pages 1–12, Seattle, Washington, June 1998.
12. J.D. Ullman. *Principles of Database and Knowledge-Base Systems, Volumes I,II.* Computer Science Press, Rockville, Maryland, 1989.
13. W. Yan and P. Larson. Eager aggregation and lazy aggregation. In *Proceedings of the 21st International Conference on Very Large Data Bases*, pages 345–357, Zurich, Switzerland, September 1995.

Morphological Disambiguation for Hebrew Search Systems

David Carmel and Yoëlle S. Maarek

IBM Haifa Research Laboratory, MATAM, Haifa 31905, Israel,
{carmel,yoelle}@haifa.vnet.ibm.com

Abstract. In this work we describe a new approach for morphological disambiguation to enable linguistic indexing for Hebrew search systems. We describe a Hebrew Morphological Disambiguator (HMD or Hemed for short) based on statistical data gathered from large Hebrew corpora. We show how to integrate HMD with a search engine to enable linguistic search for Hebrew. We report some experimental results demonstrating the the superiority of linguistic search over string-matching search, and the contribution of morphological disambiguation to the quality of search result.

1 Background and Motivation

With the advent of the Web, more and more textual information is being made available on line, and Information Retrieval (IR) systems are becoming of crucial importance to search through the vast amount of information. Most state-of-the-art IR systems operate on a canonical representation of documents called a *profile* that consists of a list (or a vector in the commonly used vector space model [13]) of indexing units and other representative terms[1]. Using a canonical representation makes the processing of documents more convenient. Profiles can be stored in an inverted index for fast retrieval, compared to each other for automatic clustering, abstracted into rules for categorization, etc. Since profiles are intended to provide a "conceptual representation" of documents, it is highly desirable that identical concepts be mapped into the same indexing unit. Thus, inflections of the same word such as plural and singular forms of a noun, or different tenses of a verb, should be represented by the same base unit (*lemma*). Indeed, a user issuing a query about "vitamins" on the Web, does not expect that only articles containing the exact string "vitamins" match his/her query but rather that any article dealing with the concept will be returned. For instance, a document dealing with "Vitamin A" should be considered relevant.

While researchers have been proposing various approaches to start addressing the problem of "conceptual ambiguity", the problem of "morphological ambiguity", at least for English, has been mostly solved by using either a stemmer or a morphological analyzer. Morphological analyzers use a set of declination rules and a dictionary, while stemmers use ad-hoc suffix stripping rules and exception

---

[1] Representative terms can be words, phrases, syntactic constructs [4], lexical affinities [8], etc.

list for these rules depending on the desired quality of the output and the language. One of the most widely used public-domain stemmers for English is the Porter's stemmer [11] which has been shown to give fast and good enough results for most applications such as search. However, stemmers, being less precise than analyzers, cannot be used for all applications. They can be less effective for other languages such as German, or even simply useless for languages such as Hebrew.

Indeed, Hebrew as well as other Semitic languages, is a highly synthetic language with rich vocalic changes such as deletion, insertion, substitution, and affixation. In standard Hebrew writing not all the vowels are represented, several letters represent both consonants and vowels, and gemination is not represented at all [10]. The major problem posed by the extensive morphology is the difficulty to identify the lexical base of a given word since for many input strings it is not clear which letters belong to the base and which have been affixed. This does not only make the definition of stemmers rules much too complex (they would require such as large exception list that it would be preferable to use a dictionary instead), but also significantly complicates the task of Hebrew morphological analyzers that typically return multiple possible analyses [6, 7]. For example, the Hebrew word *mishtara* can be analyzed as:

1. *mishtara* (police).
2. *mishtar + a* (her regime).
3. *mi + shtar + a* (from her bill).

The result of the complex morphology of the Hebrew language is a high level of word ambiguity in comparison to other languages. Highly ambiguous Hebrew words can have up to 13 different analyses. The average number of possible analyses per word is 2.15. More precisely, 55% of the words have more than one reading, and 33% of the words have more than two readings [7]. With such level of ambiguity, regular morphological analyzers cannot be used as such with indexing systems in order to generate document profiles. In a search application for instance, if all analyses returned by the analyzer are stored inside the index, the precision of the results will be very low. For example, a user looking for information about "police stations" (*mishtara* in analysis 1) will be utterly confused to get answers relevant to regimes or bills (analyses 2 and 3).

Therefore, indexing requires ideally a unique lemma (or at most a very small set of possible lemmas) in order not to reduce precision to which users are immediately sensitive. Hence, most Hebrew search engines simply disable morphological analysis to come back to a more primitive string matching search to circumvent this problem. They prefer missing relevant documents (low recall) than exposing the user to totally irrelevant ones (low precision). Note that for conceptual ambiguity, low precision is less annoying to users as they can easily figure out that the word "bank" in English[2] can be ambiguous, while morphology can be so complex that users will not understand at first sight how a document

---

[2] Bank has several senses, one refers to a financial establishment and another to the bank of a river.

dealing with the violinist *Izhak Stern* relates to their query *Mishtara*[3].

In this paper, we propose to reduce the problem of morphological ambiguity of Hebrew via a statistical approach that takes advantage of an existing morphological analyzer, as well as statistical data automatically derived from large Hebrew corpora. Section 2 describes related work on morphological disambiguation for Hebrew. In Section 3 we describe our disambiguation procedure in more detail and explain the role of its basic components. We also describe our Hebrew Morphological Disambiguation algorithm (HMD, nicknamed Hemed) and the way we gather the necessary statistical data. In Section 4, we show how Hemed has been integrated with an existing Hebrew search engine and we describe some experiments that demonstrate the necessity and contribution of morphological disambiguation to Hebrew search. Finally, Section 5 summarizes the contribution of this work.

2 Related Work

The Responsa Project at Bar-Ilan University [12] has been a twenty-year endeavor to compile an electronic database of Jewish scriptural texts. The database includes the Tanach and its commentators, the Babylonian Talmud with Rashi's commentary, the Jerusalem Talmud, Rambam, Midrashim and more. It includes a Hebrew search engine that extends the user's query by adding all grammatical forms of words included in the query, using a morphological engine. Such a query extension improves the search recall significantly but deteriorates search precision. In order to improve precision, Responsa lets the user to refine her query interactively [2].

Reducing the morphological ambiguity of Hebrew is crucial for linguistic indexing as well as for other natural language applications. Ornan [9] developed a new writing system for Hebrew called "Phonemic Script". This script enables Hebrew writing that is morphologically unambiguous. However, this script has not become popular and widely used.

Choueka and Lusignan [3] present a morphological disambiguator based on *short contexts* of words in order to resolve ambiguity, but this disambiguator depends heavily on human interaction. Levinger et al. [7] propose an approach for acquiring *morpho-lexical probabilities* from an un-tagged corpus. The probabilities can be used as an information source for morphological disambiguation. Their *context-free* approach which handles each word separately is motivated by the observation that

> "... in many cases a native speaker of the language can accurately guess the right analysis of a word, without even being exposed to the concrete context in which it appears ..." [7].

---

[3] The Hebrew term *Stern* can also be read as *Shtaran* (their bill in feminine form – an inflection of analysis 3 of the input word *Mishtara*).

In this work we describe a similar context-free approach for morphological disambiguation that reduces the Hebrew morphological ambiguity problem so as to enable linguistic indexing of Hebrew text-files.

3 The Hebrew Morphological Disambiguator, Hemed

Our Hebrew Morphological Disambiguator, Hemed, receives the output of an Hebrew Morphological Analyzer and prunes the number of candidate analyses. The chosen analyses are kept inside the index. A similar disambiguation process is performed to analyze the user's query. We propose a new method for disambiguation based on the following principle. Instead of dealing with words, we deal with morphological patterns as basic elements for disambiguation. Pruning is done by evaluating the likelihood of each analysis pattern, using statistical data which reflects the relative frequency of the morphological patterns in a typical Hebrew text. The statistical data will be gathered from a large un-tagged Hebrew corpus using only unambiguous words.

The general architecture for Hemed is illustrated in Figure 1.

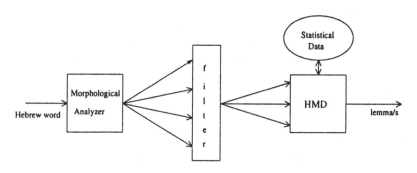

Fig. 1. The general architecture for Hemed.

The input word is analyzed by a morphological analyzer which returns all legal morphological analyses. The latter are passed to a "simple filter" which eliminates the impossible or extremely improbable ones using some basic morphological rules. The remaining analyses are fed to Hemed which does the core of the disambiguation work and returns a very limited number of most likely analyses per word. Hemed estimates the probability of each analysis by using statistical data on the relative frequency of Hebrew morphological analyses.

In a search application for instance, only the best base form(s), or lemma(s) of the analyses returned by the disambiguator are stored inside the index for later retrieval, and the same procedure is applied at querying time. A key feature of Hemed, is that the the number of valid analyses kept can be controlled via a threshold parameter ϵ, and thus the precision/recall rate can be fixed at the time the query is issued as long as enough information has been stored in the index.

Given an ambiguous word with more than one analysis, Hemed filters out all analyses with lower relative frequency than this threshold. As ϵ becomes larger, more candidate analyses are filtered out but the probability of filtering out the "true" analysis also increases. In the following, we describe the basic components of this architecture in more detail.

3.1 The Morphological Analyzer

Hemed requires the output of a morphological analyzer. In our implementation we have taken advantage of the existing *Avgad* product – a Hebrew morphological analyzer developed at IBM - Haifa Research Laboratory [1]. However, Hemed can easily be modified to work with any other morphological analyzer that provides similar information in a different format.

For each legal Hebrew string, Avgad returns all legal lexical candidates as possible analyses of the given string. The information returned by Avgad for each analysis includes:

- category – categorization of the base forms according to part of speech, gender, plural inflections, legal set of prefixes and legal set of suffixes.
- part of speech.
- prefix – attached particles.
- lemma – the base form used for indexing.
- correct form - (optional) the input word with additional vowel letters added by Avgad to enable the given analysis.
- number, gender, person.
- status – (for non verbs only) – whether this lemma is in its construct or absolute form.
- tense – (for verbs only)
- inf_num , inf_gen, inf_person – for pronoun suffix.

For example, Table 1 shows the six analyses returned by Avgad for the string *Inyany*:

lemma	pos	number	gender	person	status	example
Inyany	adj.	sing.	masc.			*Mammar Inyany* – a practical paper
Inyan	noun	sing.	masc.		const.	*Inyany Shely* – my interest
Inyan	noun	plural	masc.		const.	*Inyanay Shely* – my interests
Inyan	noun	plural	masc.		const.	*Inyaney hamedina* – the state interests
Anyen	verb	sing.	fem.	2		*Anyeny* – make them interested
Ana	verb	sing.	fem	2		*Anyny* – (*Any li* – answer me, or *Any oti* – torture/ me)

Table 1. The analyses returned by Avgad for the word *Inyany*

The sixth analysis illustrates well Avgad's feature of returning infrequent morphological patterns that are generally not used in a typical modern Hebrew text, but are yet valid ones.

3.2 The Simple Filter

The simple filter component eliminates some of the analyses that are not relevant for indexing. The first rule consists of filtering out all the corrected forms, i.e., all analyses inferred by adding vowel letters to the original string, to enable the given analysis. This rule is motivated by the assumption that only the original string is a candidate to be indexed (or to be searched). The second rule consists of filtering out all analyses with the same lemma and the same category, leaving out only one representative base form for this set. The intuition behind this rule is that different inflections of the same lemma do not add information that should be stored in the index. For example, analyses 2,3,4, in the example shown in Table 1, are all inflections of the noun *Inyan* and therefore can be represented by one single analysis inside the index. Using the simple filter reduces the average number of analyses per word from 2.15 to 1.91.

3.3 Hebrew Morphological Patterns

Our disambiguation method uses morphological patterns of the analyses returned by Avgad as the basic elements for disambiguation. The morphological disambiguator makes decisions based on the frequency of the morphological patterns associated with the analyses of the input word. Infrequent patterns are pruned using statistical data gathered from a large Hebrew corpus and only the most likely set of analyses are returned.

A morphological pattern is defined according to the information returned by the morphological analyzer. Table 2 shows all legal values for all analysis entries:

field	number	values
pos	12	*Shem Etzem, Poal, Shem Toar, Mispar, Milat Yachas, Milat Guf, Milat Shela, Milat Hibur, Mlit, Toar Hapoal, Notricon, Shem Prati*
prefix	7	*moshe-vecalev* letters (keeping only the last letter of the prefix)
number	2	*yachid, rabim*
gender	3	*zachar, nekeva, zachar/nekeva*
person	4	1, 2, 3, all
tense	5	*Avar, Hove, Atid, Tzivui, Shem Poal*
Binyan	7	*Paal, Nifal, Piel, Pual, Hitpael, Hifil, Hufal*

Table 2. Legal values of the analysis entries returned by Avgad.

For non-verbs, a morphological pattern is defined to be a tuple of (pos, prefix, number, gender, person, status, inf_num, inf_gen, inf_person). For verbs, we add the *Binyan* field to the morphological pattern.

Using morphological patterns instead of words avoids many of the problems related to accumulating word statistics. Pattern statistics are much more reliable and are much easier to manage since there are much fewer patterns than words. 2300 different patterns were found in a corpus of 10 million Hebrew words compared to 25,000 unique Hebrew words.

Pattern statistics are computed by scanning the corpus concerning only unambiguous words. Since 45% of the Hebrew words are unambiguous [6], the sample size includes approximately 4.5 million words. For each identification of an unambiguous word with one legal analysis we increment the counter of it associated pattern. The pattern counters are stored in a global hash table for efficient retrieval.

3.4 Context-Free Analysis

Pattern statistics related to the morphological patterns are used as follows. Analyses associated with infrequent morphological patterns are filtered out by the context-free Hemed algorithm which receives a threshold parameter from the user and filters out all analyses with lower relative frequency than this threshold.

The relevance score of any document retrieved for a given input query depends on the frequency of the query terms inside the document. Since we might keep more than one lemma per word inside the index, there might be a bias for ambiguous words since all their lemmas contribute to the accumulated score. In order to avoid this effect, we store each lemma with its relative frequency and this value is used while computing the relevance score for the retrieved documents.

The Context-free Hemed algorithm, described in Figure 2, takes as input a word w and a threshold parameter ϵ and returns a set of (lemma, weight) pairs:

4 Experiments with Hemed

We conducted a set of experiments to test the contribution of Hemed to Hebrew search which is the main information retrieval application[4]. In the first experiment we tested the accuracy of Hemed. In the second we added Hemed to an existing Hebrew search engine and tested the effect on the search results.

4.1 Evaluation of the Accuracy of Hemed

In order to evaluate the accuracy of Hemed we manually tagged a set of 16,000 Hebrew words. Each word was associated with its "true" analysis, chosen manually from the set of analyses return by Avgad. The accuracy of Hemed computed

---

[4] Comparable tests could be conducted for other IR applications such as categorizing but we believe that search is the application that suffers most from the ambiguity problem.

```
Context-free-HMD( word w, threshold ε)
  Analysis[] ← Avgad(w)
  n ← |Analysis|
  if n = 0 /* for illegal words we use the input word as a base form.*/
    return (w,1)
  else
    if n = 1 /* one analysis: no dilemma, use its lemma as a base form */
      return (Analysis[1].lemma,1)
    else /* more than one analysis */
      Lemmas ← {}
      for i = 1 to n
        let Freq[i] be the relative frequency of pattern(Analysis[i])
        if Freq[i] ≥ ε
          Lemmas ← Lemmas + (Analysis[i].lemma, Freq[i])
      return Lemmas
```

Fig. 2. Hemed: The Context-Free HMD algorithm

by counting the number of words for which the set of analyses returned by Hemed includes the "true" analysis.

Figure 3 shows the accuracy of Hemed as a function of the threshold parameter ϵ. The upper curve shows the results for all the tagged words. The lower curve shows the results when tested only for ambiguous words. We can see that for low thresholds, only a few analyses are pruned and the accuracy is close to 100%[5]. For large threshold parameters more analyses are pruned and the accuracy decreases. For $\epsilon = 0.5$, Hemed returns the most likely analysis and prunes all other candidates. In this case the accuracy deteriorates to 86%.

Figure 4 shows the percentage of words with different number of analyses as a function of the threshold ϵ. As ϵ becomes lower the number of ambiguous words increases as expected but only few words have more than three analyses. For example, consider $\epsilon = 0.1$, we see that the accuracy of Hemed is 95%, according to figure 3, but the average number of analyses per word is kept low: 75% of the words are assigned one analysis, 20% of the words have two and 5% of the words have more than two analyses. Only a negligible number of words has 4 analyses and no one has more than four. These are very reasonable results to be applied for linguistic indexing.

4.2 Hemed Contribution to Hebrew Search Engine

Most free-text search engines comprise two components: an indexing component and a retrieval component. The indexing component analyzes a set of documents from a given collection and extracts from each of them a set of meaningful

---

[5] The reason that the accuracy is not 100% for $\epsilon = 0$ is that the simple filter has also few errors in pruning.

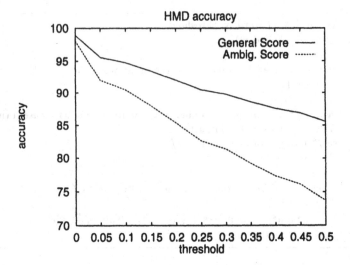

Fig. 3. The accuracy of Context-free Hemed as a function of the threshold parameter. The upper curve shows the general accuracy measured for all words. The lower curve shows the number of successes among ambiguous words.

indexing units. The retrieval component is given as input a query, and returns a list of references to those documents that are most relevant to the query. This list can be ranked according to a numerical score that represents the relevance to the query.

The performance of a search engine is usually measured by two evaluation criteria:

Recall: the ratio between the number of relevant items retrieved to the number of relevant items in collection.

Precision: the ratio between the number of relevant items retrieved to the number of retrieved items.

The most common measures used for evaluating the retrieval effectiveness of search engines in the information retrieval community are the average recall and precision of the search results and the Recall/Precision graph which shows both criteria simultaneously. Typically, when precision goes up, recall goes down and vice versa. Such measures can be evaluated for individual queries, or averaged over a set of queries as described in [14]. Recall and precision are not absolute measures in the sense that they strongly depend on the chosen test collection and therefore can only be used for comparative purpose. The performance of two search engines can be compared by comparing the average recall/precision measures of the engines for the same set of queries.

We have integrated Hemed into *BabaGuru*, a Hebrew search engine based on the search engine *Guru* [8], to evaluate its contribution. Each word in the text collection is analyzed by Hemed[6] while creating the index. We used 3 different

---

[6] Not including stop-words, i.e., common words not used for indexing.

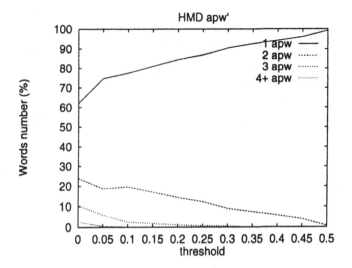

Fig. 4. The percentage of words with different analyses number (apw) as a function of the threshold parameter.

thresholds, $0, 0.1, 0.5$ to create three different repositories for the same collection of documents. For $\epsilon = 0$ all analyses are kept inside the repository (not including those filtered out by the simple filter). For $\epsilon = 0.5$ only the most likely analysis is kept inside the repository. Hemed is also applied for the query terms, using a threshold parameter determined by the user. The analyses returned by Hemed are searched inside the index repository. In addition, we experimented with a string-matching search engine which applies *precise indexing* and a simple string-matching retrieval function.

A collection of 900 news articles, including approximately 400K Hebrew words, were indexed by BabaGuru and by the string-matching search engine. Table 3 shows the search results of the different search engines for the query *Mishtara*. The string-matching search engine retrieved only 17 documents, compared to the 123 documents retrieved by Hemed versions with a threshold 0.1 and 0.5, and 162 documents retrieved by Hemed with a threshold of $\epsilon = 0$. String matching had poor results since it ignores all inflections of the query term – *Hamishtara*, (the police), *Mehamishtara* (from the police), *Mishtarot* (plural form), *Mishteret*, (constructed form), and many others. All versions of Hemed succeeded to retrieve all relevant documents dealing with *Mishtara*. However, the $\epsilon = 0$ version also retrieved 39 non-relevant documents who deal with *Mishtar* (regime) and *Shtar* (bill). Among those documents, 4 deal with the violinist *Itzhak Stern* whose name can be read as *Shtaran* (their bill in feminine form), and 10 include the adverb *Sheterem* which can be read as *Shtaram* (their bill in masculine form).

To evaluate the quality of search engines more systematically, we used a set of 22 queries, each one is associated with a relevant list of all relevant documents

String	String-matching	$\epsilon = 0.5$	$\epsilon = 0.1$	$\epsilon = 0.0$
Mishtara (police)	17	17	17	17
Hamishtara (the police), Mehamishtara, Lamishtara, Bamishtara etc.	-	100	100	100
Mishteret (constructed form)	-	50	50	50
Mishtarot (plural form)	-	1	1	1
Mishtarti (adjective)	-	6	6	6
Mishtar (regime)	-	-	-	25
Sheterem (before) (also can be read as Shtaram, their bill)	-	-	-	10
Stern (Private Name) (also can be read as Shtaran, their bill)	-	-	-	4

Table 3. The number of documents retrieved by the different search engines for the query *Mishtara*.

manually tagged by a human judge[7]. Table 4 shows the recall/precision of the Search Engine averaged over the 22 queries. The upper row shows the result of a string matching search where no analysis was done while creating the index and submitting the queries. The three lower rows show the search results of Hemed with the different threshold parameters. String matching search achieves high precision but very low recall. In contrast, Hemed versions search for the base forms and return all appearances of their inflections.

	Recall	Precision
String Matching	0.559	0.364
Hemed $\epsilon = 0$	0.836	0.248
Hemed $\epsilon = 0.1$	0.797	0.263
Hemed $\epsilon = 0.5$	0.758	0.277

Table 4. The recall/precision of different search engines averaged over 22 queries.

The search engine integrated with the Hemed versions achieves much better results but with lower precision. Using a threshold of 0 improves the recall of the search significantly since all analyses are kept inside the index. This is also

---

[7] Unfortunately, there is no forum like TREC, and no test collections like those on Ed Fox's Virginia disk for Hebrew search systems. We therefore had to "craft" our own Hebrew test collection, and the results should only be seen as encouraging until a more formal forum is established.

the reason for the deterioration in the search precision. Enlarging the threshold parameter improves the precision of the search with a little decrease in recall.

Figure 5 shows the Recall/Precision curves of the Hebrew Search Engines, averaged over the 22 queries. The results strengthen our claim that string matching search fails for Hebrew. Its performance is reflected by the recall/precision curve which is much lower than the curves of the search engines integrated with Hemed. The graph also highlights the role of the threshold parameter for Hemed procedure. It allows the user to control the tradeoff between recall and precision by changing the threshold according to required results.

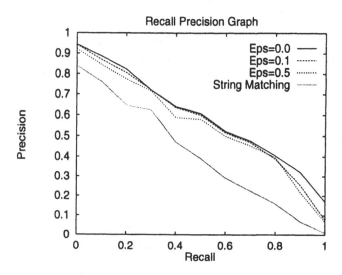

Fig. 5. The recall/precision graph of three versions of Hemed, and a string matching search engine, averaged over 22 queries.

5 Summary

In this work we describe a new approach for linguistic indexing of Hebrew text files. We showed that linguistic indexing can significantly improve the recall rate of a Hebrew search engine with low reduction in precision rate, compared to precise indexing used by a string-matching search engine. We introduced the idea of adding controllable morphological disambiguation while indexing and while analyzing users' queries. The level of disambiguation can be set dynamically to control the recall and precision of the search results.

We described Hemed, a statistical morphological disambiguator for Hebrew. Hemed exploits statistical data gathered from a large Hebrew corpus to reduce the level of morphological ambiguity. Hemed has been integrated into *BabaGuru*, a research prototype of a Hebrew search engine, and is now being integrated into

Intelligent Miner for Text (IM4T) [5], a multi-lingual search engine, to enable linguistic indexing for Hebrew.

The context-free disambiguator described in this work analyzes words without concerning their context. In many cases the "true" morphological analysis of a given word can not be determined without taking its context into consideration. Context-sensitive disambiguation function might have better results for indexing. The question how to implement such a context-sensitive disambiguator for Hebrew remains open for further research.

Acknowledgments

We are grateful to thank Victoria Skoblikov for implementing *BabaGuru*, the Hebrew search engine used in the experiments described in this work. We would also like to thank Moshe Levinger for stimulating discussions and useful suggestions concerning this work.

References

1. Esther Benture, Aviela Angle, and Danit Segev. Computerized analysis of Hebrew words. In *Hebrew Computerized Linguistics*. Isreal Ministry of Science and Technology, 1992.
2. Yaacov Choueka, A. S. Fraenkel, S. T. Klein, and E. Segal. Improved techniques for processing queries in full-text systems. In *Proceedings of ACM Conference on research and development in Information Retrieval*, pages 306 – 315. ACM press, NY, June 1987.
3. Yaacov Choueka and S. Lusignan. Disambiguation by short contexts. *Computers and Humanities*, 19:147 – 157, 1985.
4. J. L. Fagan. The effectiveness of a nonsyntactic approach to automatic phrase indexing for document retrieval. *JASIS*, 40(2):115–132, 1989.
5. Intelligent Miner for Text. *http://www.software.ibm.com/data/iminer/fortext*. IBM Corporation, 1998.
6. Moshe Levinger. Morphological disambiguation, Master thesis (in Hebrew), Technion, Israel institute of technology. 1992.
7. Moshe Levinger, Uzzi Ornan, and Alon Itai. Learning morpho-lexical probabilities from an untagged corpus with an application to Hebrew. *Computational Linguistics*, 2(3):383 – 404, 1993.
8. Yoelle Maarek and F. Smadja. Full text indexing based on lexical relations, an application: Software libraries. In N. Belkin and C. van Rijsbergen, editors, *Proceedings of SIGIR89*, pages 198 – 206. Cambridge MA, ACM press, 1989.
9. Uzzi Ornan. Phonemic script: A central vehicle for processing NL – the case of hebrew, IBM, scientific center, haifa. Technical Report 88-181, 1986.
10. Uzzi Ornan. Theoretical gemination in Israeli Hebrew. In Allan S. Kaye and Otto Harrassowitz, editors, *Semitic Studies in Honor of Wolf Leslau*, pages 1158 – 1168. 1991.
11. M. F. Porter. An algorithm for suffix stripping. *Program*, 14(3):130 – 137, 1980.
12. Responsa project. *http://www.biu.ac.il/JH/Responsa/*. Bar-Ilan univrtsity, 1998.

13. G. Salton and M.J. McGill. *Introduction to Modern Information Retrieval.* Computer Series. McGraw-Hill, New York, 1983.
14. Ellen M. Voorhees and Donna Harman. Overview of the Sixth Text REtrival conference (TREC-6). In *Proceedings of the Sixth Text REtrieval Conference.* National Institute of Standards and Technology, August 1997.

Author Index

Lecture Notes in Computer Science

For information about Vols. 1–1553
please contact your bookseller or Springer-Verlag

Vol. 1596: R. Poli, H.-M. Voigt, S. Cagnoni, D. Corne, G.D. Smith, T.C. Fogarty (Eds.), Evolutionary Image Analysis, Signal Processing and Telecommunications. Proceedings, 1999. X, 225 pages. 1999.

Vol. 1597: H. Zuidweg, M. Campolargo, J. Delgado, A. Mullery (Eds.), Intelligence in Services and Networks. Proceedings, 1999. XII, 552 pages. 1999.

Vol. 1598: R. Poli, P. Nordin, W.B. Langdon, T.C. Fogarty (Eds.), Genetic Programming. Proceedings, 1999. X, 283 pages. 1999.

Vol. 1599: T. Ishida (Ed.), Multiagent Platforms. Proceedings, 1998. VIII, 187 pages. 1999. (Subseries LNAI).

Vol. 1601: J.-P. Katoen (Ed.), Formal Methods for Real-Time and Probabilistic Systems. Proceedings, 1999. X, 355 pages. 1999.

Vol. 1602: A. Sivasubramaniam, M. Lauria (Eds.), Network-Based Parallel Computing. Proceedings, 1999. VIII, 225 pages. 1999.

Vol. 1603: J. Vitek, C.D. Jensen (Eds.), Secure Internet Programming. X, 501 pages. 1999.

Vol. 1605: J. Billington, M. Diaz, G. Rozenberg (Eds.), Application of Petri Nets to Communication Networks. IX, 303 pages. 1999.

Vol. 1606: J. Mira, J.V. Sánchez-Andrés (Eds.), Foundations and Tools for Neural Modeling. Proceedings, Vol. I, 1999. XXIII, 865 pages. 1999.

Vol. 1607: J. Mira, J.V. Sánchez-Andrés (Eds.), Engineering Applications of Bio-Inspired Artificial Neural Networks. Proceedings, Vol. II, 1999. XXIII, 907 pages. 1999.

Vol. 1608: S. Doaitse Swierstra, P.R. Henriques, J.N. Oliveira (Eds.), Advanced Functional Programming. Proceedings, 1998. XII, 289 pages. 1999.

Vol. 1609: Z. W. Raś, A. Skowron (Eds.), Foundations of Intelligent Systems. Proceedings, 1999. XII, 676 pages. 1999. (Subseries LNAI).

Vol. 1610: G. Cornuéjols, R.E. Burkard, G.J. Woeginger (Eds.), Integer Programming and Combinatorial Optimization. Proceedings, 1999. IX, 453 pages. 1999.

Vol. 1611: I. Imam, Y. Kodratoff, A. El-Dessouki, M. Ali (Eds.), Multiple Approaches to Intelligent Systems. Proceedings, 1999. XIX, 899 pages. 1999. (Subseries LNAI).

Vol. 1612: R. Bergmann, S. Breen, M. Göker, M. Manago, S. Wess, Developing Industrial Case-Based Reasoning Applications. XX, 188 pages. 1999. (Subseries LNAI).

Vol. 1613: A. Kuba, M. Šámal, A. Todd-Pokropek (Eds.), Information Processing in Medical Imaging. Proceedings, 1999. XVII, 508 pages. 1999.

Vol. 1614: D.P. Huijsmans, A.W.M. Smeulders (Eds.), Visual Information and Information Systems. Proceedings, 1999. XVII, 827 pages. 1999.

Vol. 1615: C. Polychronopoulos, K. Joe, A. Fukuda, S. Tomita (Eds.), High Performance Computing. Proceedings, 1999. XIV, 408 pages. 1999.

Vol. 1617: N.V. Murray (Ed.), Automated Reasoning with Analytic Tableaux and Related Methods. Proceedings, 1999. X, 325 pages. 1999. (Subseries LNAI).

Vol. 1619: M.T. Goodrich, C.C. McGeoch (Eds.), Algorithm Engineering and Experimentation. Proceedings, 1999. VIII, 349 pages. 1999.

Vol. 1620: W. Horn, Y. Shahar, G. Lindberg, S. Andreassen, J. Wyatt (Eds.), Artificial Intelligence in Medicine. Proceedings, 1999. XIII, 454 pages. 1999. (Subseries LNAI).

Vol. 1621: D. Fensel, R. Studer (Eds.), Knowledge Acquisition Modeling and Management. Proceedings, 1999. XI, 404 pages. 1999. (Subseries LNAI).

Vol. 1622: M. González Harbour, J.A. de la Puente (Eds.), Reliable Software Technologies – Ada-Europe'99. Proceedings, 1999. XIII, 451 pages. 1999.

Vol. 1625: B. Reusch (Ed.), Computational Intelligence. Proceedings, 1999. XIV, 710 pages. 1999.

Vol. 1626: M. Jarke, A. Oberweis (Eds.), Advanced Information Systems Engineering. Proceedings, 1999. XIV, 478 pages. 1999.

Vol. 1627: T. Asano, H. Imai, D.T. Lee, S.-i. Nakano, T. Tokuyama (Eds.), Computing and Combinatorics. Proceedings, 1999. XIV, 494 pages. 1999.

Col. 1628: R. Guerraoui (Ed.), ECOOP'99 - Object-Oriented Programming. Proceedings, 1999. XIII, 529 pages. 1999.

Vol. 1629: H. Leopold, N. García (Eds.), Multimedia Applications, Services and Techniques - ECMAST'99. Proceedings, 1999. XV, 574 pages. 1999.

Vol. 1631: P. Narendran, M. Rusinowitch (Eds.), Rewriting Techniques and Applications. Proceedings, 1999. XI, 397 pages. 1999.

Vol. 1632: H. Ganzinger (Ed.), Automated Deduction – Cade-16. Proceedings, 1999. XIV, 429 pages. 1999. (Subseries LNAI).

Vol. 1633: N. Halbwachs, D. Peled (Eds.), Computer Aided Verification. Proceedings, 1999. XII, 506 pages. 1999.

Vol. 1634: S. Džeroski, P. Flach (Eds.), Inductive Logic Programming. Proceedings, 1999. VIII, 303 pages. 1999. (Subseries LNAI).

Vol. 1636: L. Knudsen (Ed.), Fast Software Encryption. Proceedings, 1999. VIII, 317 pages. 1999.

Vol. 1638: A. Hunter, S. Parsons (Eds.), Symbolic and Quantitative Approaches to Reasoning and Uncertainty. Proceedings, 1999. IX, 397 pages. 1999. (Subseries LNAI).

Vol. 1639: S. Donatelli, J. Kleijn (Eds.), Application and Theory of Petri Nets 1999. Proceedings, 1999. VIII, 425 pages. 1999.

Vol. 1640: W. Tepfenhart, W. Cyre (Eds.), Conceptual Structures: Standards and Practices. Proceedings, 1999. XII, 515 pages. 1999. (Subseries LNAI).

Vol. 1644: J. Wiedermann, P. van Emde Boas, M. Nielsen (Eds.), Automata, Languages, and Programming. Proceedings, 1999. XIII, 720 pages. 1999.

Vol. 1649: R.Y. Pinter, S. Tsur (Eds.), Next Generation Information Technologies and Systems. Proceedings, 1999. IX, 327 pages. 1999.

Vol. 1650: K.-D. Althoff, R. Bergmann, L.K. Branting (Eds.), Case-Based Reasoning Research and Development. Proceedings, 1999. XII, 598 pages. 1999. (Subseries LNAI).

Vol. 1653: S. Covaci (Ed.), Active Networks. Proceedings, 1999. XIII, 346 pages. 1999.